OPERATING SYSTEM CONCEPTS

Covering Syllabus of BCA, MCA, B.Tech of Various Technical Universities and Other applicable courses

Ekta Walia

Ph.D. (Computer Science)
Professor & Head
Department of Information Technology
M.M. University
Mullna, Ambala (Haryana)

KHANNA BOOK PUBLISHING CO. (P) LTD.

Publisher of Engineering and Computer Books

4C/4344, Ansari Road, Darya Ganj, New Delhi-110002

Phone : 011-23244447-48 **Mobile:** +91-9910909320

E-mail : contact@khannabooks.com

Website : www.khannabooks.com

Dear Readers,

To prevent the piracy, this book is secured with HIGH SECURITY HOLOGRAM on the front title cover. In case you don't find the hologram on the front cover title, please write us to at contact@khannabooks.com or whatsapp us at +91-99109 09320 and avail special gift voucher for yourself.

Specimen of Hologram on front Cover title:

Moreover, there is a SPECIAL DISCOUNT COUPON for you with EVERY HOLOGRAM.

How to avail this SPECIAL DISCOUNT:

Step 1: Scratch the hologram
Step 2: Under the scratch area, your "coupon code" is available
Step 3: Logon to www.khannabooks.com
Step 4: Use your "coupon code" in the shopping cart and get your copy at a special discount
Step 5: Enjoy your reading!

Price: ₹ 425.00

ISBN: 978-93-80016-65-8

Operating System Concepts
by Ekta Walia

Edition: 2025

To view complete list of books,
Please scan the QR Code:

Published by:
Khanna Book Publishing Co. (P) Ltd.
CIN: U22110DL1998PTC095547

Visit us at: **www.khannabooks.com**
Write us at: **contact@khannabooks.com**

Printed in Bharat.

Dedicated to

to my parents..................

PREFACE

Today, operating system is an indispensable part of a computer system. A good realization of this fact is that there are a number of books, which give operational knowledge about various operating systems. Together with this many user manuals and online help provisions are there to facilitate the user's interaction with the operating system. But at the same time if we look into the operating system concepts, although there are many good books each of which gives detailed knowledge about few of these concepts, yet while teaching this subject, I could not find a single complete book that could impart the knowledge of all the essentials of the operating system concepts.

As rightly said "Need is the Mother of Invention", it became my duty to take up this challenge of putting the operating system concepts in simplest form and produce a complete reader friendly text book. The aim of this book is to serve all those who intend to learn operating system concepts. Since the contents of this book are based on the syllabi used in various Post Graduate and Under Graduate programmes throughout India, as a reader you will find all the theoretical aspects supplemented with practical examples, which will definitely complete your knowledge about the operating system concepts.

EKTA WALIA

Contents of This Book

The book has been divided into 14 chapters, each of which starts with a brief overview followed by the concerned text and examples. Each chapter ends with a set of exercise for the readers. Some of these exercises require only short answers and they are a sort of recall exercises, where as some are "action" exercises which test the depth of your understanding. Answer to such selected exercises are given at the end of the book.

The use of very simple illustrations to explain the difficult concepts makes this book reader friendly. The following is a brief description of the topics that are covered in each chapter :

In **Chapter 1,** an effort has been made to discuss what do we expect from an operating system. The operating system's role has been chalked out here and a brief overview of how operating systems evolved with the change in hardware and software technology has been mentioned here. It includes a good reasoning of what factors led to the development of a new kind of operating system.

Chapter 2 aims to discuss basic computer operations, I/O structure including interrupts, management of memory by an operating system and storage hierarchy. The necessity of hardware protection, memory protection and CPU protection has been discussed in detail. Various mechanisms to meet these different types of protection requirements have also been suggested. A brief mention of system calls has also been made here.

Chapter 3 describes in brief the various services that must be essentially provided by the operating system. Memory management, Process management, CPU-scheduling, Device management are amongst those services. Various operating system architectures have been discussed and their comparative study has been done in this chapter. This chapter also discusses design and implementation issues of an operating system. System generation process has also been mentioned briefly.

Chapter 4 has been framed to get to know the concept of processes. Various process states : ready, blocked, running and their transitions have been discussed in a very simple manner. This chapter also presents the description of two basic operations on processes, *i.e.,* process creation and process termination.

Chapter 5 focuses upon the needs for processor scheduling, scheduling criterion and also explains various scheduling algorithms for a uniprocessor system. A brief mention of multiple processor scheduling has been made here. This text also covers scheduling mechanisms implemented in real time systems. An effort has been made to make each and every concept clearer with the help of examples.

The first part of **Chapter 6** discusses the need of synchronization, its actual implementation and various concerns associated with it. Critical section problem and its software solutions have been explained in a very simple language. Hardware solutions and more software solutions using synchronization tools like : semaphores and monitors have been explained. The later part of this chapter deals with the concurrency control mechanisms. It explains the need of atomicity in transactions. Following this, the concurrency-control schemes to guarantee serializability in the concurrent execution of atomic transactions have been explained in depth.

Chapter 7 has been written to exclusively deal with the problem of deadlocks. It describes the methods to prevent and avoid deadlocks. Bankers' algorithm has been given in detail. Second half of this chapter deals with deadlock detection mechanisms and deadlock recovery. Algorithms for deadlock detection have been explained with examples.

The aim of **Chapter 8** is to introduce the basic concepts of address binding, relocation and address space. After making you familiar with the terms like load time, compile time and run time, it moves on to discuss very important topic of contiguous and non-contiguous storage allocations. It covers fixed partition and variable partition as contiguous storage allocation techniques. It further discusses paging and segmentation as non-contiguous storage allocation techniques. Each technique has been introduced with the help of examples. Merits and demerits associated with each of the techniques have been mentioned in detail.

Chapter 9 focuses on management of virtual memory. Demand paging is used to implement the concept of virtual memory and therefore, has been described in detail. Page replacement algorithms (like FIFO, LRU, Optimal etc.) have been discussed with a mention of their advantages and disadvantages. Demand segmentation has been described in brief.

The first part of **Chapter 10** introduces file : an abstract data type defined and implemented by the operating system. It discusses file concepts containing naming of files, file operations and file attributes. File access methods—'sequential' and 'random' have been described and their comparison has been done in brief. Directory structures, directory operations and access paths have been explained in detail. A brief notion of file protection has been introduced. The second part of this chapter deals with file system implementation issues. It involves the discussion of various methods of allocating space to the files on the disk and management of free space on the disk.

The first part of **Chapter 11** discusses the various device management functions of an operating system. It gives a brief introduction of the concept of dedicated, shared and virtual devices. It also discusses in brief, the various components of an I/O subsystem, *i.e.,* I/O channel, I/O control unit, I/O traffic controller, I/O device handler and I/O scheduler. The second part of this chapter discusses the secondary storage device-magnetic disk and tertiary storage devices-floppy disk, CD-ROM etc. The magnetic disk structure and scheduling algorithms have been explained in depth. Disk management issues like bad block recovery, low-level formatting etc. have been described next. Swap space management on the disk has also been explained with respect to the operating system's responsibilities. A brief introduction to various tertiary storage devices is being followed up by the discussion of operating system's capabilities to use these tertiary storage devices.

The first part of **Chapter 12** discusses protection issues related to various resources associated with a computer system. The concepts of domains and access rights have been explained. The access matrix has been explained as a general model of protection. A mention of its implementation using access list and capability list has been made. The second part of this chapter discusses the security issues related to the external environment within which a system operates. It also explains various user authentication mechanisms such as passwords, biometrics techniques, etc. An attempt has been made to introduce encryption as a security measure and also to chalk out the safeguards against computer viruses and worms. Methods to do threat monitoring have also been discussed.

Chapter 13 introduces the concept of Distributed Systems, their advantages over standalone PCs and centralized systems. A brief mention of their possible disadvantages has also been made. Sections 13.3 and 13.4 explain the concepts of Network operating systems and Distributed operating systems. Section 13.5 explains the issues related with the design of a distributed operating system. The last section 13.6 is a big one as it deals with all the synchronization issues related with distributed systems. Its various sub-sections explain the mechanisms for dealing with mutual exclusion requirements, concurrency control and deadlock handling in distributed systems. Various Election algorithms associated with the election of a coordinator site in a distributed system have also been explained.

The goal of the last chapter, *i.e.,* **Chapter 14** is to discuss UNIX and Windows NT with respect to their architectures, file system, memory management, process management, etc. The first part of this chapter takes up the case study of UNIX operating system. The concepts of shell and command language in UNIX have been discussed in detail. Its file management, process management, I/O management methods have also been explained. The second part of this chapter explains the NT architecture in detail. NT's various layers and their functions have been described in detail. File system, CPU scheduling and process management in Windows NT have been discussed in depth. The last section describes virtual memory management in Windows NT.

Upon completion of its reading, the reasonably motivated reader will be able to analyze the characteristics of different operating systems with respect o CPU Scheduling, Process Management, Memory Management, Device Management, Treatment of deadlocks etc. It will also enable the reader to apply various concepts learnt here like the availability of the system calls, in the development of system programs.

I hope you will enjoy reading it!

ACKNOWLEDGEMENTS

Before acknowledging any human form of GOD, I would like to thank the almighty for bringing my academic achievements and career to this level.

I acknowledge Dr. Chandan Singh, Professor, Department of Computer Science, Punjabi University, Patiala and Dr. Gurpreet Singh Lehal, Professor, Department of Computer Science, Punjabi University, Patiala for being a constant source of inspiration and motivation for me. This has enabled me to once again take up this challenge of upgrading this text book. I would further like to thank the esteemed readers, students as well as teachers who have deeply gone through and fully utilized this book. I also acknowledge the valuable suggestions received through E-Mail and other mediums. Hopefully, this will be a better book as compared to its previous versions.

The untired efforts of Ms. Kirti Sachdeva, Assistant Professor, Deptt. of Computer Science, Adesh Institute of Engineering & Technology, Faridkot have made this revised version of the book possible. Her help is deeply acknowledged by me.

I thank the supporting staff for their constant hard work and timely support. Finally, I thank Puneet Khanna, who is responsible for presenting this book in its current format.

EKTA WALIA

CONTENTS

CHAPTER 1 : OPERATING SYSTEM : AN INTRODUCTION 1–17

CHAPTER 2 : COMPUTER SYSTEM STRUCTURES 18–40

CHAPTER 5 : CPU SCHEDULING 77–94

CHAPTER 6 : PROCESS SYNCHRONIZATION 95–121

CHAPTER 7 : DEALING WITH DEADLOCKS 122–136

CHAPTER 8 : MEMORY MANAGEMENT BASICS 137–155

CHAPTER 9 : MANAGING VIRTUAL MEMORY 156–174

CHAPTER 11 : DEVICE MANAGEMENT AND STORAGE STRUCTURES 196–221

CHAPTER 12 : PROTECTION AND SECURITY 222–237

CHAPTER 13 : OPERATING SYSTEM FOR DISTRIBUTED SYSTEMS 238–267

CHAPTER 14 : CASE STUDIES—UNIX AND WINDOWS NT 268–307

CHAPTER

1

Operating System : An Introduction

OVERVIEW

In this chapter, an effort has been made to discuss what do we expect from an operating system. The operating system's role has been chalked out inthis text and a brief overview of how operating systems evolved with the change in hardware and software technology has been mentioned here. This chapter includes a good reasoning of what factors led to the development of a new kind of operating system.

1.1. WHAT IS AN OPERATING SYSTEM

In has been rightly said that operating system is the first software we see when we turn on the computer and the last software we see when the computer is turned off.

More appropriately, we can define operating system as a program (in fact a system program) that, after being initially loaded into the computer by a boot program, manages all other programs in a computer. The other programs managed by it are usually application programs.

The application programs make use of the operating system by making requests for services through a defined Application Program Interface (API). In addition, users can interact directly with the operating system through a user interface, such as a comand language or a graphical user interface.

The most common operating systems are the windows family of operating systems (Windows 95, 98, 2000, NT), the UNIX family of operating systems (which includes Linux, BSD UNIX and many other derivatives) and the Macintosh operating system. Many other operating systems are available for special purpose applications including specializations for mainframes, robotics, manufacturing, real-time control systems and so on.

1.2. BOOTING PROCESS

Booting is the process used to load operating system in memory. We know that data and programs remain stored in disk as permanent storage. But because of slow access speed of disks, CPU interacts with main memory (temporary storage) to perform a task. Any program that has to be run must be swapped in from disk to main memory. Operating system is the first system program to get executed and remains in memory till the system execution.

Before actual loading of operating system, BIOS routines plays an important role. These routines perform a check for reliability and accessibility of the hardware attached. System BIOS is hardwired code on the motherboard chip. The very first step is the POST (power on self test). It checks the validity of all the hardware devices attached with the computer like keyboard, mouse, monitor etc. Then another check is being performed on the memory area and non standard peripherals. Then, Boot strap loader program is made available in the first physical sector of bootable disk by the master boot record. The purpose of master boot record is to find out the primary partition to load the boot strap loader for further processing. In case of booting with floppy disk, this step is a miss because floppy disk do not have any partition in it.

1.2.1 MS-DOS Booting Process

MS-DOS operating system has three parts

- IO.SYS
- MSDOS.SYS
- COMMAND.COM

IO.SYS contains the device drivers for various devices attached to the computer like keyboard, printer, monitor etc.

MSDOS.SYS is the interface between user and the hardware. All the major resource management roles performed by operating system are the part of this interface like process management, file management, memory management etc.

COMMAND.COM is the command line interface of MS-DOS called shell. It makes execution of all the commands possible by the user.

Now, Bootstrap loader loads the first part of MSDOS Operating System i.e. IO.SYS. This file contains information necessary to understand the commands of input output devices attached. It is also called DISK BIOS as it helps in managing the input output devices in the operating system. The other part of IO.SYS which helps in loading the kernel area i.e. MSDOS.SYS is SYSINIT.

MSDOS.SYS contains the resource management functions. Then with the help of CONFIG.SYS, the command line interface gets loaded in the memory but if CONFIG.SYS is not present in the operating system file then by defalut COMMAND.COM is loaded into the memory. After that AUTOEXEC.BAT (, if present) is loaded and the operating system starts working properly.

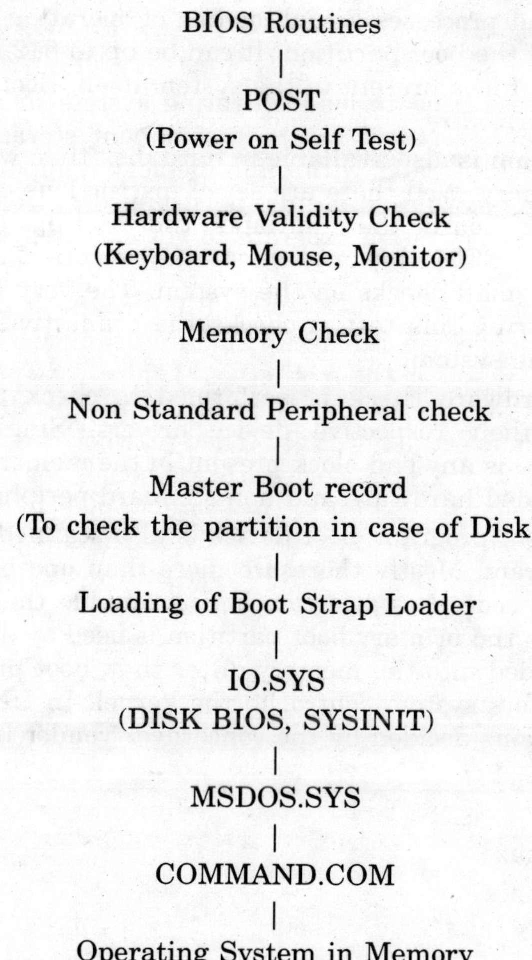

Figure 1.1 : Booting sequence for MS-DOS operating system

The two files AUTOEXEC.BAT and CONFIG.SYS are optional files. If these files are not available with operating system then COMMAND.COM manages the execution on its own part. And after loading of COMMAND.COM, operating system becomes ready to accept the user commands.

During this process, any error encountered is being handled by BIOS routines. A part of these routines helps in managing the error state in case some hardware is not correctly attached with the system.

1.2.2 UNIX Booting Process

Booting is the first process that executes when we switch on our computer system. During this process system goes through small checks for the connected hardware and finally loads operating system into main memory. The sequence of steps performed during booting is called boot strapping.

It is boot program that processes actual loading of operating system and it is made available in the block 0 of the boot partition. It can be up to 512 bytes in size. It is also called master boot record if it is present in the system itself. Boot program can be made available in the form of firmware.

Now if the boot program is also available in hard disk then what makes the loading of all these things in memory. Well there are set of instructions coded on the ROM chip available on the system board that initiates the booting process. This code is permanently coded in the ROM chip and starts its execution the moment system is switched on. It performs small checks on the system. The very first step is the Power On Self Test (POST). During this test it checks the connectivity of all the hardware devices connected with the system.

After that small hardware check is performed to check the standardization of connected devices and their respective device drivers. Similarly memory test is performed to check if there is any bad block present in the memory. In addition, resident code checks the newly added hardware and non-standard peripheral devices.

Before loading the boot program, boot device is also scanned to find out the actual position of the boot program. Mostly there are more than one boot device available in the system. The resident code uses selection logic to decide the actual boot device. In case of failure in doing so, the primary boot partition is used by default for this purpose. Boot program is then loaded into the memory. After that, boot program loads operating system kernel and transfers system control to the kernel. In UNIX variants, kernel is present at different locations decided by the concerned vendor like :

AIX	/unix
LINUX	/boot/vmlinuz
HP-UX	/stand/vmunix
Solaris	/kernel/unix
IRIX	/unix
TRU64	/vmunix

Here '/' represents the root drive of Unix operating system and Unix variants. Root drive here works like primary partition in Windows operating system i.e. C : drive.

When kernel gets the system control it starts initializing the system hardware. During this process it performs check on availability of memory with the system. With this information it sets the internal tables in RAM to keep track of the processes and the required memory allocations. It checks newly added hardware devices and loads respective device drivers.

After the successful execution of this phase, kernel mounts the root file system and enters into process 0 state. The UNIX variants like BSD and System V generates the processing of process 0 to control and coordinate processes for in and out from memory and processor allocation to them. Some variants do not execute this process and directly initialize the process 1 (PID 1). This is the first program that executes after kernel installation. PID 1 processes exec system call and executes '/etc/init' program. This program is named PID 1 because it provides initialization to all successive processes.

The process acts like a dispatcher after process 0 (scheduler) to spawn other processes. Init reads '/etc/inttab' file to decide which process to execute next. This file contains information regarding processes present in the system. The process information like process id, process state, memory status and other process characteristics are being provided through this file.

Init executes command like exec, wail, getty etc to provide efficient process execution. The UNIX system has various run levels. The moment system is executing under a particular run level, it performs the respective system functions associated with that mode. The run levels provided are :

0	Halt
1	Single User Mode
2	Multi User More with no NFS
3	Multi User Mode with NFS support
4	Not Used
5	Hardware State or Graphical Mode (in few like X11)
6	Shut Down and Reboot

The main activities involved with init are :

1. Testing the file system with fsck utility.
2. Remounting the file system.
3. Types of processes supported under init are : system processes, user processes and daemon processes. User processes are sometimes named as non-dummy as they are associated with their state information at each step.
4. Checking network activities related to the configuration of remote activities.

After all these activities, booting is said to be complete and user can log in to start further processing with system.

1.3. ROLE OF OPERATING SYSTEM

When the power to a computer turned on, the first program that runs is usually a set of instructions kept in the computer's Read-Only Memory (ROM) that examines the system hardware to make sure everything is functioning properly. This Power-On Self-Test (POST) checks the CPU, memory, and basic input-output systems for errors and stores the result in a special memory location. Once the POST has successfully completed, the software loaded in ROM (sometimes called firmware) will begin to activate the computer's disk drives. In most modern computers, when the computer activates the hard disk drive the first piece of a system program it finds, is the bootstrap loader.

The bootstrap loader is a small program that has a single function : It loads the operating system into memory and allows it to begin operation. In the most basic form, the bootstrap loader sets up the small drive programs that interface with and control the various hardware sub-system of the computer. It sets up the divisions of memory that hold the operating system, user information and applications. It establishes the data structures that will hold the signals, flags and semaphores that are used to communicate within and between the sub-systems and applications of the computer. Finally, it turns control of the computer over to the operating system.

The operating system's tasks, in the most general sense, fall into six categories :

— Processor management

— Memory management

— Device management

— Storage management

— Application Interface

— User Interface

While there are, some who argue that an operating system should do more than these six tasks, and some operating system vendors that build many more utility programs and auxiliary functions into the operating systems, these six tasks define the core of essentially all operating systems.

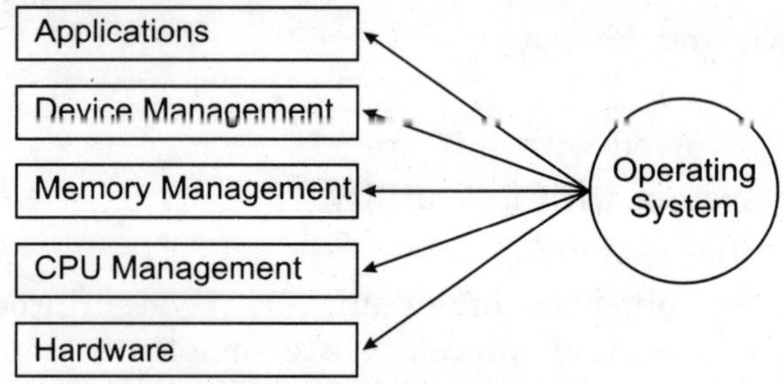

Figure 1.2. Role of an Operating System.

1.4. EVOLUTION OF OPERATING SYSTEM

Let us try to understand the reasons behind the development of operating systems from one form to another and so on.

1.4.1 Batch Processing

The computers in the past were very large in size and their input devices were very different from those that are there today. There never used to be an interactive job processing as such. In fact the programmers had nothing to do with the computer's input-output operation. The programmers' responsibility was to prepare a program, data, control information etc. and to submit it to a computer operator. This computer operator's job was to submit this program (usually in the form of punch cards) to the computer, take out the result of the program, dump of memory and registers in case of errors.

The role of operating system in these days was to transfer control automatically from one job to the next.

In order to use this system effectively, a batch of these programmed cards instead of the single card would be given to the computer operator. Usually, batch jobs would be stored up during working hours and then executed during off time or whenever the computer is idle.

Advantages of Batch Processing

- Batch processing is particularly useful for operations that require the computer or a peripheral device for an extended period of time and very little user interaction.

Disadvantages of Batch Processing

- No interaction is possible with the user while the program is being executed.
- Job setup time was real problem. It took a lot of time for mounting of tapes or cards.
- CPU sat idle during the transition from one job to another.

In order to reduce the wastage of time during job transition, automatic job sequencing was developed. First operating system known as Resident monitor came into existence. Initially, resident monitor was invoked, and then it would transfer control to a program. When the program terminated, it would return control to the resident monitor. Then the control will go to the next program. Thus, resident monitor would automatically sequence the execution of jobs one after the other.

Resident monitor had many identifiable parts—Major part was control-card interpreter that was responsible for reading and carrying out the instructions on the cards at the point of execution.

But even in this set up with Resident monitor, CPU used to be mostly idle because Input-Output devices are slower as compared to the CPU.

In order to overcome the problem of speed-mismatch, the concept of SPOOLing (Simultaneous Peripheral Operation On-line) was introduced. To free the CPU for useful work, the output was sent to a magnetic tape drive, which was much faster than a printer and much cheaper than a computer. After the job was finished, the tape was removed from the tape drive attached to the computer and mounted on a tape drive connected to a printer. The printer could print the data without holding up the computer. Similarly, instead of inputting the program from the card reader, it was first copied to a tape and the computer then read the tape. This system solved the problem of speed mismatch and reduced the unnecessary hold of computer by the slow peripheral devices.

Examples : Operating Systems like DOS, UNIX, Windows 95/98, NT all support batch file processing. A user can prepare a batch file that the operating system should execute without interacting with the user.

1.4.2 Multiprogramming

Though SPOOLing solved the problem of speed mismatch between CPU and peripheral devices, still CPU was not fully utilized by a single user.

Therefore, aroused the need of a system that could keep the CPU always busy with either the input-output processing or with the execution of other instructions of one program or the other. This system was termed multi-programming system.

The key idea was :

The operating system could support for keeping several jobs in memory at one time. The operating system could pick and start the execution of one of the jobs in the memory. Whenever the job does not need CPU, *i.e.,* the job has to interact only with the input-output devices, and the CPU is idle at that time, the operating system switches to another job in the memory and CPU executes a portion of it till this job issues a request for Input/output or the first one has finished its Input/output and so on.

Here, the operating system in this case had to be very complex. A very high-level memory management operation was expected from this operating system. Switching from one job to another, involves a huge effort on the part of operating system as it has to keep track of where did it left the execution of previous job and from where did it take up the execution of next job.

Advantages of multiprogramming

- High CPU utilization
- It appears that many programs are allotted CPU almost simultaneously.

Problems with Multiprogramming

- Jobs may have different sizes therefore, memory management is needed to accommodate them in memory.
- Many jobs may be ready to run on the CPU, which implies that we need CPU scheduling.

Examples : Operating Systems like UNIX, Windows 95/98, NT.

1.4.3 Multiprocessing

An old saying "many hands make light work", expresses the idea that led to the development of multi-processor systems. At any given time, there is a technological limit on the speed with which a single processor chip can operate. If a system's workload cannot be handled satisfactorily by a single processor, one response is to apply multiple processors to the problem and this is known as multiprocessing environment.

Symmetrical Multiprocessing System

In symmetrical multiprocessor system, all of the processors are essentially identical and perform identical functions.

Characteristics of such system can be specified as :

- Any processor can initiate an I/O operation, can handle any external interrupt, and can run any process in the system.
- All of the processors are potentially available to handle whatever needs to be done next.

Asymmetric Multiprocessing System

Asymmetry implies imbalance, or some difference between processors. Thus, in asymmetric multiprocessing, different processors do different things. From design point of view, this is often implemented so that one processor's job is to control the rest, or it is the supervisor of the others. Sometimes, a processor is specialized to the point where it is responsible for doing only one thing in the system (like handling a task like sound, video or some other specialized input or output).

Some advantages and disadvantages of this approach are :

- In some situations, I/O operation or application-program processing may be faster because it does not have to contend with other operations or programs for access to a processor, *i.e.,* many processors may be available for a single job.
- In other situations, I/O operation or application program processing can be slowed down because not all of the processors are available to handle peak loads.
- In asymmetric multiprocessing, if the supervisor processor handling a specific work fails, the entire system will go down.

The diagrams in Figures 1.3 (a) and 1.3 (b) elaborate the differences between asymmetric and symmetric multiprocessing.

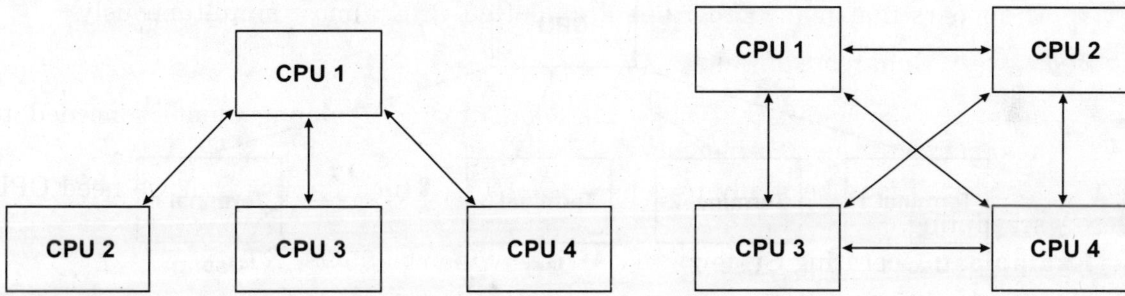

Figure 1.3(a) : Asymmetric Multiprocessing

Figure 1.3(b) : Symmetric Multiprocessing

1.4.4 Time Sharing

Time sharing feature of operating system allow users to run multiple tasks concurrently. It usually provides each user his own terminal for input output and an impact that only he/she is the one who is running his/her processes on the system (the presence of other user processes is transparent to a user). This implies that CPU's time is shared between many user processes.

The question arises here that what was the need for a time sharing system ? In the era of mainframe systems, multiple users were supposed to work simultaneously with single processor. The resources (like memory, processor and I/O devices) gets attached to all the user terminals in such a way that user can access any one of them by sensing its idle state. Otherwise it has to wait in a queue for its turn. We know that the processor works faster than other resource units. During processing, task completion needs to be done by other units like memeory fetch or I/O execution. In that case, processor remains idle to wait for its input from those units. The timesharing approach proved to be a better option for CPU utilization. Here CPU time gets sliced up among different user processes. The scheduling algorithms are used to manage time sliced processing. The subsystem involved in this process along with operating system kernel is known as schelduler. Mainly round robin scheduling technique is used to handle time sharing processes. A user can use its own time slice and wait for the next one if it needs more time to process its work. This wait is always a negligible time duration which generally is not sensed by the user. In this way every user gets a feel that he/she has full access of all the resources while processing. UNIX is the best example of time sharing systems.

Along with above mentioned positive results for CPU utilization, time sharing mechanism has its negative effects also. Major disadvantages of time sharing systems are :

1. The scheduling technique makes all processes get executed according to their turn, but in case of preemptive scheduling where priority is a main consideration, process can stay starved in the queue for resources.
2. With the increase in number of user processes, processor throughput gets decreased.
3. Memory protection is also a major issue, as users must not enter into another user's memory space. This has to be handled out with kernel mode processing.

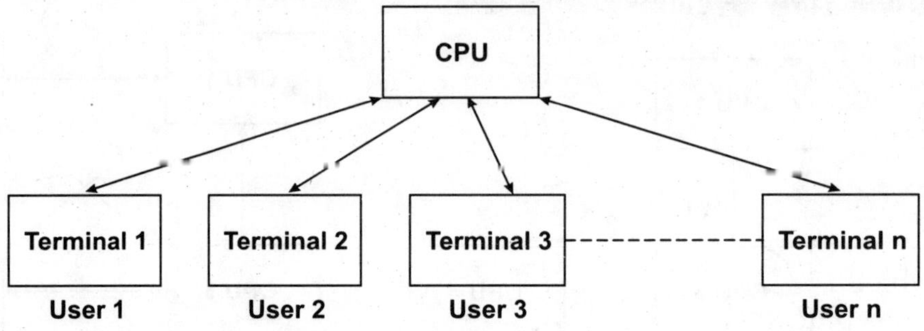

Figure 1.4 : Timesharing system (multitasking for multiple users)

1.4.5 Real Time Systems

There are several definitions of real-time systems and most of them are contradictory. Unfortunately the topic is controversial, and there does not seem to be 100 per cent agreement over the terminology. We can state that :

- "A real-time system is one in which the correctness of the computations not only depends upon the logical correctness of the computation but also upon the time at which the result is produced. If the timing constraints of the system are not met, system failure is said to have occurred."
- "Hence, it is essential that the timing constraints of the system are guaranteed to be met. **Guaranteeing timing** (Deadline) behaviour requires that the system should be predictable. It is also desirable that the system should attain a high degree of utilization while satisfying the timing constraints of the system".

Real Time Operating System (RTOS)

Real time operating system has well defined fixed time limit, *i.e.,* processing must be done within the defined time limit otherwise the system will fail.

Areas where RTOS is useful

A Real time system is often used as a central device in a dedicated application like those that have been listed here :

1. Systems that control scientific experiments
2. Medical-imaging systems
3. Some display systems, e.g., display screen of an airplane
4. Fuel-injection systems
5. Robotics
6. Air-traffic control
7. Control systems

Next generation system will include the automated land rover, controller of robots with elastic joints, the space stations, and undersea exploration.

Example of Real Time Systems

A good example is a robot that has to pick up something from a conveyor belt. The job is moving, and the robot has a small window to pick up the object. If the robot is late, the piece won't be there anymore, and thus the job will not be done correctly, despite the fact that the robot went to the right place. If the robot is early, the piece won't be there yet, and the robot may block it.

Let us first identify, what is a real time task?

A task, which is attempting to control or react to the events (occurring in real time) and is able to keep up with the event with which it is concerned, is known as Real Time Task.

This control is possible only when task has a deadline (which specifies either start time or completion time). Most of the time deadline refers to the completion time.

Now, these real time tasks can be classified into two categories—Hard Real Time Tasks and Soft Real Time Tasks.

In case of Hard Real Time task, meeting the deadline is must otherwise, undesirable and unforeseen damages can occur. Whereas, in case of Soft Real Time Task, meeting the deadline is desirable but not mandatory. For such tasks, if the deadline could not be met, there is a possibility to reschedule the task and complete it.

Real time operating system should support the functioning of a system, which is specialized to cater to the deadline requirements of a particular real time task.

Examples of real time operating system are : Harmony (Developed by National Research Council of Canada), Maruti (University of Maryland), OS9 (Microwave Systems Corporation), RTEMs (Real Stone Military Arsenal), etc.

1.4.6 Multitasking

Multitasking is closely related to the concept of time sharing. Time sharing technique was implemented on mainframe systems where more than one user worked together to complete one task. Multitasking makes multiple task execution possible in microcomputers. Multitasking implies that multiple tasks can be handled simultaneously by the system user. For example, in windows environment, one can work in word editor, excel sheet and can surf internet at the same time. With multithreading, it has become possible running more than one light weight process with in a window (like within word editor, managing printing and editing on the same time).

A processor executes one process at a time. While a job is busy with memory or I/O unit, the processor stays idle. But this scheme provides an illusion of multiple task execution. During this technique scheduler decides the next process to be executed based on the scheduling algorithm. Multitasking comes in two flavours :

1. **Cooperative Multitasking :** This appears to be a basic scheme for multitasking, in which process voluntarily give up the access of processor to another process in queue. The main drawback of this scheme is that total hold of processor is given to the active program. While going through I/O processing or memory access if that process denies giving up the processor time to other system processes then they have to wait till the current process execution. This leads to improper use of resources and involves risk in process execution if one process denies giving up the control.

   Examples : MAC OS (up to MACOS 8), Windows 3.1

2. **Preemptive Multitasking :** A more mature form of multitasking comes to us with this technique. In this technique scheduler keeps all the control to itself. It prevents any one process to keep the total control with itself. The preemption can occur in many different ways : Round Robin Scheduling with preemption, Priority based execution

   Examples : Windows NT, LINUX

Real time Multi tasking

Real time operating system is required for time critical programming applications. These days, we rarely find any sequential application running on computer system. Multiprogramming is the demand of the day. This means for real time applications, we must manage the executions of multiple tasks. Before going into the detail we need to know the complexities of applying multiple applications run in this case. As real time applications are having time constraint attached to them, it means resource requirements must be met on time. The preemptive multitasking technique is the optimal approach to handle multi task execution for real time systems. The preemptive scheduler keeps time critical tasks busy with processor as per the requirement. During preemption, context information of running application gets stored on to stack and processor performs execution of the current task. The best examples of real time operating systems are : QNX, RTX, and VxWorks.

Advantages

1. Multiple real time tasks can be handled simultaneously.
2. Preemptive scheduler helps managing the context switch.
3. Priority listing handles execution of hard real time applications efficiently.

Disadvantages

1. Context switch put extra overhead on operating system.
2. Priority preemption can results in starvation.

1.4.7 Network Operating System

An operating system, which includes software to communicate with other computers via a network, is called network operating system. This allows resources such as files, application programs and printers to be shared between computers.

Such operating systems are specialized to provide the networking services. The first network operating systems really were add-on packages that supplied the networking software for existing operating systems such as MS-DOS or OS/2. More recent operating systems come with the networking components built in to them.

Network operating system examples are :

BSD (Berkeley System Distribution) Unix, Novell, Lantastic, MS LAN Manager, Windows NT etc. Network operating system can be specialized to serve as peer-to-peer operating system or as client/server operating system.

1.4.7.1 Client/Server Support

Client server machines require specific software components. Redirector and Server services are two types of services that must be provided by client and server operating system respectively. Redirector service forwards the I/O requests (of the clients) for accessing remote files, where as a server satisfies them. A computer that is strictly a server often cannot provide any client functionality. On a Novell server or a Banyan server, a user cannot run word processing application whereas on Microsoft's NT server and UNIX server, user can run client programs.

1.4.7.2 Peer-to-peer Support

A computer in a peer-to-peer network functions as both client and a server, thus, it requires both client and server software. Operating systems such as **Windows NT Workstation** and **Windows 95**, both of which are peer-to-peer network operating systems, include dozen of services and utilities that facilitate networking.

1.4.8 Parallel Processing System

Many people conceive that the notion of parallel processing is very complicated stuff for them... but here, an attempt has been made to explain it in very simple words...

In Layman's terms, if you have lot of clothes piled up for washing, you can wash them in your washing machine at home by spending several hours on this job. Another way to do this job is to distribute these clothes among many laundries, which will do their job simultaneously. Thus, you can shrink your time commitment by several hours.

These same principles are behind parallel processing, in which lots of processors—either in one computer or inside several linked machines gang up to work on a single problem at one time. A typical desktop PC has one processor; a computer built to handle parallel processing can have several hundred of processors.

Specific areas where parallel processing is required are scientific industries, although its reach is slowly extending to the business world. The best candidates for parallel processing are projects that require many different computations. Single processor computers perform each computation sequentially. Using parallel processing, a computer can perform several computations simultaneously, drastically reducing the time it takes to complete a project. The medical community uses parallel processing supercomputers to analyze MRI images and study models of bone implant systems. Airline uses parallel processing to process customer information, to forecast demand and to decide what fares to charge.

Parallel processing is not that easy to implement, a special operating system and a special programming language are few things that are required to implement such a system.

The task of an operating system designed to support parallel processing is to manage how to divide a program so that it runs on more than one processor at a time.

Similarly, the programming language meant to code parallel processing programs must have special constructs to specify different parts of a program that should run on different processors for achieving parallelism.

Example. UNIX (Digital UNIX, IBM AIX), LINUX, Windows NT

1.4.9 Distributed Processing

A large central computer with a number of remote terminals connected to it is sometimes conceived as distributed processing environment. However, it is not like that until it has a component of processing that is distributed or data that is distributed over a number of computers connected across a network.

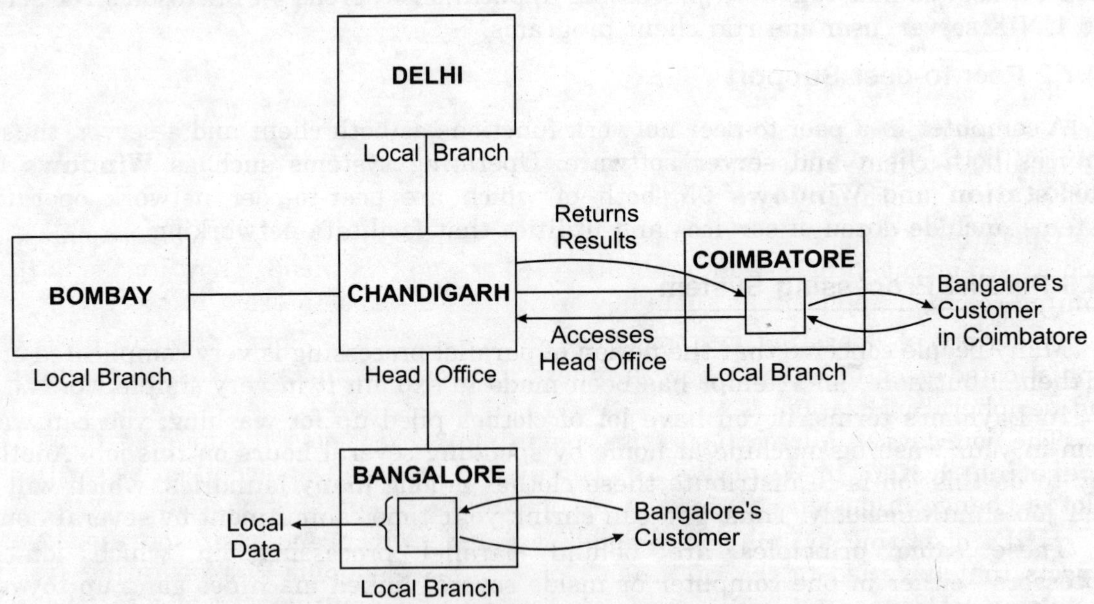

Figure 1.5 : Examples of Distributed Processing

The concept of distributed processing will be more clear if we consider the examples of a bank having its branches throughout India and its head office in Chandigarh. Let us assume that this bank maintains the local data at the local branch and the copy of data of all branches at Chandigarh. Thus, we say that the data is distributed throughout the country. This is basically to facilitate the query processing for local customers of a branch and also for global customer (one who moves from Bangalore to Coimbatore). Figure 1.5 shows the clear pictures of distributed processing.

Distributed processing is thus, a form of on-line processing that allows a single transaction to be composed of application programs that access one or more databases on one or more computers across a network. This type of transaction in which multiple application programs cooperate, is called a distributed transaction. The computer in distributed system can vary in size and even in their platforms. They may include microprocessors, workstations, minicomputers and large general-purpose computer systems. Resource sharing, increased throughput, communication, reliability are few reasons to have distributed processing systems. Using distributed processing, related data at regional and branch locations can be synchronized; updated simultaneously with guaranteed results.

In Chapter 13 of this book, an attempt has been made to discuss almost all the issues related to distributed systems.

The job of distributed operating system is to allow the user to access remote resources in the same manner as they do local resources, control the data and process migration from one site to another, detecting idle CPUs on the network etc.

Many operating systems have been developed to support distributed processing. **Alpha Kernel, Amoeba, Angle, Chorus, Mach** are few examples of distributed operating systems.

1.4.10 Personal Computer System

For a personal computer (PC) the operating system should perform some basic tasks such as recognizing information from the keyboard and mouse, sending information to the monitor, storing and retrieving information from memory and controlling peripheral devices such as printers and scanners.

Operating systems are responsible for running assistive technology applications such as screen magnifiers, and applications that read text aloud. They are the basis for running common applications such as word processors and Internet browsers.

A variety of operating systems have evolved for PCs. Some of them have more sophisticated user interface whereas others have more emphasis on maximizing CPU and peripheral utilization.

The journey of Microsoft in this regard has been quoted to range from **Disk Operating System** to **Windows XP**. However, therefore, this evolution has witnessed a lot of change in design criterion for an operating system.

UNIX operating system has a lot of variants, which emphasize on the different aspects that have led to the continuous process of developing new operating systems. Protection, multitasking, multi-user, user interaction, multiprocessing are few issues that have now become a mandatory part of the operating system's role.

Windows NT, Windows 95, Windows 98, Window XP, Windows 2000, Linux, Macintosh, are few operating systems commonly used on personal computers. The author has recently attended a workshop on an open source operating system "Bharat Operating System Solutions" developed by C-DAC (Center for Development of Advanced Computing). It is a Linux based operating system popularly known as BOSS. Other than all important required features it has something very special, *i.e.*, its interface is available in almost all the Indian languages such as Assamese, Bengali, Punjabi, Sanskrit, Tamil, Manipuri etc. It will enable the mainly non-english literate users in the country to be exposed to ICT and to use the computer more effectively.

1.4.11 Operating System for handheld devices

Handheld devices have emerged from a personal information organizer to a feature rich device in just a couple of years. These days' handheld devices are named as : Personal Digital Assistant (PDA), Palm Tops, Pocket PC and Smart Phones. Earlier handheld devices provided features like information organizer, calculator, notepad and text messaging. Wireless technology has changed the way information is being transferred from one place to another. With the advent of internet enabled devices, handheld devices started managing web surfing, e-mail and multimedia support. The handheld devices used for simple telephonic purposes are now getting involved in audio and video transmission, gaming and third party application exchange. Everyday we are having new vendors and models with more mature functionalities in their devices. It has been the operating system with in these devices which makes provision of functionalities possible in this small package. With effect of various mobile telephony systems used across regions no one has yet designed a standard mobile operating system which can be accepted all over the world in same proportion. The main challenges faced by developers in designing operating system for such devices are :

The small size of handheld devices make it difficult to manage a strong graphical user interface which should provide loading a complete web page. Similarly working on word documents and excel sheets is not a simple task. The resolution adjustments create complexities for designers.

Handheld devices had limited amount of memory in their earlier models. So single task processing was done mostly. But today mobile devices are provided with huge amount of memory (in GB's). Now, it becomes possible to handle multiple task execution in handheld devices. With the addition of such schemes, the complexity of operating system design has also increased.

Internet surfing has made developers taking care of the security provision with in the handheld devices. To safeguard one's information during exchange using e-mail or messaging, authentication techniques need to be managed to provide secure transmission.

The main competitors in mobile operating system race are Palm OS, Windows Mobile, Blackberry, Symbian and Linux. Palm OS is simple and easy to use operating system which provides single tasking environment. It provides huge amount of third party application support along with Personal Information Management (PIM) functionality. It also gives easy navigation facility through menus with touch screen.

Windows Mobile gained popularity because of its user friendly graphical user interface. It provides office capabilities in addition to the Outlook express.

Blackberry compete Windows mobile in provision of Push email facility and QWERTY keyboard that makes it popular gadget among handheld device users. Symbian has captured a whole lot of mobile market with its multitasking functionality along with latest e-mail and multimedia facilities. Linux is an open platform which is freely available to developers with its extensibility feature.

Many vendors and developers are individually working on Linux platform like MontaVista, Access Linux Platform and Google. Now some of them have grouped together as LIMO (Linux Mobile) foundation to provide strong market competition to other platforms. More than 30 mobile-phone companies are members of LIMO, including heavy weights Samsung, Motorola, Vodafone, NTT DoCoMo, and Texas Instruments. Apple's iPhone was launched last year in US and has become quite a popular device among US handheld users. Still iPhone is struggling for its better image in Asian Markets. Today the handheld market is growing at a fast speed and more value added features are expected in near future.

EXERCISES

1.1 Differentiate between parallel processing and symmetric multiprocessing.

1.2 Explain the term SPOOLing and state the advantages of this technique.

1.3 What is the fundamental difference between network and distributed operating systems?

1.4 Identify the various requirements to set up a parallel processing system.

1.5 Describe the various criteria that led to the development of new operating systems.

1.6 Explain the evolution of the operating systems from a simple operating system to today's popular operating systems.

1.7 What are supposed to be special features of a network operating system?

1.8 Explain how multiprogramming contributes towards higher CPU utilization and increased throughput.

1.9 Identify some situations where multiprocessing becomes mandatory.

1.10 Explain with the help of an example, the purpose of distributed processing.

1.11 What are the challenges associated with operating systems for hand held devices?

○○○○○

CHAPTER

2

Computer System Structures

OVERVIEW

This chapter aims to discuss basic computer operations, I/O structure including interrupts, management of memory by an operating system and storage hierarchy. The necessity of hardware protection, memory protection and CPU protection has been discussed in detail. Various mechanisms to meet these different types of protection requirements have also been suggested. A brief mention of system calls has also been made here.

2.1. COMPUTER SYSTEM OPERATION

A computer's functional diagram is as shown in Figure 2.1. Basically, CPU, memory and number of devices make our modern general-purpose computer system.

A brief description of different parts of computer goes like this :

2.1.1 CPU

It is the brain of the computer. All information goes through the CPU to be processed. IBM compatibles are CPUs from Intel (and others) with names like 8086, 80286, 80386, 80486, and Pentium (80586). Apple computers use CPUs from Motorola with names like 6502, 68000, 68020, 68030. The latest CPUs execute many millions of instructions per second. The type of operations that the CPU can do include :

(a) Retrieving data from memory
(b) Outputting data to memory or ports
(c) Logical operations such as AND, OR, NOR
(d) Mathematical operations such as add, subtract, multiply and divide
(e) Comparisons such as equal to, greater than, and less than
(f) Program control operations such as jump to a new spot, skip the next instruction, and "if-then" statements
(g) Response to special external impulses ("interrupts")

A CPU does not have to run a whole computer. There are specialized CPUs made that are explicitly geared to do specific tasks, such as to run the electronics in a car, or a VCR, or microwave oven. In fact, inside the computer itself are a number of these "embedded" CPUs that run the keyboard, the video controller, the serial ports, the network card, and the disk controller.

2.1.2 Memory

Memory is where the information is stored. Memory is organized in little cubbyholes, each of which needs an **address.** The description of various parts goes like this :

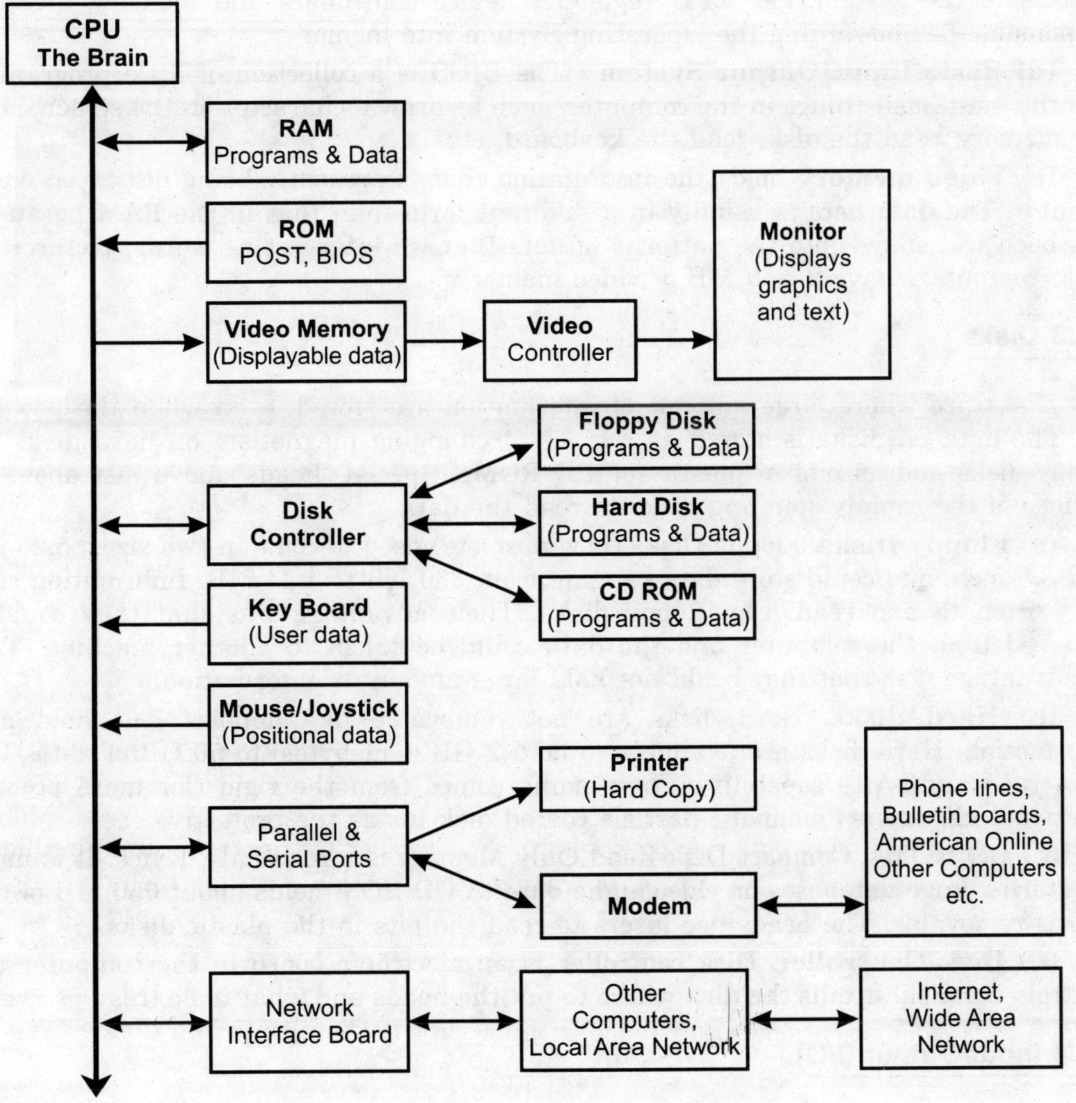

Figure 2.1 : Computer Functional Block Diagram

(a) RAM : Random Access Memory stores programs and data as it is used. The information in RAM is lost when the power is turned off. Information can be written to and read from RAM. A modern computer usually has from 128 MB to 1 GB (Gigabytes) of RAM.

(b) ROM : Read Only Memory stores start up and basic operating information. Information can be read from, but not written to ROM. The information in ROM is not lost when the power is turned off. Computers generally have about 400-500 KB (Kilobytes) of ROM.

(c) Bootstrap Program is an initial program stored in ROM which initialized all aspects of the system, *i.e.,* CPU registers, device controllers and memory, etc. It is responsible for forwarding the Operating System into memory.

(d) Basic Input Output System : The BIOS is a collection of little programs to run the most basic things in the computer, such as draw a character on the screen, check the memory, read the disk, read the keyboard, etc.

(e) Video memory holds the information that is presently being displayed on the monitor. The data here is usually in a different form than that in the RAM because it has been translated into the patterns of dots that we interpret as words, pictures etc. Most computers have 2 to 8 MB of video memory.

2.1.3 Disks

Disks are where large amount of information are stored, even when the power is off. The data on disks is stored as regions of changing magnetism on hard disks and floppy disks and as pits in plastic for CD ROMs. Special "heads" move just above the surface of the rapidly spinning disks to read the data.

(a) Floppy Disks. Floppy Disks (now obsolete) used to come in two sizes, 5.25 inch and 3.5 inch, and could store data ranging from 360 KB to 1.44 MB. Information could be written to and read from floppy disks. Their advantage was that they could be removed from the computer and the data could be taken to another machine. Their disadvantage was that they could not hold large amount of information.

(b) Hard disks. Hard disks are not removable like floppies, but hold more information. Hard disks are available to hold 2 GB (Gigabytes) to 50 GB of data. They have read and write capability. Their name comes from the rigid (for more accurate positional alignment) magnetic-particle coated disk inside the protective case.

(c) CD ROMs. Compact Disk Read Only Memory is a read only device. It is useful for storing huge databases or video/audio data. A CD ROM holds about 650 MB of data and is removable. The heads use lasers to read the pits in the plastic disks.

(d) Disk Controller. Disk controller is an electronic board in the computer that controls the disk. It tells the disk where to put the heads and what to do (read *vs.* write).

2.1.4 Input/Output (I/O)

I/O components allow a computer to communicate with the outside world. Every I/O component in the computer has its own address, just like memory.

(a) Keyboard is used to enter information from the user to the computer. It is not inherently connected to anything. The computer only responds to keyboard if the CPU is looking at the keyboard to see if someone had pressed a key. If the CPU is not looking, the person can hit the keyboard all they want and nothing will happen.

(b) Monitors are used to display information that the computer wishes to tell us. All monitors can show a pattern of coloured dots known as pixels. Monitors know nothing about letters or pictures.

(c) Video controller is a board in the computer that controls the monitor. It translates the data in the video memory. It can thus draw letters and graphs on the screen.

(d) Parallel/Serial Ports allow the computer to send data to and receive data from printers, modems, etc.

(e) Mouse and Joysticks are used to input positional information to the computer. They usually have their own ports, though the mouse often uses the serial port to connect to the computer.

(f) Network Interface Card—A NIC connects the computer to local area networks (LANs) like CLUNet. Networks are a high-speed method of transferring data from one computer to another.

2.1.5 Bus Lines

Bus lines are the data highways inside the computer through which the information moves from one spot to another.

(a) Data bus wires actually carry the information around the inside of the computer.

(b) Address bus wires carry the addresses of where the data is coming from or where it is going. This tells the various components in the computer whether they should receive data from or supply data onto the data bus wires.

(c) Control bus wires carry information regarding what to do with data, such as read or write or what kind of data it is. They also carry timing information for synchronizing the various parts of the computer so they are all doing the right thing at the right time.

As mentioned earlier, when the computer is started—bootstrap program initializes all aspects of the system and finally load the operating system in memory. The operating system now starts executing an initial process like "init" process and waits for the occurrence of some event. The occurrence of this event is indicated by an interrupt from either the hardware or the software.

The event can also be signaled by the occurrence of a trap. Trap and Interrupt are closely related terms with a marginal difference. Interrupts serve a very important purpose—if there were no mechanism of interrupts, one would have to manually check in the main program whether the timers have over flown, whether we have received another character via the serial port, or if some external event had occurred. Besides making the main program ugly and hard to read, such a situation would make our program inefficient. Since, we would be wasting precious "instruction cycles" checking up for events that usually do not happen.

Trap and Interrupt

Trap is actually a software-generated interrupt caused either by an error (for example division by zero, invalid memory access, etc.), or by a specific request for an operating system service generated by a user program. Trap is sometimes called Exception. The hardware or the software can generate these interrupts. When the interrupt or trap occurs, the hardware therefore, transfers control to the operating system which first preserves the current state of the system by saving the current CPU register contents and program counter's value. After this, the focus shifts to the determination of which type of interrupt has occurred. For each type of interrupt, separate segments of code in the operating system determine what action should be taken and thus the system keeps on functioning by executing computational instructions, I/O instructions, storage instructions etc.

Modern operating systems are interrupt driven i.e., if there are no processes to execute, no I/O devices to service, no users whom to respond then operating system will be idle and wait for something to happen.

2.2. INPUT/OUTPUT STRUCTURE

As the block diagram of Figure 2.1 indicates, CPU and device controllers all use a common bus for communication. Each controller controls specific types of device, e.g., tape drive, line printer, disk drive, etc. A device controller has a local buffer storage and a set of multipurpose registers like input register, output register, control register and status register. The device controller will be moving data between the peripheral device and its local buffer storage.

Let us go through Figure 2.2 which explains various steps involved in an I/O operation.

2.2.1 Asynchronous and Synchronous Input/Output

The I/O operation discussed in Figure 2.2 is typically asynchronous I/O operation because after the start of I/O, control is returned to the user program without waiting for the I/O to complete. The I/O continues and on its completion, an interrupt is generated by the controller to attain CPU's attention. The other option to deal with I/O is :

CPU execution waits, while I/O proceeds, in which case, there is a possibility that at most one I/O request is outstanding at a time. This is known as synchronous I/O. Synchronous I/O is achieved by polling. CPU starts an I/O operation, and continuously polls (checks) that device until the I/O operation finishes. Thus synchronous I/O keeps CPU idle in the sense that it cannot execute any other process, while an I/O operation is going on. Asynchronous I/O is more advantageous as it increases system efficiency. Asynchronous I/O is the best way to compensate the speed differences between slow I/O devices and fast processor.

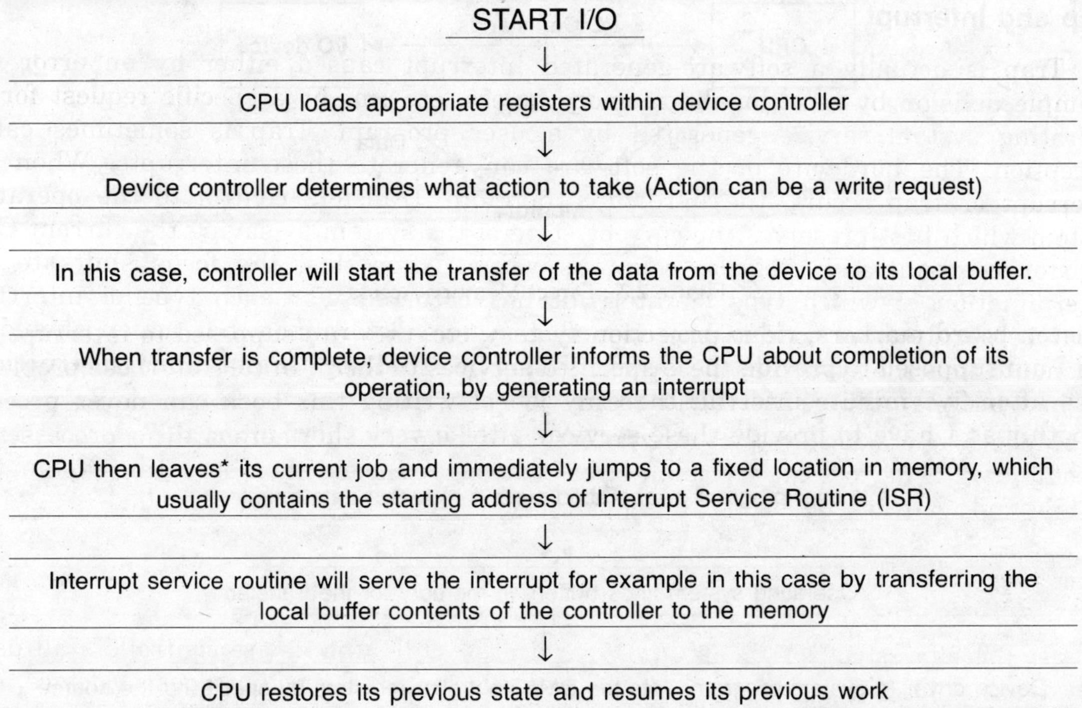

Figure 2.2 Input Output Operation

2.2.2 Direct Memory Access (DMA)

Direct Memory Access is another advanced mechanism where I/O device is given full freedom to transfer block of data to/from memory without going through the CPU. Figure 2.3 explains this concept. This method is known to increase the speed of overall computer operation.

Usually, a specified portion of memory is designated as an area to be used for direct memory access (e.g., in ISA bus standard, up to 16 MB of memory) can be addressed for DMA. The EISA and micro channel architecture standards allow access to the full range of memory addresses (assuming they are addressable with 32 bits)).

After going through all this matter about DMA, an obvious question that might arise in your mind is—What was the necessity of DMA?

The answer is—If the I/O operation becomes very fast then CPU faces a situation in which it receives more and more interrupts within a given time interval and thus CPU is left with hardly any time to execute a process.

This situation can be compared with real life situation. Suppose I am writing a book in my cabin, and I am also supposed to conduct a course where I have assigned lectures to my fellow teachers. Whenever they have a problem *e.g.,* they want to take attendance

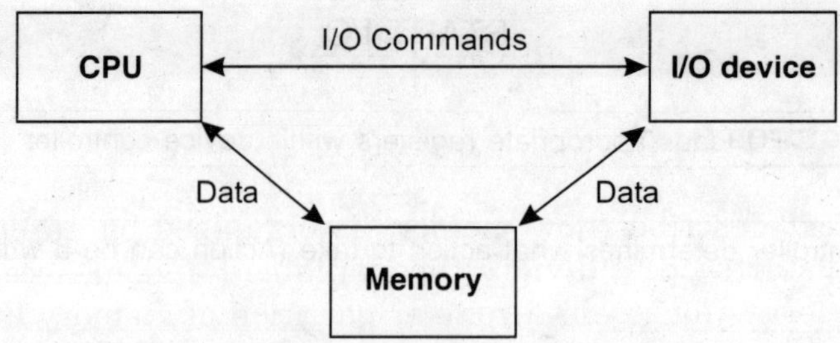

Figure 2.3 : Direct Memory Access

register, board markers, video projection system, etc. they are supposed to interrupt me and I am supposed to provide these specified services to them. In case all these problems arise after five minute interval, then my job of writing this book can never proceed smoothly as I have to provide these services after a very short interval.

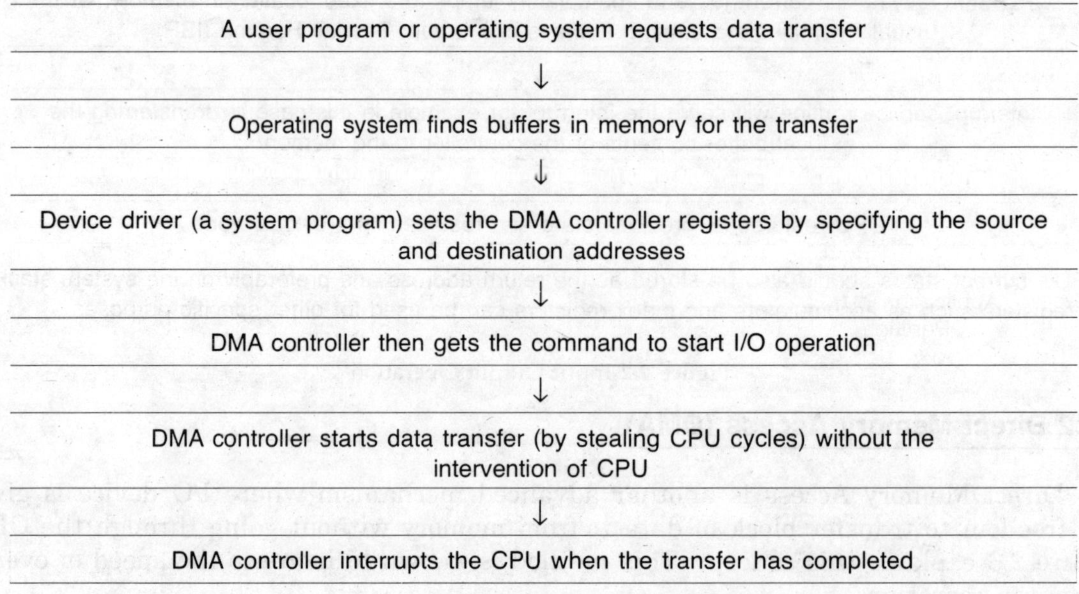

Figure 2.4 : I/O Operation Using DMA

The solution to this can be :

Give them direct access to the attendance register, video projection system etc. so that they do not interrupt me at any given time. They are then left with only one job of intimating that they have successfully completed their lectures (say after an interval of 2 hours).

Based on this analogy the invent of DMA can be justified. Thus, DMA is used for high-speed I/O devices. The device controller transfers an entire block of data directly to or from its local buffer to memory, without any intervention of CPU. Only the interrupt is generated per block rather than one interrupt per byte generated for the low-speed devices. Figure 2.4 explains the steps involved in I/O operation using DMA.

2.3. STORAGE STRUCTURE AND STORAGE HIERARCHY

2.3.1 Storage Structures

The following text describes how memory is organized by an operating system. As an operating system starts up, it divides the available Random Access Memory into two broad sections. It reserves for itself, a zone or partition of memory known as the system partition. The system partition always begins at the lowest addressable byte of memory (memory address 0) and extends upward. The system partition contains a system heap and a set of global variables, described later in this text.

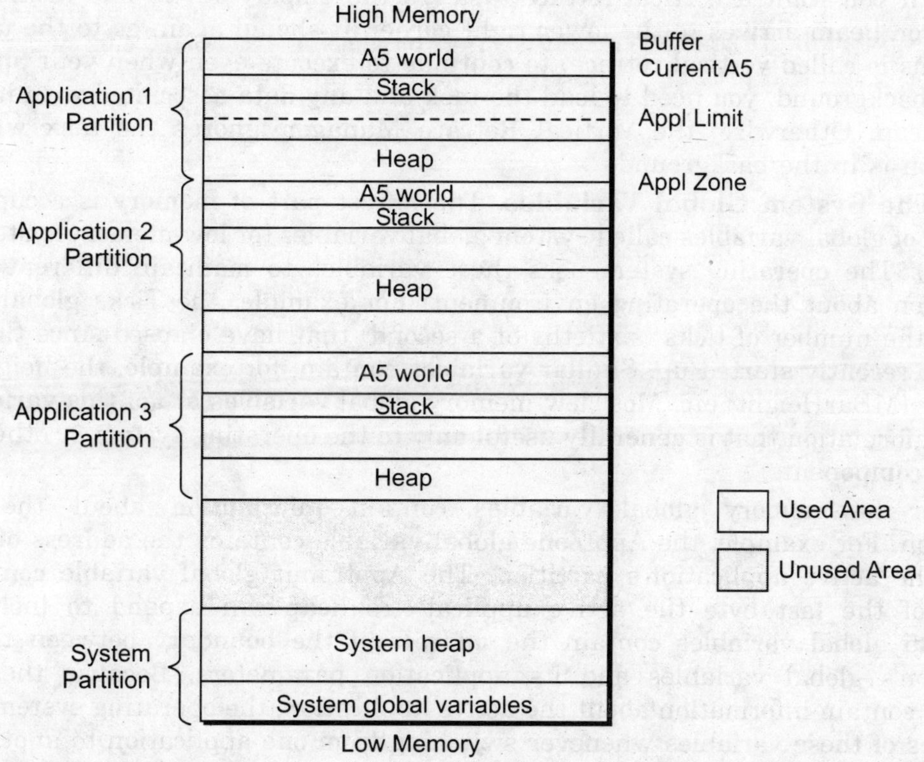

Figure 2.5 : Memory Organization when several Applications are open on the system

Figure 2.5 illustrates the organization of memory when several applications are open at the same time. The system partition occupies the lowest position in memory. Application partition occupies part of the remaining space. Note that application partitions are loaded into the top part of memory first.

In Figure 2.5, three applications are open, each with its own application partition. The application labeled Application 1 is the active application (The labels on the right side of the figure are system global variables, explained later in the text).

2.3.1.1 Organization of Memory in System Partition

(a) The System Heap. The main part of the system partition is an area of memory known as the system heap. In general, the system heap is reserved for exclusive use by the operating system and other system software components, which load into it various items such as system resources, system code segments, and system data structures. All system buffers and queues, for example are allocated in the system heap.

The system heap is also used for code and other resources that do not belong to specific applications, such as code resources that add features to the operating system or that provide control of special-purpose peripheral equipment. Device drivers (system programs that enable operating system to recognize and communicate with a piece of hardware) are loaded into the system heap.

Most applications do not need to load anything in the system heap. In certain cases, however, you might need to load resources or a part of code into the system heap. For example, if you want a vertical retrace task (In the display device like monitor, when the electron beam arrives to the lower right corner, it should again go to the upper left corner, this is called vertical retrace) to continue to execute even when your application is in the background, you need to load the task and any data associated with it into the system heap. Otherwise, the Vertical Retrace Manager ignores the task when your application is in the background.

(b) The System Global Variables. The lowest part of memory is occupied by a collection of global variables called system global variables (or low-memory system global variables). The operating system uses these variables to maintain different kinds of information about the operating environment. For example, the Ticks global variable contains the number of ticks (sixtieths of a second) that have elapsed since the system was most recently started up. Similar variables contain, for example, the height of the menu bar (MBarHeight) etc. Most low-memory global variables are of this variety : they contain information that is generally useful only to the operating system or other system software components.

Other low-memory global variables contain information about the current application. For example, the ApplZone global variable contains the address of the first byte of the active application's partition. The ApplLimit global variable contains the address of the last byte the active application's heap can expand to include. The CurrentA5 global variables contain the address of the boundary between the active application's global variables and its application parameters. Because these global variables contain information about the active application, the operating system changes the values of these variables whenever switching from one application to another takes place.

In general, it is best to avoid reading or writing low-memory system global variables. The results of changing their values can be unpredictable. Usually, when the value of a low-memory global variable is likely to be useful to applications, the system software provides a routine that you can use to read or write that value. For example, you can get the current value of the Ticks global variable by calling the TickCount function.

2.3.1.2 Organization of Memory in an Application Partition

When your application is launched, the operating system allocates for it a partition of memory, called its application partition. That partition contains required segments of the application's code as well as other data associated with the application. Figure 2.6 illustrates the general organization of an application partition.

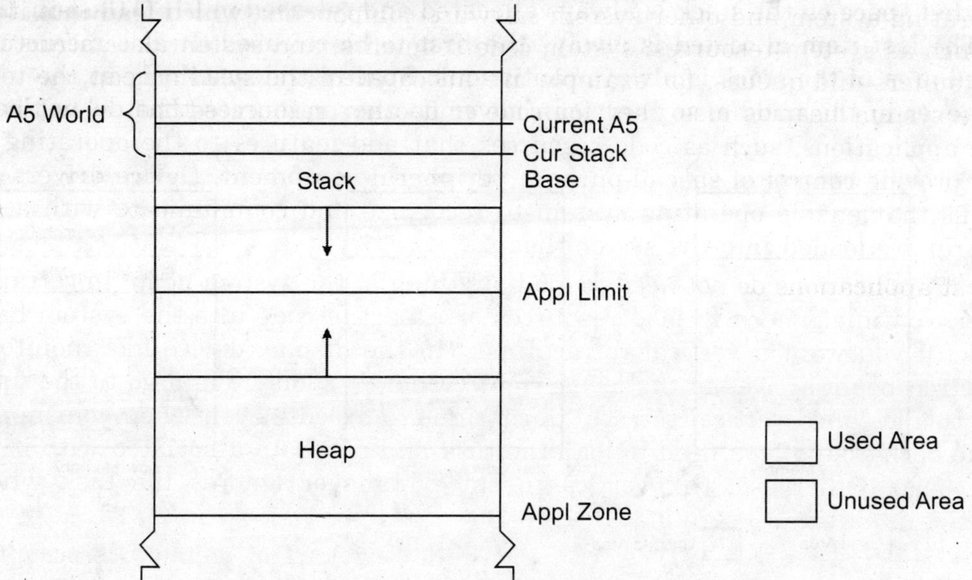

Figure 2.6 : Organization of an application partition

Your application partition is divided into three major parts :

- the application stack
- the application heap
- the application global variables and A5 world

The heap is located at the low-memory end of your application partition and always expands (when necessary) toward high memory. The A5 world is located at the high-memory end of your application partition and is of fixed size. The stack begins at the low-memory end of the A5 world and expands downward, toward the top of the heap.

As you can see in Figure 2.6 there is usually an unused area of memory between the stack and the heap. This unused area provides space for the stack to grow without encroaching upon the space assigned to the application heap. In some cases, however, the stack might grow into space reserved for the application heap. If this happens, it is very likely that data in the heap will become corrupted.

Unlike the heap, the stack is not bounded by ApplLimit. If your application uses heavily nested procedures with many local variables or uses extensive recursion, the stack could grow downward beyond ApplLimit. Because you do not use Memory Manager routines to allocate memory on the stack, the Memory Manager cannot stop your stack from growing beyond ApplLimit and possibly encroaching upon space reserved for the heap. However, a vertical retrace task checks approximately 60 times each second to see if the stack has moved into the heap. If it has, the task, known as the "stack sniffer", generates a system error. This system error alerts you that you have allowed the stack to grow too far, so that you can make adjustments.

(a) The Application Stack. The stack is an area of memory in your application partition that can grow or shrink at one end while the other end remains fixed. This means that space on the stack is always allocated and released in LIFO (last-in, first-out) order. The last item allocated is always the first to be released. It also means that the allocated area of the stack is always contiguous. Space is released only at the top of the stack, never in the middle, so there can never be any unallocated "holes" in the stack.

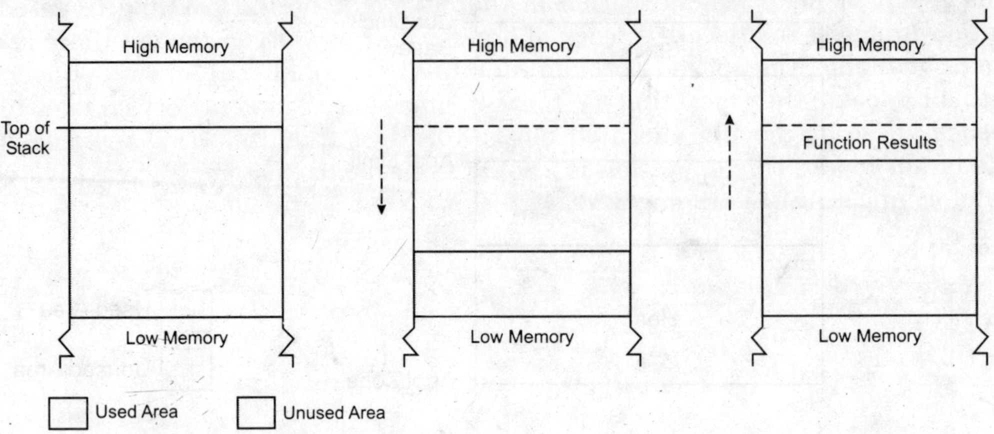

Figure 2.7 : The application stack

By convention, the stack grows from high memory toward low memory addresses. The end of the stack that grows or shrinks is usually referred to as the "top" of the stack, even though it is actually at the lower end of memory occupied by the stack.

Because of its LIFO nature, the stack is especially useful for memory allocation connected with the execution of functions or procedures. When your application calls a routine, space is automatically allocated on the stack for a stack frame. A stack frame contains the routine's parameters, local variable, and return address. Figure 2.7 illustrates how the stack expands and shrinks during a function call. The leftmost diagram shows the stack just before the function is called. The middle diagram shows the stack expanded to hold the stack frame. Once the function is executed, the local variables and function parameters are popped off the stack. If the function is a Pascal function, all that remains is the previous stack with the function result on top.

Note : Dynamic memory allocation on the stack is usually handled automatically if you are using a high-level development language such as Pascal. The compiler generates the code that creates and deletes stack frames for each function or procedure call.

(b) The Application Heap. An application heap is the area of memory in your application partition in which space is dynamically allocated and released on demand. The heap begins at the low-memory end of your application partition and extends upward in memory. The heap contains virtually all items that are not allocated on the stack. For instance, your application heap contains the application's code segments and resources that are currently loaded into memory. The heap also contains other dynamically allocated items such as window records, dialog records, document data, and so forth.

The operating system memory management Service does all the necessary housekeeping to keep track of blocks in the heap as they are allocated and released. Because these operations can occur in any order, the heap does not usually grow and shrink in an orderly way, as the stack does. Instead, after your application has been running for a while, the heap can tend to become fragmented into a patchwork of allocated and free blocks, as shown in Figure 2.8. This fragmentation is known as heap fragmentation.

One result of heap fragmentation is that it might not be possible to satisfy your application's request to allocate a block of a particular size. Even though there is enough free space available, the space is broken up into blocks smaller than the requested size. When this happens, the Operating System's memory management service tries to create the needed space by moving allocated blocks together, thus collecting the free space in a single larger block. This operation is known as heap compaction. Figure 2.9 shows the results of compacting the fragmented heap shown in Figure 2.8.

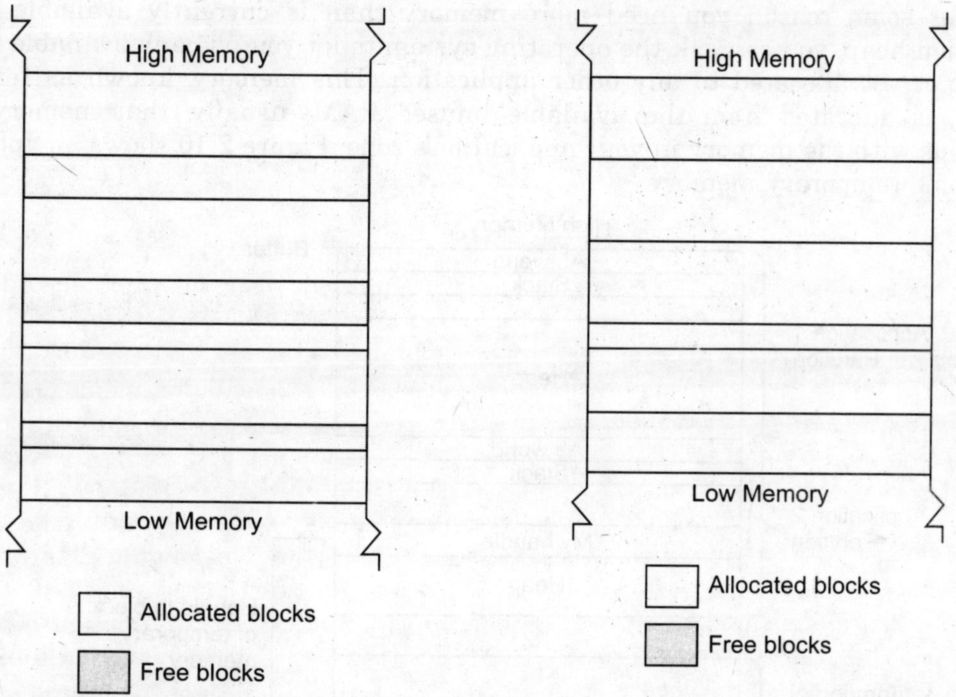

Figure 2.8 : A fragmented heap

Figure 2.9 : A compacted heap

Heap fragmentation is generally not a problem as long as the blocks of memory you allocate are free to move during heap compaction.

(c) The Application Global Variables and A5 World. Your application's global variables are stored in an area of memory near the top of your application partition known as the application A5 world. The A5 world contain four kinds of data :

- application global variables
- application QuickDraw global variables
- application parameters
- the application's jumps table

Each of these items is of fixed size, although the sizes of the global variables and of the jump table may vary from application to application.

2.3.1.3 Temporary Memory

In a multitasking environment, each application is limited to a particular memory partition (whose size is determined by information in the 'Size' resource of that application). The size of your application's partition places certain limits on the size of your application heap and hence on the size of the buffers and other data structures that your application uses. In general, you specify an application partition size that is large enough to hold all the buffers, resources, and other data that your application is likely to need during its execution.

If for some reason you need more memory than is currently available in your application heap, you can ask the operating system to let you use any available memory that is not yet allocated to any other application. This memory, known as temporary memory, is allocated from the available unused RAM; usually, that memory is not contiguous with the memory in your application's zone. Figure 2.10 shows an application using some temporary memory.

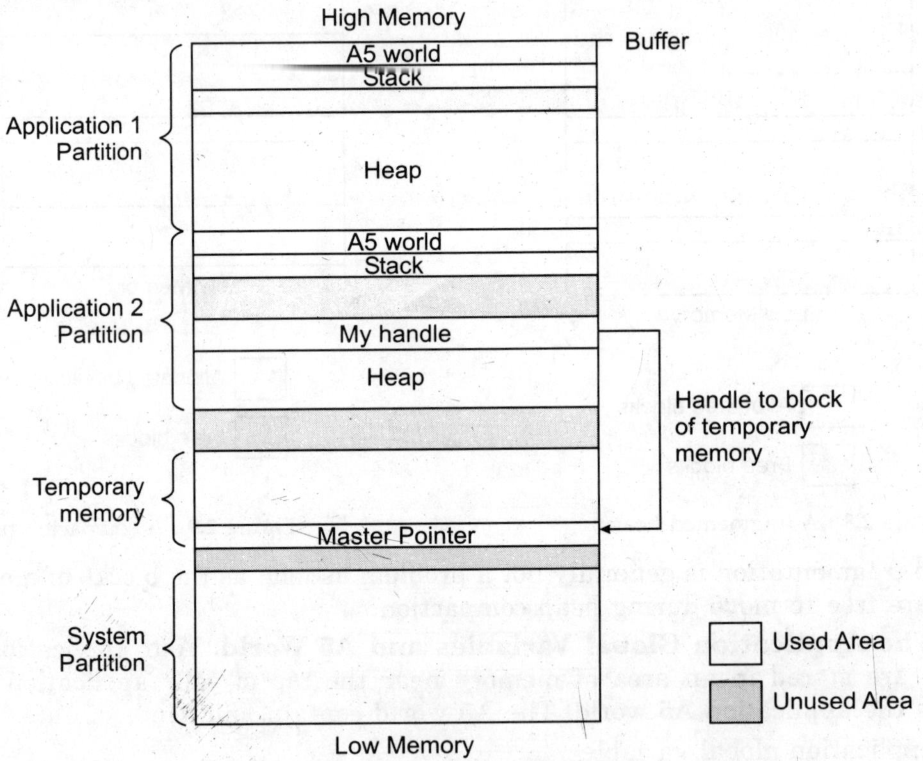

Figure 2.10 : Using temporary memory allocated from unused RAM

Application 1 has almost exhausted its application heap. As a result, it has requested and receive a large block of temporary memory, extending from the top of Application 2's partition to the top of the allocatable space. Application 1 can use the temporary memory in whatever manner it desires.

Your application should use temporary memory only for occasional short-term purposes that could be accomplished in less space, though perhaps less efficiently. For example, if you want to copy a large file, you might try to allocate a fairly larger buffer of temporary memory. If you receive the temporary memory, you can copy data from the source file into the destination file using the large buffer. If, however, the request for temporary memory fails, you can instead use a smaller buffer within your application heap. Although using the smaller buffer might prolong the copying operation, the file is nonetheless copied.

One good reason for using temporary memory only occasionally is that you cannot assume that you will always receive the temporary memory you request. For example, in Figure 2.10 all the available memory is allocated to the two open applications; any further requests by either one for some temporary memory would fail.

2.3.2 Storage Hierarchy

The Figure 2.11 shows, the hierarchy of various kinds of memory available for use by the operating systems, application programs and other system programs loaded in a system.

The Figure 2.11 indicates that there is always a tradeoff between size and speed of the memory. As the size grows, the memory becomes slow in its speed. Another concept is that of storage volatility, main memory is a volatile memory. It implies that its contents are lost when power supply to the system is stopped. Therefore, we say that non-volatile memories are useful for taking backups. All the storage systems above the main memory are (and including it) volatile and all the storage systems below it are non-volatile.

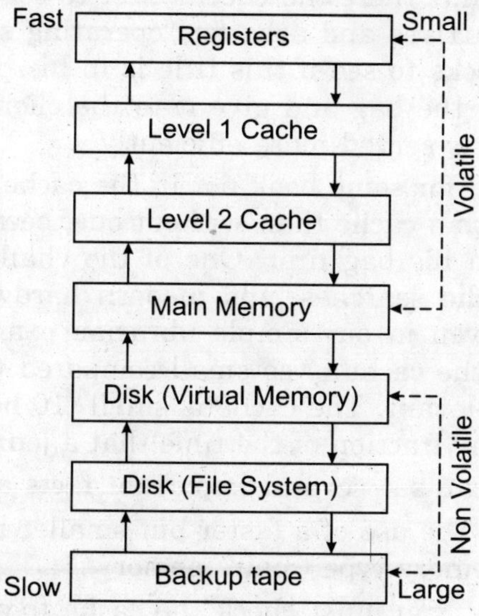

Figure 2.11 : Storage Hierarchy

Caching is a technology based on the memory subsystem of your computer. The main purpose of a cache is to accelerate your computer while keeping the price of the computer low. Caching allows you to do your computer tasks more rapidly.

To understand the basic idea behind a cache system, let's start with a super-simple example that uses a librarian to demonstrate caching concepts. Let's imagine a librarian behind his desk. He is there to give you the books you ask for. For the sake of simplicity, let's say you can't get the books yourself—you have to ask the librarian for any book you want to read and he fetches it for you from a set of stacks in a storeroom. First, let's start with a librarian without cache.

The first client arrives. He asks for a popular book "operating system". The librarian goes into the storeroom, gets the book, returns to the counter and gives the book to the client. Later, the client comes back to return the book. The librarian takes the book and returns it to the storeroom. He then returns to his counter waiting for another client. Let's say the next client asks for "operating system" (you saw it coming...). The librarian then has to return to the storeroom to get the book he recently handled and give it to the client. Under this model, the librarian has to make a complete round trip to fetch every book—even very popular ones that are requested frequently. Is there a way to improve the performance of the librarian?

Yes, there is a way—we can put a cache on the librarian. Let's give the librarian a bag into which he will be able to store 10 books (in computer terms, the librarian now has a 10-book cache). In this bag, he will put the books the clients return to him, up to a maximum of 10. Let's use the prior example, but now with our new-and-improved caching librarian.

The day starts. The bag of the librarian is empty. Our first client arrives and asks for "operating system." No magic here—the librarian has to go to the storeroom to get the book. He gives it to the client. Later, the client returns and gives the book back to the librarian. Instead of returning to the storeroom to return the book, the librarian puts the book in his bag and stands there (he checks first to see if the bag is full—more on that later). Another client arrives and asks for "operating system", before going to the storeroom, the librarian checks to see if this title is in his bag. He finds it ! All he has to do is take the book from the bag and give it to the client. There is no journey into the storeroom, so the client is served more efficiently.

What if the client asked for some book not in the cache (the bag)? In this case, the librarian is less efficient with a cache than without one, because the librarian takes the time to look for the book in his bag first. One of the challenges of cache design is to minimize the impact of cache searches, and modern hardware has reduced this time delay to practically zero. Even in our simple librarian example, the latency time (the waiting time) of searching the cache is so small compared to the time to walk back to the storeroom that it is irrelevant. The cache is small (10 books), and the time it takes to notice a miss is only a tiny fraction of the time that a journey to the storeroom takes.

For this example, you can see several important facts about caching :

- Cache technology is the use of a faster but smaller memory type to accelerate a slower but large memory type (main memory).
- When using a cache, you must check the cache to see if an item is in there. If it is there, it is called a cache hit. If not, it is called a cache miss and the computer must wait for a round trip from the larger, slower memory area (i.e., main memory).

- A cache has some maximum size that is much smaller than the larger storage area of RAM and secondary storage devices.
- It is possible to have multiple layers of cache. With our librarian example, the smaller but faster memory type is the bag, and the storeroom represents the larger and slower memory type. This is a one-level cache. There might be another layer of cache consisting of a shelf that can hold 100 books behind the counter. The librarian can check the bag, then the shelf and then the storeroom. This would be a two-level cache.

2.3.2.1 Computer Caches

A computer is a machine in which we measure time in very small increments. When the microprocessor accesses the main memory (RAM), it does it in about 50 nanoseconds (60 billionth of a second). That is pretty fast, but it is much slower than the typical microprocessor. Microprocessors can have cycle times as short as 2 nanoseconds, so to a microprocessor 50 nanoseconds seems like an eternity.

What if we build a special memory bank, small but very fast (around 30 nanoseconds)? that is already two times faster than the main memory access. That is called a level 2 cache or an L2 cache. What if we build an even smaller but faster memory system directly into the microprocessor's chip? That way, this memory will be accessed at the speed of the microprocessor and not the speed of the memory bus. That is an L1 cache, which on a 233-megahertz (MHz) Pentium is 3.5 times faster than the L2 cache (which has two times faster access than the access to main memory).

There are a lot of subsystems in a computer; you can put cache between many of them to improve performance. Here is an example. We have the microprocessor (the fastest thing in the computer). Then there is the L1 cache that caches the L2 cache that caches the main memory, which can be used (and is often used) as a cache for even slower peripherals like hard disks and CD-ROMs. The hard disks are also used to cache an even slower medium—your Internet connection.

Your Internet connection is the slowest links in your computer. So your browser (Internet Explorer, Netscape, Opera, etc.) uses the hard disk to store HTML pages, putting them into a special folder on your disk. The first time you ask for an HTML page, your browser downloads it and a copy of it is also stored on your disk. The next time you request access to this page, your browser checks if the date of the file on the Internet is newer than the one cached. If the date is the same, your browser uses the one on your hard disk instead of downloading it from Internet. In this case, the smaller but faster memory system is your hard disk (i.e., Hard disk becomes cache) and the larger and slower one is the Internet.

Cache can also be built directly on peripherals. Modern hard disks come with fast memory, around 512 kilobytes, hardwired to the hard disk. The computer does not directly use this memory—the hard-disk controller does. For the computer, these memory chips are the disks itself. When the computer asks for data from the hard disk, the hard-disk controller checks into this memory before moving the mechanical parts of the hard disk (which is very slow compared to memory). If it finds the data that the computer asked for in the cache, it will return the data stored in the cache without actually accessing data on the disk itself, saving a lot of time.

Here is an experiment you can try. Your computer caches your floppy drive with main memory, and you can actually see it happening. Access a large file from your floppy—for example open a 300-kilobyte text file in a text editor. The first time, you will see the light on your floppy turning on, and you will wait. The floppy disk is extremely slow, so it will take 20 seconds to load the file. Now, close the editor and open the same file again. The second time (do not wait 30 minutes or do a lot of disk access between the two tries) you would not see the light turning on, and you would not wait. The operating system checked into its memory cache for the floppy disk and found what it was looking for. So instead of waiting 20 seconds, the data is found in a memory subsystem much faster than when you first tried it (one access to the floppy disk takes 120 milliseconds, while one access to the main memory takes around 60 nanoseconds—that is a lot faster). You could have run the same test on your hard disk, but it is more evident on the floppy drives because it is so slow.

To give you the complete picture of it all, here is a list of normal caching system :

- **L1 cache—**Memory accesses at full microprocessor speed (10 nanoseconds, 4 kilobytes to 16 kilobytes in size).
- **L2 cache—**Memory access of type Static RAM (around 20 to 30 nanoseconds, 128 kilobytes to 512 kilobytes in size).
- **Main Memory—**Memory access to type RAM (around 60 nanoseconds, 32 megabytes to 128 megabytes in size).
- **Hard disk—**Mechanical, slow (around 12 milliseconds, 1 gigabytes to 40 gigabytes in size).
- **Internet—**incredibly slow (between 1 second and 3 days, unlimited size).

As you can see, the L1 cache caches the L2 cache, which caches the main memory, which can be used to cache the disk subsystem, and so on.

One common question asked at this point is, "Why not make all of the computer's memory run at the same speed as the L1 cache, so no changing be required?" That would work, but it would be incredibly expensive. The idea behind caching is to use a small amount of expensive memory to speed up a large amount of slower, less-expensive memory.

In designing a computer, the goal is to allow the microprocessor to run at its full speed as inexpensively as possible. A 500 MHz chip goes through 500 million cycles in one second (one cycle every two nanoseconds). Without L1 and L2 caches, an access to the main memory takes 60 nanoseconds, or about 30 wasted cycles accessing memory.

When you think about it, it is kind of incredible concept that such relatively tiny amounts of memory can maximize the use of much larger amounts of memory. Think about a 256-kilobyte L2 cache that caches 64 megabytes of RAM. In this case, 256,000 bytes efficiently caches 64,000,000 bytes. Thus, it really works!

2.3.2.2 Locality of Reference

In computer science, we have a theoretical concept called locality of reference. It means that in a fairly large program, only small portions are ever used frequently at any one time. As strange as it may seem, locality of reference works for the huge majority of programs. Even if the executable is 10 megabytes in size, only a handful of bytes from that program are in use at anyone time, and their rate of repetition is very high. For example, a set of statements is executed within a loop many times as compared to other set of statements without any loop control structure. Let us consider that a word processor spends 95 per cent of the time waiting for your input and 5 percent for displaying it on the screen. The later part of word-processor program is in the cache. This 5 per cent is what we call locality of reference, and that is why a cache works so efficiently.

2.3.2.3 Coherency of Data

As mentioned in this text, copy of the same data is maintained by the cache and main memory and may be by the hard disk also. What can happen, if one copy of this data (in cache) is updated and rest remain unchanged? There is a possibility that stale (not current) data is obtained by an application (if the desired data is not there in the cache data is to be fetched from main memory). Thus, there arises a necessity to keep the data "at all levels", consistent. This is known as cache coherency problem. Cache coherency is critical for multiprocessing environment. In this case, any change in the data should be immediately notified to the other caches.

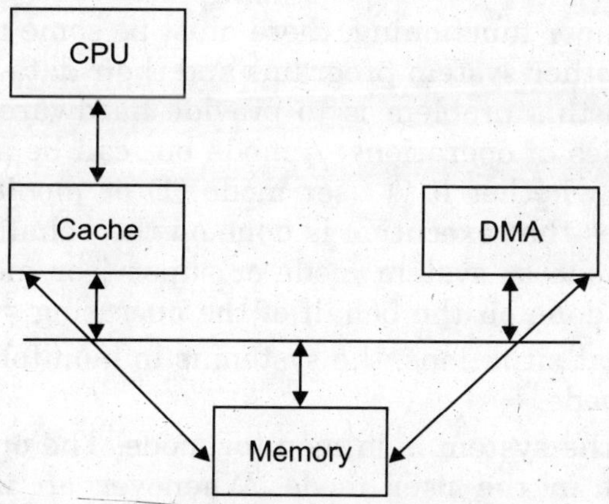

Figure 2.12 : Depicts the cache Write-through method

The situation becomes worse in a distributed environment, where several replicas (copies) of the same data are kept on different computers, which are located, geographically far apart. Again a mechanism of notifying an update (in one of the copies) to other systems so that they have latest copy of the data is mandatory. Cache or write through method is one solution to this problem. This method provides for propagating all updates of caches to the main memory and thus making main memory always consistent with the cache. But this method has a disadvantage that increased memory utilization will affect the performance of the system, as each cache update will involve two simultaneous operations : updating the cache and updating the main memory.

Many protocols have been proposed to deal with the problem of cache coherency.

2.4. HARDWARE PROTECTION

As we have learnt about the evolution of operating systems, we have also come across the fact that operating system gained more and more control over the system with the passage of time. With this hold of the operating system over the computer system, arised the necessity that an operating system must ensure that an incorrect program do not cause incorrect execution of the other programs, i.e., there should not be a possibility of an erroneous program to modify another program or data of some other program or the operating system itself. MS-DOS, Macintosh operating system, both are the examples of the operating systems that do not take any care of such errors.

The hardware can detect many programming errors. These errors are handled by the operating system. In case of an error like trying to jump to an invalid address or executing an illegal introduction, hardware generates trap to the operating system. The trap, just like an interrupt, transfers control to the operating system.

Thus, the point here is that in order for an operating system to serve as an adequate controller of the hardware, the hardware must also provide some kind of support.

2.4.1 Dual-Mode Operation

In order to ensure proper functioning, there must be some mechanism to protect the operating system and all other system programs and their data from any malfunctioning program. An approach to this problem is to provide hardware support to differentiate between at least two modes of operations. A mode bit, can be added to the hardware of the computer to indicate whether it is user mode (1) or monitor mode (0). User mode indicated by bit '1', implies that execution is done on the behalf of a user. Monitor mode (also known as Kernel mode or system mode or supervisor mode), indicated by bit '0', implies that execution is done on the behalf of the operating system.

Let us find out in what situations, the system is in monitor mode and in what other situations, it is in user mode.

When system boots, the system is in monitor mode. The operating system is loaded and user processes start in the user mode. Whenever an interrupt or trap occurs, hardware switches to the monitor mode. Thus, whenever the operating system gains control of the computer, it is in the monitor mode and before passing control to a user program, the mode is changed to user mode.

Some of the machine instructions termed as privileged instructions, can cause harm if executed in user mode. Therefore, hardware allows their execution to be done in the monitor mode only. (Let us try to know what happens if privileged instruction is forced to be executed in user mode?) If an attempt is made to execute a privileged instruction in a user mode, the hardware does not execute it and treats it as an illegal instruction and traps to the operating system.

Thus, the hardware supported dual mode operation is must for the proper functioning of an operating system. Windows NT, Windows98, Windows95 etc., are few operating systems that ensure greater protection for the operating system by supporting this feature.

2.4.2 I/O Protection

(a) In order to prevent a user from performing illegal I/O, all I/O instructions should be defined as privileged instruction.

(b) Another mechanism which is required to achieve I/O protection is that user program should never be given control of the computer in monitor mode because if the user program can get control of the system in monitor mode then all the I/O instructions (which we have been made privileged) can be executed according to user's wish which can lead to undesired results in the system.

In order to implement mechanism stated in (b), memory protection should also be provided. Memory protection has been discussed thoroughly in the following text.

2.4.3 Memory Protection

It becomes essential to protect interrupt service routine (ISRs) and interrupt vectors from modification, as there is a possibility that a user program can store a new address in the interrupt vector which can be an address in the user program itself. Thus, when a corresponding trap or interrupt will occur, the hardware will switch to monitor mode and through the interrupt vector will transfer the control to the user program. As an essence, there is a possibility of a user program gaining control over the computer in monitor mode. Similarly, if interrupt service routine (ISR) is modified, it will lead to undesired results. Therefore, there arises the necessity to protect the system program and each of the user programs from each other. This is achieved by determining the range of legal addresses that the program may access. There are two methods of doing this :

(a) Base and Limit Registers : The simplest method of enforcing memory protection is adding two registers to the CPU, a "base" and a "limit" that demarcate a range of memory to which valid references can be made. References outside that range cause a trap to the operating system. Figure 2.13 depicts memory protection by base and limit registers. It indicates that the base register contains the base address of the process and the limit register contains the size of the range.

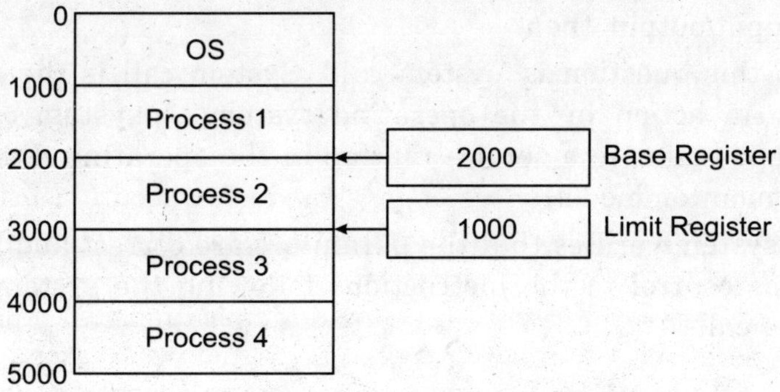

Figure 2.13 : Base and Limit

Advantage : This is the simplest and best method of memory protection as long as memory is allocated contiguously to a user program.

Disadvantage : Non-contiguous memory is harder to protect by this mechanism.

Figure 2.13 indicates that process 2 has the legal range of addresses starting from 2000 (Base Register) to 2000 (Base Register) + 1000 (Limit Register) = 3000.

The contents of Base Register and Limit Register can only be modified in the monitor mode.

(b) Memory Keys. A second approach (from IBM/360) is to break up all of the memory into 2K pages and assign a 4-bit key to each. Add a register to the CPU that holds the process's current key. Reference is allowed where the process's key and the page's key match, otherwise trap is generated to the operating system. The key can only be changed in the supervisor mode or monitor mode.

2.4.4 CPU Protection

In order to prevent a user program from getting stuck in an infinite loop, and never returning control to the operating system, timer mechanism must be implemented. A timer should interrupt the process execution after a specified period. This period can be fixed or variable. Timer's value is set by the operating system and is decremented every clock tick. Whenever, the timer reaches the value 0, an interrupt occurs.

In case, the timer interrupts, the operating system should get the control of the system and now it is at the discretion of the operating system whether to abort the user program or give it some more time to execute. It should again be kept in mind that the instructions, which modify the operation of timer, should be defined as privileged.

2.5. GENERAL SYSTEM ARCHITECTURE

As we have discussed the necessity and implications of privileged instructions, we come to a conclusion that instructions which manipulate a timer, which turn on and off the interrupts, which halt the computer system are all privileged. Other than these, I/O instructions should also be privileged. This leads to a question that how does the user program perform input/output then?

The answer to this question is 'system call'. System call is the method used by a process to request an action by the operating system. A system call control passes through the interrupt vector to a service routine in the operating system and the mode bit is to set to the monitor mode.

The operating system verifies that the paramters are correct and legal, executes the request, and returns control to the instructions following the system call. Figure 2.14 explains the system calls.

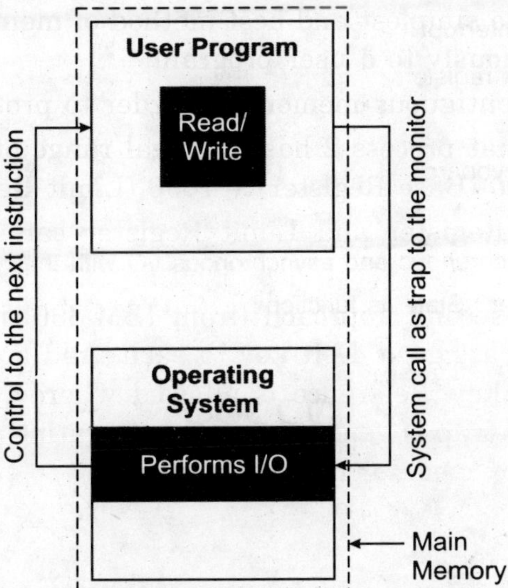

Figure 2.14 : User program executes System call to request that Operating System should perform I/O on its behalf

For a detailed notion of system calls, you can refer Section 3.2 (Chapter 3).

EXERCISES

2.1 What is the purpose of having a mode bit?

2.2 Contrast trap and interrupt. What is the function of each of them?

2.3 Explain the advantage of DMA over Interrupt based I/O system.

2.4 List the advantages and disadvantages of caching.

2.5 Explain how application programs are accommodated in main memory.

2.6 What is system heap? State its purposes.

2.7 What is temporary memory? State its purpose.

2.8 Which of the following instructions should be privileged?

(a) Set value of a timer

(b) Read the clock

(c) Clear memory

(d) Turn off interrupts

(e) Switch from user to monitor mode

(f) Set the priority of an interrupt

(g) Set the base and limit registers

(h) Halt the system

(i) Read data from the keyboard

(j) Write data to a printer.

2.9 Differentiate between synchronous and asynchronous I/O with the help of an example.

2.10 What is a device controller? State its functions.

CHAPTER

3

Operating System Structures

OVERVIEW

This chapter describes in brief the various services that must be essentially provided by the operating system. Memory management, Process management, CPU-scheduling, Device management are amongst those services. Various operating system architectures have been discussed and their comparative study has been done in this chapter. This chapter also discusses design and implementation issues of an operating system. System generation process has also been mentioned briefly.

3.1. OPERATING SYSTEM SERVICES

An operating system provides an environment for the execution of programs. All its services are meant to serve the users *i.e.,* each service is responsible to reduce the user's programming burden e.g., the user need not specify where should the program be loaded in the memory, it should be decided by the memory management service. Similarly, the user should not be required to give a set of commands to find the path of his file. The Graphical user Interface of the operating system should provide the facility to travel through the system directories just by mouse clicks. Each service should be provided by an independent component of an operating system. Brief mention of its services is as follows :

- Process Management service
- Main-memory management service
- File management service
- I/O operations management service
- Secondary storage management
- Network management

There can be many other services, (e.g., providing a good graphical user interface) depending upon the kind of operating system.

Each of the above mentioned services have been discussed in detail in the chapters following this chapter. Still it has been realized that a brief mention of each of these services should be provided here. It goes like this :

Process Management. Operating system is responsible for the following activities with respect to process management :

- The creation, deletion, suspension and resumption of both user and system processes.
- Handling process synchronization and inter-process communication.
- Deadlock handling.

Main-memory Management. Operating system is responsible for the following activities in connection with management of memory :

- Allocation and de-allocation of memory as and when needed.
- Keeping track of used and unused memory space.
- Deciding what process to be loaded into memory in case space becomes available.

File Management. The operating system provides a file system interface and a mechanism for its implementation.

- It should handle creation and deletion of file and directories.
- It should also support wrapping of files into secondary storage.
- It should provide mechanisms to protect files.

I/O Operations Management. The operating system should be able to keep the user unaware of the specific details of hardware devices. In effect, only a device driver (a system program that enables operating system to recognize and communicate with a piece of hardware) should know the internal details of the specific device for which it has been designed. Chapter 11 deals with the details of the device management service of an operating system.

Network Management. With the advent of micro and mini-computers, distributed processing is becoming more and more popular. For distributed processing, the operating system has to be structured in a very different way to deal with the routing and connection strategies, problems of contention and security in a distributed environment etc. Thus some sort of network management mechanisms must be provided by the operation system.

Besides, the services mentioned here, the operating system must be capable of reporting the errors occurring in the CPU, memory hardware, I/O devices or in a user program. These errors can be memory error, parity error, access to an illegal memory location, printer out of paper, infinite looping by a user program etc.

3.2. OPERATING SYSTEM COMPONENTS

Operating System works as a resource manager and control program. The major components involved in managing system resources are :

User Interface : Operating system acts as an intermediary between application programs and computer hardware. Computer is a digital device and understands the language of binary numbers i.e. 0 and 1. The program written in binary form is known as machine language construct. But user finds it difficult to write complex programs in machine language. The next generation languages are more user-friendly and less machine dependent. The software used to convert user friendly language into machine language is called system software. Operating system is one system software that acts as the base for all computer executions. It makes user unaware of the complexities of the computer hardware. The environment provided by the operating system for a user to enter commands is called user interface. There are two major categories of user interfaces : Command Line Interface (CLI) and Graphical User Interface (GUI).

In CLI, user has to enter predefined commands to perform any task. The environment of CLI is called Shell. Here users can enter commands to start a new job, create or delete file or directory, modify and retrieve the contents and change the current path. The operating system like DOS and UNIX are totally command based while other operating systems provides command line interface as an extra functionality.

Graphical user interface makes application software appear like an icon to the user. It requires just a mouse click or the enter command from the keyboard to initiate the process. It is also called as what you see is what you get environment. Users feel more convenient working on GUI environment. The commands initiated in the form of program are also written in high level language which appears more user friendly. The system software like compiler, assembler, linker and loader help converting these commands into machine language. So user need not deal with any complexities regarding internal hardware.

Process Management :

A process represents the working state of a system program. A program keeps its stay in disk as a static unit. While getting asociated with the system resources like processor, memory or I/O devices, it enters into an active state with its stay in main memory. During execution, process maintains its attributes like identity of a process, current state, memory limits and register values. The information about a process resides in the process control block. Operating system performs a major role in managing the execution of a process. It helps in creation and deletion of a process. Like wise modification and retrieval is also being managed. During execution all the process states like blocked, wait and suspension state where risk factors are involved are also managed. Also scheduling of process to provide maximum system utilization and any bottleneck that result in deadlock state is also avoided. From its initial stage to final stage, process moves across various queues. At the entry level, operating system stores the attributes of the concerned process in Process control block.

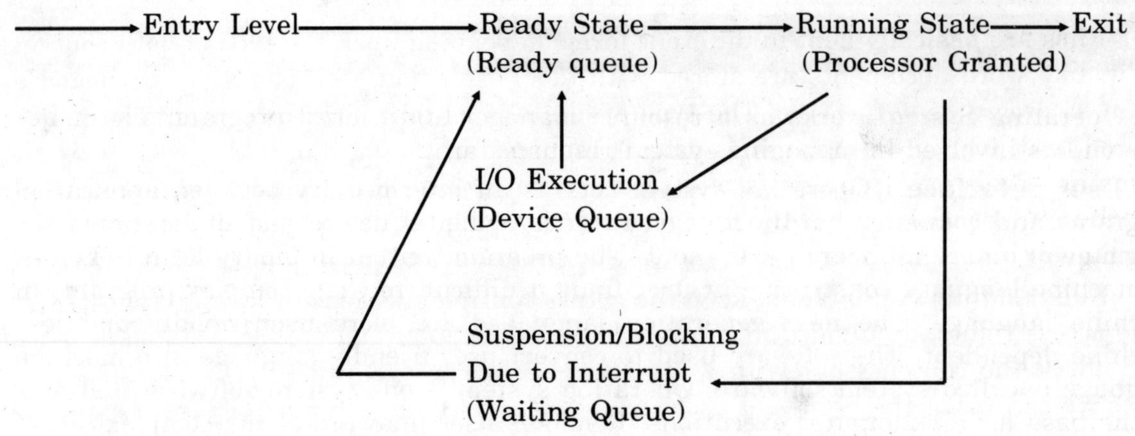

Figure 3.1 : Queue listing for a process while in execution

When the sufficient memory becomes available for keeping the process in main memory, it gets shifted in the ready queue. Here long term scheduler manages the multiprogramming limit. Based upon the scheduling algorithm, short term scheduler assigns the processes to processor for execution. In case process requires some input from an external device, it needs to wait in the device queue for its turn. In another case if some high priority process suspends its working for some time, the process gets shifted to the suspended/wait state. It gets the CPU time at its turn and finally the result of execution gets stored in memory or provided through some output device. The memory space of that particular process is made available to other processes for execution.

File Management :

File is a unit of data storage in computer system. Files are used to store data and programs for various applications. We are provided with different types of data representations and like wise the files to store them. Files are stored in permanent storage so that user can retrieve, modify or delete them at its convenience. Also access modes must be defined for particular user at specific files to keep them protected from unauthorized access. These operations regarding file handling must be managed by operating system.

The operating system starts managing files in the system from its creation time to its placement in the disk, while modifying the data contents to placement of file in some other directory. The main task involved behind all these operations is the location search and file retrieval. To place a file onto the disk whole path needs to be searched. Similar is the case with retrieval. Efficient search and access algorithms need to be implemented by the file handling subsystem. In case of any damage, the restoration and backup facilites must be made available.

Files are basically kept in different forms depending upon the type of data contents in it, like word documents are stored with (doc) extension, web pages are managed as html, C programs with C etc. The type of file tells us that how the contents have been stored in it. e.g. In database, files data is managed in the form of tables with rows and columns. Every row represents one record of an object while column represents their attribute fields. Collectively the file gives information about the object and its properties. With every file management system we can create, delete, modify or move a file.

File handling system must keep the access control of various users on data contents. The access rights are divided into two categories : Read or Write. With read access, user can check the contents but with write access user can even modify the contents. Like wise we can make the groups of users who can access particular set of files. This is one way of keeping individual files. Another way comes as an organized form of groups of files using Directory structure. Directories are used to store set of files under one name. Directories keep the file attributes like file name, type, content size, access mode etc. intact.

With the help of directories, similar files can be placed under one heading. Directories are managed in single level, multiple level, hierarchical view, tree or graph• structures.

I/O Management : The operating system manages the communication between computer hardware and the outside world with the help of I/O devices. Whenever it is required to have data elements from user or to present results in the form of soft or hard copy content, I/O devices provide the functionality. Important input devices include keyboard, mouse, joystick and scanners. Output devices are printer, tape drive and hard disk. All these devices differ in type of data contents to handle, transfer rate, error handling and complexity of execution. Due to this diversity, no standard software is available with operating system to manage these devices. Operating system provides device drivers to make communication among I/O devices and hardware/system software possible. The figure 3.2 shows the hierarchy of the adjustment level, which makes working of all the user application programs possible.

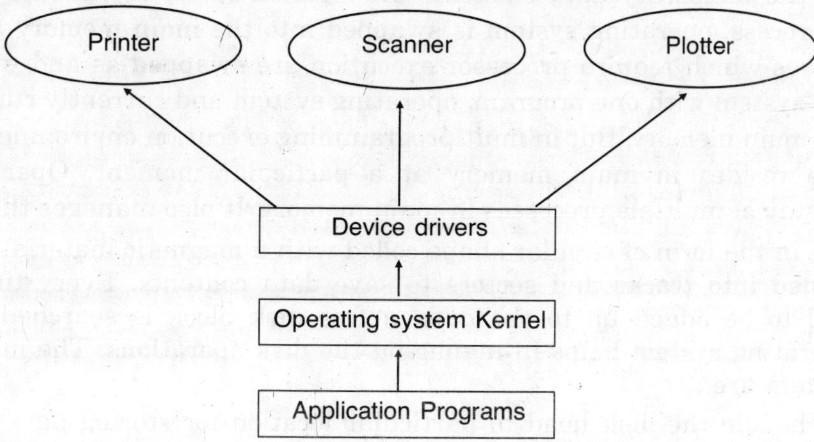

Figure 3.2 : The Hierarchy of I/O devices adjustment level

During a process execution, most of the times processor remains busy in handling I/O demands. The slow speed of these devices greatly affects the overall performance measure. This problem generally results in deadlock or bottleneck among processes and resources involved in the execution. Operating system provides I/O processor to handle complexities regarding these external devices. The first solution is using Direct Memory Access (DMA) technique; with this scheme I/O processor need not ask CPU every time executing a task. It just needs to take permission at the beginning and end of a job. Rest it handles through direct communication with memory device. This has been discussed in previous chapter.

Another solution is provided with the multiprogramming provision within I/O devices. Here more than one task execution is managed by operating system with the help of scheduler subsystem. Concurrency among multiple jobs is managed by the synchronization and lock based protocols. Also buffering is provided with every I/O device to handle the slow speed execution. When more than one job requests approach for same device access, to avoid busy waiting the requests are placed in device queue. The moment device becomes free from current job request the next request is assigned to it.

Storage Structure Management : Storage structures are provided to keep the information in its original form and make it available to the user whenever it is required during processing. In computer system there are two major types of storage structures:

Hard Disks (Permanent Storage)

Main Memory (Temporary Storage)

Hard disk is the permanent storage area where huge amount of data and programs remains intact. Disks come in large sizes of upto hundreds of GB. The only negative point of disks is that the data retrieval is slow. It is difficult for processor to fetch data elements from disks while execution. Due to fast execution speed of processor it has to wait a lot for disk processing to come to an end. So processor works in direct communication with main memory. Main memory is the temporary storage unit that keeps user data till the concerned program is in memory. The moment it gets shifted to hard disk all the temporary data elements are washed out of the memory. During the system boot process, operating system is swapped into the main memory and like wise all the processes which require processor execution are swapped as and when they are required. In a system with one program, operating system and currently running process resides in the main memory. But in multiprogramming execution environment more than one processes resides in main memory at a particular moment. Operating system manages the stay of multiple processes in main memory. It also manages their execution.

Disks are in the form of circular shape coded with a magnetic material. The circular shape is divided into tracks and sectors to save data contents. Every time new data contents need to be added up to the disk, a free disk block is searched to store the contents. Operating system helps in managing the disk operations. The major duties of operating system are :

1. To schedule the disk head to particular location for storing data contents and while retrieving any information from disk. Main scheduling algorithms being

used are First-in-First-out, Shortest-seek-time-first, SCAN, C-SCAN and LOOK. All these scheduling techniques are provided to make disk operations efficient.

2. Free space management is handled to utilize the free disk blocks.

Network Management : A network constitutes interconnected computers for sharing of information. Every computer present in the network has its individual identity i.e. IP address. This IP address comprises network id, host id and node id. The connection among the devices can be of two types : centralized and distributed.

In case of centralized system there is client-server strategy. A client has to take permission from the server whenever it wants to access information from another computer. On the other hand in distributed system, all systems have peer-to-peer relationship amongst each other. To share information, they just need to get logged onto network once and can access data from any system connected to it. Unlike centralized system, every system in the network possesses its own processing element and memory unit. After getting connected to the network, user can access information from any other system in communication. The major hardware elements included are wires, ports, switches, buses and connectors. All these collectively make the information exchange among diferent systems possible. Every system present in the network possesses different hardware and software configurations. One system can work on UNIX platform while other can work with Windows and so on. Systems follow some standard set of rules to make communication possible. These rules are known as protocols. Some of the important protocols are : Transmission Control Protocol (TCP), Internet Protocol (IP), Domain Name Server (DNS), Simple Mail transfer Protocol (SMTP), Hyper Text Transfer Protocol (HTTP) and File Transfer Protocol (FTP). The risk factors involved in transmission within a network are : Bandwidth or data transfer rate, speed, security, reliability and maintenance. Operating system helps mananging the risk factors inspite of all the diverse configurations present in the network. Operating system keeps the details of system configurations and protocols to provide efficient communication amongst the system. Security is provided using encryption, authentication and authorization schemes. The network device drivers present in the operating system handle the incoming and outgoing data requests. The network traffic is managed using traffic management techniques.

Protection and Security : The entities involved in the execution of a task are user processes, data elements and system resources. Protection means the ability to manage valid involvement of these entities in an execution. In single task execution only operating system and one user program resides in memory at a particular moment. So it is quite easy to manage allocation of resources to that very process. But in case of multiprogramming, more than one user processes are made to stay in main memory for their concurrent execution. Operating system helps providing memory space to each process. The process requirements are mentioned at the entry level itself. Accordingly the operating system provides the access of resources to processes available in the main memory. The user processes are provided authorization to access any resource facility in a particular access mode for some predefined time requirement. The access matrices are designed to store information regarding user processes, requested resources and accesss mode provided to a particular process for that resource. In case of any erroneous state, operating system shifts system control to monitor mode to manage further execution.

Basically computer is a data processing device. Here one can work along or in a group to produce the required information. While communicating in a group, security is the major concern. Security deals with providing authorized data/resource access to the users. Operating systems manage security provision through authorization techniques. Users are divided into groups with predefined privileges. Similarly intruder detection systems are provided to stop any malicious access. Other techniques like firewall, password protection, encrypted password, all these are used for secure transmission across a network.

3.3. SYSTEM CALLS

As mentioned earlier in the previous chapter, the purpose of a system call is to request the operating system to perform some activity. This means that system call provides an interface between a process and the operating system.

The execution of a system call requires the user process to save its current state, let the operating system take control of the CPU and perform some function. Then operating system should save its state and give control of the CPU back to the user process.

System calls are generally available as assembly language instructions but as assembly language programmers are becoming rare and as assembly language programming is considered difficult, therefore, high level languages such as 'C', Bliss, PERL, etc., allow these system calls to be made directly. A very simple example of how a system call is used is—we know that all operating system have a routine for creating a directory. If you want to execute this operating system routine from your program, you must make a system call. Figure 3.3 shows the system calls available in UNIX for almost every service that UNIX operating system provides. Figure 3.4 indicates how a system call serves in achieving protection of operating system from user program.

There are different system calls for performing different kinds of tasks :

- File manipulation system calls for example are : open, close, read, write, seek etc.
- There can be system calls for process control. These can be like abort, execute, create process, terminate a process, allocate and free memory for a process etc.
- For device management, the system calls that can be there are—request device, release device, read, write, reposition, get and set device attributes, etc.
- For managing the information, the system calls that can be there are—get and set time, get and set file or device attributes etc.

PROCESS CONTROL			
fork( )	exec( )	wait( )	abort( )

FILE MANIPULATION			
chmod( )	link( )	stat( )	creat( )

DEVICE MANIPULATION			
open( )	close( )	ioctl( )	select( )

INFORMATION MAINTENANCE		
time( )	acct( )	gettimeofday( )

COMMUNICATIONS			
socket( )	accept( )	send( )	recv( )

Figure 3.3 : System Calls in UNIX

3.4. SYSTEM STRUCTURE

Before we discuss the structure of UNIX and Windows NT Operating systems later in this text, let us understand what does actually an operating system comprise of? It contains mainly a Kernel, command processor or shell and graphical user interface to make a user's life simple.

Kernel. It is the control module of an operating system. It is that part of the operating system, which loads first and remains in the main memory. Because, it stays in the memory, it is important for the kernel to be as small as possible while still providing all the essential services required by other parts of the operating system and applications. Typically, a kernel is responsible for memory management, process and task management, and disk management.

Command Processor. Command processor of an operating system is that part which receives and executes operating system commands. Whenever a command prompt is displayed the command processor waits for a command. After you enter a command, the command processor makes sure that command is valid and then either executes it or issues an error message. For operating systems with graphical user interface, the command processor interprets mouse operations and executes the appropriate command. It is also known as command line interpreter.

Shell. Shell is an exclusive feature of UNIX. It is a process that accepts the command line input and after expanding wild cards, aliases etc. executes whatever programs have been called. The shell is not only a command line interpreter and line editor, but also a language with variables, arrays, functions, and control structures. Command lines can be put into a file and executed. These files also known as shell scripts can be quickly written and tested and should be tried in association with other

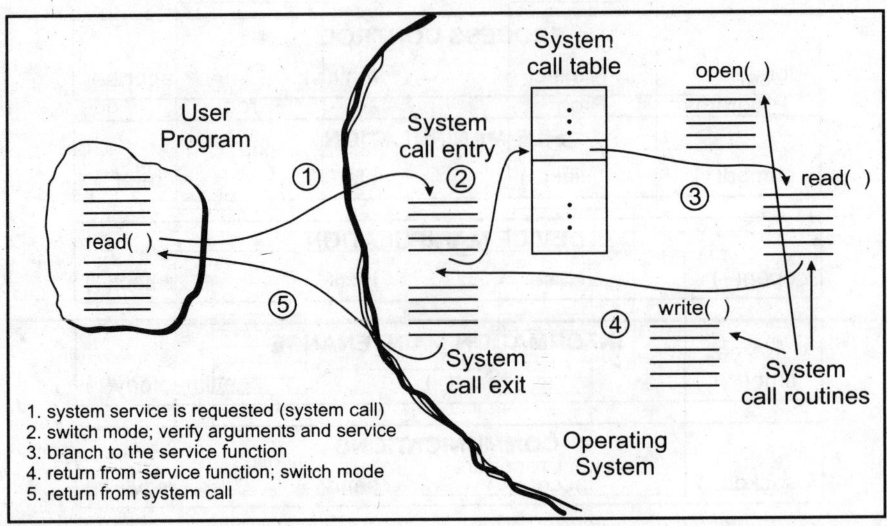

Figure 3.4 : Protection Provided by System Call

standard UNIX utilities before embarking on a higher level language, at least for prototyping purposes.

Graphical User Interface. It is provided so that the user need not remember tedious syntax of the command language, instead pointing to an option by means of a mouse can do his/her job. This should not be confusing to understand that actually, the command processor executes all these selected commands at the back end. GUI is there to relieve the user from the burden of remembering commands.

Now, let us see what are the possible ways of arranging these components to develop an operating system. This leads to the concept of operating system architecture.

3.4.1 Monolithic Architecture for OS

Figure 3.5 shows the monolithic architecture of an operating system. It is the oldest architecture used for developing an operating system. In general, it is considered that monolithic kernels are not preferred because of the fact that code has to be rewritten for all new hardware architecture that the operating system is to be ported on. In other words, the monolithic kernel is not portable.

The key features of the monolithic kernels are :

- Monolithic Kernel interacts directly with the hardware.
- Monolithic Kernel can be optimized for particular hardware architecture.
- Monolithic Kernel is not very portable.
- Monolithic Kernel gets loaded completely into memory at boot time.
- Most system calls are made by trapping to the Kernel, having the work performed there, and having the Kernel return the desired result to the user process.

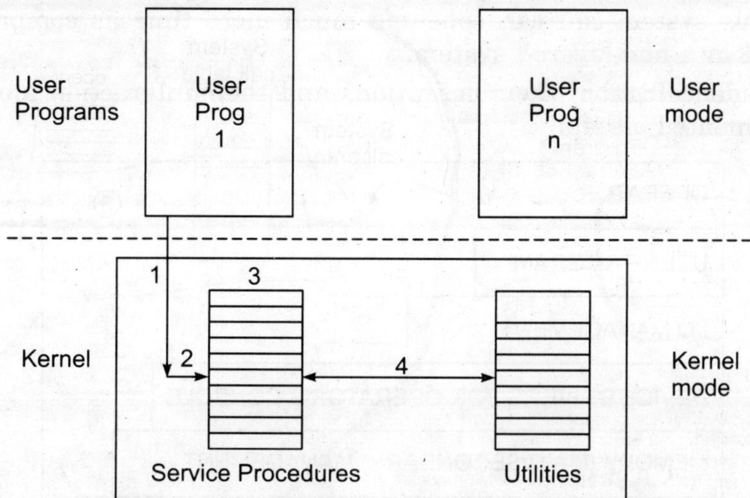

1. System call (User –> Kernel Mode) 2. Check parameters 3. Call service routine 4. Service routine call utilities Reschedule/Return to user

Figure 3.5 : Monolithic Architecture

3.4.2 Layered Architecture for OS

Dijkstra introduced the layered architecture for operating systems when he developed in the 60's an operating system named "THE".

The main benefit of this approach is modularity. The layers are selected such that each uses services and functions of its lower layers. All the benefits of modular programming can be achieved with this architecture. The layered architecture of THE operating system has been shown in Figure 3.6. At the lowest level, it has hardware, layer 1 has processor allocation and support for multiprogramming, layer 2 implements memory management, layer 3 contains the device drivers for operator's console, layer 4 contains I/O buffering support.

OS/2 operating system has a layered architecture. Earlier versions of Windows NT had a layer-oriented organization.

Disadvantages of this approach

- It requires appropriate definition of the various layers and a careful planning for the proper placement of the layers. For example the disk driver (infact all other secondary storage drivers) should be normally above the CPU scheduler as the driver may have to wait for the I/O and the CPU can be assigned to some other process by the scheduler, during this time.
- Sometimes, it is felt that each layer adds an overhead to the system call executed by a user program for a specific purpose. For example, a system call issued by user program for an I/O operation will be trapped to the I/O layer, which calls the memory management layer by modifying the parameters and data, which may further be passed on to some other layer and ultimately to the hardware.

Thus, this system call can consume much more time as compared to the one executed in a non-layered system.

Thus layer identification; their definitions and their interaction among each other should be implemented carefully.

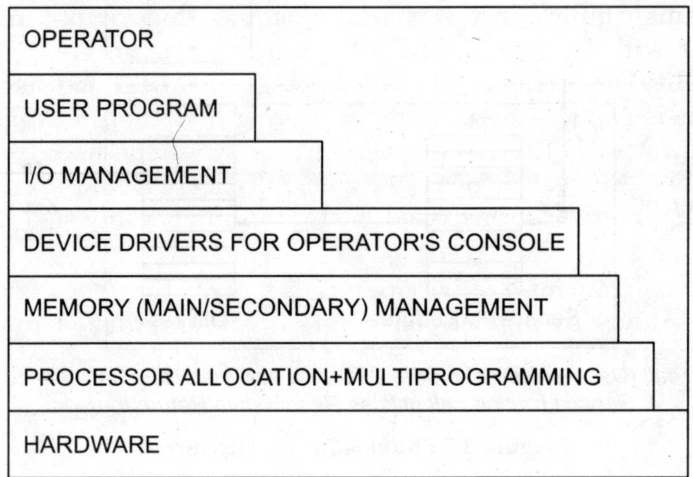

Figure 3.6 : Layered Architecture

3.4.3 Virtual Machine Architecture for OS

Virtual machine architecture is sometimes, also known as enterprise system architecture. Virtual machine operating system for IBM systems is the best example of Virtual machine concept, because IBM pioneered the work in this area. The VM operating system is built on the virtual storage concept to subdivide a single computer system into multiple, virtual computer systems, each with its own processor, disk storage, tape storage, and other I/O devices. That is, VM uses software techniques to make a single computer appear to be multiple smaller computer systems. Each of these small computers, simulated in software, acts as an independent and complete computer system. It manages a real computing system so that all of its resources—CPU, storage and I/O devices are available to many users at the same time. Each user has at his disposal the functional equivalent of a real, dedicated computing system. Figure 3.7 shows the virtual machine architecture of an operating system. Because this functional equivalent is simulated by virtual machine and does not really exist, it is called a "virtual" machine.

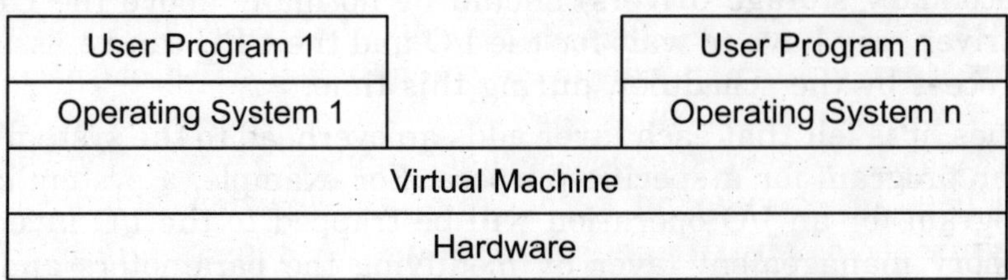

Figure 3.7 : Virtual Machine Architecture

Virtual machine has two main components :

—The control program (CP) controls the real machine

—The conversational monitor system (CMS) controls virtual machine

The CP creates a virtual machine image in 'software' for each user of the computer system. To the programs running in the virtual machine, that virtual machine appears to be actual computer with its own hardware, operating system etc. Since the control program has the ability to create a software image identical to that presented by computer hardware, it is called a hypervisor. By giving a virtual machine to each user, the Control Program provides effective protection to prevent one user from accidentally interfering with another. All real devices are controlled by CP and are made available to virtual machines on a more or less shared basis. Terminals connected to CP can logon on virtual machines.

The CMS is a single-user interactive operating system that runs on top of CP and interacts with the user and any application program running that virtual machine.

Disadvantages of this approach. This architecture is difficult to implement, as it requires lot of effort to provide an exact duplicate of the underlying machine.

3.4.4 Micro-Kernel Architecture for OS

A very modern architecture is the micro-kernel architecture. This architecture strives to take out of the kernel as much functionality as possible, so as to limit the code executed in privileged mode and to allow easy modifications and extensions. It does so by moving many operating system services from the kernel into the "user space". Thus, making kernel as small as possible and therefore, it is called Micro Kernel.

This is one advantage as it always stays in the main memory and thus consumes less memory of the system.

Some other advantages of this architecture are :

Robustness. If there is a problem with a particular service, it normally can be reconfigured and restarted without having to restart the complete OS. This should be helpful for situations requiring high availability. Moreover, since services would now run in completely independent memory spaces (which is not the case for kernel-level services), bugs and misconfiguration will not be able to corrupt the kernel.

Moreover, the "true kernel" winds up being smaller in scope, and thus is easier to understand and verify.

Security. By running the services as lower level user processes, their access to system resources (*e.g.*, the ability to mess things up) is far more restricted.

Configurability. Services can be changed without need to restart the whole system.

Makes Coding Easier. Kernel code usually requires the use of special "memory allocation and input/output" routines since the kernel cannot depend on a lower level to manage these things for it. User-mode code is thus simpler to write than "kernel" code, because it does not need to worry about kernel-specific restrictions.

Simplifies Symmetric Multiprocessing code. Managing multiple processors requires a fair bit of internal book-keeping. The more services that sit in the kernel, the more book-keeping work code is required, and the less effective use can be made of the additional processors. Changing a large, single-threaded monolithic kernel to make effective use of SMP (Symmetric Multi Processing) hardware is very difficult.

If the operating system has a microkernel specifically written to make effective use of SMP, then SMP support does not need to be obtrusive in the 'main' kernel.

Are there any downsides to the use of micro kernels? Yes, indeed.

- Most microkernels are not tiny, despite the name. (QNX being a notable exception).
- Communication between components of the extended "operating system" requires the use of formalized message-passing mechanisms (like those explained in a section on "Inter-process Communication" in chapter 4).
- New kinds of error conditions are possible between system components that would not be possible with a monolithic kernel.

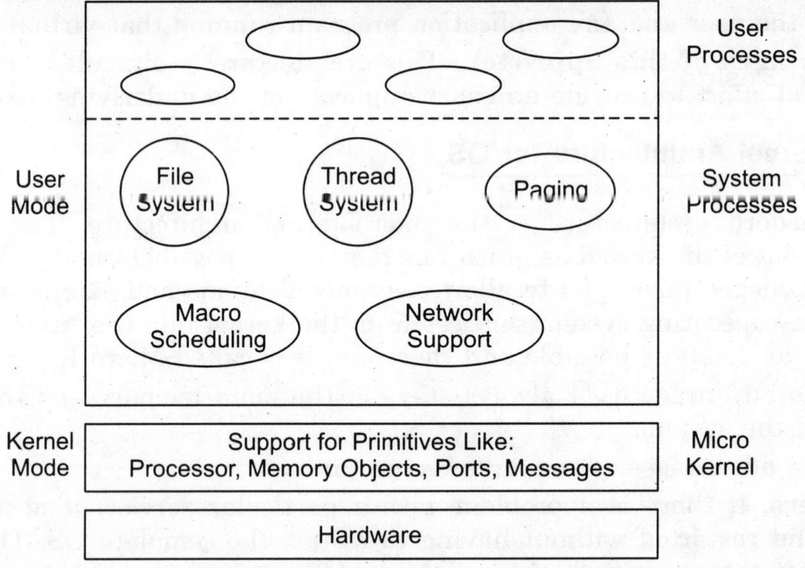

Figure 3.8 : Micro Kernel Architecture

Probably the fundamental consideration encouraging microkernel development is the growth of interest in SMP and other multiprocessing applications. Figure 3.8 shows micro-kernel architecture.

3.4.5 Exokernel Architecture for OS

Exokernel is a further extension of the microkernel approach where the "kernel" per se is almost devoid of functionality; it merely passes requests for resources to "user space" libraries.

This would mean that (for instance) requests for file access by one process would be passed by the kernel to the library that is directly responsible for managing file systems. It results in significant performance improvements, as it does not force data to even pass through kernel data structure.

This architecture is at present largely in "research mode". MIT exokernel operating system is one of them to name.

Figure 3.9 shows a table that compares these architectures in brief.

	Monolithic	Micro Kernel	Exo Kernel
Implementation of operating system abstractions	All are implemented in kernel space	Only Lower level operating system facilities are implemented in Kernel	Nothing is implemented in kernel space

Figure 3.9 : *Comparison of Kernel implementation of various OS architectures*

3.5. SYSTEM DESIGN, IMPLEMENTATION AND GENERATION

3.5.1 System Design

The design of an operating system will depend upon the following factors :

- Type of system—Batch, Time sharing, Single user, Multi-user, Distributed, Real time, etc.
- Architecture of the system
- Users' Expectations—Convenient to use, Easy to learn, Easy to use, Reliable, Safe and Fast.
- Designer's convenience—Easy to design, implement and ultimately much easy to maintain.

Even though, we have tried to identify few factors that are involved in the design of the system, it is worth mentioning here that it will always depend much upon the actual task given to the designer, i.e., the actual requirements specified by the customer or company for the design of a domain specific operating system.

3.5.2 System Implementation

At the implementation level, the concerns are :

- Language to be used—Traditionally, operating systems have been written in assembly language. But nowadays, coding of an operating system is done even in a high level language. The level of language chosen contributes to the attributes of the resulting operating system.

If high level language is used to code an operating system, it can reduce the speed and increase the storage requirements of the resulting operating system. But at the same time it is easier to port (move to some other hardware) the operating system if it is written in a high level language. On the other hand, an assembly language coding can result in a small sized operating system having high speed but it may not be that easy to understand and debug this code as compared to high level language code.

- Algorithms and data structure—Performance can be improved by incorporating better data structures and algorithms.

- Identify the services used mostly—Services like memory management and CPU scheduling are demanded in higher frequency as compared to others, therefore, the routines written to implement them should be refined for performance purposes.

3.5.3 System Generation

The process of configuring an operating system for each specific computer site is called system generation. The operating system now-a-days is provided to users on the CD-ROM media. But for installing an operating system, a special program SYSGEN is used. It reads from a given file or asks the systems operator not only about the hardware configuration of the systems but also tries to collect some other information also.

The information will be like :

- Kind of CPU
- Amount of memory available
- Devices available
- Device number, device interrupt number and device type and model of each device.

SYSGEN program used to be very time consuming in the past and used to take hours together but now it has been improved considerably.

After determining this information, system is generated (probably complied with some changes in its source code depending upon the information gathered or simply the setup file is executed and this information is used here at the execution time). Now, the operating system is ready to provide its services. The computer is booted by Bootstrap loader program (stored in ROM) which locates the kernel, loads it into main memory and starts its execution.

EXERCISES

3.1 List the services of an operating system.

3.2 List and Explain the various components of an operating system.

3.3 Compare monolithic, microkernel and exokernel operating system architecture with respect to memory requirement, portability, kernel's size, ease of modification etc.

3.4 What is a virtual machine? What are the advantages of implementing a virtual machine?

3.5 Explain with the help of a diagram how a system call serves the purpose of I/O protection.

3.6 List the major activities of an operating system with respect to memory management, secondary-storage management and process management.

3.7 What is the purpose of the command interpreter and why it is usually separate from the kernel?

3.8 What is the main advantage of layered approach to operating system design?

3.9 What factors should be kept in mind while designing an operating system?

3.10 Contrast the coding of an operating system in high level language with the coding in assembly language.

3.11 While coding an operating system, what methods can be adopted to improve its performance?

CHAPTER

4

Introduction to Processes

OVERVIEW

This chapter has been framed to get to know the concept of processes. A process is an active entity whereas a program is a passive entity. A program in execution becomes a process. Various process states such as ready, blocked, running and their transitions have been discussed in a very simple manner. This chapter also presents the description of two basic operations on processes : Processes creation and process termination.

A discussion of short term versus medium term and long term schedulers has been done. An introduction to cooperating processes has been laid down. These processes and their synchronization issues have been taken up in detail in chapter 6 of this text. The concept of thread has been introduced here. In chapter 1 multithreading was not discussed, therefore here it has been presented together with its advantages and its implementation issues. Inter-process communication has been explained at the end of this chapter.

4.1. CONCEPT OF PROCESS

A process is a program in execution.

- The command interpreter is a process.
- When we execute a program we have just compiled, the operating system generates a process to run the compiler.

As mentioned "process" is not the same as "program", it is infact a program in execution. We can distinguish between a passive program on disk and an actively executing process, very easily. Many people can run the same program; and each copy of this program corresponds to a distinct process.

Let us now see, what does a process contain other than a program? A program is only one part of a process; the process also contains the execution state of the program. Let us now identify the reasons for process creation and process termination. Reasons for process creation can be :

- User logs on the system
- User starts a program
- Operating system creates a process to provide a service (e.g., printer daemon to manage printer)
- Program starts another process

Reasons for process termination can be :

- Normal completion of process (Exit)
- Arithmetic error, or data misuse (e.g., wrong type of data)
- Invalid instruction execution
- Insufficient memory available, or memory bounds violation
- Resource protection (e.g., : memory protection error, CPU protection error (e.g., Infinite looping process))
- I/O failure

All the above stated reasons fall in the category of internal completion. It can be external completion (forced completion : by operator or by parent process of the child process).

4.2. PROCESS STATES AND THEIR TRANSITIONS

At any time, a process is in one of the states mentioned below :

1. Running
2. Ready to Run
3. Blocked

Running state implies that process is currently run by the CPU. **Ready to run** means that it needs CPU attention and time to run, otherwise it is not blocked in any sense or in other words, process is waiting to be assigned to a processor. **Blocked state** implies that process is not running currently and is waiting for some event to occur (such as I/O completion or reception of a signal).

Figure 4.1 shows state transitions of a process, in general. Some possible reasons for these transitions are :

1. Ready to Running : A process is selected out of the ready queue (i.e., scheduled to be run) and is dispatched to the running state.

2. Running to Blocked : A process starts a time consuming **I/O operation** or is **swapped out** of the main memory or makes a spontaneous request to sleep or is blocked due to synchronization operations. I/O operation is infact the most common reason for this type of transition. Here, since a process is waiting for I/O completion and thus do not need CPU for executing any other instructions, CPU is freed by it and CPU in the meantime takes up some other ready process and starts its execution.

3. Blocked to ready : The reason for a process to remain blocked is no longer applicable *e.g.,* I/O completes, timer goes off etc. Thus, the process becomes ready for its execution.

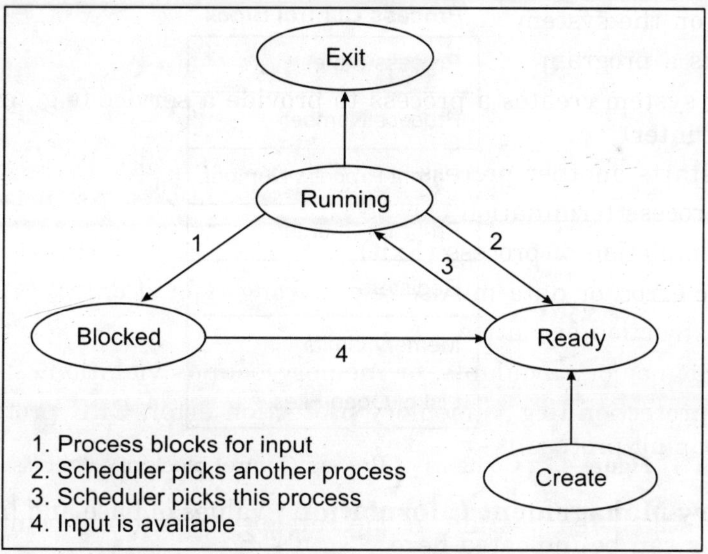

Figure 4.1 : Process State Transitions

4. Running to Ready : The running process is pre-empted because some other process of higher priority has become ready.

4.3. PROCESS CONTROL BLOCK

Each process is represented by a process control block, also known as task control block. It contains information regarding the execution state of the program, memory management information and CPU scheduling information etc. Figure 4.2 shows the contents of a process control block. The description of this information is as follows :

(i) Process State : It can be ready, running and blocked. It is useful to indicate the current state of the process.

(ii) Process Number : Unique number is allocated to a process at the time of its execution. This is helpful in referring to the process through shell commands or other commands of the command language of the operating system.

(iii) Parent Process Number : If this process has been originated as a sub-process of a process, then its parent's process number is also mentioned so that the output of this process can be returned back to the parent process.

(iv) Program Counter : It contains the address of the next instruction to be executed and thus is useful in indicating the status of a process.

(v) CPU Registers : CPU registers depend upon the computer architecture. They can be index registers, accumulators, general-purpose registers etc. They are used to save other information e.g., when an interrupt occurred, whether the current instruction was fully executed or not etc., at the time of state transition of a process.

(vi) CPU Scheduling Information : Priority of the process is mostly indicated here.

Process Control Block

Process State
Process Number
Parent Process Number
Program Counter
Registers
Memory Limits
List of Open Files

Figure 4.2 : Contents of Process Control block of a Process

(vii) Memory Management Information : Values of base and limit registers, page or segment tables can be indicated here.

(viii) Accounting Information : The information like amount of CPU time used, process numbers, time limits etc. fall into this category.

(ix) I/O Status Information : It includes the names of I/O devices used by a process, list of open files etc.

4.4. PROCESS SCHEDULING

Let us first understand why and where do we need to do process scheduling? In a uniprogramming environment (the environment where only one process is ready for its execution at one moment of time) there is no question of process scheduling. It becomes a necessary activity in a multiprogramming environment.

Refer to state transitions in section 4.2 where it has been mentioned that a process, which is ready, becomes a running process when it is selected out of a ready queue. Let us first concentrate on this concept of ready queue and device queue.

Ready Queue : It is a doubly linked list of processes, which are ready to run. They are ordered by priority, the highest priority process is at the front of the queue. As we all know queue has FIFO structure, therefore, whenever the CPU takes up a new process, it actually picks up the process with the highest priority.

When we say processes are listed together, it means that actually their PCBs (Process Control Blocks) are linked together. The header of the queue contains two pointers. The first pointer points to the first PCB and the second points to the last PCB in the list. Each PCB has a pointer to point to the next process in the ready queue.

Device Queue : The processes, which are blocked due to unavailability of an input/output device, constitute this queue. There is a separate queue for each I/O device. Figure 4.3 shows the structure of a ready queue. A process when created is initially put in the ready queue. Once it is picked up by the CPU for its execution, there may occur one of the many events that cause a transition in its state from running to ready or running to blocked or running to final completion (exit). If its state is changed to blocked, it is added to the device queue of the device whose services are required by it.

In case, its state is changed to ready again, it is put back to the ready queue. In case, it terminates after its successful completion, it is removed from all the queues and its PCB and other resources are deallocated.

Now, let us find out who is responsible for taking a process out of a ready queue and assign it to CPU for its execution? The answer is process scheduler. Process scheduler is a part of the operating system that is responsible for changing the state of processes. In other words, it is that component, which is responsible for scheduling of the processes to be executed by the CPU.

A scheduler infact should compromise between certain desirable things :

- Make sure that each process gets a fair share of the CPU
- Keep the CPU busy 100% of the time
- Minimize Response Delays

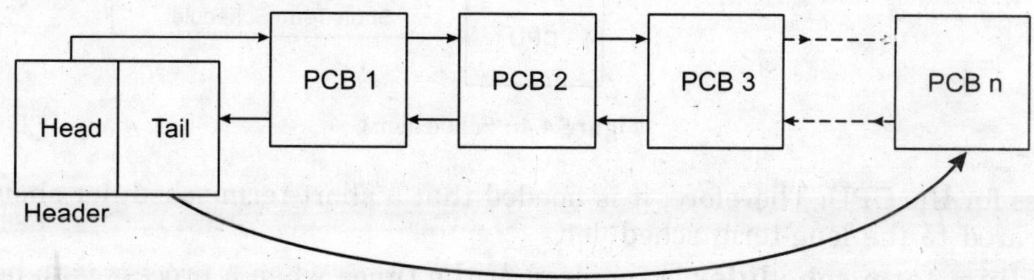

Figure 4.3 : Ready Queue

Schedulers are defined to be of three types :

(i) Long-term scheduler
(ii) Short-term scheduler
(iii) Medium-term scheduler

Long-term scheduler selects processes from secondary storage device e.g. disk and loads them into memory for execution.

Short-term scheduler selects from among the processes that are ready to execute, and allocates the CPU to one of them.

Long-term scheduler is known as "long-term" because time for which the scheduling is valid is long. In other words, it executes less frequently as it takes from minutes to hours for the creation of new processes in the system. The primary job of long-term scheduler is to run the multi-programming environment smoothly. thus, its job is to ensure that there are always a fixed number of ready processes in the memory of the system.

Short-term scheduler on the other hand, must have to work very often. A process must be executing for only a very short duration (e.g. in few milliseconds) before it gets blocked (due to some I/O operation etc.). This requires that CPU should immediately take up another process for execution and thus the scheduler should immediately select

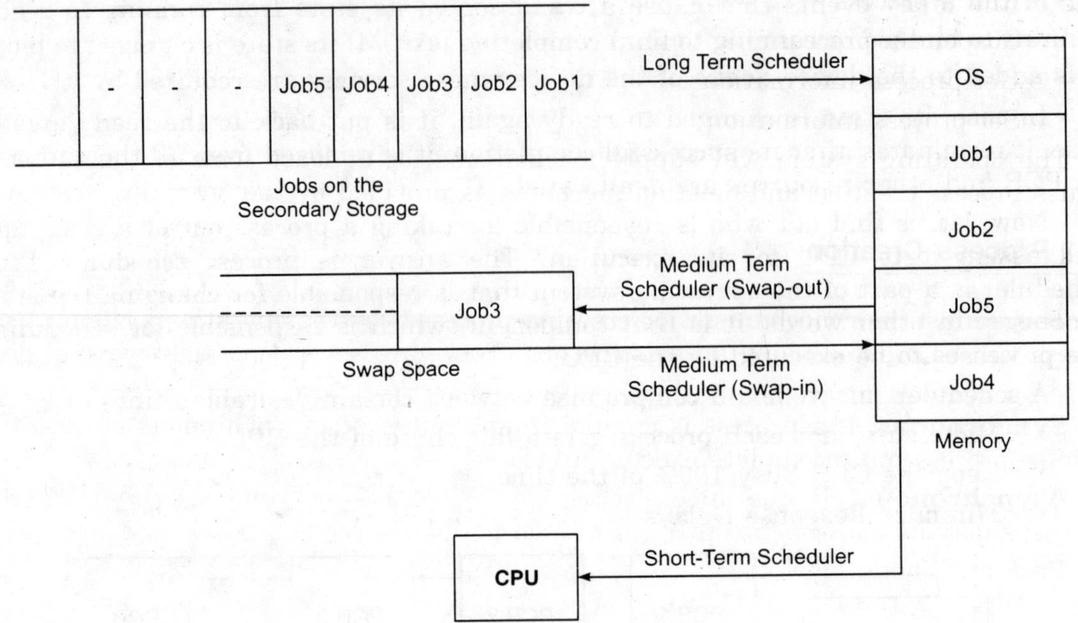

Figure 4.4 : Schedulers

a process for the CPU. Therefore, it is needed that a short-term scheduler should be fast as compared to the long-term scheduler.

Medium-term scheduler is required at the times when a process is to be removed from the memory (due to some performance reasons) and thus to reduce the degree of multiprogramming. Later on, this process may be put into the memory again and its execution can be again started from where it was left off. This process of moving a process in and out of the memory is called swapping. Sometimes, swapping becomes essential to deal with the situation when a running process requests more RAM. It can be given by moving (swapping) a ready process to the disk and making RAM available to the requesting process. Later on, when the requirements of this process are over, the swapped out process can be swapped back into the memory. All versions of Windows operating system use swapping. Working of schedulers has been depicted in Fig. 4.4.

4.5. OPERATIONS ON A PROCESS

A process is usually sequential and consists of a sequence of actions that take place one at a time. When a set of processes is run on a single CPU, using time slicing to multitask them, this is referred to as concurrent sequential processing or pseudo-parallel processing. If there is more than one CPU available, then processes may be run in parallel.

The set of operations on processes includes :

- Create a process
- Destroy a process

- Run a process
- Suspend a process
- Get process information
- Set process information

The operating system will supply mechanisms for at least some of these. Let us discuss process creation and deletion mechanisms provided by the operating systems.

4.5.1 Process Creation

There must be a mechanism for creating processes by the operating system. A new process will be created using an existing one. There are several possible ways of doing this.

Synchronous. If a process is created from another as a synchronous process then the new process must complete execution before the old one can resume.

Asynchronous. If the new process is created asynchronously, then the two processes may be run concurrently (in pseudo-parallel way).

Parent. When a new process is created, it may use the old one as "parent". This is done in MSDOS and UNIX. Alternatively, there may be no relation between the original and the new process, as in Windows NT.

As each newly created process will use some of the physical and logical resources (e.g., input data to the program), therefore, we should also analyze how these resources will be shared by the parent and child processes? There are infact three possibilities :

- Parent and children share all resources
- Children share a subset of parent's resources
- Parent and child share no resources.

Similarly, there are two possibilities regarding the address space of the new process :

- The child is duplicate of parent
- The child has a program loaded into it.
- Let us see, how a process is created in UNIX.

UNIX's Application Programming Interface (API)

UNIX API allows creation of asynchronous processes where each process has a parent. Each process has a process ID (a number) that can be used to tell them apart. This PID (Process ID) is shown by executing the user-level command "ps". Because the parent process can resume execution before a child terminates, the parent can continue to create processes. The children can also create processes as shown in Figure 4.5(a).

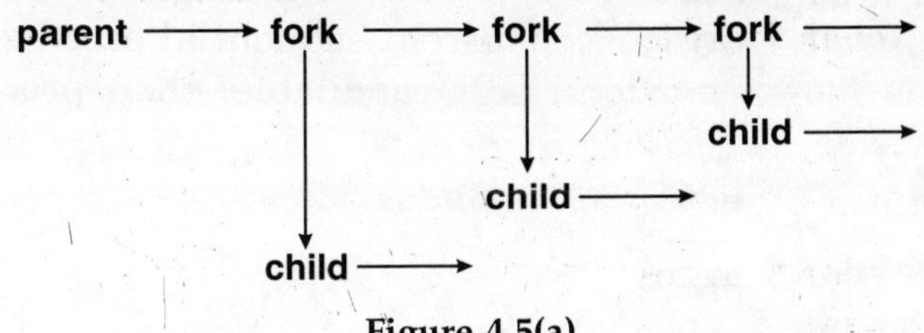

Figure 4.5(a)

This can also create a tree of processes as shown below in Figure 4.5 (b).

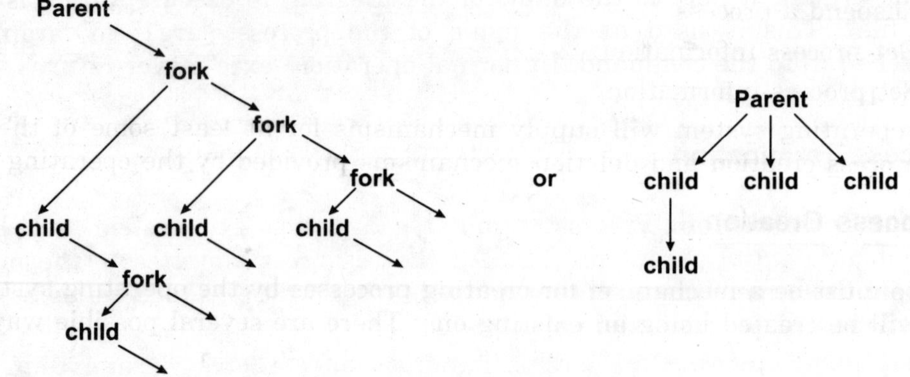

Figure 4.5(b)

Fork() is infact provided as a system call by UNIX. This splits the current process into two almost identical copies. The major difference is that one has the PID of the parent; the other has a new PID. The fork system call returns a value that is a PID. The return value of fork() is zero if a process is child, or is PID of the child if a process is parent.

Exec

If we want to replace one of these processes so that it uses a different program. For example, suppose the process creates a file that it wants to be printed. In UNIX it cannot print it itself, because it does not have access to the line printer device. The program "1pr" must be used. One way is

system ("1pr myfile");

This runs synchronously, so until the line printer program terminates, the calling program suspends. A preferable way may be to fork a new process and let the parent continue with the main piece of work, while the child prints the file asynchronously. This is possible but may require good length of code to be written like :

```
if (form ( ) == 0)
    system ("1pr myfile");
else { / * parent * / }
```

But it does nothing and waits for the "system" to finish. Better is to replace the child with the "1pr" program. This is the job of the "exec" functions.

```
int exect 1p  (  (char * file
                  char * arg0,
                  char * arg1,
                         ,
                         ,
                         ,
                  char * argn)
                  (char * ) 0 );
```

The file argument here is the name of the program to execute. "argo" is often the same as "file". This is used as the name of the process. "arg1" to "argn" are the arguments(1 to n) to the command. In normal operation "exec" never returns. If it fails, it returns - 1.

4.5.2 Process Termination

Normal Termination. Process terminates by using exit system call. It returns some output data to its parent process. All the resources allocated to the process are freed by it, at this time. This is all that happens when a process terminates by executing its last statement, i.e., completion on its own.

Forced Termination. On the other hand, it can be a forced termination. A process may be forcefully terminated by its parent process by executing an abort system call. A parent may want to abort its child's execution due to the following reasons :

- Child has exceeded allocated resources.
- Task assigned to the child is no longer required.
- Parent is terminating and operating system does not allow a child to continue if its parent terminates (this is known as cascading termination).

In case of UNIX, a process may terminate by using exit system call and its parent process may wait for that event by using wait system call. UNIX supports cascading termination.

In UNIX, there is a possibility that user can straight away terminate a process provided he knows the process ID of that process. This is possible by a system call "kill". It takes two arguments :

(i) Process ID (pid) of the process that user wants to kill, and

(ii) Signal (sig) that you want to send to that process.

If kill is successful, it returns 0; otherwise it returns a negative value.

4.6. COOPERATING PROCESSES

Let us now understand the concept of cooperating processes.

"The processes which execute concurrently and affect or get affected by other processes executing in the system are called cooperating processes."

The processes can affect or get affected by other processes by sharing data or by sharing other resources in the system. Thus, any process which shares data with other process is a cooperating process. The need of such processes is obvious. They will be required to speed up the computation, sharing of information, user convenience, etc.

Breaking up of one task into subtasks such that each of them can run in parallel and thus give faster computation results may be one of the requirements. Similarly, it may be required to allow several users to share the same piece of information (e.g., some data may be common to many user programs). This makes it compulsory for the operating system to provide support for the execution, synchronization and communication amongst cooperating processes.

Producer	Consumer
Person A	**Person B**
Look in fridge—Pizza	Look in fridge—Pizza !
Leave for store	consume Pizza
Arrive at store	and wash hands
Buy Pizza	
Arrive Home	
Put Pizza in fridge	

Figure 4.6 : *Pizza Problem*

To illustrate the concept of cooperating processes, let us have a look at Figure 4.6 indicating "Pizza" problem. Let us consider two persons—Person A and Person B. Both of them are family members and one is producing while another is consuming pizzas.

Here, person A is a producing process whereas person B is a consuming process. In order that both can do their jobs concurrently, we must have a buffer (here fridge) of pizzas that can be filled in by the person A (producing process) and emptied by the person B (consuming process). The producer and consumer should be synchronized in their actions. This implies that person B (consumer) should not try to eat pizza that has not been bought from the store yet, by the person A. In such situation, the person B (consumer) should wait. Now this buffer (fridge in our example) can be taken to be bounded or unbounded. In case of unbounded buffer there is no limit on the size of buffer and therefore, it is possible that consumer has to wait sometime for new pizzas but the producer can always keep on producing new pizzas. Thus, we can say that person A will never fall short of fridge space, whereas in case of bounded buffer when buffer size is fixed, both person A and B can have to wait if buffer is full and if buffer is empty respectively.

If person A and person B are processes executing in the operating system and have a producer-consumer relation, then the buffer that has been talked about here, is provided by either the operating system or by the code written by the application programmer in the form of shared memory. Chapter 6 of this text deals with the synchronization problems (of cooperating processes) in the shared-memory environment.

4.7. THREADS

All programmers are familiar with writing sequential programs. You have probably written a program that displays or sorts a list of names, or computes a list of prime numbers. These are sequential programs : each has a beginning, an end, a sequence, and at any given time during the runtime of the program there is a single point of execution.

A thread is similar to a sequential program : a single thread also has a beginning, an end, a sequence, and at any given time during the runtime of the thread, there is a single point of execution. However, a thread itself is not a program—it cannot run on its own—but runs within a program.

Definition : A thread is a single sequential flow of control within a program.

There is nothing new in the concept of a single thread. The real concern surrounding threads is not about a single sequential thread, but rather about the use of multiple threads in a single program all running at the same time and performing different task. This is known as multithreading.

The HotJava browser is an example of a multithreaded application; within the HotJava browser you can scroll a page while it is downloading an applet or image, play animation and sound concurrently, print a page in the background while you download a new page, or watch three sorting algorithms race to the finish. You are used to life operating in a concurrent fashion ... so why not your browser? This concurrent execution is possible by virtue of multithreading.

Thread is also known as lightweight process. A thread is similar to a real process as a thread and a running program are both a single sequential flow of control. However, a thread is considered lightweight because it runs within the context of a full-blown program and takes advantage of the resources allocated for that program and the program's environment.

As a sequential flow of control, a thread must carve out some of its own resources within a running program (it must have its own execution stack and program counter for example). The code running within the thread only works within that context. Thus, other texts use "execution context" as a synonym for "thread".

4.7.1 Threads and Processes

An idea of how threads and processes can be related to each other is depicted in Figure 4.7. Threads are almost similar to process in many ways.

Similarities between Threads and Processes are :

(i) They also have almost the same states as processes—ready, running, blocked.

(ii) They also share CPU.

(iii) Each thread has its own stack and program counter.

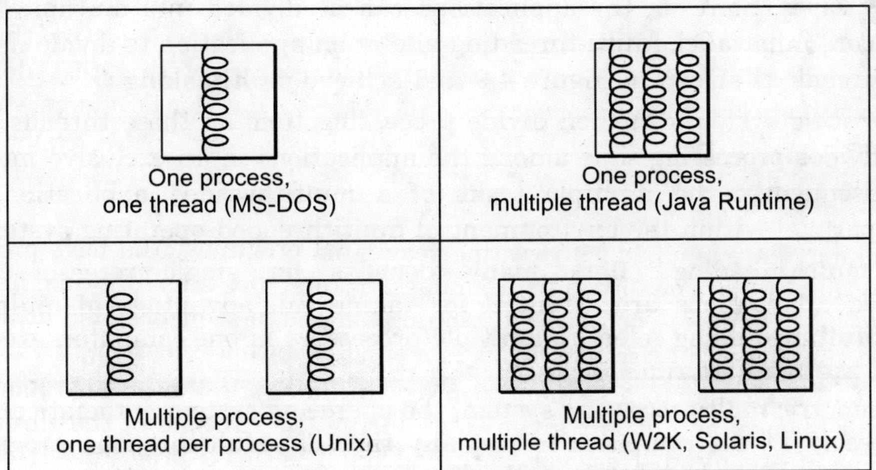

Figure 4.7 : Threads and Processes

(iv) Threads can create child threads.
(v) If one thread is blocked, the other thread can run.
(vi) A thread (within a process) executes sequentially.

Dissimilarities between Threads and Processes are

(i) Unlike processes, threads are not independent of one another.
(ii) There is no concept of protection as in processes. All threads share the address space of a task and therefore, a thread can read/write over any other thread's stack.
(iii) Processes may originate from different users, and may be hostile to one another whereas an individual task with multiple threads will always be owned by a single user.
(iv) It takes less time to create a new thread in an existing process than to create a new process.
(v) It takes less time to terminate a thread than to terminate a process.
(vi) It takes less time to switch between two threads within the same process than to switch between two processes.
(vii) Threads enhance efficiency in communication between different executing programs—since threads within the same process share memory and files, they can communicate with each other without invoking the operating system's kernel.

4.7.2 Multithreading

In a single-threaded environment like Windows 3.1, a task is an application such as Microsoft Word, Excel, or Access. These applications take turns running on the computer processors, with each application using a small time slice of the processor, then yielding to the next application as shown in Figure 4.8.

In many cases, however, the applications can be divided into multiple tasks that can also execute in parallel. Multi-threading allows an application to divide its task into individual threads as shown in Figure 4.9 and achieve multitasking.

The operating system can then divide processing time on these threads similar to the way it divides processing time among the applications in an exclusive multitasking system. Consequently, the multiple tasks of a multithreaded application can also progress in parallel within the environment of multithreaded operating system.

While multithreading offers many benefits on single-processor machines, multithreaded applications are essential for taking full advantage of multiprocessor computers. Multiprocessing refers to multiple processors in one computer, executing the threads that are ready to run.

In a symmetric multiprocessing system, the operating system automatically uses all of the processors in the computer to run any threads. Multithreaded programs with parallel executing threads can take full advantage of any number of processors within the system. With multiprocessing power, your multithreaded application can run multiple threads simultaneously on different processors, finishing more task in less time.

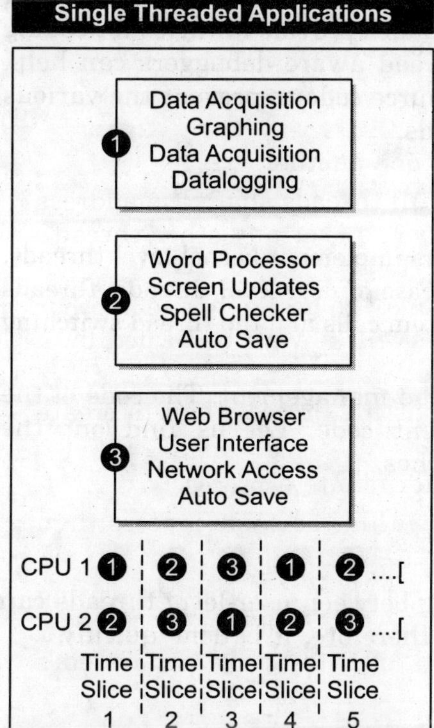

Figure 4.8 : Any subtask in a single threaded application will prevent the execution of other subtasks

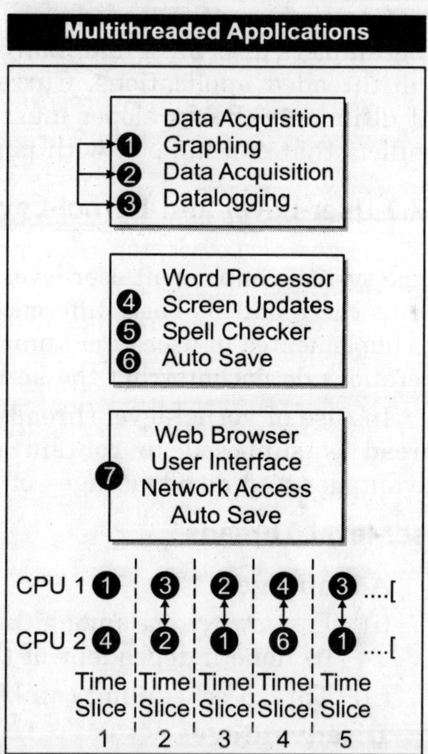

Figure 4.9 : Multithreaded application takes advantage of multiprocessors to execute multiple threads in one time slice

Thus, to achieve maximum performance from multithreaded operating systems and multiprocessor machines, an application must be multithreaded.

Advantages of Multithreading

Windows NT, Windows 95, and some variants of UNIX operating system are multithreaded and run on either a single-processor machine or a multiprocessor computer. The multithreading software and multiprocessor computers are readily available today, but what does that really offer?

Multithreading brings numerous benefits, especially in PC-based data acquisition (DAQ) and instrument I/O applications. On single-processor machines, multithreading can help applications where :

1. Some task takes much longer to execute than others.
2. Some task needs a better deterministic outcome than others.
3. Some user interface activity is to be run concurrently with hardware communications.

On multiprocessor systems, multithreading of an application takes advantage of the additional hardware and can result in greatly improved overall performance.

Creating multithreaded applications can be difficult for even very experienced programmers also. Java and many other upcoming languages provide libraries for coding multithreaded applications. Current tools like multithread aware debuggers can help, but ultimately the developer must carefully track the source code to prevent the various conflicts that can happen with parallel executing threads.

4.7.3 User-Level and Kernel-Level Threads

Some systems implement user-level threads where as others implement kernel-level threads. Let us check out the basic difference between the two. In case of user-level threads, threads are implemented in user-level libraries rather than via system calls and the thread switching operations do not interrupt the kernel.

In case of kernel-level threads, the kernel does thread management. The code of the thread is supposed to contain no thread management code. Let us find out the advantages and disadvantages of each of these approaches.

User-level Threads

Advantages

(i) Fast switching among threads—since switching between user-level threads can be done independent of the operating system, therefore, it is done quickly.

(ii) Thread scheduling can be application specific.

Disadvantages

(i) When a user level thread executes a system call, not only that thread is blocked but also all of the threads within the process are blocked. This is because operating system is unaware of the presence of threads and only knows about the existence of a process actually constituting these threads.

(ii) Multithreaded application using user level threads cannot take advantage of multiprocessing since kernel assigns one process to only one processor at a time. This is again because operating system is unaware of the presence of threads and it schedules processes not threads.

Kernel Level Threads

Advantages

(i) The operating system is aware of the presence of threads in the processes, therefore, even if one thread of a process gets blocked, the operating system chooses the next one to run, either from the same process or from the different one.

(ii) The operating system can also schedule multiple threads from the same process on multiple processors.

Disadvantages

(i) Switching threads is time consuming because the kernel (via an interrupt) must do the switching.

A third approach to implement threading is a hybrid approach in which both user level and kernel level threads are implemented. Solaris 2 (a version of UNIX) is an example of such operating system. Figure 4.10 shows all the three approaches to implement threads.

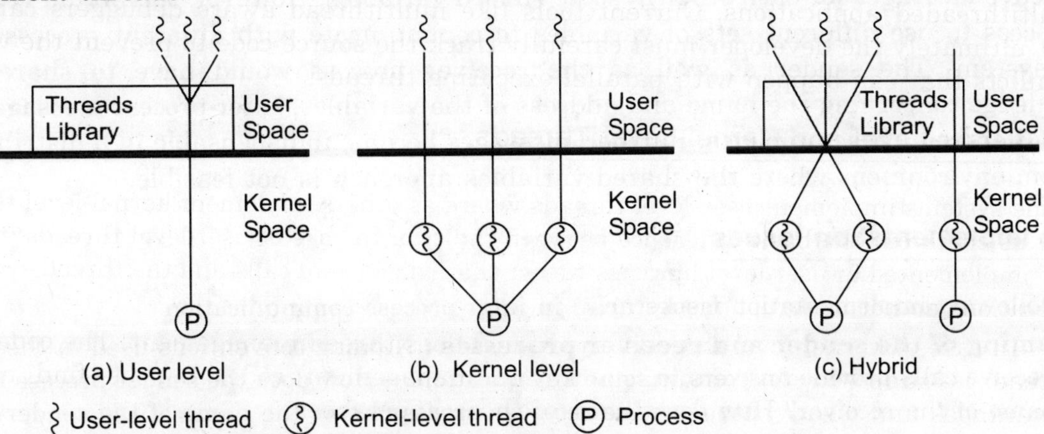

Figure 4.10 : User level and kernel level threads

4.8. INTER-PROCESS COMMUNICATION

Inter-process Communication (IPC) is a facility provided by an operating system via which cooperating processes can communicate with each other. This facility can allow the processes to cooperate and synchronize their actions. IPC is provided by a message system. Some operating systems can use both message system (IPC) and shared memory/buffer (as discussed in Section 4.6) to establish communication and synchronization among the processes.

4.8.1 Inter-process Messages (Direct Communication Method)

If a process A sends a message to process B by executing the operating system call *send*, then the operating system copies the message into a buffer and awaits execution of a *receive* call by process B. When B executes a *receive*, the operating system delivers the message to B. Process B interprets the message and takes appropriate action determined by its contents. This may result in a reply being sent to A. If no message has been sent to B by the time B executes a receive call, the operating system blocks B till a message arrives for it. If many messages have been sent to B, the operating system queues them and delivers them in FIFO order when B executes *receive* calls. In this method, processes A and B will look like as shown in figure 4.11.

Figure 4.11 : *Direct Communication where Processes name each other*

Such communication can be performed using shared variables. Processes A and B can leave messages for each other in some shared variables. However, this would require a process to use different sets of variables to communicate with different processes in the system. The sender as well as the receiver process would have to share the knowledge concerning the name and address of the variables. Inter-process messages do not suffer from these problems. Further, messages become indispensable in a distributed system environment where the shared variables approach is not feasible.

4.8.2 Implementation Issues

The following implementation issues arise in inter-process communication :

1. Naming of the sender and receiver processes : Naming conventions used in the send and receive calls provide answers to some key questions—How does the sender process know the name of the receiver? How does the receiver process know the name of the sender?

2. Message delivery protocols : Protocols determine the message data formats and action of processes while sending and receiving messages.

3. Operating system responsibilities : Buffering of messages, blocking and waking of processes, etc.

These issues are discussed in the following sub sections.

4.8.2.1 Naming

Typical formats for the send and receive calls are :

send (Id_1, *message*);
receive (Id_2, *ad* (*message_area*));

where

- Id_1, Id_2 are names of the receiver and sender processes, respectively (these are typically process id's assigned by the operating system).
- *message* is the textual form of the message to be sent
- *ad*(*message_area*) is the address of a memory area in which the receiver wishes to receive the message.

This naming scheme is symmetrical since both sender and receiver processes name each other. The convention used for naming the sender and receiver processes gives rise to the following issues :

1. *How do the sender and receiver processes know each other's id?*

This issue concerns the scope of process names in the system. It is easy for concurrent processes within a program to know each other's names. However, processes belonging to different programs do not possess this ability. The operating system must provide some arrangement by which a process can find the name of any other process in the system.

2. *Is it essential to name the sender and receiver process?*

This issue concerns the need for communicating processes to know each other's names. When two user processes communicate, it is natural to expect knowledge of each other's names. However, this is inconvenient for server processes. For example, if a print server is only required to print the files deposited in its queue, knowledge of sender's name is unnecessary. For this reason, an asymmetric naming convention is often used in practice. The send and receive calls in this form of communication have the following formats :

send (*Id*1, *message*);

receive (*ad* (*message_area*));

Here the receiver does not name the process from which it wishes to receive a message, however, the sender process must still know the name of the receiver process.

4.8.2.2 Message Delivery Protocols

We know that a protocol is a set of rules and conventions shared by communicating entities. A message delivery protocol has the following elements :

1. Conventions concerning data formats.
2. Rules concerning actions to be performed by a sender and receiver process until a message is delivered.
3. Rules for handling exceptional conditions.

Elements 2 and 3 have been discussed here :

Blocking and Non-blocking Protocols

In a **blocking protocol**, a sender process is blocked till the message is delivered to the receiver. A blocking protocol has certain nice properties for both user processes and the operating system. A sender process has a guarantee that the message sent by it is delivered before it continues its execution. The operating system responsibilities are also simpler since it can allow a message to remain in the sender's memory area until it is delivered. However, blocking of the sender may pose unnecessary waits in certain situations—for example, while communicating with a print server—resulting in poor response times.

A **non-blocking protocol** permits a sender to continue execution after performing a send irrespective of whether the message is delivered. In both (blocking and non-blocking) protocols a process performing a *receive* must wait till a message can be delivered to it. A non-blocking protocol has the advantage that a sender is free to continue its execution immediately after sending a message. However, a sender has no means of knowing when (and whether) its message is delivered to the receiver; a sender does not know when it is safe to reuse the memory area containing the text of a message. To overcome this problem, the operating system does not hold undelivered messages in a sender's memory area. It allocates a buffer in the system area and copies the message into the buffer. This involves substantial memory commitment when many undelivered messages exist. It also consumes CPU time as a message has to be copied twice–once into a system buffer at a send, and later into the message area of the receiver at the time of message delivery.

Exceptional Conditions

Message delivery protocols should provide for handling of exceptional conditions during *send* and *receive* calls. A list of few such conditions in the order of reducing security is as follows :

1. In symmetric communication the process from which a message is to be received does not exist.
2. The process to which a message is to be sent does not exist.
3. The operating system cannot accept a send call because it has run out of buffer memory.
4. No message exists for a process when it executes a receive call.

In cases 1 and 2, the process executing the *send* or *receive* call (which leads to the exception) may be cancelled and its termination code may be set to describe the exceptional conditions. In case 3, the sender process may be blocked till some buffer space becomes available due to *receive* calls executed by other processes. Case 4 is really not an exception as *receive* calls are generally blocking but it may be treated as an exception to provide some flexibility to the receiving process. For example, the operating system may return from a *receive* call with an appropriate status code. If the status code is 'no message is available', the receiver process has the choice to wait for the arrival of a message, or attempt a receive after performing some other actions. In the former case, it may repeat the receive call with a flag to indicate that occurrence of this condition should be suppressed. More severe exceptions may also occur but their description is out of the scope of this book.

4.8.3 Mailboxes (In-direct Communication Method)

As the name suggests, a mailbox (or port) is a repository for inter-process messages. It has the following features :

1. A mailbox has a unique identity.
2. A mailbox has an owner, which is typically the process, which created the mailbox. Only the owner can receive messages from a mailbox.
3. Any process, which knows the identity of a mailbox, can send messages to it. These processes are called the users of a mailbox.

Figure 4.12 illustrates creation of a mailbox by process A, and its use by process B to send a message. The creator process, *i.e.,* A mentions a unique name to be given to the mailbox. Process B uses the mailbox name, instead of a process-id, in its send.

Figure 4.12 : *Mailbox example*

4.8.3.1 Implementation of a Mailbox

Answers to two key questions motivate alternative implementations of mailboxes;

1. How does a process know the name of a mailbox?
2. Where does the system buffer the message sent to a mailbox?

An operating system may provide a set of pre-fixed mailbox names, or may permit user processes to create names of their choice. A process creates a mailbox through a *create_mailbox* call. A user of a mailbox can simply send a message to a mailbox. Both calls would return with status codes to indicate the success or failure of a call. The operating system may associate a fixed set of buffers with each mailbox, or may allocate buffers from a common pool of buffers when a message is sent. For better control over creation and destruction of mailboxes, an operating system may require a user to explicitly 'connect' to a mailbox before starting to use it, and to 'disconnect' at the end of its communication.

Apart from creation and use of mailboxes, the operating system may permit the ownership of a mailbox to be transferred to another process. Operating system may also permit an owner to destroy a mailbox. In that case, it has the responsibility to inform all users of the mailbox accordingly.

4.8.3.2 Advantages of Mailboxes

Inter-process communication using mailboxes (indirect communication) differs from (direct communication) where the sender and receiver processes directly name each other in the following respects :

1. Mailboxes permit anonymity of the receiver process; a sender need not know the name of the receiver.
2. A process may own many mailboxes. This permits it to segregate different kinds of messages sent to it.

EXERCISES

4.1 What is a process? What are the operations defined on a process?

4.2 What are the different states a process can be in at a particular time? What factors can lead to the transition of process states?

4.3 List the differences among short-term, medium-term and long-term schedulers.

4.4 What will you create (if you are given a choice out of a thread and a process) as a subset of a current process and why?

4.5 What is the purpose of fork () and exec () system call in UNIX?

4.6 Differentiate between user-level and kernel-level threads.

4.7 What are cooperating processes? What support do you think the operating system should provide for the concurrent execution of processes?

4.8 List the names of operating systems that support multithreading.

4.9 Differentiate between single threaded and multithreaded system.

4.10 What do you understand by the following terms?

(i) Swapping

(ii) Cascading termination

(iii) Synchronous process creation

(iv) Asynchronous process creation

(v) Ready Queue

4.11 What is the direct communication method in Inter-process Communication? How is it different from indirect method?

4.12 Compare the blocking and non-blocking message delivery protocols in Inter-process direct communication method.

4.13 What sort of exceptions should be handled by message delivery protocols?

4.14 Justify that multithreading can take the best advantage of multiple processors.

CHAPTER

5

CPU Scheduling

OVERVIEW

This chapter focuses upon the need for processor scheduling, scheduling criterion and also explains various scheduling algorithms for a uniprocessor system. A brief mention of multiple processor scheduling has been made here. This text also covers scheduling mechanisms implemented in real time systems. An effort has been made to make each and every concept clearer with the help of examples.

5.1. INTRODUCTION

Before going on to understanding various CPU scheduling criteria and algorithms, let us first try to understand what is CPU scheduling? It is the process of determining which processes will actually run when there are multiple runnable processes. The next thing that comes to our mind is, is it really that important? Yes, it is. Because, it can have a big effect on the resource utilization and overall performance of the system.

By the way, world went through a long period (late 80's to early 90's) in which the most popular operating systems (DOS, Mac) had no sophisticated CPU scheduling algorithms. They were single threaded and ran one process at a time until the user directed them to run another process. But now as the operating systems became more sophisticated (e.g., Windows NT), they started supporting multiprogramming for maximizing CPU utilization. Multiprogramming environment led to the development and implementation of sophisticated CPU scheduling algorithms.

Basic assumptions behind most of the scheduling algorithms are :

- There is a pool of runnable processes contending for the CPU.
- The processes are independent and compete for resources.

- The job of the scheduler is to distribute the scarce resource of CPU to the different processes "fairly" and in a way that optimizes some performance criteria.

The behaviour of a process plays a key role in CPU scheduling. Let us now see, how do processes behave? It is depicted by CPU-I/O burst cycle. A process will normally run for a while (known as the CPU burst), perform some I/O, (known as the I/O burst) then run for a while more (the next CPU burst) and so on. The duration of interval between CPU burst and I/O burst depends upon the following :

- If the process is I/O bound—(A process is an I/O bound process if it performs lots of I/O operations as compared to other computation operations). Each I/O operation is followed by a short CPU burst to process the I/O. Thus, more I/O happens.
- If the process is CPU bound—(A process is known as CPU bound process if it performs lots of computation and has very less I/O operations to do), there will be long CPU bursts with I/O bursts of very short duration.

5.2. TYPES OF SCHEDULING

Basically, there are two types of scheduling algorithms—Preemptive and Non-preemptive algorithms.

Non preemptive scheduling. Once the CPU has been allocated to a process, the process keeps the CPU until its termination or its transition to the blocked state. This means that once CPU is allocated to a process, this process can use the CPU for its own execution till it willingly surrenders or leaves the CPU.

Preemptive scheduling. Here, even if the CPU has been allocated to a certain process, it can be snatched from this process any time either due to time constraint or due to priority reasons. It implies that if a process with higher priority becomes ready for its execution, the process which is currently using the CPU will be forced to give up the CPU so that higher priority job can run fast.

Preemptive scheduling is costly as compared to Non-preemptive scheduling. For time constraints, time support is needed. Also when two processes share some data and one is in the midst of updating the data when the second process preempts it, then second process might access the inconsistent data left in between by the first process. For coordinating access to the shared data, special mechanisms must be provided by the operating system and this is again a costly affair.

Dispatcher

This is another component involved in CPU scheduling. It is a program responsible for assigning the CPU to the process, which has been selected by the short-term scheduler. Assigning the CPU to a ready process involves three major steps :

Step 1. Context Switching. As the name indicates, it implies the switching of CPU from one process to another. This involves saving the state of the old process (one that was running previously) and loading the saved state, if any, for this ready process (scheduled to be run now). This implies that there will be no saved state in case this ready process has been newly created and is being allocated the CPU for the first time. But if this ready process was previously in the blocked state (due to I/O etc.), then the process' registers and memory must be loaded with all the previously saved data.

Step 2. Switching to user mode from monitor mode. As we know, a user process must be run in user mode therefore, mode must be changed from monitor mode to user mode.

Step 3. Restart the execution of process. The execution of process should be restarted by jumping to the instruction that was supposed to be executed when this process was last interrupted or to the first instruction if this ready process is to be executed for the first time after its creation.

Out of the three operations mentioned above, context switching consumes more time and therefore, an effort should be made to minimize context switch time. The overall time taken by the dispatcher is the sum of time consumed in all these operations.

5.3. SCHEDULING CRITERIA

The possible metrics for determining "How good a scheduling algorithm is?" are:

- **CPU utilization.** CPU should remain as busy as possible.
- **Throughput.** Throughput is defined as the number of processes that are completed per unit of time and it should be as high as possible. It is usually dependent on the job mix-i.e., the number of CPU bound and I/O bound processes. If all the processes are CPU bound, throughput will be less as compared to I/O based processes (which require CPU for less time and hence more of them can be finished in a given time). Thus, the two types of the jobs should be properly mixed to improve the throughput.
- **Turnaround time.** Turn around time is defined as interval between the time of submission and completion of the job and it should be as less as possible. It is a metric for batch systems.
- **Waiting time.** It is the sum of the time intervals for which the process has to wait in the ready queue. The CPU scheduling algorithm should try to make this time as less as possible for a given process.

- **Response time.** In an interactive system, response time is the best metric. It is defined as the time interval between the job submission and the first response produced by the job. Response time should be minimized in an interactive system.

As we have seen, most of these metrics are applicable to one process e.g., waiting time of a process, response time of a process etc. but actually, we have to consider the general performance of a scheduling algorithm. Therefore, we optimize the average measure. For example, average of waiting times of all the processes should be kept minimum and this can be taken to be one criterion to prove that the performance of a scheduling algorithm is good. On the other hand, the variance not average of the response time of the processes should be minimized, because the idea is not to have a process having very long response time as compared to all other processes.

After having discussed the various types of scheduling and the scheduling criteria, let us explore the scheduling algorithms in detail.

5.4. SCHEDULING ALGORITHMS

5.4.1 First-come First-served scheduling algorithm (FCFS)

It is the simplest of all the scheduling algorithms. Key concept of this algorithm is "allocate the CPU in the order in which the procceses arrive". It assumes that ready queue is managed as FIFO (First in first out). When the CPU is free, it is allocated to the process, which is occupying the front of the queue. Once this process goes into running state, its PCB is removed from the queue. This algorithm is non-preemptive.

Advantages of this algorithm are :

1. It is simple to understand and code.
2. Suitable for Batch Systems.

Disadvantages of this algorithm are :

1. Waiting time can be large if short requests wait behind the long ones.
2. It is not suitable for time sharing systems where it is important that each user should get the CPU for an equal amount of time interval.
3. A proper mix of jobs (I/O based and CPU based jobs) is needed to achieve good results from FCFS scheduling.

Example : Consider the following set of processes having their CPU-burst time (mentioned in milli-seconds). CPU-burst time indicates that for how much time, the process needs the CPU.

Process	Time for which CPU is required CPU-Burst (Milli-seconds)
P_1	10
P_2	5
P_3	5

If the processes have arrived in order P_1, P_2 and P_3, then the average waiting time for the process will be obtained from the chart shown below :

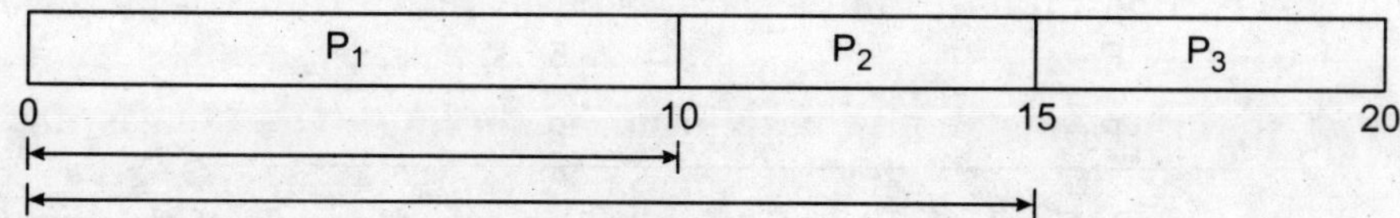

Waiting time for P_1 = 0 milli-second

Waiting time for P_2 = 10 milli-seconds

Waiting time for P_3 = 15 milli-seconds

$$\text{Average waiting time} = \frac{0 + 10 + 15}{3} = \frac{25}{3} = 8.33 \text{ milli-seconds}$$

In case, the processes have arrived in the order P_2, P_3, P_1, then

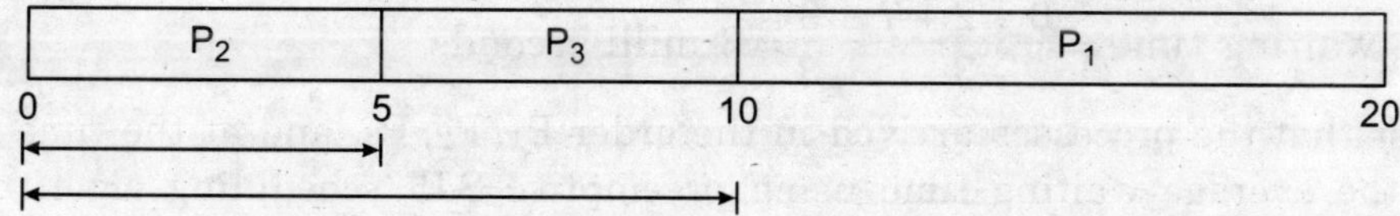

$$\text{Average waiting time} = \frac{0 + 5 + 10}{3} = \frac{15}{3} = 5 \text{ milli-seconds}$$

Thus, average waiting time will always depend upon the order in which the processes arrive and will greatly vary depending upon whether the processes having less CPU-burst arrive first in the ready queue. Overall, this algorithm is never recommended wherever performance is a major issue.

5.4.2 Shortest-Job First Scheduling

Key concept of this algorithm is :

"CPU is allocated to the process with least CPU-burst time"

Amongst the processes in the ready queue, CPU is always assigned to the process with least CPU burst requirement. If there are two processes with same CPU burst, the one which arrived first, will be taken up first by the CPU. This algorithm can be either preemptive or non-preemptive.

Advantage of this algorithm is :

This is usually considered to be an optimal algorithm, as it gives the minimum average waiting time.

Disadvantage of this algorithm is :

The problem is to know the length of time for which CPU is needed by a process. A prediction formula can be used to predict the amount of time for which CPU may be required by a process.

Example : Let us consider, the following set of processes having their CPU-burst time (mentioned in milli-seconds) and having arrived almost at the same time.

Process	CPU-burst (Milli-seconds)
P_1	10
P_2	5
P_3	2

Using the non-preemptive SJF scheduling, the waiting times for each of the processes will be as shown below :

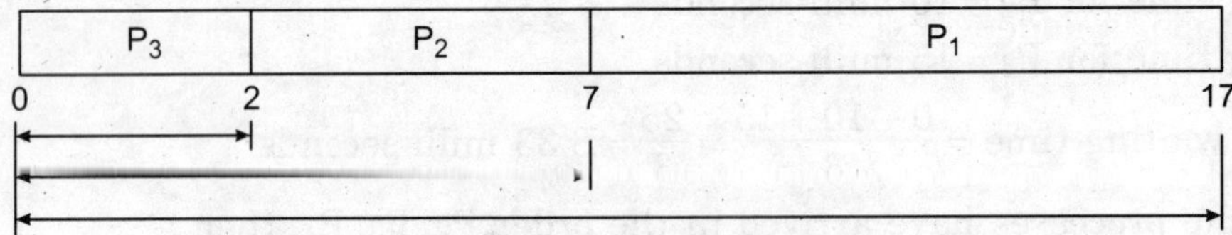

$$\text{Average waiting time} = \frac{0+2+7}{3} = \frac{9}{3} = 3 \text{ milli-seconds}$$

If we consider that the processes arrived in the order P_1, P_2, P_3, and at the time mentioned below, then the average waiting time using preemptive SJF scheduling algorithm will be calculated as :

Process	CPU-burst	Time of Arrival
P_1	10	0
P_2	5	1
P_3	2	2

P_1	P_2	P_3	P_2	P_1
0–1	1–2	2–4	4–8	8–17

P_1 (1 to 8), P_2 (0 to 1), P_2 (1 to 4), P_3 (0 to 2)

In this, the CPU will be taken away from the currently executing process whenever a process with less CPU burst time (as compared to the time remaining for the current process) arrives. As in example shown above, the time when process P_2 arrives, P_1 needs 9 milli-seconds more to finish. As P_2's CPU burst is 5 milli-seconds < 9 milli-seconds, therefore, P_1's execution will be preempted and P_2 will be executed but again as P_3

arrives, P_2's execution needs 3 more milli-seconds where as P_3 needs only 2 milli-seconds to execute, thus P_3 takes over P_2 and so on.

Waiting time for $P_1 = 0 + (8 - 1) = 7$ milli-seconds

Waiting time for $P_2 = 1 + (4 - 2) = 3$ milli-seconds

Waiting time for $P_3 = 2$ milli-seconds

Average waiting time $= \frac{7+3+2}{3} = \frac{12}{3} = 4$ milli-seconds

5.4.3 Priority Scheduling

Each process in the system if given a priority, then the scheduling must be done according to the priority of each process. A higher priority job should get CPU whereas lower priority job can be made to wait. Key concept of this algorithm is "Priority scheduling is necessarily a form of prremptive scheduling where priority is the basis of preemption". Some systems implement it is a non-preemptive scheduling also, where a higher priority job is added to the front of the ready queue so that it can be executed next, but it cannot preempt the currently executing process.

Example : Let us consider, a set of processes P_1, P_2 and P_3 having priorities ranging from 1 to 3. Let us assume that 1 is the highest priority whereas 3 is the least priority. Let us also assume that P_1 arrives first and P_3 arrives in the last.

Process	**Burst time**	Priority	Arrival time
P_1	10	3	0
P_2	5	2	1
P_3	2	1	2

P_1	P_2	P_3	P_2	P_1

0 1 2 4 8 17

$$\text{Average waiting time} = \frac{0 + (8-1) + 1 + (4-2) + 2}{3}$$

$$= \frac{7+1+2+2}{3} = \frac{12}{3}$$

$$= 4 \text{ milli-seconds}$$

Here, the prremption is based on the priority. When P_1 executes, P_2 arrives with priority 2, which is higher than priority 3 of P_1, and thus P_1 is preempted. Similarly when P_2 executes, P_3 arrives with priority 1 which is the highest priority and thus P_2 is preempted and so on.

A natural question that arises here is—what if two processes have been assigned same priorities? (Priorities may be assigned by the user or by the operating system depending upon the importance of the process). The tie will be broken by comparing their CPU-burst times. The process with short CPU burst time will be executed first.

Problems with this scheduling algorithm are :

Preemptive priority scheduling some times becomes the biggest cause of starvation of a process. If a process is in ready state but its execution is almost always preempted due to the arrival of higher priority processes, it will starve for its execution. Therefore, a mechanism like aging has to be built into the system so that almost every process should get the CPU in a fixed interval of time. This can be done by increasing the priority of a low-priority process after a fixed time interval so that at one moment of time it becomes a high priority job as compared to others and thus, finally gets CPU for its execution.

5.4.4 Round-Robin Scheduling

All the above mentioned algorithms are good for non-interactive systems. What about the interactive systems, then? Another scheduling algorithm whose key concept is to give response to the users in a reasonable time is known as Round-Robin Scheduling algorithm. The basic purpose of this algorithm is to support time-sharing systems. This algorithm is similar to FCFS algorithm but now it is a preemptive FCFS scheduling. The preemption takes place after a fixed interval of time called time quantum or time slice. Its implementation requires timer interrupts based on which the preemption takes place.

Key concept of this algorithm is :

Consider a set of processes lined up in the ready queue. The processes are taken out of the ready queue in FCFS order. Let us consider that a process has been taken up for execution now. Keep in mind that the execution cannot go beyond the time-slice (implemented by timer interrupt). This process may either finish up its execution (if its CPU burst is less than time quantum) before the timer goes off or CPU will be preempted from it after the timer goes off and this causes an interrupt to the operating system. At this time, context switching will take place. The next process will be taken up from the ready queue (this process, which is left by the CPU, will be added to the tail of the ready queue now).

Let us first understand the concept of its working with the help of the following example.

Example : Let there be three processes P_1, P_2 and P_3, with their CPU burst times mentioned in milli-seconds. Let us assume a time sharing system in which all of the processes arrive almost simultaneously. Let the time quantum be of 2 milli-seconds.

Process	CPU-Burst time
P_1	10
P_2	5
P_3	2

P_1	P_2	P_3	P_1	P_2	P_1	P_2	P_1	P_1
0–2	2–4	4–6	6–8	8–10	10–12	12–13	13–15	15–17

Waiting time for P_1 will be : $= 0 + (6 - 2) + (10 - 8) + (13 - 12)$

$= 4 + 2 + 1 = 7$ milli-seconds

Waiting time for P_2 will be : $= 2 + (8 - 4) + (12 - 10)$

$= 2 + 4 + 2 = 8$ milli-seconds

Waiting time for P_3 will be 4 milli-seconds

Thus, the average waiting time will be :

$$= \frac{7 + 8 + 4}{3} = \frac{19}{3}$$

$= 6.33$ milli-seconds.

As shown in the figure above, first P_1 gets the CPU and gets executed for 2 milli-seconds, then context switching occurs and P_2 gets CPU for 2 milli-seconds, then again context switching occurs and P_3 gets CPU for 2 milli-seconds, since its CPU burst time is 2 milli-seconds only, therefore, it completes its execution here and thus do not get the CPU again. P_1 and P_2 similarly continue to share the CPU in the same fashion till they are done.

As we have seen here, this algorithm is purely preemptive.

The performance of this algorithm depends upon many factors :

1. Size of time quantum

- If time quantum's size is large then this algorithm becomes same as FCFS algorithm and thus performance degrades.
- If time quantum's size is very small then the number of context switches increases considerably and the time quantum almost equals the time taken to switch the CPU from one process to another. Therefore, 50 percent of overall time spent in the execution of a set of processes will be due to context switching among the processes which is not desirable at all.

  Thus, the time quantum should not be very large and also should not be too small to achieve good system performance.

2. Number of context switches—As mentioned above, the number of context-switches should not be too many to slow down the overall execution of all the processes. Time quantum should be large with respect to the context switch time. This is to ensure that a process keeps CPU for a considerable amount of time as compared to the time spent in context switching.

5.4.5 Multilevel Queue Scheduling

Key concept of this algorithm is "Multilevel Queue Scheduling was created for situations in which processes are easily classified into different groups".

Multilevel Queue Scheduling has the following characteristics :

- Processes are divided into different queues based on their types. For example, interactive (foreground) versus batch (background) system, these two types of processes have different response-time requirements. In addition, processes have different priority. The foreground queue processes may have higher priority over background queue processes. In Multilevel Queue Scheduling, processes are permanently assigned to a particular queue.

- Each queue has its own scheduling algorithm. For example, interactive processes at the foreground may use the Round-Robin Scheduling methods while batch jobs at the background may use the FCFS method.
- There must be a scheduling algorithm between the queues. Usually this is a fixed-priority preemptive scheduling. For example, the foreground queue may have absolute priority over the background queue. A percentage-based time sliced approach can also be used. Each queue gets a certain portion of the CPU time, which it can then schedule among the various processes in its queue. For instance, in the foreground-background queue examples, the foreground queue can be given 85 percent of the CPU time for Round Robin scheduling among its processes, whereas the background queue receives 15 percent of the CPU time to allocate to its processes in a FCFS manner.

Example : Let us look at an example of a multilevel queue scheduling algorithm with four queues as shown in Figure. 5.1.

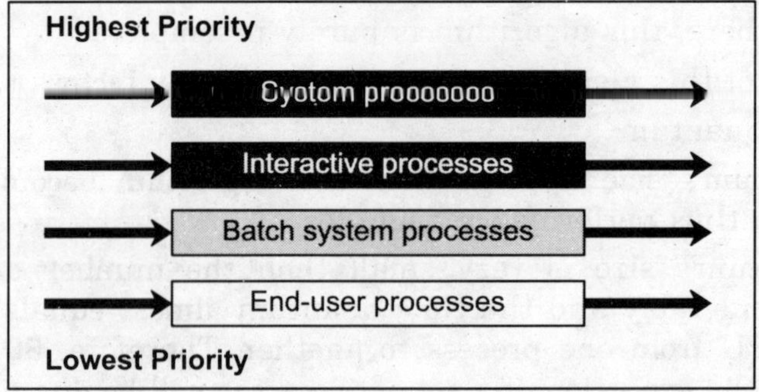

Figure 5.1 : Multilevel queue scheduling

1. System processes
2. Interactive processes
3. Batch processes
4. End-user processes

Here each queue has absolute priority over lower-priority queues. No process in the batch queue, for example, could run unless the queues for system processes and interactive processes were all empty. If an interactive process entered the ready queue while a batch process was running, the batch process would be preempted.

Advantages of this algorithm are :

In a Multilevel Queue algorithm, processes are permanently assigned to a queue on entry to the system. Since processes do not change their foreground or background nature, this set up has the advantage of low scheduling overhead.

Disadvantages of this algorithm are :

It is inflexible as the process can never change their queues and thus may have to starve for the CPU if one or the other higher priority queues are never becoming empty.

5.4.6 Multilevel Feedback Queue Scheduling

Key concept of this algorithm is :

"It is an enhancement of multilevel queue scheduling where processes can move between queues". In this approach to process scheduling, the ready queue is partitioned into multiple queues of different priorities. The system tends to assign processes to queues based on their CPU burst characteristics : if a process consumes too much CPU time it is placed into a lower priority queue. Thus I/O-bound and interactive processes stay in the higher priority queues and CPU-bound processes gravitate to the lower priority queues. A technique called "aging" (discussed earlier in section 5.4.3) promotes lower priority processes to the next higher priority queue after a suitable interval of time.

In Figure 5.2, the process queues are displayed from top to bottom in order of decreasing priority. The top priority queue has the smallest CPU-time quantum. After a process from the top queue exhausts this time quantum on the CPU, it is placed on the next lower queue. Similarly, a process, which consumes the larger CPU-time quantum of the next-to-highest priority queue, will be demoted to the third queue. The queue's time quota is scaled by a factor of 2 with each decreasing step in priority until the lowest priority queue is reached. This queue has a large time quantum which effects FCFS scheduling in contrast to the round robin scheduling on the other queues. We assume that a new process arriving on the top priority queue will preempt an active process originating from a lower priority queue and require it on its queue of origin. A process that spends an amount of elapsed time exceeding the aging interval will be promoted to the next higher priority queue.

How to define this algorithm?

The following things should be determined for the implementation of this type of algorithm :

- Number of queues
- Scheduling algorithm for each queue
- Method for upgrading a process to a higher-priority queue
- Method for downgrading a process to a lower-priority queue
- Method for assigning a process to a queue initially.

The **advantages** of Multilevel Feedback Queue Algorithm are :

1. Multilevel feedback queue scheduling allows a process to move between queues. This is fair for I/O-bound processes, they do not have to wait too long.
2. A process that waits too long in a lower-priority queue may be moved to a higher-priority queue, this form of aging prevents starvation.
3. The definition of a multilevel feedback queue scheduling makes it the most general CPU scheduling algorithm. It can be configured to match a specific system under design.
4. It is more flexible.

The **disadvantages** of this algorithm are :

1. It requires some means of selecting values for all the parameters to define the best scheduler.
2. Moving the processes around the queues produces more CPU overheads.
3. It is the most complex scheduling algorithm.

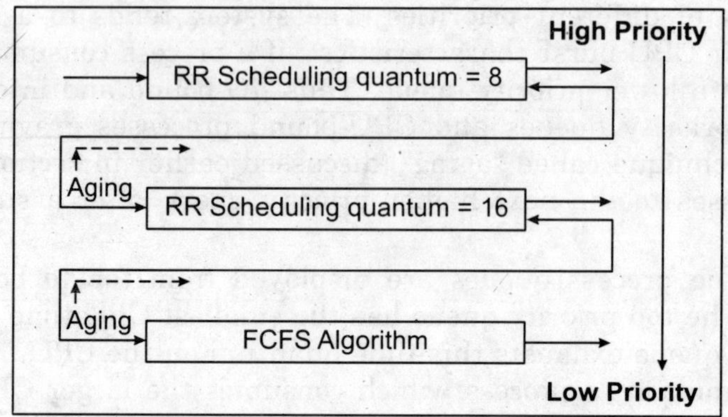

Figure 5.2 : Multievel feedback queues

Consider the following set of processes with their CPU-burst times and arrival times mentioned here :

Processes	Arrival time	Burst time
	Time in milli-seconds	
P_1	0	17
P_2	12	25
P_3	28	8
P_4	36	32
P_5	46	18

Consider a multilevel feedback queue scheduling with three queues, numbered as Q1, Q2, Q3. The scheduler first executes processes in Q1, which is given a time quantum of 8 milli-seconds. If a process does not finish within this time, it is moved to the tail of the Q2. The scheduler executes processes in Q2 only when Q1 is empty. The process at the head of Q2 is given a quantum of 16 milli-seconds. If it does not complete, it is preempted and is put into Q3. Processes in Q3 are run on an FCFS basis, only when Q1 and Q2 are empty.

A process that arrives in Q1 will preempt a process in Q2, a process that arrives in Q2 will preempt a process in Q3. The chart shown here depicts the multilevel feedback queue scheduling of process P_1 to P_5.

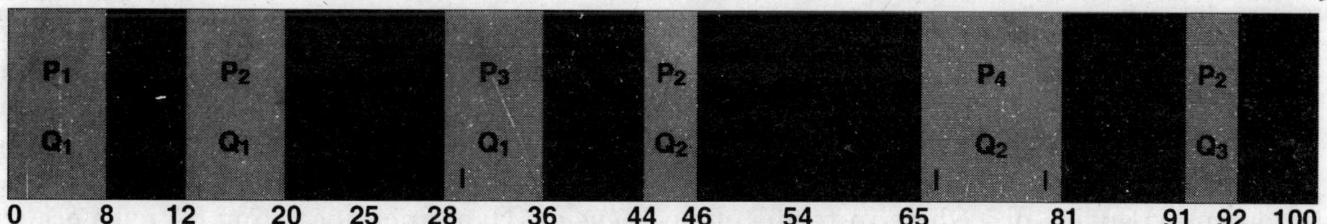

The waiting time for each process will be as mentioned below :

Process	Arrival time	CPU Burst	Waiting time
P_1	0	17	8
P_2	12	25	55
P_3	28	8	0
P_4	36	32	32
P_5	46	18	27

Round Robin with multilevel feed back queue scheduling is used in UNIX system.

5.5. MULTIPLE-PROCESSOR SCHEDULING

All the algorithms, discussed here were to deal with the scheduling of one processor (CPU) among various processes in the system. What, if multiple CPUs are available in the system? Probably, a very different kind of scheduling mechanism needs to be incorporated. Without looking into the details of such scheduling mechanisms, it can be mentioned that such scheduling will be much more complex.

Terminology

Understanding multiprocessing, like understanding any other technology, requires a familiarity with some important terms. As explained in chapter 1 also, in Symmetric Multiprocessing (SMP) systems, CPUs share system resources, including the bus to a common memory space. CPUs communicate to one another by sharing information in this memory space. This setup is also referred to as a tightly coupled architecture.

Conversely, in Parallel Processing (PP) systems, each CPU has its own memory and often a unique set of system resources. As a result, CPU's must communicate externally over some type of network scheme. This setup is also referred to as a loosely coupled architecture.

One other way to classify multiprocessor systems is by the type of CPUs that are utilized. Heterogeneous systems use different types of CPUs, whereas Homogeneous systems use identical CPUs.

5.5.1 Static and Dynamic Scheduling

As we know, concurrent execution of a program on multiple processors used to be the sole domain of large, expensive supercomputers running complex scientific or financial applications. Since, there were no general-purpose operating systems to manage task for these machines, the scheduling issues had traditionally been resolved before runtime during the program design phase. Set theory, task graphs, mathematical proofs, and other forms of numerical analysis were used to determine the optimum method of allocating processors and ordering events. This form of static scheduling required prior knowledge of the program's behaviour and resource requirements, and was an expensive procedure in terms of clock cycles. Dynamic scheduling of tasks occurs at the time of execution, so it seeks to minimize this overhead. As a result, dynamic scheduling differs from static scheduling in its objectives as well as its operation.

5.5.2 Dynamic Scheduling Goals

Whereas the focus of static scheduling was primarily to minimize execution time, dynamic scheduling in a multiprocessor system seeks to :

- minimize execution time
- minimize communication delays between processors
- maximize resource utilization
- maximize processor utilization

Communication delays and resource utilization are primarily relevant in distributed systems. Most distributed systems are difficult to program due to the message passing that is required between processing elements. As a result, communication overhead can become a bottleneck.

Resource utilization becomes an issue in distributed heterogeneous systems, where different processors may have sole access to specific hardware, software, or data. The scheduler must keep track of all these resources and assign the tasks accordingly.

The majority of multiprocessor systems are used for their high performance, fault tolerance (redundancy in case of failure), and scalability (increased performance with additional processors). Each of these requires that the scheduler should maximize processor usage. This is done through a procedure called load balancing, where tasks are redistributed from heavily loaded to lightly loaded processors.

5.5.3 Performance Issues

In order for a multiprocessor system to run at all, a program must be divided into smaller steps that can run concurrently. Developing applications for multiprocessing computers requires that a lot of thought be put into this process. If the steps are small (fine grain tasks), the overhead for CPU communication and operating system intervention will severely degrade performance. However, if the steps are large (coarse grain tasks), parallelism is reduced. The goal then is to find the right ratio for task granularity to maximize overall performance. As with static scheduling, there are many complex algorithms available to generate an ideal size of steps into which a process must be divided but the overhead of these operations makes it impractical for the operating system to incorporate them.

5.5.4 An Example : Windows NT

The simplest approach to dynamic scheduling balances the load across 'n' processors by running the global scheduler on an additional processor. The global scheduler dispatches tasks on a first-in-first-out (FIFO) basis to the other n processors. As shown in Figure 5.3, each of these processors maintains its own private waiting queue of tasks it has been assigned. When it finishes execution of a task, it gets the next one from the queue and runs it to completion. If a task needs the services of another task, it sends this request to the scheduler queue. The scheduler in turn uses a FIFO rule to dispatch these requests to the processor with the currently shortest waiting queue, thereby balancing the load.

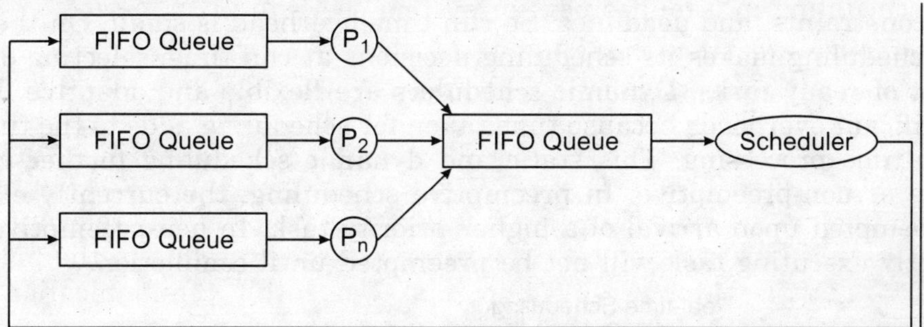

Figure 5.3 : A Simple Scheduler

Windows NT uses an SMP version of this model to schedule threads on multiple processors. With this model, any thread can be assigned to any processor. Therefore, scheduling threads on a computer with multiple processors is similar to scheduling threads on a computer with a single processor. However, the scheduler has a pool of available processors so it can schedule threads to run concurrently. One difference in the NT model is that scheduling order is determined by thread priority (a number assigned by either the programmer or the operating system designating the relative importance of the thread).

5.6. REAL-TIME SCHEDULING

As we have already made a brief mention of real time systems and real time operating systems (RTOS) in chapter 1, we will like to look into the processor scheduling in such systems. Depending upon the type of real time systems (hard or soft), the scheduling process will also differ. For example, in case of hard real time systems, the scheduler if decides to take up the execution of a hard real time task will have to ensure its completion within the prescribed time whereas in case of soft real time systems, the scheduler can implement priority scheduling with Real-Time tasks having higher priroity as compared to others. Let us concentrate on hard-real time scheduling first.

5.6.1 Hard-Real Time Scheduling

Real time scheduling can be categorized into hard vs. soft. Figure 5.4 represents taxonomy of real-time scheduling algorithms. A hard-real time system must execute a set of concurrent real-time task in such a way that all time-critical tasks meet their specified deadlines. Every task needs computational and data sources to complete the job. The scheduling problem is concerned with the allocation of the resources to satisfy the timing constraints.

Hard Real-Time scheduling can be broadly classified into two types; static and dynamic. In static scheduling, the scheduling decisions are made at compile time. A run-time schedule is generated off-line (statically) based on the prior knowledge of task-set parameters, e.g., maximum execution times, precedence constraints, mutual exclusion constraints, and deadlines. So run-time overhead is small. On the other hand, dynamic scheduling makes its scheduling decisions at run time, selecting one out of the current set of ready tasks. Dynamic schedulers are flexible and adaptive. But they can cause significant overheads because time taken for scheduling adds to the time consumed in the run-time processing. This static and dynamic scheduling further can be either preemptive or non-preemptive. In preemptive scheduling, the currently executing task will be preempted upon arrival of a higher priority task. In non-preemptive scheduling, the currently executing task will not be preempted until completion.

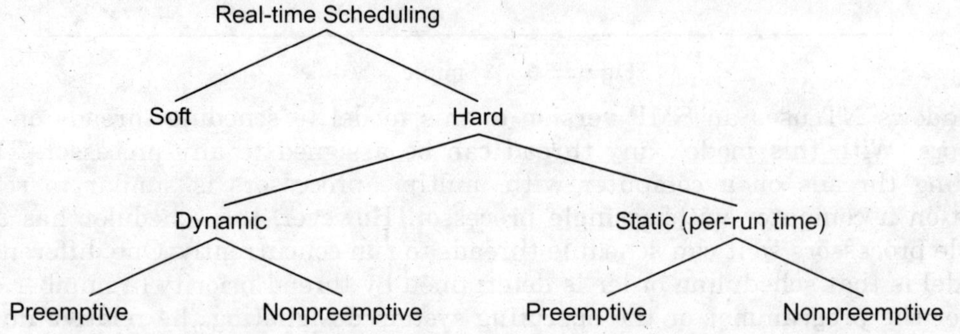

Figure 5.4 : Taxonomy of Real-Time Scheduling

5.6.1.1 Dynamic Scheduling Algorithms

Schedulability test is often used by dynamic schedulers to determine whether a given set of ready tasks can be scheduled to meet their deadlines. Different scheduling algorithms and their schedulability criteria is explained below.

Rate Monotonic Algorithm (RMA)

Rate monotonic algorithm is a dynamic preemptive algorithm based on static priorities. The rate monotonic algorithm assigns **static priorities** based on task periods. Here task period is the time after which the tasks repeat and inverse of period is task arrival rate. For example, a task with a period of 10 ms repeats itself after every 10 ms. The task with the shortest period gets the highest priority, and the task with the longest period gets the lowest static priority. At run time, the dispatcher selects the task with the highest priority for execution.

Earliest Deadline-First (EDF) Algorithm

EDF algorithm is an optimal dynamic preemptive algorithm based on **dynamic priorities.** In this after any significant event, the task with the earliest deadline is assigned the highest dynamic priority. A significant event in a system can be blocking of a task, invocation of a task, completion of a task etc. The processor utilization can go up to 100 percent with EDF. The dispatcher operates in the same way as the dispatcher for the rate monotonic algorithm.

5.6.1.2 Static Scheduling Algorithms

In static scheduling, scheduling decisions are made during compile time. This assumes parameters of all the tasks is known a priori and builds a schedule based on this. Once a schedule is made, it cannot be modified on-line. Static scheduling is generally not recommended for dynamic systems. There are no explicit static scheduling techniques except that a schedule is made to meet the deadline of the given application under known system configuration. Most often, there is no concept of priority in static scheduling. Based on task arrival pattern, a time line is built and embedded into the program and no change in schedules is possible during execution.

5.6.2 Soft Real-Time Scheduling

In case of soft real time scheduling—Regular processes (not real time) should be given less priority as compared to real time processes. Real time processes should never be taken over by any non-real time process whose priority has been increased by aging mechanism. Dispatch latency (which is the time elapsed from the moment the process becomes runnable to the moment it actually begins to run) for a real time process shall be as small as possible. Keeping the dispatch latency small is possible by making the system calls (used by processes) preemptible. This again can be achieved in two possible ways :

1. Preemptive points
2. Making kernel preemptive

Preemptive point can be inserted in the system calls that take long time for execution. At this point, a checking can be done to see whether a higher priority Real-Time task needs to run or not. If yes, CPU can take up that higher priority job and leave this current job for some time. After the completion of higher priority job, the interrupted process can continue with the system call. Preemption points should be placed at those points where it is known that kernel data structures will not be modified.

Kernel can be made preemptible to achieve low dispatch latency. This implies that now a non real time process can always be preempted (even if it is in midst of executing a system call) to make dispatch latency low for a real time task. Complicated mechanisms are needed to make a kernel preemptible as its data structures need to be protected by incorporating various mechanisms. Solaris 2 is the example of an operating system which uses kernel preemption to make dispatch latency low.

EXERCISES

5.1 Define the term "CPU Scheduling".

5.2 What are the different scheduling criteria?

5.3 What do you understand by CPU-bound and I/O bound processes? What is the meaning of CPU-burst time?

5.4 Differentiate between preemptive and non-preemptive scheduling.

5.5 What is a dispatcher? What are its functions?

5.6 What are the disadvantages of FCFS scheduling algorithm as compared to shortest job-first (SJF) scheduling?

5.7 What factors can lead to the degradation of performance of RR (Round and Robin) scheduling?

5.8 How is multilevel queue scheduling different from multilevel feed back queue scheduling? What are the advantages of multilevel feed back queue scheduling over multilevel queue scheduling?

5.9 What is dynamic scheduling in multiprocessor system? How does it differ from static scheduling?

5.10 What is load balancing in multiprocessor systems? How does scheduler perform the job of load balancing?

5.11 Contrast dynamic scheduling with static scheduling in Hard Real Time Systems.

5.12 What is dispatch latency in soft-real time systems? How can it be kept low?

5.13 Consider a system with a set of processes P_1, P_2 and P_3 and their CPU burst times, priorities and arrival times being mentioned as below :

Process	CPU burst time	Arrival time	Priority
P_1	5	0	2
P_2	15	1	3
P_3	10	2	1

Assume 1 to be the highest priority and calculate the following :

1. Average waiting time using FCFS, SJF (preemptive and non-preemptive) and priority (preemptive and non-preemptive) scheduling mechanisms.
2. Average turn around time using FCFS, SJF (preemptive and non-preemptive) and priority (preemptive and non-preemptive) scheduling mechanisms.
3. Assume time quantum to be 2 units of time. Calculate average waiting time and average turn around time using Round Robin Scheduling.

OOOOO

CHAPTER

6

Process Synchronization

OVERVIEW

This first part of this chapter discusses the need of synchronization, its actual implementation and various concerns associated with it. Critical section problem and its software solutions have been explained in a very simple language. Hardware solutions and more software solutions using synchronization tools like : semaphores and monitors have also been explained. The later part of this chapter deals with the concurrency control mechanisms. It explains the need of atomicity in transactions. Following this, the concurrency-control schemes to guarantee serializability in the concurrent execution of atomic transactions have been explained in depth.

6.1. CONCURRENCY

We can call this as concurrent execution of CPU and the I/O devices. We can have a look into the ways in which concurrency can be achieved :

(i) **Hardware Parallelism.** CPU can be computing while one or more I/O devices are running at the same time. This is the one, which is actually implemented, in multiprogramming environment.

(ii) **Pseudo Parallelism.** Rapid switching (back and forth) of the CPU among processes is known as pseudo parallelism as it gives the effect that many processes are running concurrently. This is actually implemented in time sharing environment.

(iii) **Real Parallelism.** Actual parallelism (concurrent execution) is achieved by having multiple CPUs, each executing a different process or a part of a process simultaneously.

Concurrent processes. In a multiprogramming environment, processes executing concurrently are either competing for the CPU and other global resources, or co-operating with each other for sharing some resources. The concept of co-operating processes has already been introduced in Chapter 4 of this text.

An operating system deals with the competing processes by carefully allocating resources and properly isolating processes from each other. For co-operating processes, on the other hand, the operating system provides mechanisms to share some resources in certain ways and allowing the processes to properly interact with each other. As mentioned earlier also, cooperation is achieved either by sharing or by communication. Examples of co-operating processes are transaction processes in airline reservation system. They share a common database; update and read same data on a sharing basis.

The properties of cooperating processes are :

- They share (or exchange) something : a common object (or a message).
- They are non-deterministic.
- They may be irreproducible.
- They are subject to race conditions.

Let us see what is this race condition?

Instructions of co-operating processes can be interleaved arbitrarily. Hence the order of instructions is irrelevant. However, certain instruction combinations must be eliminated. For example, consider two co-operating processes (sharing variables A and B) and having the following set of instructions in each of them :

Process 1	**Process 2**	**Concurrent access**
A = 1	B = 2	does not matter
A = B + 1, B = B + 1	B = B ∗ 2	important !

Suppose our intention is to get A as 3 and B as 6 after the execution of both the processes. The interleaving of these instructions should be done in order to avoid race condition. If the order of execution is like :

A = 1
B = 2
A = B + 1
B = B + 1
B = B ∗ 2

A will contain 3 and B will contain 6, as desired, whereas if the order of execution is like :

A = 1
B = 2
B = B ∗ 2
A = B + 1
B = B + 1

A will contain 5 and B will contain 5 which is not desired. Thus, the output of the interleaved execution depends on the particular order in which the access takes place and this is called race condition. To solve this problem, shared variables A and B should not be updated simultaneously by process 1 and 2. Only one process at a time should manipulate the shared variable.

But, if we want the processes to execute concurrently, how can we stop them from manipulating the shared data simultaneously? It is very much possible through synchronization mechanism, which must be provided by the operating system.

6.2. CRITICAL SECTION

A section of code or set of operations, in which process may be changing shared variables, updating a common file or a table etc., is known as critical section of that process. For the processes that execute concurrently, it should be ensured that execution of critical section should be made atomic. Atomic means that either an operation in the critical section should happen in its entirety or not at all, i.e., it couldn't be interrupted in the middle. (Thus critical section of a process should not be executed concurrently with the critical section of another process. This should be ensured by the synchronization mechanism). The remainder section of code or set of operations of a process that do not belong to its critical section is called remainder section. Figure 6.1 indicates these two sections of the process 1 and 2 discussed in Section 6.1.

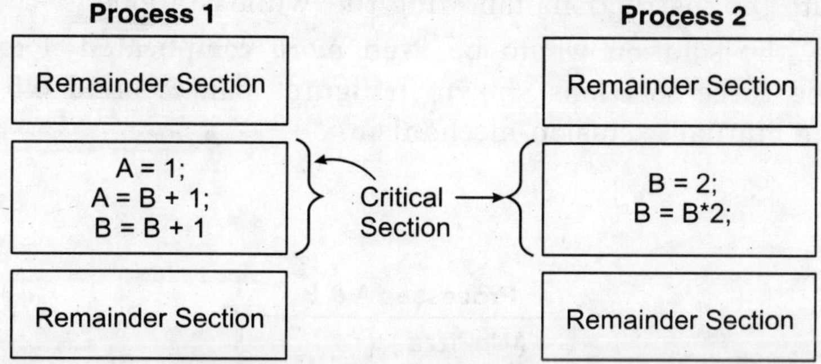

Figure 6.1 : Structure of Process 1 and 2

Atomic operations are used to ensure that co-operating processes execute correctly. Mutual Exclusion mechanisms are used to solve the critical section problem.

Mutual Exclusion is a mechanism to ensure that only one process is doing certain things at one time and the others are prevented from modifying shared data until the current process finishes. Let us consider the example of "too much pizza" problem. Let there be two persons A and B having their schedules as shown in Figure 6.2.

This problem shows that when co-operating processes are not synchronized, they may face unexpected errors. Mutual Exclusion mechanism when applied to this problem will ensure that only one person buys pizza at one time.

Time	Person A	Person B
3:00	Look in Fridge (out of pizza)	
3:05	Leave for store	
3:10	Arrive at store	Look in Fridge (out of pizza)
3:15	Buy pizza	Leave for store
3:20	Leave the store	Arrive at sotre
3:25	Arrive home, put pizza away	Buy pizza
3:30		Leave the store
3:35		Arrive home OH! OH!

Figure 6.2 : Too much Pizza problem

Let us look into the possible solutions of this problem. It is assumed that a note can be put by either of them to indicate that they are leaving for store to buy pizza. The solution 1 to this problem is good for people but not for processes. This is because the solution 1 mentioned in figure 6.3 should be exercised by executing all the first three steps atomically which is possible for people but not for processes where each instructions can be interleaved with the other instructions of some other process. The solution 2 shown in figure 6.4 can leave the two processes in a state where both the processes if leave their own notes simultaneously, then their "if" statements will return false and thus none of them will be able to execute its instructions for buying pizza. The solution 3 shown in Figure 6.5 is complicated. This asymmetric solution is very complex and tends to leave process B in a state where it consumes CPU cycles while waiting for its turn to execute the instructions following the 'while' statement.

In any case, the solution would be even more complicated if extended to many processes. All the three solutions shown in figures 6.3, 6.4 and 6.5 are obtained by implementing the mutual exclusion mechanism.

Solution 1

Processes A & B

```
if ( NoPizza ) {
  if ( NoNote ) {
        Leave Note;
        Buy Pizza;
        Remove Note;
  }
}
```

Figure 6.3 : Solution 1 the "too much pizza" problem

Solution 2

Process A

```
Leave NoteA ;
if ( NoNoteB ) {
  if ( No Pizza ) {
     Buy Pizza;
  }
}
Remove NoteA;
```

Process B

```
Leave NoteB ;
if ( No Note A ) {
  if ( No Pizza ) {
     Buy Pizza;
  }
}
Remove NoteB;
```

Figure 6.4 : Solution 2 for the "too much pizza" problem

Solution 3

```
Process A                         Process B
Leave NoteA ;                     Leave NoteB ;
while ( NoNoteB ) {               while ( NoteA ) {
  // do nothing                   // do nothing
 if ( NoPizza ) {                 if ( NoPizza ) {
    Buy Pizza; }                  Buy Pizza;
}                                   }
Remove NoteA;                     Remove NoteB;
```

Figure 6.5 : Solution 3 the "too much pizza" problem

6.3. SOLUTIONS TO CRITICAL SECTION PROBLEM

The fundamental requirements to be met by concurrent processes in order to cooperate correctly and efficiently using the shared data are :

(i) Mutual exclusion—no two processes will simultaneously be inside (executing) their critical section.

(ii) Progress—a process wishing to enter its critical section will eventually do so in finite time. This implies that every process will be fairly dealt with by being given an opportunity to enter its critical section in finite time.

(iii) No assumptions—should be made about relative speeds or the number of processors.

(iv) Efficiency—Each process should be treated fairly for the execution of its critical section.

Now, we will look into the solutions to the critical section problem mentioned in the previous section. We will also check up each solution algorithm to see whether it satisfies all the above mentioned requirements or not?

Let us have a look on our attempt 1 (shown in figure 6.6) to solve this problem of synchronizing the execution of concurrent processes. Our attempt 1 uses 'proc' as a global variable which is initialized to A (or B). Both the processes start execution concurrently. The problem with this attempt is : there is a strict alternation between process A and process B which implies that an execution of process A should always be followed by the execution of process B.

```
Process A                      Process B
. . .                          . . .
while( TRUE) {                 while( TRUE) {
. . .                          . . .
While( proc ==B ) ;            While( proc ==A ) ;
// do nothing                  // do nothing
<criticalA>                    <criticalB>
proc = B;                      proc = A;
. . .                          . . .
}                              }
. . .                          . . .
```

Figure 6.6 : Attempt 1

What if process B does not want to execute its critical section? This means that if process B does not execute its critical section and make proc = A, process A cannot take its turn again. This attempt fails, as "progress" requirement is not met by this solution.

The solution shown in figure 6.7 is our attempt 2 to solve this problem. This solution uses two global variables pAinside and pBinside which are initialized to false. This attempt fails when "while (pBinside)" and "while (pAinside)" instructions are executed simultaneously, thus enabling both the processes to enter into their critical sections at the same time. Thus, it may lead to violation of requirement for Mutual Exclusion, in the solution to this problem.

Process A

```
. . .
while( TRUE) {
. . .
While( pBinside ) ;
// do nothing
pAinside = TRUE;
<critical_A>
pAinside = FALSE;
. . .
}
. . .
```

Process B

```
. . .
while( TRUE) {
. . .
While( pAinside ) ;
// do nothing
pBinside = TRUE;
<critical_B>
pBinside = FALSE;
. . .
}
. . .
```

Figure 6.7 : Attempt 2

Another attempt is made by swapping second and third instructions in attempt 2. This attempt 3 is shown in figure 6.8. This attempt again fails because if simultaneous execution of instructions that set the value of pAinside and pBinside, takes place then progress stops. Thus, we can say that concurrent execution of the code, mentioned in attempt 3 might become a cause of failure.

Process A

```
. . .
while( TRUE) {
. . .
pAinside = TRUE;
// do nothing
While( pBinside ) ;
<critical_A>
pAinside = FALSE;
. . .
}
. . .
```

Process B

```
. . .
while( TRUE) {
. . .
pBinside = TRUE;
// do nothing
While( pAinside ) ;
<critical_B>
pBinside = FALSE;
. . .
}
. . .
```

Figure 6.8 : Attempt 3

Peterson's Algorithm

An established algorithm known as **Peterson's algorithm** shown in figure 6.9 provides the correct solution to this problem. In this algorithm the global variables pAinside and pBinside have been renamed to pAtrying and pBtrying respectively. There is another global variable "turn" which depicts the turn of a process to execute its critical section.

This algorithm is self-explanatory. It allows a process to make its 'trying' variable to be set to true but to assume that turn is that of another process. It then makes the process wait till the turn is that of another process and the other process is also trying to enter its critical section. Only when it ensures that the other process is not attempting to execute its critical section, a process will be allowed to execute its critical section. This algorithm meets all the requirements mentioned in the beginning of this section. The reader is advised to check up whether all the requirements are really met or not, by making an attempt to trace the run of these processes. This algorithm provides a good solution but works only for two processes. Similar to the last solution of the "too much pizza" problem, this algorithm can be generalized for N processes, but, N must be fixed (known a priori). Again, the algorithm becomes too much complicated and expensive when extended for more than two processes.

Process A

```
...
while( TRUE) {
...
pAtrying = TRUE;
turn = B;
While( pBtrying &&
          turn == B ) ;
          // do nothing
<criticalA>
pAtrying = FALSE;
...
}
...
```

Process B

```
...
while( TRUE) {
...
pBtrying = TRUE;
turn = A;
While( pAtrying &&
          turn == A ) ;
          // do nothing
<criticalB>
pBtrying = FALSE;
...
}
...
```

Figure 6.9 : Peterson's algorithm for sychronization of concurrent processes

Peterson's algorithm is based upon the following assumptions :

- That a variable (memory location) can only have one value; never "between values" e.g., turn variable will be either A or B at one moment of time. It cannot be something in between A and B.
- If process A and B write a value to the same memory location at the "same time", either the value from A or the value from B will be written rather than some scrambling of bits.

Information common to both processes A & B is :

turn = A
pAtrying = FALSE
pBtrying = FALSE

Process A	**Process B**
pAtrying = TRUE turn : = B • check pBtrying = TRUE and turn = B • Since condition is false, no waiting in while loop • Enter the critical section • Process B happens to loss the processor	
	• pBtrying = TRUE • turn = A • check pAtrying = TRUE and turn = A • Since conditoin is true, B keeps busy waiting until it gets the processor
• Process A resumes and continues until it finishes in the critical section • Leave critical section • pAtrying = FALSE • Start executing the remainder (anything else a process does besides using the critical section) Loss the processor	
	• check pAtrying = TRUE and turn = A • This condition fails because pAtrying = FALSE • No more busy waiting • Enter the critical section

Figure 6.10 : Sample execution of process using Peterson's algorithm

In essence, Peterson's Algorithm has the following characteristics :

- A simple algorithm that can be run by two processes to ensure mutual exclusion for one resource (say one variable or data structure).
- Does not require any special hardware.
- It uses busy waiting (a spinlock, discussed later in the text of this chapter).

A sample execution of two processes using this algorithm has been shown in Figure 6.10.

Bakery Algorithm

A better solution for more than one process can be obtained from Bakery algorithm. In this algorithm, every process receives a number before entering its critical section. The process with the lowest number enters the critical section next. In case, two processes P_i and P_j receive the same number and $i < j$, then P_i is served next (*i.e.*, process names are unique and totally ordered). When exiting from its critical section, the process sets its number to 0. This algorithm uses two shared data structures :

- Choosing – Array of Boolean values – Initialized to False
- Number – Array of integer values – Initialized to 0

This algorithm has been shown in Figure 6.11 and it has been established that it satisfies all the requirements mentioned in the beginning of section 6.3 of this text. Let us check how?

Mutual Exclusion : If P_i is in the critical section, it implies that any other process P_k will have a number k! = 0 and number [k] will be greater than number [i] and thus at this time only P_i can execute its critical section. If P_k tries to enter its critical section, it will be looping in the second while statement as its number is greater than number of P_i.

```
repeat
choosing[i] = true;
number[i] = max(number[0],..., number[i-1])+1;
choosing[i] = false;
for (j=0; j < n; j++)
{while (choosing[j]);
while ((number[j]! = 0) && ((number[j],j) < (number[i],i))); }
< critical section of Pi ; >
number[i] = 0;
<Remainder section of Pi; >
until false;
```

Notation : (number[j],j) < (number[i], i) implies
that the above relation is true if
number [j] < number[i] or if
number [j] = number[i] and j<i

Figure 6.11 : Multiple-Process Solution by Bakery Algorithm for any Process P_i

Progress : It is there because a process after exiting from its critical section, makes its number 0 and it needs to take a new number (which is obviously going to be larger as compared to the existing numbers) to contest with other processes trying to enter their critical section. Therefore, every process will be fairly dealt with by being given an opportunity to enter its critical section after a finite time (As done in a bakery by assigning tokens to its customers).

In this algorithm no assumptions have been made regarding the relative speed of processes. Since the processes are served in first-come-first-served order and all the processes are fairly dealt, therefore, efficiency is also achieved here.

6.4. HARDWARE SOLUTIONS

Let us look at all the software solutions that have been mentioned in the preceding section. These solutions have some common drawbacks :

- All these solutions are complicated to program (code).
- With these solutions, processes that are requesting to enter in their critical section are busy waiting, thus consuming processor's time needlessly.

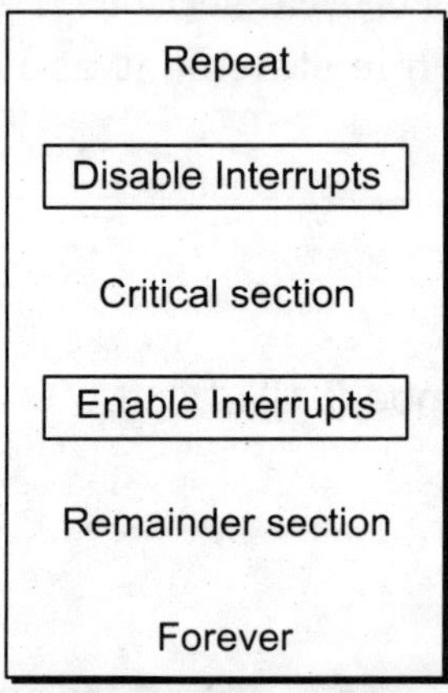

Figure 6.12 : hardware Solution 1

If the critical section which is currently being executed is long, then it is desirable to block process that are waiting (instead of wasting CPU cycles) to enter into their critical section.

Thus, instead of exploring software solutions only, it will be better to explore what does the hardware provide to solve the problem of process synchronization?

Disable Interrupts : The first solution is to disable interrupts while a process is modifying a shared variable. This ensures that no other process will make unexpected modifications to the shared variables. Figure 6.12 shows the structure of this solution. This solution is a correct solution for uniprocessor machine. During the execution of critical section, multiprogramming is not utilized by this solution. Thus the disadvantages of this solution are :

- Performance of the system is degraded, as multiprogramming is not utilized during the execution of critical section.

- This solution is not correct for a multiprocessor machine, because to disable interrupts, all processors will have to inter-communicate with each other which will be a time consuming effort and thus will have a negative effect on system efficiency.

Hardware Instructions

Many CPUs today provide hardware instructions to read, modify and store a word atomically. Most common instructions with this capability are :

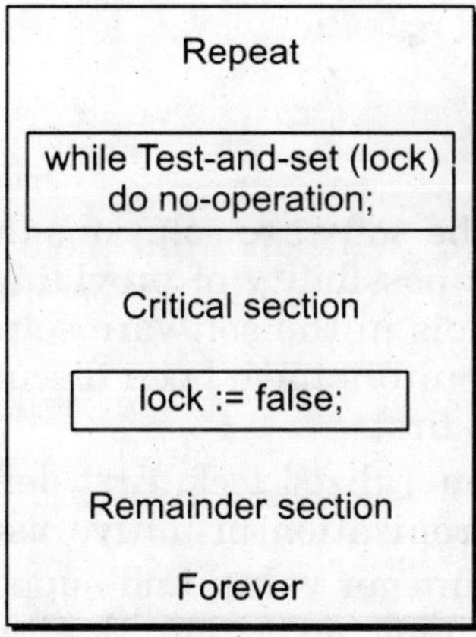

Figure 6.13 : Solution Using Test - and - Set Instruction

—TAS : test-and-set (in Motorola 68 K)

—CAS : Compare-and-swap (in IBM 370 and Motorola 68 K)

—XCHG : Exchange (in X 86)

The basic idea is to be able to readout the contents of a variable (memory location), and set it to something else in one execution cycle atomically.

Figure 6.13 shows the structure of a process using Test-and-set instruction. The instruction itself is defined as a function, which returns a boolean value (True or False).

```
Function Test-and-set (var target : boolean) : boolean
begin
Test-and-set : = target;
target : = True;
end.
```

There is a shared variable used in this solution. The shared variable is "lock". It is of the type boolean and is initialized to "False".

Let us now see, what requirements does this solution satisfy? Mutual Exclusion is met because if first process is in critical section, it sets the value of lock to True (by executing test-and-set function). Thus, the second process will always have a true value for test-and-set instruction and therefore, it will not come out of the while loop till the lock is set to false by the first process currently executing its critical section. Progress is there because if the second process does not want to enter its critical section now, the solution does not stop the first process to enter its critical section again. It is an efficient solution because it is not biased with a particular process. Every process gets a fair chance to enter in its critical section and that too in a finite time.

The **disadvantage** of this solution is :

- Implementation of such hardware instructions on multiprocessors is a difficult task.

6.5. SEMAPHORES

Till now, we have explored the software solutions (in section 6.3 of this text) for the critical section problem. Another possibility of providing solutions to this problem is by implementing synchronization tools in the software solutions. Two such synchronization tools namely semaphores and monitors have been discussed in this chapter. Let us take up the discussion of semaphores first.

Semaphores are a kind of generalized lock, first defined by Dijkstra in the late 60's. Semaphores are the main synchronization primitive used in UNIX.

A Semaphore has a positive integer value, and support the following two operations :

- semaphore->P() : an atomic operation that waits for semaphore to become positive, then decrements it by 1. It is also known as wait operation.
- semaphore->V() : an atomic operation that increment semaphore by 1. It is also known as signal operation.

Semaphores have following characteristics :

1. Semaphores are like integers, except that they have no negative values.
2. Only operations possible on semaphores are P and V—they cannot read or write a value, except to set it initially.
3. The operations (P and V) must be atomic (*i.e.,* the instructions in each of the operation should be executed in a single execution cycle).
4. Wait and signal operations are defined as follows :

Semaphore → P() : While semaphore ≤ 0
do nothing;
semaphore : = sempahore – 1;
Semaphore → V() : Sempahore : = Semaphore + 1;

Semaphore can be used to implement synchronization among process as stated below :

Mutual exclusion

When sempahores are used for mutual exclusion, the semaphore has an initial value of 1, and P() is called before the critical section, and V() is called after the critical section as shown below :

semaphore → P();
critical section
semaphore → V();
remainder section

Let us see how this structure shown above works to achieve mutual exclusion. Let us suppose that one process A is already executing its critical section then it implies that semaphore value at that time is zero (as wait signal must have been executed for the process A). If process B now tries to enter its critical section, it cannot enter the critical section because it will have to wait before semaphore becomes greater than zero. This is possible only when process A executes its signal operation, after executing its critical section.

Scheduling constraints

Semaphores can also be used to express generalized scheduling constraints—in other words, semaphores provide a way for a process to wait for something. Usually, in this case, the initial value of the semaphore is 0, but not always! It implies that suppose you want to run a process B only when process A finishes its execution, semaphore can provide a very good solution for such synchronization.

Let the initial value of semaphore be zero and the processes A and B can be made to use the semaphore as shown below :

Process A	**Process B**
Execute its code	
Semaphore → V()	Semaphore → P()
	Execute its code

It implies that if process B wants to execute before process A, then it is not possible because by definition of wait operation, it will come out of the while loop only when semaphore value is greater than 0. Since, in this case, semaphore value is initialized to 0. Thus, process B has to wait for executing signal operation so that semaphore's value becomes 1.

Problems

The main problem of the software solution discussed here (and in section 6.3) is that all of them require busy-waiting. Busy waiting means that while a process is in its

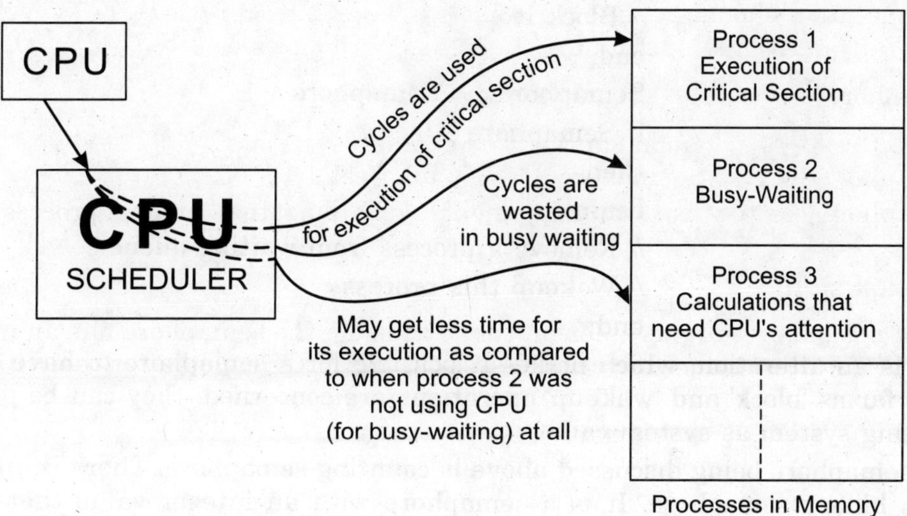

Figure 6.14 : Busy-waiting leads to wastage of CPU cycles

critical section, any other process that tries to enter in its critical section must loop continuously till it can enter the critical section. This leads to the wastage of CPU cycles, which could have been used by some other process to do some very important task as compared to continuous waiting. Figure 6.14 explains the concept more clearly.

Such semaphores are called spinlocks. They are undesirable in uniprocessor environment. However, they are useful (in multiprocessor environment) where the critical section of the currently executing process is small and therefore, not much of the time is consumed in waiting as compared to the time consumed in context-switching (which is done when CPU leaves this waiting process and takes up the execution of some other process).

To overcome this problem of busy waiting, the semaphore operations can be redefined.

If a process like process 2 of Figure 6.14, executes the wait operation and finds that value of semaphore is currently not greater than 0, then instead of busy-waiting (and thus wasting CPU cycles), it can be forced to change its state to "blocked". By a change in its state, it is automatically appended to a waiting queue associated with the semaphore. The CPU has full freedom to choose another process like process 3 of our Figure 6.14, to execute without being unnecessarily held by process 2.

This blocked process 2 should be restarted when process 1 executes a signal operation. Some operations like wakeup operation can be implemented to change the state of process 2 from blocked to ready state. It is then upto the CPU scheduling algorithm to decide when does this process 2 get the CPU next?

The redefined semaphore operations will be like :

```
Semaphore → P()        Semaphore : = Semaphore – 1;
                       if Semaphore < 0
                       then
                       begin
                       // Add this process to waiting queue of semaphore
                       // Block it
                       end;
Semaphore → V()        Semaphore : = Semaphore + 1;
                       if Semaphore ≤ 0
                       then
                       begin
                       // Remove a process from waiting queue
                       // Wakeup this process
                       end;
```

This is an alteration, which makes it possible for a semaphore to have a negative value. As far as 'block' and 'wakeup' operations are concerned, they can be provided by an operating system as system calls.

The semaphore being discussed above is counting semaphore. There is another type known as binary semaphore. It is a semaphore with an integer value that can range only between 0 and 1. A binary semaphore can be easier to implement than a counting semaphore, depending on the underlying hardware architecture.

Example

Let us see, how can we use semaphore to solve the bounded—buffer pizza problem mentioned in chapter 4. Synchronization required is that person A (producer) should wait if the Fridge (buffer) is full, person (B) (consumer) should wait if the Fridge (buffer) is empty. Thus the solution to this synchronization problem should have an implementation for two scheduling constraints (person B waits if Fridge is empty and person A waits if Fridge is full) and the mutual exclusion constraint (person A and B cannot access the Fridge (buffer) at the same time). This solution uses three semaphores one for each constraint :

Semaphore full buffers; // For Consumer's constraint. If 0, no pizza in Fridge.

Semaphore empty buffers; // For Producer's constraint. If 0, no space in fridge to put more pizza.

Semaphore mutex; // For mutual exclusion

We have to implement what is shown in the following figure 6.15 :

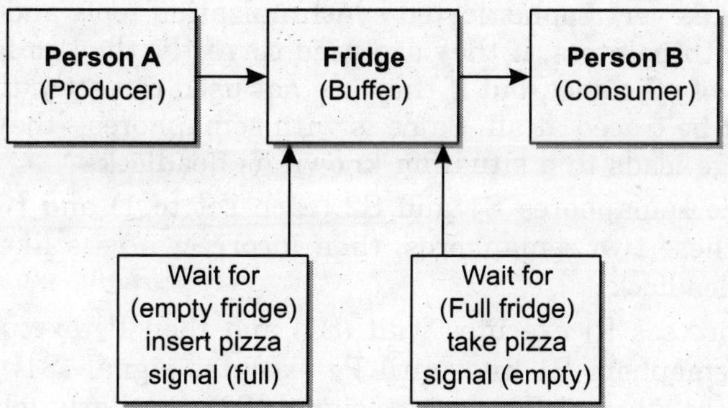

Figure 6.15 : Desired bounded buffer solution to pizza problem

The actual solution of this problem by using semaphores is as follows :

Semaphore fullBuffers = 0 // initially, no pizza!

Semaphore emptyBuffers = numBuffers; // Initially, number of empty slots in Fridge.

This semaphore is used to count how many slots there are!

Semaphore mutex = 1; // no one using the Fridge

Producer ()

{

emptyBuffers → P(); // check if there's space for more pizza

mutex → P(); // make sure no one else is using Fridge

put 1 pizza in fridge

mutex → V(); // ok for others to use Fridge

```
fullBuffers → V();                // tell consumers there's now a
                                     pizza in the fridge
}
Consumer ()
{
fullBuffers → P();                // check if there's pizza in the Fridge
mutex → P();                      // make sure no one else is using Fridge
take out 1 pizza
mutex → V();                      // ok for others to use Fridge
emptyBuffers → V();               // tell producer we need more
}
```

Semaphore and Performance Issues

We have seen that the possible uses of semaphores are : Mutual Exclusion, Synchronization of co-operating processes and managing multiple instances of a resource (as shown in bounded buffer pizza problem). It is worth mentioning that some authors classify semaphores as very sophisticated synchronization tools and compare them with pointers in C. As with pointers, if they are used correctly, they go far ahead from other constructs in terms of efficiency, but if they are not used correctly, they can lead to such errors which cannot be traced at all. Same is with semaphores—they are mistake prone. Their incorrect usage leads to a situation known as deadlock.

If there are two semaphores S1 and S2 (each set to 1) and two processes P_1 and P_2 each focussing these two semaphores, then incorrect access like the one mentioned below will lead to deadlock.

Suppose that process P_1 executes wait (S1) and then P_2 executes wait (S2). Here, P_1 is waiting for semaphore S1 and until P_2 executes signal (S1) and similarly, P_2 is waiting for semaphore S2 until P_1 executes signal (S2). Similarly, when P_2 executes wait (S1), it must wait until P_1 executes signal (S1). Since, these signals cannot be executed, it leaves the process P_1 and P_2 in a state where each one of them is waiting to get a signal from the other one and thus, none of them can proceed. Such a state is called deadlock. Both the processes P_1 and P_2 are deadlocked.

Process P_1	**Process P_2**
P (S1) ;	P (S2) ;
P (S2) ;	P (S1) ;
'	'
'	'
'	'
V (S1) ;	V (S2) ;
V (S2) ;	V (S1) ;

Thus, with improper use, semaphores made the two processes to block indefinitely and therefore, an improvement was sought over semaphores. Therefore, monitors were invented.

6.6. MONITORS

A monitor is a high level (programming language) abstraction that combines (and hides) the following :

—Shared data

—Operations on data

—Synchronization with condition variables

Programming languages such as concurrent Pascal, Modula, Mesa, and Java provide monitors. Figure 6.16 shows a monitor abstraction. As seen earlier, mutual exclusion is not sufficient for concurrent programming. An additional way to block processes (e.g., when resource is busy or buffer is full) is also needed. Monitors use condition variables to provide user-tailored synchronization and manage each with a separate condition queue. The only operations available on these condition variables are wait and signal. How are they different from a semaphore then?

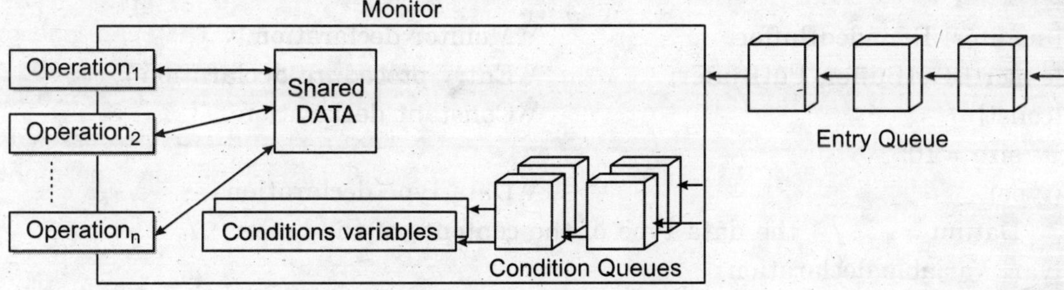

Figure 6.16 : Monitor Abstraction

A condition variable is like a semaphore, with two differences :

1. A wait on a condition variable always blocks the calling process. Thus instead of busy waiting (as in case of semaphore), process will be blocked automatically.
2. The signal operation resumes exactly one suspended process. If no process is suspended, then the signal operation has no effect, thus, the state of a condition variable is as though the operation was never executed. Whereas in case of semaphores, signal operation always affects the state of semaphore (by incrementing its value by 1).

It is like a Module in the following respect : Declares data (access to which is to be mutually excluded), procedures that manipulate these data, and an initialization code. The procedures can be exported to other modules, which may import them.

It is unlike a Module in following respect : Can declare certain procedures as entry procedures, which have the property that no matter how many processes are running, only one process is allowed to execute an entry procedure at a time. Thus, if a monitor declares two-entry procedures *e*1 and *e*2, then while *e*1 is being executed by a process, another process cannot call *e*1 or *e*2. A process that invokes an entry procedure while the monitor is 'busy' (that is some other process is executing an entry procedure in it) is put on an entry queue.

Bounded Buffer Problem

Let us see how can monitor solve the bounded buffer problem. To accommodate a solution to the synchronization problem, they are associated with *conditions* associated with the *wait* and *signal* operations. A call to *wait* places the process in a condition queue associated with the signal. It is removed from this queue when some other process does a signal on the condition. Any state associated with a condition must be explicitly managed by the monitor programmer.

We can use a monitor to implement the bounded buffer problem (also called the producer-consumer problem) stated as follows :

Any number of producer and consumer processes are running. A producer puts data in a buffer whose size is finite (hence a bounded buffer). A consumer removes data from this buffer. A producer blocks when the buffer is full and a consumer blocks when the buffer is empty.

The following is a monitor solution to this problem :

```
{monitor} BoundedBuffer;                  \\Monitor declaration
{export} GetBuffer, PutBuffer;            \\Entry procedure declaration
{const}                                   \\Constant declaration
    size = 10;
{type}                                    \\Data type declaration
    Datum = . . . / * the data type of the contents of the buffer * /
{var} Variable declaration
    buffer : array 0 .. size-1 of Datum;
    count : 0 . . size; / * number of elements in buffer * /
    nextIn, nextOut: 0...size –1; / * index of next datum to place in buffer * /
    nonEmpty, nonFull : { condition };
{ entry procedure } PutBuffer (what : Datum) ;
  begin
    if count = size then
      {wait} nonFull;
    end ;
    buffer [nextIn] ← what;
    nextIn ← (nextIn + 1) mod size;
    count ← count + 1;
    { signal } nonEmpty;
  end ;
```

```
{ entry procedure } GetBuffer (var result : Datum) ;
 begin
   if count = 0 then
     { wait } nonEmpty;
   end;
   result ← buffer [nextOut] ;
   nextOut ← (nextOut + 1) mod size;
   count ← count – 1 ;
   { signal } nonFull ;
end ;
begin / * initialization code * /
count ← 0;
nextIn ← 0;
nextOut ← 0;
end ;
```

A producer waits on the signal *nonFull* before adding new data and signal *nonEmpty* when it successfully adds data. Conversely, a consumer waits on *nonEmpty* before consuming new data and signals *nonFull* when it successfully adds new data.

Assume that a consumer is waiting on a condition, and a producer does a signal. When is the consumer allowed to execute? If immediately, then we may have two processes in the monitor at the same time, and our careful mutual exclusion is ruined. If later, then some other process may have taken the last datum, and the assumption made by the first consumer that an execution of the *wait nonEmpty* statement guarantees a non-empty buffer is wrong.

Not all definitions of monitors in the literature agree on the answers to these questions. The following is a common approach to this problem. We associate a monitor with an urgent queue. Thus, a monitor is associated with an entry queue, a condition queue for each condition, and an urgent queue. Processes that are blocked are placed in these queues. Here are the rules that govern placement and removal of processes from these queues :

New processes wait in the entry queue. When a process exits a monitor (that is, finishes execution of an entry procedure), a process from the urgent queue is allowed to execute if the queue is not empty. Otherwise, a process from the entry queue is removed if the queue is not empty. A process that does a *wait* enters the appropriate condition queue. When a process executes *signal*, the signalled condition queue is inspected. If some process is waiting on the queue, the signaller enters the urgent queue and some waiting process is allowed to execute. If no process is waiting in that queue, then the signaller proceeds without leaving the monitor. The signal is ignored.

All queues are ordered first in, first out. These rules ensure that a waiting consumer is unblocked immediately when a producer signals *Nonempty*, and the producer is blocked in the urgent queue until the consumer has taken the datum. We have maintained the rule that at most one process occupies the monitor.

People who use monitors have noticed that the signal operation is almost always the last operation in an entry procedure. The above rules will often make the signaller with in the urgent queue and then return to the monitor just to get out of it. Thus, these rules, while they work, are often inefficient. Thus some people require that signal *must* be the last operation executed in an entry procedure.

Another alternative is to make the *signal* operation a *hint* to a waiting process; it causes execution of some process waiting on the condition to resume at some convenient future time. There is no guarantee that some other process will not enter the monitor before the waiting process. Under these semantics, the waiting process has to reestablish the condition for which it was waiting still holds when it wakes up. The proper pattern for usage is :

while not <ok to proceed> do
{wait} c
instead of
if not <ok to proceed> then
{wait} c

Thus in the bounded-buffer problem, the code

if count = 0 **then**
{ wait } nonEmpty

is replaced by

while count = 0 **do**
{ wait } nonEmpty

The last alternative results in an extra evaluation of the <ok to proceed> predicate after the wait. In return there are fewer process switches compared to the first alternative, and it is more flexible than the second alternative. Moreover, it allows dequeueing of all processes waiting on a signal. (why?). Thus a special operation **broadcast** can be defined on signals.

The queues maintained under the hint semantics are the same as above except that it is the signalled process that goes into the urgent queue rather than the signalling process.

Java implements a simplified version of these hint-based monitor semantics. In Java, a class may declare certain methods to be declared as entry procedures (by using the keyword **synchronized**). Each instance of a class with entry procedures behaves as a monitor. A monitor, however, is associated with a single condition variable and queue, in which both signalled and new processes are placed. Java supports both signal (called **notify**) and broadcast (called **notifyAll**) operations.

In either case, the notified process is supposed to check for itself if its condition has been satisfied.

6.7. ATOMIC TRANSACTIONS

This section deals with the situation where we would like to make sure that critical section forms a single logical unit of work that either is performed in its entirety or is not performed at all. For example, in case of funds transfer in which one account is debited and the other is credited, we will like to ensure that either both debit and credit take place in entirety or that neither occur. This implies that an attempt should be made to ensure that data is always consistent at all times. This is basically a concept related to the field of database system. But proposal is there to use this technique even in the operating systems and therefore, it has been mentioned in the following subsections.

Let us now understand what a transaction is :

A transaction is a unit of work that performs single logical function. When we talk of atomic transactions we imply that the transaction should be executed either in its entirety or not at all. A transaction that has completed its execution successfully is committed; otherwise it is aborted. But when a transaction is aborted (for example, due to certain system failure), then the data modified by it will be left in an inconsistent state. Thus, the state of the data accessed by an aborted transaction must be restored to what it was just before the transaction started executing. This means that a transaction should be roll backed. Thus, the system should ensure that when a transaction is aborted, it should also be rollbacked. We know that storage media is volatile (e.g., Main Memory), Non-volatile (e.g., magnetic disks, magnetic tapes, etc.), Stable storage (A storage media where the information never gets lost and therefore, this can be implemented by replicating information in several non-volatile caches (usually disks)). The transactions talked about here may be executed on any of them. But, we deal with mechanisms to ensure the atomicity of transactions executed on volatile storage.

6.7.1 Log-Based Recovery

Atomicity can be ensured by recording on stable storage all the actions, which are performed by a transaction. The most widely used method for this is write ahead logging. Before the transaction performs any modification, the following data is written to the stable storage :

- Transaction Name
- Data-item Name
- Old value of data-item
- New value of data-item.

Other special log records are used to record significant events during transaction processing such as start of transaction, commit or abort of transaction etc. As a log record should be written before an actual update or write is done, therefore, it is an overhead associated with every update or write operation of a transaction.

This log, however, serves very important purpose of recovery in case when a transaction gets aborted. The recovery algorithm uses two procedures :

1. Undo
2. Redo

Undo(T)—removes the impact of the actions of a transaction T

Redo(T)—repeats the actions of a transaction T

Which of the above two procedures should be involved for recovery is another important issue. Suppose that a transaction T starts executing and the system fails then transaction T should be undone if the log shows that T started but could not be committed. Otherwise, if the log shows that T started and was also committed before the failure occurred, then transaction T should be redone.

6.7.2 Checkpoints

There are two drawbacks of log based recovery :

1. It takes a lot of time to search the log for determining which transactions have to be undone and which have to be redone.
2. The transactions which have to be redone, must have already updated the data therefore, redoing the things that have already been done will make the recovery process too slow.

To overcome these drawbacks, the concept of checkpoints is introduced. In addition to the write ahead log, the system maintains a periodic placement of checkpoints. The placement of checkpoint requires the following sequence of actions to take place :

1. Output all log records residing in volatile storage on to stable storage.
2. Output all modified data residing in volatile storage to the stable storage.
3. Write a log record (telling that checkpoint has been placed) on the stable storage.

Checkpoint is a way of periodically committing the executed portions of transactions. This is a very helpful method for recovery. The use of redo operation is reduced to a great extent. It works as follows :

At any time when the system fails, the log is checked to determine the most recent transaction that started executing before the most recent checkpoint took place (because all other transactions that were started and committed before the checkpoint must already have written to the stable storage. Therefore, the impact of these transactions will never be lost and hence they must not be redone or undone). Once this transaction T is identified, the undo and redo operations will have to be applied to it and to all other transactions that started after T. Thus, now out of all these transactions including T, only those will be undone for which there is no commit entry in the log and those for which the commit entry is there in the log will be redone. Therefore, the redone operation is applied to a smaller number of transactions.

6.8. CONCURRENT EXECUTION OF ATOMIC TRANSACTIONS

Now the question is how to achieve concurrent execution of atomic transactions. The concurrent execution of transactions must be equivalent to the case where these transactions are executed serially in some arbitrary order. This is known as serializability. This is possible by applying mutual exclusion to the execution of atomic transactions.

However, it is possible to attain serializability, even by allowing the transactions to overlap their execution, *i.e.*, without mutual exclusion. The following sub-sections discuss various concurrency control algorithms to ensure serializability.

Before moving next, let us now understand what is serializability? A sequence of actions related to many transactions is called a schedule. A schedule is called a Serializable Schedule, if the actions of different transactions are never interleaved. Consider two transactions T_0 and T_1 described as below :

T_0	T_1
read (A)	read (A)
A = A – 50	Temp = A ∗ 0.1
write (A)	A = A – temp
read (B)	Write (A)
B = B + 50	Read (B)
write (B)	B = B + temp
Commit	Write (B)
	Commit

Suppose that A and B contain 1000 and 2000 respectively. No matter T_0 is followed by T_1 or T_1 is followed by T_0, the sum of A and B is always preserved. If we intermix the execution of these transactions as :

T_0	T_1
read (A)	
A = A – 50	
Write (A)	
	read (A)
	temp = A ∗ 0.1
	write (A)
read (B)	
B = B + 50	
write (B)	
Commit	
	read (B)
	B = B + temp
	write (B)
	Commit

This sequence does not look like a serial schedule but behaves as a serial schedule only, as the sum A + B is preserved. Such a schedule is called serializable schedule. This is not always the case. Not all interleaved execution sequences will be serializable. For example, if T_0 and T_1 are again executed non-atomically as shown below, it is found that the schedule is not identical to a serial schedule and thus it is called a non-serializable schedule.

T_0:	T_1:
read (A)	
A = A – 50	
	read (A)
	temp = A ∗ 0.1
	A = A – temp
	write (A)
	read (B)
write (A)	
read (B)	
B = B + 50	
write (B)	
Commit	
	B = B + temp
	write (B)
	Commit

Thus, when several transactions overlap their execution, the resulting execution may no longer be equivalent to an execution, where these transactions execute atomically (i.e., serial schedule). To ensure correct execution, concurrency control schemes should be used. The following sub-sections discuss various concurrency control mechanisms to ensure serializability.

6.8.1 Locking Protocols

This protocol ensures that each data item used by a transaction should be locked. There are two types of locks - shared and exclusive. If a transaction has a shared lock on a data item, it can read this data item but cannot write it. If a transaction has an exclusive lock on a data item, then that transaction can both read and write this data item. Thus, every transaction should first lock the data item, depending upon the type of operations to be performed on it.

If transaction T_0 has locked a data item which transaction T_1 also wants to lock, then following possibilities are there :

1. If T_0 has a shared lock on a data-item, T_1 can also lock it in shared mode.
2. If T_0 has exclusive lock on a data item, T_1 cannot lock it unless T_0 releases this data item.
3. If T_0 unlocked the data item then T_1 can lock it either in shared or in exclusive mode, whichever is required.

A transaction cannot unlock a data item as long as it accesses that data item. Even after the transaction has undergone last access of that data item, it may not release it (until its other operations are over) to ensure serializability.

Two-phase locking protocol which is used to ensure serializability, requires that each transaction should issue lock and unlock requests in two phases :

1. Growing phase : A transaction may obtain locks, but may not release any lock.

2. Shrinking phase : A transaction may release locks, but not obtain any new locks.

In the beginning, a transaction is in the growing phase. The transaction can acquire all the needed locks in this phase. Once the transaction releases a lock, it enters the shrinking phase in which no new locks can be obtained. Although, the protocol ensures serializability, this is not free from deadlock.

6.8.2 Time Stamp-based Protocols

In the locking protocols, the order between pair of conflicting transactions is determined at execution time by the first lock that they both request. Another method for determining serializability order is to select an ordering among transactions in advance. This is done by time stamp ordering scheme. Each transaction T in the system is associated with a unique fixed timestamp, denoted by TS(T). This time stamp is assigned by the system before T starts execution.

If a transaction T_0 has been assigned a timestamp and later on a new transaction T_1 enters the system, then TS (T_0) < TS (T_1).

The timestamps of the transactions determine the serializability order. Thus, if TS (T_0) < TS (T_1), then the system must ensure that the produced schedule is equivalent to a serial schedule in which transaction T_0 appears before transaction T_1.

To implement this scheme, we associate with each data item, two time stamp values :

- **W-timestamp,** which denotes the largest timestamp of any transaction that has written on the data item successfully.
- **R-timestamp,** which denotes the largest timestamp of any transaction that has read the data item successfully.

These timestamps are updated whenever a new read or write instruction is executed.

The timestamp-ordering protocol ensures that any interleaved read and write operations are executed in timestamp order. This protocol operates as follows :

- Suppose that transaction T_0 issues read command on a data item D.
  - — If TS (T_0) < W-timestamp (D), then this state implies that T_0 needs to read a value of D which was already overwritten. Hence, the read operation is rejected, and T_0 is rolled back.
  - — If TS (T_0) ≥ W-timestamp (D), then the read operation is executed, and R-timestamp (D) is set to the maximum of R-timestamp (D) and TS (T_0).
- Suppose that transaction T_0 issues write command on a data item D.
  - — If TS (T_0) < R-timestamp (D), then this state implies that the value of D that T_0 is producing was needed previously and T_0 assumed that this value would never be produced. Hence, the write operation is rejected, and T_0 is rolled back.
  - — If TS (T_0) < W-timestamp (D), then this state implies that T_0 is attempting to write an obsolete(old) value of D. Hence, this write operation is rejected, and T_0 is rolled back.
  - — Otherwise, the write operation is executed.

A transaction T_0, which is rolled back by the concurrency-control scheme as a result of the issuing of either a read or write operation, is assigned a new timestamp and is restarted.

T_2	T_3
read (B)	
	read (B)
	write (B)
read (A)	
	read (A)
	write (A)

To illustrate this protocol, we consider the following schedule with transactions T_2 and T_3. Here, TS (T_2) < TS (T_3), and thus the schedule is possible under the timestamp protocol.

EXERCISES

6.1 List the various ways in which concurrency can be achieved.

6.2 What are concurrent processes?

6.3 Explain the term `race condition' associated with cooperating processes.

6.4 What do you understand by critical section problem? What requirements should be met by its solution?

6.5 Explain Peterson's Algorithm to solve the critical section problem. Justify that it meets all the requirements of the critical section problem's solution.

6.6 What hardware solutions are possible for critical section problem?

6.7 How do semaphores provide better solution as compared to the other software solutions for the critical section problem?

6.8 What is a spin-lock?

6.9 How can busy-waiting be avoided by proper use of semaphores ?

6.10 What problem can occur with the incorrect usage of semaphores?

6.11 What are monitors? How do condition variables differ from semaphores?

6.12 Compare the semaphore solution of bounded buffer problem to the solution that uses monitor.

6.13 Show that, if the wait and signal operations of a semaphore are not executed atomatically, then mutual exclusion may be violated.

6.14 The following figure 6.17 shows Dekker's algorithm, which provides software solution to the critical section problem for two processes. The variables used are :

flag : array of boolean

turn : which takes value 0 or 1

```
Repeat
    flag [ i ] = true
    while flag [ i ]
    if turn = j then
        begin
        flag [ i ] = false;
        while turn = j do no-operation;
        flag [ i ] = true
        end;
<critical section>
    if turn = j ;
    flag [ i ] = false;
<remainder section>
Forever
```

Figure 6.17. The structure of process Pi in Dekker's algorithm

Prove that the above algorithm satisfies all the three requirements for the critical section problem.

6.15 What is the purpose of the checkpoint mechanism? How often should the checkpoints be placed? How does the frequency of checkpoints affect the following :

- System performance when no failure occurs.
- Time taken to recover from system crash.

6.16 Explain the concept of transaction atomicity.

CHAPTER

7

Dealing with Deadlocks

OVERVIEW

This chapter has been written to exclusively deal with the problem of deadlocks. As mentioned in the previous chapter, a state can arise in the system when one process waits for the other to release the required resources and the other process waits for the first one to release the required resources. Such a state is known as Deadlock State. This chapter describes the methods to prevent and avoid deadlocks. Bankers' algorithm has been given in detail. Second half of this chapter deals with deadlock detection mechanisms and deadlock recovery. Algorithms for deadlock detection have been described with examples.

7.1. INTRODUCTION

A deadlock is a situation in which two processes sharing the same set of resources are effectively preventing each other from accessing the resource, resulting in both programs ceasing to function.

The earliest computer operating systems ran only one program at a time. All of the resources of the system were available to this one program. Later, operating system with multiprogramming support ran multiple programs at once, interleaving them. Programs were required to specify in advance what resources they needed so that they could avoid conflicts with other programs running at the same time. Eventually, some operating systems offered dynamic allocation of resources. Programs could request further allocation of resources after they had begun running. This led to the problem of the deadlock. Here is the simplest example :

- Program 1 requests resource A and receive it.
- Program 2 requests resource B and receive it.
- Program 1 requests resource B and is queued up, pending the release of B by program 2.
- Program 2 requests resource A and is queued up, pending the release of A by program 1.

The resources talked about here could be of the type memory space, CPU cycles, files and I/O devices (such as printers and tape drives etc.). Now neither program can proceed until the other program releases a resource. The operating system cannot know what action to take. At this point the only alternative is to abort (stop) one of the processes.

Learning to deal with deadlocks had a major impact on the development of operating systems and the structure of databases. Thus, data has to be structured and the order of requests has to be constrained to avoid deadlocks.

If there are multiple resources of the same type, each is called an instance of that resource type. A system table records whether or not a resource is free. So, if a request is made, a lookup operation is done in the table. If a requested resource is being use by some other process, then the requesting process is added to a queue for that resource. Thus, a queue is maintained for each resource.

7.2. DEADLOCK CHARACTERISTICS

We can tell when a deadlock will occur. If these four conditions occur simultaneously, then we have deadlock :

1. **Mutual Exclusion :** a resource can be used by only one process at a time.
2. **Hold-and-wait :** at least one process is holding a resource, and needs to acquire other resources that are being held by other processes.
3. **No preemption :** If a process holds a resource, it can not be preempted (forced to release that resource).
4. **Circular wait :** There must exist a set $\{P_0, P_1, \ldots, P_n\}$ of waiting processes such that P_0 is waiting for a resource that is held by P_1. P_1 is waiting for a resource held by P_2 ... and so on ... and finally P_n is waiting for a resource held by P_0.

7.2.1 Recognition methods

A tool for recognizing deadlock is "Resource-allocation graph" (RAG). This graph has vertices representing the processes and the resources in the system. Its edges are of two types :

1. Request edge : This edge indicates the request of a process for acquiring a particular resource. It is a directed edge like $P_i \rightarrow R_j$. It indicates that process P_i has requested an instance of resource R_j.

2. Assignment edge : This edge indicates the allocation of a resource to a particular process. It is also a directed edge like $R_j \rightarrow P_i$. This edge here indicates that an instance of resource R_j has been allocated to the process P_i. Circles represent processes and rectangles represent resources. Figure 7.1 shows a typical resource allocation graph (RAG).

Notice the dots in rectangles of Figure 7.1. Each is an instance of the resource.

- There is one instance of R_1
- There are two instances of R_3
- There is one instance of R_2

• There are four instances of R_4

Thus, in Figure 7.1, P_1 is holding an instance of R_3 (since there is the assignment edge $R_3 \rightarrow P_1$) and is waiting for an instance of R_1. Similarly, P_2 is holding an instance of R_3 and is waiting for an instance of R_2, which is now held by P_3.

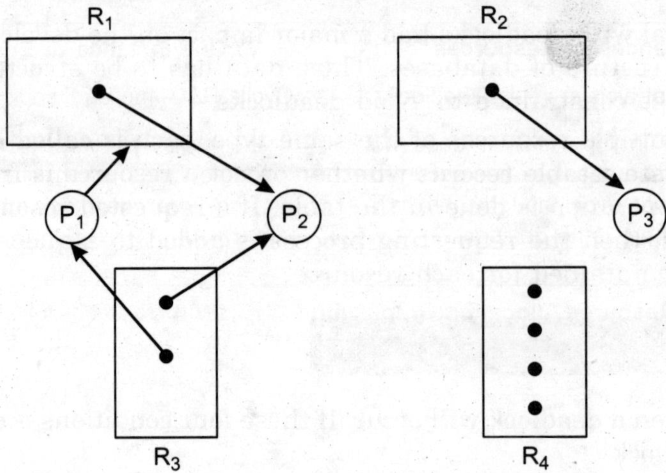

Figure 7.1 : Example of a Resource Allocation Graph (RAG)

Can we_determine if deadlock exists by using the RAG? Not necessarily, if a cycle exists in the RAG, there may or may not be deadlock. HOWEVER... it is sure that if no cycle exists (that is, if the graph is acyclic) then deadlock will not exist.

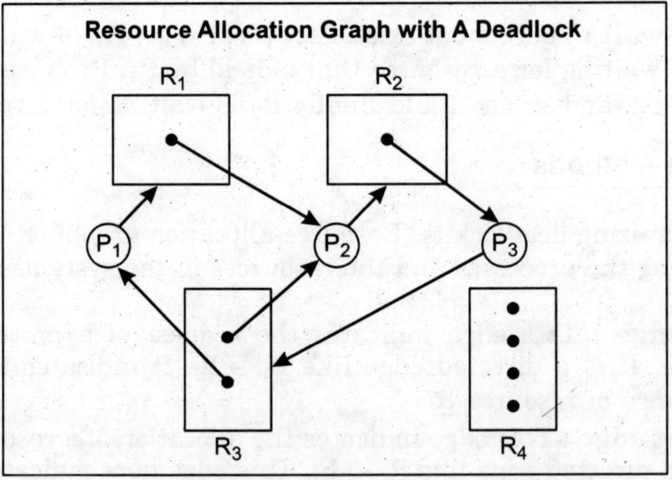

Figure 7.2 : Deadlock system

Therefore,

Acyclic RAG ⇒ no Deadlock

But it is not true that

No Deadlock ⇒ Acyclic RAG

As mentioned above that an acyclic Resource Allocation Graph (RAG) always implies the non-existence of a deadlock whereas if the deadlock does not exist, in the system then, it is not necessary that there are no cycles in the Resource Allocation Graph. This means that cycles can be there even if there is no deadlock. Taking into consideration the number of instances of each resource type can further specify this condition.

Multiple Instances of Resources	One Instance of Every Resource
• Cyclic RAG need not always imply Deadlock	• Cyclic RAG implies Deadlock
• If there is a cycle in the RAG, it does not necessarily imply that a deadlock has occurred. Figure 7.3 shows that even though there is a cycle in the RAG, there is no deadlock.	• If the cycle in RAG involves only a set of resource types, each of which has a single instance, then deadlock must have occurred.

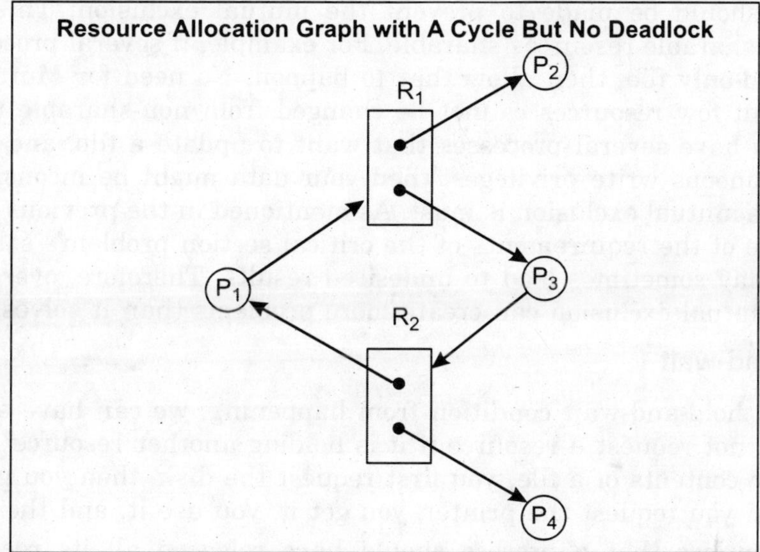

Figure 7.3 : No Deadlock

In Figure 7.3, notice that P_2 holds an instance of R_1, and P_4 holds an instance of R_2. Neither of these processes is waiting for a resource in the set R. P_2 and P_4 can release their resources. If they do then R_1 and R_2 will both have free instances, so there will be no deadlock, as those free instances can be assigned to P_1 and P_3, respectively, and the arrows will be reversed. The request edges will turn into assignment edges. Then the graph will be acyclic, and acyclic RAG $\Rightarrow$ no deadlock.

7.3. DEALING WITH DEADLOCKS

Once we have come to know that a deadlock exists in the system, we should now understand the methods of dealing with the deadlocks.

These methods are :

- Deadlock prevention—Do not let the deadlock occur.

- Deadlock recovery—Let the deadlock occur in the system and then attempt to recover the system from deadlock.
- Do not do anything for deadlock prevention and recovery. Let the deadlocks occur in the system and deteriorate the system performance, leading to a situation where system will have to be restarted manually.

7.3.1 Deadlock prevention

Deadlock can be prevented, if one of the necessary conditions (mentioned in section 7.2 of the text) is prevented from occurring. Let us see how can we prevent the occurrence of each of these conditions :

7.3.1.1 Mutual Exclusion

An effort should be made to prevent the mutual exclusion. This is possible by making all the sharable resources sharable. For example, if several processes would like to access a read-only file, then allow that to happen. No need for Mutual Exclusion in such a case. But few resources cannot be changed from non-sharable to sharable. For example, if you have several processes that want to update a file, and you allow them to have simultaneous write privileges, then your data might be inconsistent. This is a condition where mutual exclusion is must. As mentioned in the previous chapter, mutual exclusion is one of the requirements of the critical section problem's solution also, thus preventing it may sometimes lead to undesired results. Therefore, overall conclusion is that denying mutual exclusion can create more problems than it solves.

7.3.1.2 Hold-and-wait

To prevent hold-and-wait condition from happening, we can have a rule that says, "a process may not request a resource if it is holding another resource". So, to take the print out of the contents of a file, you first request the disk, then you get it, use it and release it. Then you request the printer, you get it, you use it, and then you release it.

Thus, it implies that a process should have released all its resources before it requests for additional resources. Or another rule can be there that "a process should request and acquire all the requested resources before its execution begins". For example, to take the print out of the contents of a file, the disk and printer should be requested before hand.

In either case, there are two problems :

1. **Low Resource Utilization :** If a process follows the second rule, it will acquire all the resources like disk, tape and printer at the very beginning of its execution, no matter that it might need the printer at the end of its execution. This will stop other processes from accessing the printer and thus printer utilization will be very low.

2. **Starvation :** A process that needs many resources to start its execution, may be waiting for one or the other resource (allocated to other processes) for an indefinite time.

7.3.1.3 No Preemption

To ensure that this condition does not happen, preemption of the resources should be allowed. A rule like "if a process that is holding some resources requests another resource that cannot be immediately allocated to it, then all the resources currently being held by it are preempted". The process will now have to wait for the allocation of resources that have been preempted in addition to those for which it was already waiting. This process is restarted only when it can regain its old resources as well as the new ones it is requesting. This method can be applied only to the resources whose state can be easily saved and restored later, such as CPU registers and memory.

7.3.1.4 Circular wait

In order to prevent circular waiting, resources can be numbered and it may be made compulsory that each process can request the resources in the increasing order of numbers. Suppose we have three resources namely, tape drive, disk drive and printer and suppose that the numbers allocated to them are 1, 2 and 6 respectively. A process, which wants to access disk drive and printer, should first request the disk drive and then printer. This rule can be extended to say that once a process has some resources assigned to it, it can acquire a new resource only if number of all its acquired resources is less than the number of the newly requested resource.

A process requesting disk drive numbered 2 will be allotted a disk drive only if all its existing resources have number less than 2. This implies that a process having a printer cannot acquire disk drive until it releases the printer (because printer's number 6 is greater than disk drive's number 2).

It can be proved that these rules ensure that circular wait do not hold in the system. The numbering of the resources should be done appropriately. Facts like, "tape drive will be needed before a printer is needed by a process" should be kept in mind while numbering the resources.

Thus, we have seen that by preventing one of these conditions, we can prevent the deadlock.

7.4. AVOIDANCE METHODS

Is there any other way to prevent the deadlocks? Yes, it is. Let us explore a deadlock-avoidance algorithm that ensures that circular-wait condition never happens in the system. This algorithm requires knowing maximum number of resources that each process needs to acquire. Based on this information, it can calculate what resources can be granted immediately and for which of them should the process wait?

Basically, this algorithm checks that after allocating the resources, will the system be in a safe state or not? A system is in safe state if the system can allocate resources to each process in some order and still avoid a deadlock. This implies that the sequence in which the requests of the processes should be fulfilled, must be a safe sequence. Let us see what is a safe sequence? A sequence of processes $<P_1, P_2, \ldots, P_n>$ is safe if the request of each process P_i can be granted from the pool of currently available resources and the resources held by the processes preceding it i.e., by P_j where $j < i$. In case P_i's request could not be satisfied, it can wait for those resources till all the processes preceding it (all P_j's) finish their job and release their resources. System is said to be in unsafe state, if no safe sequence exists. A deadlock state is a form of unsafe state. This implies, the moment it is ensured that system is in unsafe state, there arises a probability of deadlock. Preventing the system from entering in an unsafe state can thus prevent deadlock.

Example : Consider that there are total 12 tape drives.

Process P_0 needs total 10, currently has 5 and thus needs 5 more.

Process P_1 needs total 4, currently has 2 and thus needs 2 more.

Process P_2 needs total 9, currently has 2 and thus needs 7 more.

At time t_0, the system is in safe state, as a safe sequence <P_1, P_0, P_2> exists. This implies that first grant 2 tape drives to P_1 (from the pool of 12 – (5 + 2 + 2) = 3 available tape drives) so that it has all the four necessary for its execution.

Then, when P_1 also releases its tape drives we will have (4 released by P_1 and 1 left in the pool), 5 available for meeting the requirement of other process. Now P_0 can be granted these 5 tape drives. After P_0 finishes, number of available tape drives will be 10. Now, 7 tape drives can be granted to P_2 for its execution. Thus, the system is in safe state. But it is in safe state at a time point t_0. It is not necessary that the system be in safe state for always. Whenever a new process enters the system, or when an existing process asks for more resources, the safe state can remain to be safe or can be changed to an unsafe state.

If the process P_0 here requests two more tape drives and is allotted two tape drives. Let us see whether the system is still in safe state or not? The status will be like :

Process P_0 needs total 12, currently has 5 and thus needs 7 more.

Process P_1 needs total 4, currently has 2 and thus needs 2 more.

Process P_2 needs total 9, currently has 2 and thus needs 7 more.

Now first P_1's request can be easily granted as available tape drives are 12 – 9 = 3. Now P_1 releases tape drives and we have 5 available for allocation. These 5 cannot serve the purpose of P_0 (which needs 7 more) and P_2 (which also needs 7 more). Thus, the system is in an unsafe state.

This is all that should be done by deadlock avoidance algorithm. It should be able to tell whether the system is left in the safe state or not, after the request of particular process is granted. If the algorithm finds that granting the request immediately will lead to an unsafe state, then the process must be asked to wait.

7.4.1 Banker's Algorithm

This algorithm's purpose is deadlock-avoidance. It considers each request and examines if it leads to a safe state. It does the following to examine the state of the system.

1. Check if there are enough resources to satisfy at least one process.
2. Sum the resources of the process to those available, marks the process and iterate.
3. If at the end there are processes that are left unmarked, the system would be in an unsafe state.

These steps ensure whether the system is in safe state or not? This part of the algorithm is known as safety algorithm. Another part of this algorithm ensures whether a process requesting a resource should be granted that resource immediately or should wait. This depends upon whether processing of this request leads to a safe or unsafe state? If granting the request leaves the system in an unsafe state, then the request should not be granted and the process must wait. This portion of the algorithm is called Resource Request Algorithm.

Data structures used in this algorithm are :

Let there be n processes and m resource types.

1. Maximum—Request matrix of the order of $n \times m$. It indicates the maximum demand of each of the process.
2. Alloc—Matrix of the order $n \times m$. It indicates the number of resources currently allocated to each of the processes.
3. Avail—Vector of the order m. It indicates the number of resources (of each type) that are currently available.
4. Need—Matrix of the order $n \times m$. It indicates the number of resources that a process may need in the future.
5. Finish—Vector of the order n. It contains the Boolean value (True or false) to indicate if a process has been allocated the required resources and has released all of its resources after using them.

The steps of safety part of this algorithm—that ensures whether a system is in a safe state or not are :

1. Initialization

    Set Finish (i) = False for all i ranging from 1 to n.

2. Compute avail and need

    Avail vector can be obtained directly from given conditions

    Set Need (i, j) = Maximum (i, j) — Alloc (i, j)

    for all processes i and for all resource type j.

3. Find a process i such that

    Set Finish (i) = False and need (i, j) $\leq$ Avail (j) for all resource types.

    (This implies that P_i needs the resources, which the system can easily grant as its need is less than available resources).

    If no such i exists, go to step 5.

4. Schedule process i for execution so that it can utilize the resources and then free up its resources by doing the following

    Set Avail (j) = Avail (j) + Alloc (i, j)

    Set Need (i, j) = 0 for all j

    Set Finish (i) = True

    Go to step 3.

5. If finish (i) = True for all i, return (safe) else return (unsafe).

Resource—Request part of this algorithm, ensures whether the request of a process P_i on being granted, will leave the system in a safe state or not?

Let Request be a matrix of order $n \times m$. It indicates the number of resources of each type requested by a particular process, at some moment of time.

The steps will be :

1. If Request (i, j) ≤ Need (i, j), for all resource types j, go to step 2 (here 'i' is a process which has made a request)
2. If Request (i, j) ≤ Avail (j), go to step 3. Otherwise process P_i must wait, since the resources are not available.
3. Assume that the requested resources have been allocated to process P_i. Do the following updations :

   Set Avail (j) = Avail (j) – Request (i, j), for all j

   Set Alloc (i, j) = Alloc (i, j) + Request (i, j), for all j

   Set Need (i, j) = Need (i, j) – Request (i, j), for all j
4. Now apply the safety part of the algorithm, if the resulting state is safe, the transaction shown in step 3 should be completed otherwise, the transaction shown in step 3 should be rollbacked and the process P_i must wait.

The Banker's algorithm has good results. This algorithm makes the following assumptions :

1. The system has a limited number of resources.
2. Each process must use the resource for a finite amount of time.
3. Each process declares in advance, the amount of resources it will need.
4. A process may have to wait for a resource but is guaranteed to eventually get the resource.

An Example : Assume that there are five processes in the system and 4 resources namely, TD-Tape Drives, DD-Disk Drive, PR-Printer, SC-Scanner. Let the number of available resources be TD → 1, DD → 0, PR → 2 and SC → 0.

Need matrix can be obtained as under :

Process	Resources Allocated				Maximum Number of Resources Required			
	TD	DD	PR	SC	TD	DD	PR	SC
P_1	3	0	1	1	4	1	1	1
P_2	0	1	0	0	0	2	1	2
P_3	1	1	1	0	4	2	1	0
P_4	1	1	0	1	1	1	0	1
P_5	0	0	0	0	2	1	1	0

Need Matrix

Process	TD	DD	PR	SC
P_1	1	1	0	0
P_2	0	1	1	2
P_3	3	1	0	0
P_4	0	0	0	0
P_5	2	1	1	0

The system is in safe state because the process could finish in the order P_4 (which needs no more resources to finish), then P_1, P_2, P_3, and P_5. After P_4 finishes, Avail vector will have the value (2, 1, 2, 1). After P_1 finishes, Avail vector will have (5, 2, 3, 2). After that P_2 finishes to make avail as (5, 2, 3, 2) and finally P_3 finishes to make (6, 3, 4, 2) available. P_5's request is also easily granted and all are done! Thus, a safe sequence <P_4, P_1, P_2, P_3, P_5> is obtained after the execution of Banker's safety algorithm. This ensures that the system is in safe state.

Now, suppose that a request from P_5 arrives for (1, 0, 1, 0). Can the whole request be safely granted immediately?

Yes, the resulting state is safe if P_5's request is granted, and therefore, the request should be immediately granted. How do we determine this? As Request of P_5 (1, 0, 1, 0) $\leq$ need of P_5, which is (2, 1, 1, 0). We move on to check whether Request i.e., (1, 0, 1, 0) is $\leq$ Avail, which is (1, 0, 2, 0). This is also true. Then, we try to simulate allocating the requested resources to P_5 and find out a safe sequence for the system. This makes Avail to be (0, 0, 1, 0), Alloc to contain (1, 0, 1, 0) for process P_5 and need of P_5 to contain (1, 1, 0, 0). Thus, <P_4, P_1, P_2, P_3, P_5> is a safe sequence that can be obtained by applying the algorithm. Therefore, granting the request of process P_5 will leave the system in a safe state.

7.5. DEADLOCK RECOVERY

In case the system takes no measures to prevent and avoid the deadlock, then at some time deadlock may occur in the system. In order to recover from the deadlock state, the first thing that should be done is deadlock detection. There should be mechanisms to detect whether a deadlock exists in the system and if yes, methods to recover the system from such a state should be known.

7.5.1 Deadlock Detection

There are two algorithms for deadlock detection. These algorithms periodically determine whether a deadlock has occurred in the system? The first algorithm deals with the case where there is only one instance of each resource type and the other algorithm deals with the situation where there are multiple instances of each resource type.

7.5.1.1 Deadlock detection algorithm for single instance of each resource type

1. Maintain a wait—for graph : Nodes in this graph represent processes. If process i is waiting for a resource held by process j, then there is an edge from i to j.
2. Periodically invoke an algorithm that searches for cycles in the graph. Complexity of algorithm, which detects cycle in a graph, will be n^2, where n is the number of vertices in the graph. If there is a cycle in the wait-for-graph a deadlock is said to exist in the system.

Figure 7.4 shows a wait-for-graph, where P_1 is waiting for a resource held by P_2. P_2 is waiting for a resource held by P_3 and P_3 is waiting for a resource held by P_1. There is a cycle in the graph and thus the processes are deadlocked.

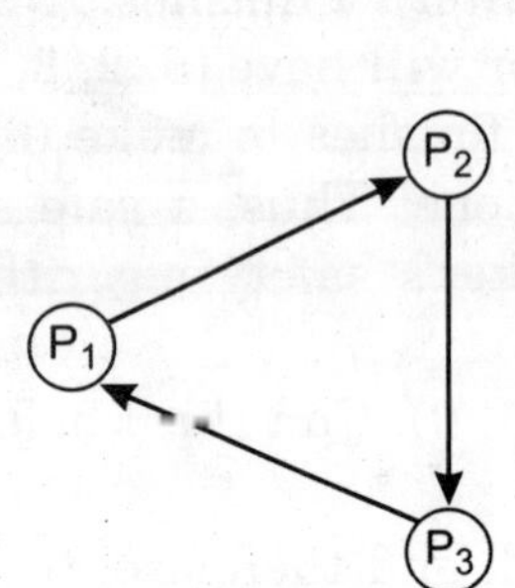

Figure 7.4 : Wait-for-graph

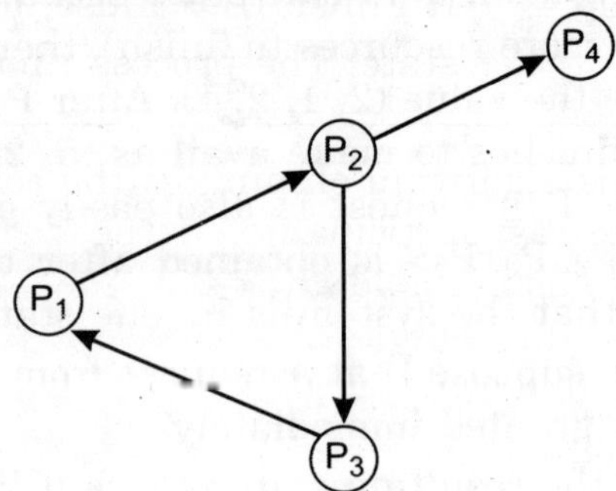

Figure 7.5 : Wait-for-graph of a system

What can you say about the system whose wait-for-graph is shown in Figure 7.5. Is the system dead locked?

Yes, the system is in deadlock state as it contains a cycle between P_1, P_2 and P_3. The processes involved in the deadlock are P_1, P_2 and P_3.

7.5.1.2 Deadlock detection algorithm for a multiple instances of each resource type :

This algorithm is almost the same as safety part of the Banker's algorithm with few semantic differences. It uses almost the same data structures as Banker's algorithm. As mentioned in the previous section, Avail, Alloc, Finish and Request are the data structures used in Banker's algorithm and here also m is the number of resources and n is the number of processes in the system. Let us go through the steps of this algorithm.

Step 1. If Alloc (i, j) ≠ 0, then
Set Finish (i) = false;
else
Set Finish (i) = True;
for all processes i = 1 to n
and all resources j = 1 to m.

Step 2. Find a process i such that both the conditions

Finish (i) = false

and Request (i, j) ≤ Avail (j)

(This means that request of process i for all resources j should be less than the available amount of resources j)

if no such i exists, go to step 4.

Step 3. Set Avail (j) = Avail (j) + Alloc (i, j)

Set Finish (i) = True;

Go to step 2.

Step 4. If Finish (i) = False, for some process, then the system is in deadlock state. The process i for which Finish (i) = False, is deadlocked.

This algorithm eliminates the consideration of those processes (which do not hold a resource) as participants in the deadlock state of the system. This implies that if a process i do not hold any resource at this time, it will not contribute towards deadlocking the system. Therefore, it is assumed in the step 1 of the algorithm and such processes are not taken into consideration any further.

Example

Process	Allocation (Alloc)			Request			Available (Avail)		
	TD	DD	PR	TD	DD	PR	TD	DD	PR
P_0	0	1	0	0	0	0	0	0	0
P_1	2	0	0	2	0	2			
P_2	3	0	3	0	0	0			

Now, we can see that in this instance the system is not deadlocked. By our algorithm, safe sequence for this set of processes can be <P_0, P_2, P_1>. Now suppose that process P_2 makes an additional request for printer. If the Request matrix now becomes:

Process	Allocation (Alloc)		
	TD	DD	PR
P_0	0	0	0
P_1	2	0	2
P_2	0	0	1

Now, let us execute our algorithm again. Process P_0 whose request is less than equal to the available vector, avail, can be allowed to finish first. After P_0 executes, avail vector will be (0, 1, 0). Now neither P_1, nor P_2 can be allowed to finish, as its request is not less than equal to available. Thus for P_1 and P_2, finish is still false, and therefore, P_1 and P_2 are deadlocked.

How often should detection-algorithm be used?

- In the extreme case, this algorithm can be executed every time, a new request (for a resource) arrives in the system. This frequency of invoking the algorithm will enhance the overall computation time.
- Another possible way is to invoke the algorithm periodically after some period of time. This period can be short enough to detect which particular process's new request has caused deadlock. This information (that which process caused deadlock) can be helpful for recovering the system from deadlock. Another possibility is that this period can be long (so that cost-factor becomes less), but once deadlock is detected after a long time, it will be difficult to know the exact cause of this deadlock and many processes may have to restarted altogether.

7.5.2 Recovery from deadlock

Once the deadlock has been detected in the system, the system should now be recovered from this state. This is must because it will continuously degrade the system's performance and if no correction mechanism is applied, there is a possibility of total system failure, some time later. Let us look into the options of recovering the system from deadlock state. One option is process termination and other is resource preemption.

7.5.2.1 Process termination

One way is to abort all the dead locked processes. This technique is fast but a lot of the work done by all the deadlocked processes will be lost.

Another way is to abort one deadlocked process at a time and check for deadlock's presence again. This technique involves more work to resolve a deadlock. Because choosing the order in which processes should be aborted is a very complicated job. Also, after aborting a process, detection algorithm will have to be invoked again and so on.

The advantage of this method is that there is a possibility that not all the deadlocked processes will have to be aborted and thus, not the work done by all these processes will be lost.

7.5.2.2 Resource preemption

This technique favours the preemption of resources from the processes and allocation of these resources to other processes till the deadlock cycle is broken. There are three issues pertaining to resource preemption :

(i) Which resources and which process should become the target of preemption? If a process has completed almost 95 percent of its execution, then it should not be our choice for preemption. Other factor can be the number of resources held by a process.

(ii) What should be done with the preempted process? One possibility is to roll back this process to some earlier safe state and restart its execution from that point. This again involves lots of effort on the part of the system, as it may have to keep more information about the state of each process.

(iii) How to ensure that starvation will not occur in the system? This means that a mechanism must be there which looks into the fact that a particular process should not be deprived of resources again and again i.e., it should not always become the target of resource preemption. A counter can be associated with each process to count the number of times its resources have been taken away. This information should be used by the deadlock recovery mechanism so that count of preemption also becomes a factor in deciding which process should become the next target of preemption. An approach can be to select a process having this counter's value 'least'.

EXERCISES

7.1 What are the necessary conditions for the occurrence of a deadlock?

7.2 What does a cycle in the Resource Allocation Graph (RAG) indicate :

(a) When there is a single instance of each resource type.

(b) When there are multiple instances of each resource type.

7.3 Is there a possibility of deadlock in a system with only one process?

7.4 Prove that the safety algorithm part of the Banker's algorithm requires operations of the order $m \times n^2$.

7.5 How can starvation of a particular process be detected by a system?

7.6 List the methods of deadlock recovery.

7.7 Consider a system consisting of m resource types being shared by n processes. Resources can be requested and released by processes only one at a time. Show that the system is deadlock free if one the following condition holds :

1. The maximum need of each process is between 1 and m resources.
2. The sum of all maximum needs is less than $m + n$.

7.8 Consider the following snapshot of a system.

Process	Allocation			Maximum Requirement		
	A	B	C	A	B	C
P_0	0	1	0	7	5	3
P_1	2	0	0	3	2	2
P_2	3	0	2	9	0	2
P_3	2	1	1	2	2	2
P_4	0	0	2	4	3	3

Let the available number of resources be given by avail vector as (3, 3, 2).

Use the Banker's algorithm to answer the following

1. Find out the contents of the matrix `Need'?
2. Is the system in a safe state?
3. If a request from process P_4 for (3, 3, 0) arrives, can it be granted immediately?

7.9 Explain with the help of an example, how can you prevent deadlock by preventing circular-wait condition.

CHAPTER

8

Memory Management Basics

OVERVIEW

The intention of this chapter is to introduce the basic concepts of address binding, relocation and address space. After making you familiar with the terms like load time, compile time and run time, it moves on to discuss very important topic of contiguous and non-contiguous storage allocations. The storage talked about here is main memory. It covers fixed partition and variable partition as contiguous storage allocation techniques. It further discusses paging and segmentation as non-contiguous storage allocation techniques. Each technique has been introduced with the help of examples. Merits and demerits associated with each of the techniques have been mentioned in detail. This chapter serves as a base of the next chapter and therefore, it should be studied thoroughly before going through Chapter 9.

8.1. INTRODUCTION

The memory management service of an operating system is one of the basic services, as it is needed :

- To ensure protection of different processes from each other (so that they do not interfere with each other's operations).
- To place the programs in memory (such that memory is utilized to its fullest and high degree of multiprogramming can be achieved).
- The memory protection part has been covered in Chapter 2. We will be totally concentrating upon the memory allocation in this chapter. But before knowing various memory allocation schemes, an idea about the various phases of program execution, address-binding, logical and physical address is must. The following subsections deal with the above said notion.

8.1.1 Address Binding

Just think about running a program and the steps involved in its execution. We know program is a set of instructions. Each instruction of the program is saved in RAM (Random Access Memory) when it is executed and thus each instruction has its location/address in the memory. Each instruction gets executed in a systematic manner known as instruction execution cycle. Instruction Execution Cycle has three steps :

- Fetch the instruction from memory
- Decode the instruction
- Get operands from the memory and then execute.

Thus, instruction gets executed and its output (if any) is stored (by the operating system) into memory.

The entire execution phase of a program is shown in figure 8.1. It divides the entire execution phase of a program into three parts :

1. Compilation phase
2. Loading phase
3. Run phase

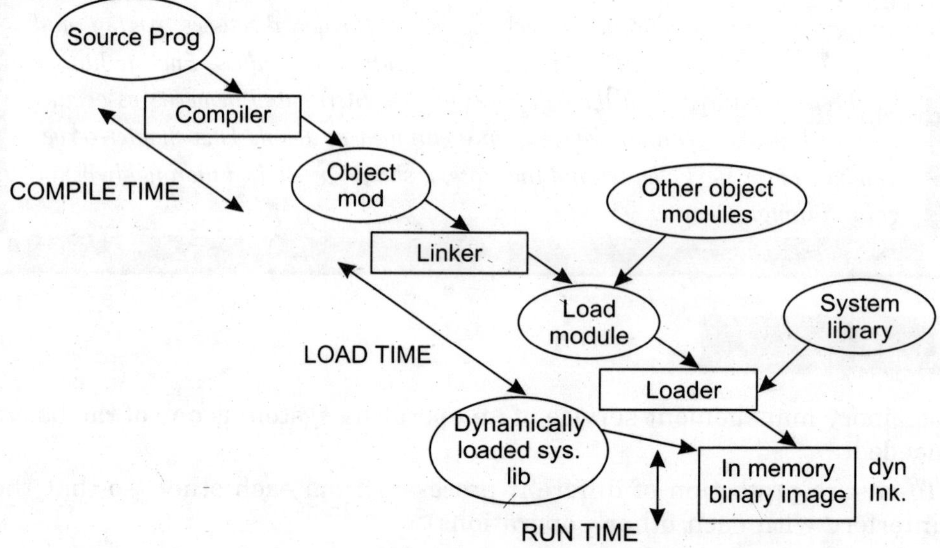

Figure 8.1 : Processing of a User Program

The problem that arises is how does the operating system know that where in the memory should the result be placed? Of course, the user whose program is getting executed must provide this. For example, if we have an instruction b = a + 5; it implies that the output of a + 5 should be stored in b. However, the user cannot tell where will 'b' be stored in the memory and where will 'a' get stored? But from user's point of view, he has tried to mention where should the output be stored. Such addresses used by a user in his/her programs are called symbolic addresses or logical addresses. Address binding is done to map these logical addresses to real physical addresses in memory.

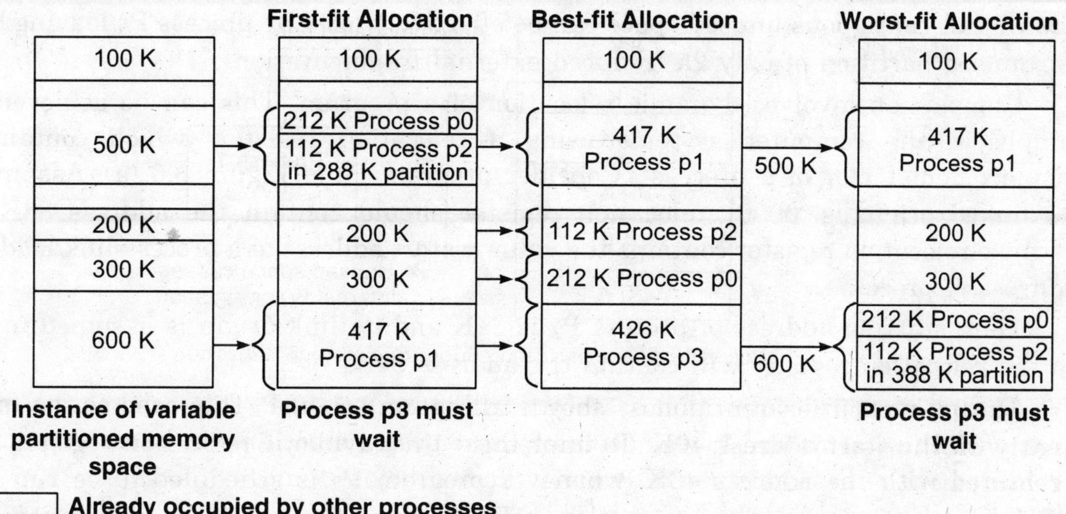

Figure 8.5 : Example of best fit, first fit and worst fit schemes

Figure 8.6 gives a clear picture of external fragmentation problem and its solution by compaction method. Compaction means to move the processes in the memory in such a way that scattered pieces of unused (free) memory can be placed together so that any other process demanding contiguous memory for it can use it.

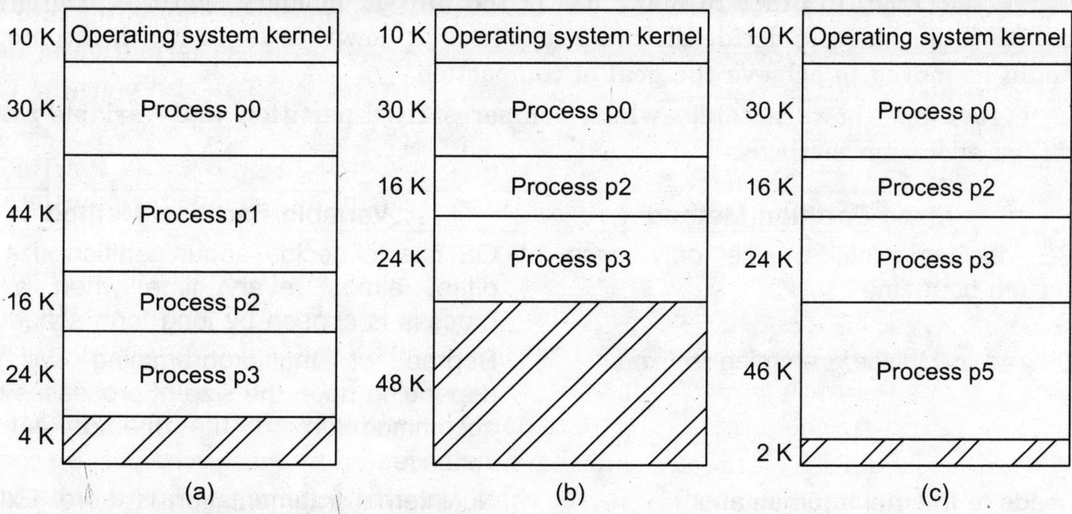

Figure 8.6 : Illustrates Memory Compaction

Figure 8.6 (a) shows processes P_0, P_1, P_2 and P_3 in execution. Figure 8.6(b) shows compaction is performed when P_1 terminates by moving P_2 and P_3 upwards. Figure 8.6(c)

shows that contiguous unused space can be effectively used by process P_5 leaving behind an unused partition of only 2k (reduced external fragmentation).

Compaction involves dynamic relocation of a program. This can be achieved quite simply in the computer systems using a relocation register (which contains the displacement factor of a process). Consider program P_2 of Figure 8.6 (a). Assume that its linked origin is '0000', relocation register should contain the address 84K. It is because relocation register contains the value = start address of a process-link/load origin address of process.

Here starting address of process P_2 is 84K and its link origin is assumed to be 0K so the relocation register will contain the address 84K.

During memory compaction as shown in Figure 8.6 (b) P_2 is moved to the memory area with the start address 40K. To implement this, dynamic relocation register should be loaded with the address 40K, whenever program P_2 is scheduled to be run by the CPU. This is because, every instruction in P_2 referring to some other instruction should use the relocation register's value to know the actual address of the referred instruction.

The problem with the compaction method is that it needs the relocation of addresses and that too dynamic relocation at the execution time of a process. Thus, Compaction is not possible if relocation is done statically (*i.e.,* at load time).

The cost of compaction increases with the increase in the number of processes to be moved (relocated) in order to make use of the unused memory space. A strategy may have to be designed to decide direction (upwards or downwards) in which the processes should be moved to achieve the goal of compaction.

Figure 8.7 shows a table, which compares fixed-partition and variable-partition storage allocation methods.

Fixed Partition Method	Variable Partition Method
OS decides partition size only once at system boot time	OS has to decide about partition size very often, almost every time when a new process is chosen by long term scheduler
Degree of Multiprogramming is fixed	Degree of multiprogramming will vary depending upon the size of processes being accommodated in the memory at one instance
Leads to internal fragmentation	No internal fragmentation is there. External fragmentation exists.
IBM/360 DOS and OS/MFT operating systems uses this approach	IBM OS/MFT used this approach also.

Figure 8.7 : A comparative study of fixed-partition and variable-partition storage allocation methods

Before, we move on to Section 8.2.2 to discuss non-contiguous storage allocation, let us have a look on the advantages and disadvantages of contiguous storage allocation method.

Advantages

- It is a simple method because the entire process is allocated contiguous memory. This makes addressing (within a process) very simple.

Disadvantages

- There is no possibility of sharing data and instructions among the processes (which are loaded into entirely different portions of the memory).
- Degree of multiprogramming is dependent on the availability of a partition that can accommodate a process wholly. This reduces the number of ready processes in the memory.

8.2.2 Non-contiguous Storage Allocation

To resolve the problem of external fragmentation and to enhance the degree of multi-programming to a greater extent, it was decided to sacrifice the simplicity of allocating contiguous memory to every process. It was decided to have a non-contiguous physical address space of a process so that a process could be allocated memory wherever it was available. Figure 8.8 shows the non-contiguous memory allocation strategy. Paging

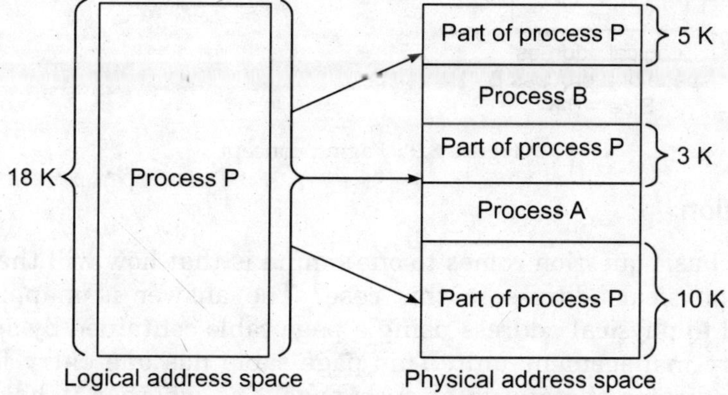

Figure 8.8 : Non Contiguous Storage Allocation

and segmentation are such mechanisms with which a process can be efficiently allocated non-contiguous memory. These mechanisms have been discussed in the subsequent sections :

8.2.2.1 Paging

In this approach, physical memory is divided into fixed-size blocks called frames and the logical memory is divided into the fixed-sized blocks called pages. The size of a page is same as that of frame. The key idea of this method is to place the pages of a process into the available frames of memory, whenever, this process is to be executed. Figure 8.9 shows the key concept of paging.

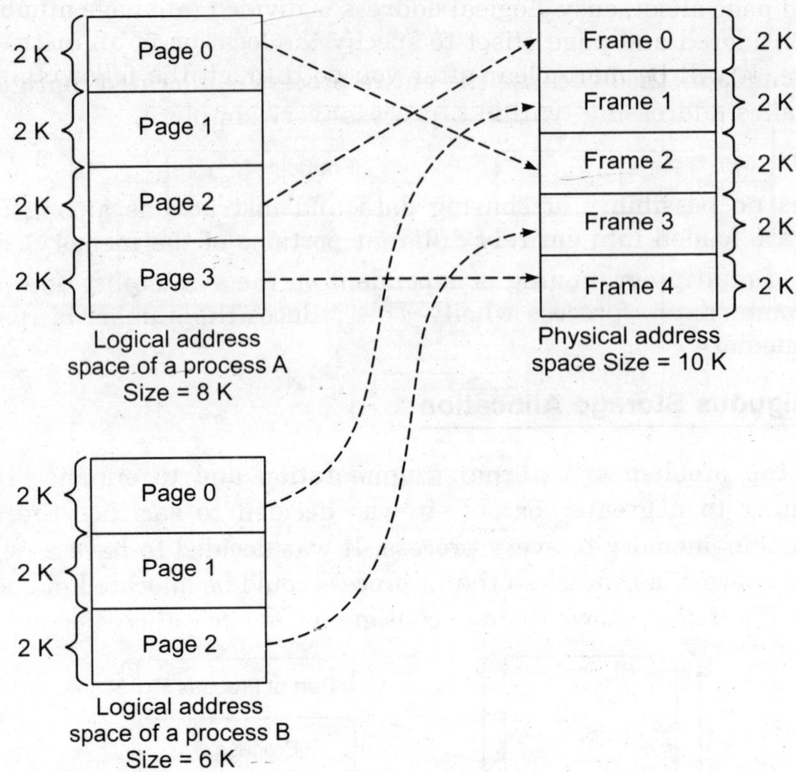

Figure 8.9 : Paging concept

Address Translation

The next very basic question comes to one's mind is that how will the logical address get converted to physical address in this case? The answer is mapping. The logical address is mapped to physical address using a page table contained by special hardware unit called memory management unit. This page table has one entry for each page of the process and indicates the status of each page, *i.e.,* whether it has been allocated space in the physical memory or not? If yes, which frame it is currently occupying?

Each table entry contains a "valid" bit which if set indicates that the associated page is in the process's logical address space otherwise it is not. It contains some other bits also. These other bits include :

Protection bit : This bit is used to flag the page as read-only or read/write or execute only.

Modified bit : This bit, usually called the dirty bit, is set whenever the page is referenced by a write (store) operation i.e., when a page is modified.

Referenced bit : This bit is set whenever the page is referenced for any reasons, whether read, load or store.

Figure 8.10 shows the page table structure. The page size or the frame size is defined by the hardware and is always a power of 2. Can you guess why is the page or frame size always a power of 2? This is to make the division of a logical address into page number and page offset, easy. Logical address is divided into page number to specify which page is considered and page offset to specify the location of an instruction within a particular page. It will be more clear after you go through the following example :

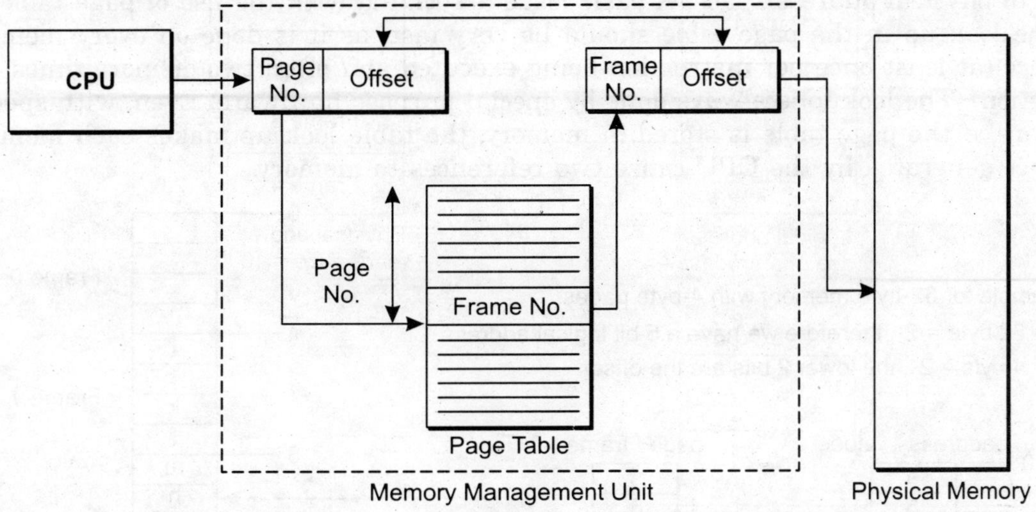

Figure 8.10 : Mapping a logical address to physical address

Let us consider the IBM/370 machine uses 24-bit logical addresses. The page size could be 2K or 4K bytes. When 2K byte pages are used, size of page = 2^{11} bytes. This implies that 11 bits are adequate to address the bytes in the pages. The remaining 24 – 11 = 13 bits will be used as page number to specify the address of a particular page. Now, consider that the size of physical memory is 1 M bytes. This implies size of physical memory = 2^{20} bytes. A typical physical address will have 20-bits. As 11 bits are used to indicate the bytes in a page, the same number is used to address bytes in a frame (as pages and frames are of same size). The remaining 20 – 11 = 9 bits specify the address of an individual frame in the physical memory.

The above example can be generalized to state that if size of logical address space is $\mathbf{2^1}$ and size of each page is $\mathbf{2^p}$, then the high-order **1 – p** bits of logical address specify the page number and the **p** lower-order bits designate the page offset i.e.,

Page No.	Page off set
1 – p	p

Logical address

The same holds true for the physical address space of 2^m size and having same frame size as the page size mentioned above.

Frame No.	Frame off set
m – p	p

Physical address

Figure 8.10 gives the complete picture of mapping a logical address to its corresponding physical address using page table.

Example : A good paging example is being shown in figure 8.11.

Problems with paging

1. Fast lookup in page table. It uses a page table per process for translating logical to physical address space. A basic issue associated with the use of page table is, that the look up in the page table should be very fast, as it is done on every memory reference (at least once per instruction being executed and often two or more times per instruction). The lookup is always done by special purpose hardware. Even, with special hardware, if the page table is stored in memory, the table look up makes each memory reference generated by the CPU cause two references to memory.

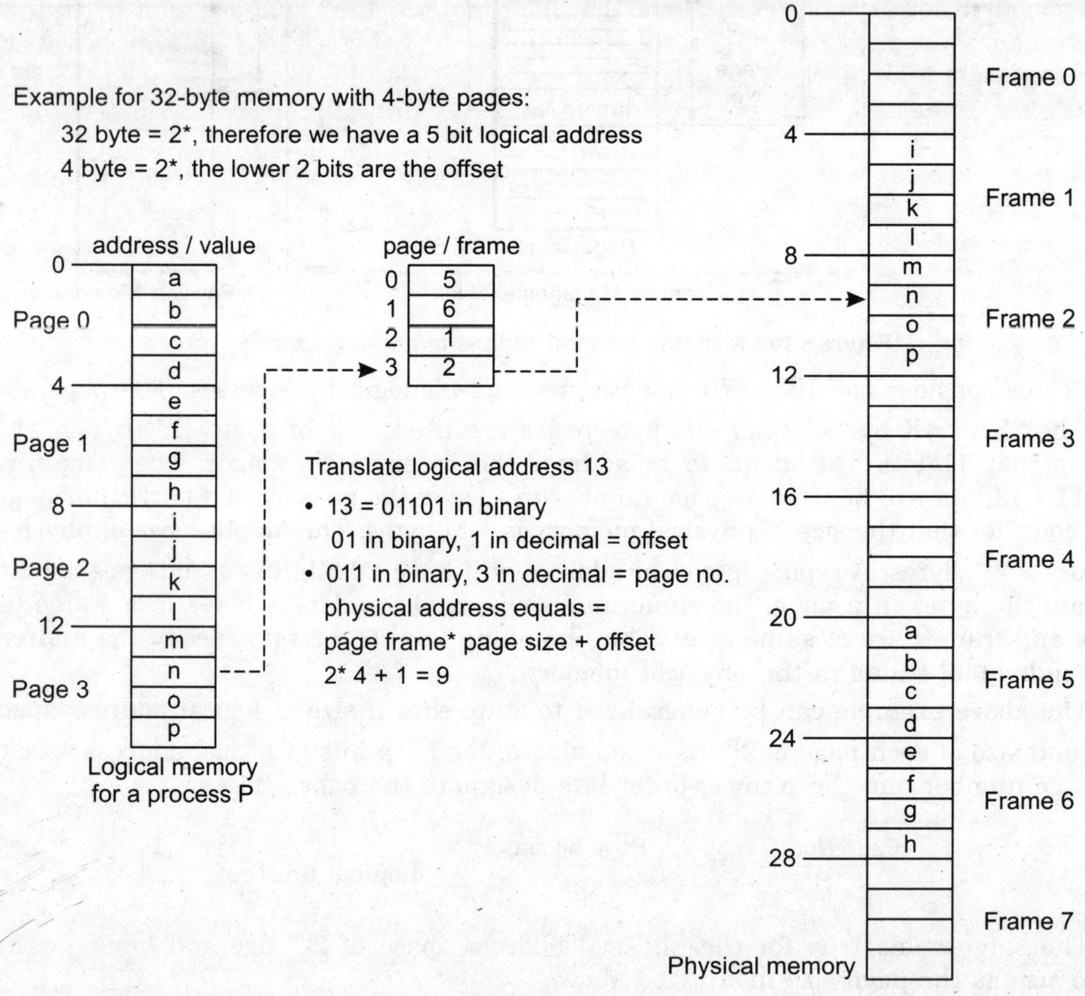

Figure 8.11 : Paging Example

To make the look up time less, caching is used. Caching has been discussed in chapter 2 of this text. It has been said that caching is the only technique in computer science used to improve performance. In this case, the specific cache device is called a translation look aside buffer (TLB). The TLB contains a set of entries, each of which contains a page number, the corresponding frame number, and the protection bits. There is special hardware to search the TLB for an entry matching a given page number. If the TLB contains a matching entry, it is found very quickly and nothing more needs to be done. Otherwise we have a TLB miss and have to fall back on one of the other techniques to find the translation. However, we can take that translation which we found with great difficulty and put it into the TLB so that we find it much more quickly the next time. The TLB has a limited size, so to add a new entry, we usually have to throw out an old entry. The usual technique is to throw out the entry that has not been used the longest. The reason this approach works so well is that most programs spend most of their time accessing a small set of pages over and over again. For example, a program often spends a lot of time in an "inner loop" in one procedure. Even if that procedure, the procedures it calls, and so on are spread over 40 K bytes, 10 TLB entries will be sufficient to describe all these pages, and there will be no TLB misses provided the TLB has at least 10 entries. This phenomenon is called locality of reference. In practice, the TLB hit rate for instruction references is extremely high. The hit rate for data reference is also good, but can vary widely for different programs. Figure 8.12 shows the use of TLB in paging. If the TLB performs well enough, it almost does not matter how TLB misses are resolved.

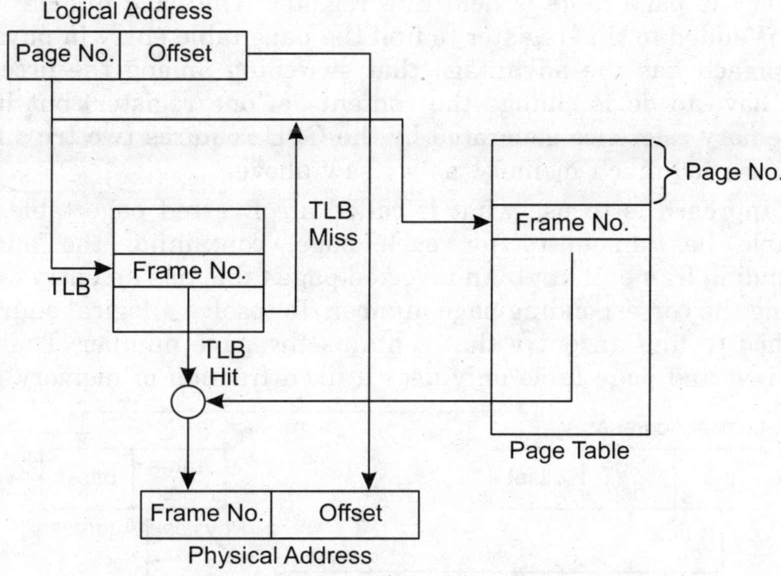

Figure 8.12 : Address translation using TLB

Two processes may map the same page number to different frames. Since the TLB hardware searches for an entry by page number, there would be an ambigutiy if entries corresponding to two processes were in the TLB at the same time. There are two ways to solve this problem. Some systems simply flush the TLB (set a bit in all entries marking them as unused) whenever they switch processes. This is very expensive, not because of the cost of flushing the TLB, but because of all the TLB misses that will happen when the new process starts running. An alternative approach is to add a process identifier to each entry. The hardware then searches on for the concatenation of the page number and the process id of the current process.

2. What to do when a page table gets large? Suppose the page size is 4 K bytes and a logical address is 32 bits long. Then the logical address would be divided into a 20-bit page number and a 12-bit offset (because $2^{12} = 4096 = 4K$), so the page table would have to have $2^{20} = 1{,}048{,}576$ entries. If each entry is 4 bytes long, that would use up 4 megabytes of memory. And each process has its own page table. Newer machines being introduced now generate 64-bit addresses. Such a machine would need a page table with 4,503,599,627,370,496 entries!

There are several different page table organizations used in actual computers.

- One approach is to put the page table entries in special registers. This was the approach used by the PDP-11 minicomputer introduced in the 1970's. Putting page table entries in registers helps make the Memory Management Unit run faster (the regsiters were much faster than main memory), but this approach has a downside as well. The registers are expensive, so it works for very small page-table size. Also, each time the operating system wants to switch processes, it has to reload the registers with the page-table entries of the new process.
- A second approach is to put the page table in main memory. The (physical) address of the page table is held in a register. The page number of the logical address is added to this register to find the page table entry in physical memory. This approach has the advantage that switching among the processes is easy (all you have to do is change the contents of one register) but it means that every memory reference generated by the CPU requires two trips to memory. It also can use too much memory, as we saw above.
- A third approach is to use what is called an inverted page table. An ordinary page table has an entry for each page, containing the address of the corresponding frame (if any). An inverted page table has an entry for each frame, containing the corresponding page number. To resolve a logical address, the table is searched to find an entry that contains the page number. The good news is that an inverted page table only uses a fixed fraction of memory. For example,

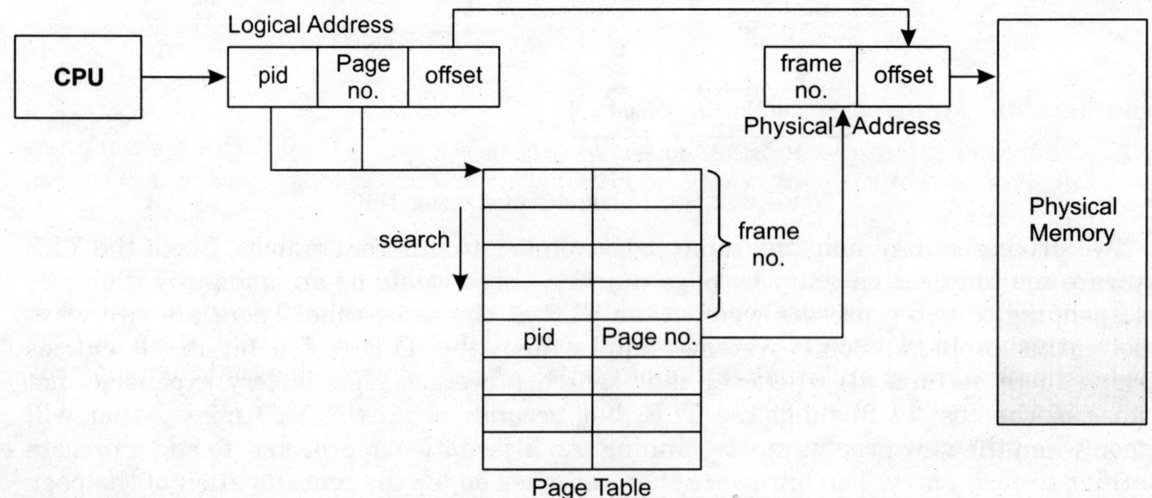

Figure 8.13 : Inverted Page Table

if a page is 4K bytes and a page-table entry is 4 bytes, there will be exactly 4 bytes of page table for each 4096 bytes of physical memory. In other words, less than 0.1% of memory will be used for page tables. This is by far the slowest of the methods, since it requires a time consuming search of the page table for each reference. A special hardware to search the table in parallel can be implemented. Figure 8.13 shows an inverted page table. Here 'pid', refers to the process identifier.

3. Internal Fragmentation. Paging also suffers from this problem. This may occur when the process size is not an exact multiple of page size. Let us say that we have a page size of 4K and the size of logical address space of a process is 133K then it can be divided into 133 K/4 K = 34 pages. When accommodated in frames, the last frame will not be completely full. Figure 8.14 explains this. The extent of internal fragmentation depends on the size of frames or pages. If we keep very large page size, it causes more internal fragmentation. If we have very small page size, there will be a lot of pages and thus more overhead will be involved e.g., more disk I/O operations will be required to move a page from disk to memory. Similarly, number of page table entries will increase leading to an increase in the page table size.

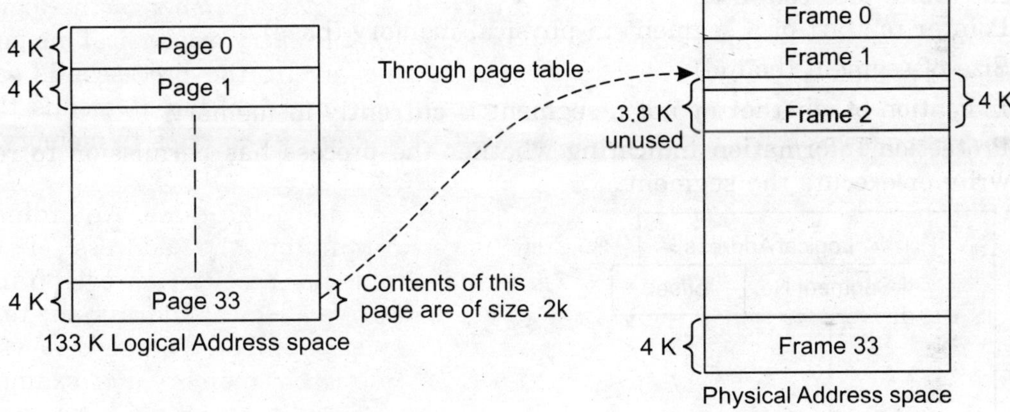

Figure 8.14 : Simplified diagram to explain internal fragmentation in paging

Advantages of paging

1. There is never a possibility of external fragmentation, it really achieves a higher degree of multiprogramming as compared to contiguous storage allocation strategies.
2. Sharing of common code among the processes is now possible. Single copy of some commonly used program such as compilers, editors, database systems can be kept in the physical memory. Many processes can share it, by making the page table of each of the processes such that it maps to the frames having shared data or programs in the physical memory. This means that many logical addresses will be mapped to one physical address.

8.2.2.2 Segmentation

As mentioned in the beginning of this section, segmentation is another technique for the noncontiguous storage allocation. It is different from paging as it supports users' view of his program. We know that users (programmers) think of their program as a collection of routines, libraries and piece of data. The programmer interprets the logical address space of a program according to his own viewpoint rather than as an array of bytes.

For a programmer it might be more relevant to divide the logical address space of his program into variable sized segments (with respect to his view of main program, subroutines, data, etc.) than to divide it into fixed size pages. Such variable sized segments, which are a collection of logically related information, are the basis of segmentation technique. In this technique, logical address space is a collection of such segments. The logical address comprises of segment number and segment offset. Normally, the compilation of a user program leads to the construction of segments. Thus a compiler may create separate segments for the global variables, the procedure call stack (that stores parameters and return addresses), the code of each procedure and the local variables of each procedure. The loader would assign numbers to these segments.

Address Translation. Let us now see, how does the mapping take place between logical and physical address? It is done by memory management unit, which uses segment tables. A segment table contains an entry for each segment of a process. Entries in segment tables also contain :

- Pointer to start of a segment in physical memory (base)
- Size of segment (bound)
- Indication of whether or not a segment is currently in memory
- Protection Information indicating whether the process has permission to read, write or execute the segment.

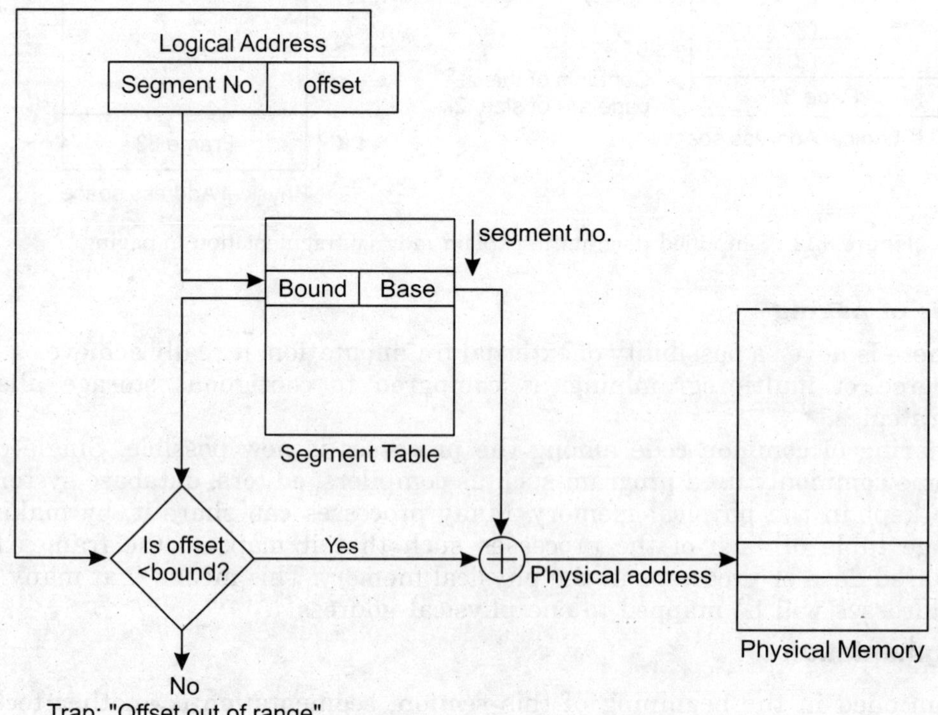

Figure 8.15 : Address translation using segment table

Figure 8.15 shows the use of segment table. The following steps are involved in address translation :

1. Segment number is extracted from logical address by dividing the address into segment number and offset. If there are 2^n segments, then n higher order bits in the logical address space specify the segment number and the remaining bits give the offset.
2. If segment number is greater than the maximum number of segments, a trap is generated to the operating system. It indicates that an attempt has been made to access an illegal segment.
3. Otherwise, segment table entry is accessed :
   (i) If segment offset is greater than the segment size (i.e., value of bound), a trap indicating "offset out of range" will be generated.
   (ii) If process does not have permission to access that segment, a trap indicating "protection violation" will be generated.
4. Otherwise, physical address (segment base + offset) is returned.

Figure 8.16 shows an example of segmentation.

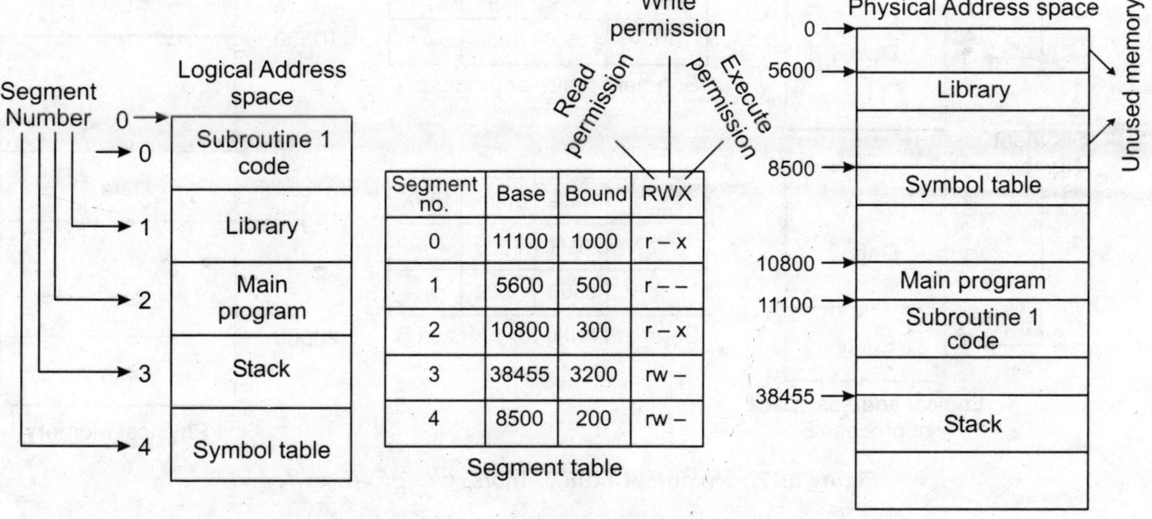

Figure 8.16 : Segmentation Example

Problem with Segmentation

1. As with paging, this mapping requires two memory references per logical address, which slows down the computer system by a factor of two. Caching is the method used to solve this problem.
2. In cases, where there are more number of segments, segment table size will grow. Thus, it cannot be accommodated in any of the registers and has to be kept in memory. Keeping it in memory needs a good hardware support from the underlying architecture.

3. Segmentation is prone to external fragmentation. This may occur when all the blocks in the memory are too small to accommodate a segment. Compaction, if possible, may sometimes be applied to solve the problem of external fragmentation.

Advantages of segmentation

1. Protection bits are associated with segments, which check that attempt to write a read-only segment should fail. They can also be used to check that attempt to use an execute-only segment, as a data segment should be prohibited.
2. As with paging, sharing of code or data is possible even with the segmentation technique. Here, entries in two different segment tables can be made to point to a common physical location. Figure 8.17 shows the sharing of common program among two different processes A and B.

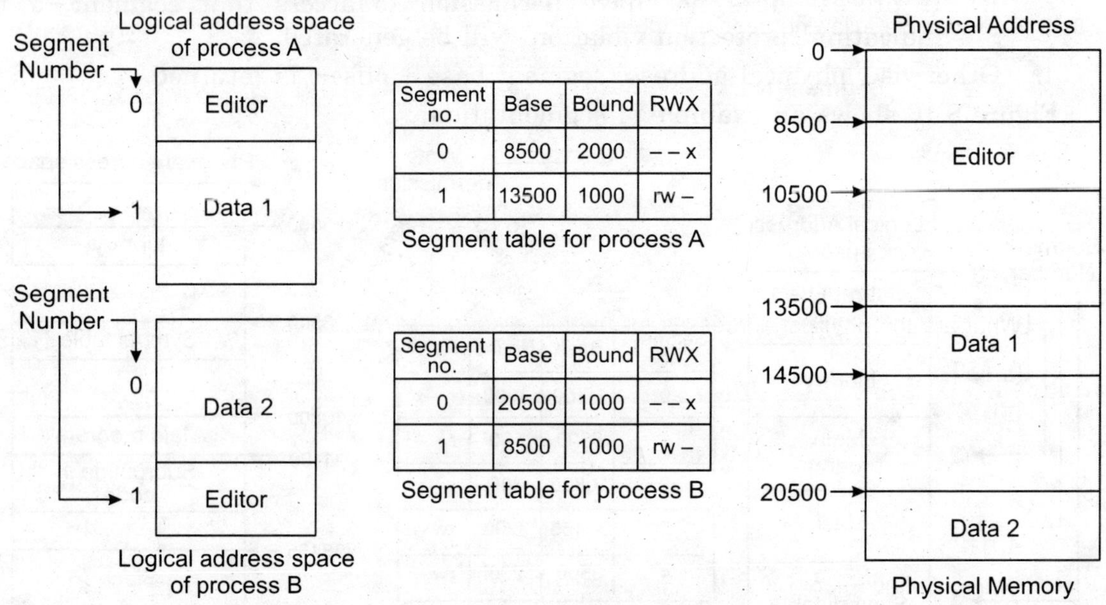

Segment no.	Base	Bound	RWX
0	8500	2000	– – x
1	13500	1000	rw –

Segment table for process A

Segment no.	Base	Bound	RWX
0	20500	1000	– – x
1	8500	1000	rw –

Segment table for process B

Figure 8.17 : Sharing of Editor among two processes A and B

EXERCISES

8.1 Explain address binding at compile time, load time and run time.

8.2 How is relocation used in run-time address binding of a program?

8.3 Differentiate between internal and external fragmentation.

8.4 Compare fixed-partition allocation strategy with variable-partition scheme for contiguous memory allocation.

8.5 Compare best-bit, worst-fit and first-fit allocation algorithms.

8.6 What is compaction? How is it implemented?

8.7 What are the problems associated with paging?

8.8 Why is TLB (Translation look aside buffer) used in a paging scheme?

8.9 List the advantages of paging.

8.10 Do you think there is any necessity of fixed-partition and variable-partition schemes, in a uniprogramming environment?

8.11 How is protection ensured in paging mechanism?

8.12 Consider a logical address space of eight pages of 1024 words each, mapped on to a physical memory of 32 frames. Find out the number of bits in the logical address and the number of bits in the physical address.

8.13 Describe using a diagram how a logical address consisting of 18 bits could be converted to a physical address where each page was 1 K byte. How many pages would there be?

8.14 How is sharing possible with segmentation?

8.15 Consider the following segment table :

Segment No.	Base	Bound	r w x
0	219	600	r w x
1	2300	14	r w x
2	90	100	r w –
3	1327	580	r w –
4	1952	96	r w –

What are the physical addresses for the following logical addresses?

0, 430

0, 10

2, 500

3, 400

4, 112

Where 0, 430 implies 430th instruction/data in 0th segment.

○○○○○

CHAPTER 9

Managing Virtual Memory

OVERVIEW

This chapter focuses on management of virtual memory. Virtual memory is an important concept with which every user program gets a feeling of being allocated the needed main memory in one go whereas actually, it is not like that. In reality, the operating system and user programs taken together may need total memory space, which exceeds the actually available one. Virtually, each user program seems to be accommodated inthe main memory. Demand paging is used to implement the concept of virtual memory and therefore, has been described in detail. Page replacement algorithms (like FIFO, LRU, Optimal etc.) have been discussed with a mention of their advantages and disadvantages. Demand segmentation has been described in brief. Thus, the idea is to discuss the virtual memory management techniques.

9.1. INTRODUCTION

Today, operating systems and applications occupy space in excess of 200 MB! With the relatively substantial cost of main memory (system RAM) and most systems being limited to 64 MB or 128 MB of RAM how does it all fit in a comparatively small main memory? Well, actually, it does not. A virtual effect is however possible by virtue of something known as "Virtual Memory".

Virtual memory is a technique of executing program instructions that may not fit entirely in system memory. This is done by calling instuctions as and when the application requires it. Virtual memory is implemented by using secondary storage to augment the main memory. Data is transferred from secondary to main storage as and when necessary and the data modified is written back to the secondary storage according to a predetermined algorithm.

Virtual memory, thus enhances the CPU utilization and throughput by executing as many programs as possible, almost simultaneously. Thus, it appears to the user that operating system and application programs are easily getting accommodated in small main memory of the system. This is actually a virtual effect because, now instead of holding the entire program, main memory holds only a portion of the program, which is currently being executed. Before moving on, here are a couple of things you should be familiar with :

Address translation is done by Memory Management Unit in paging and segmentation techniques. Both these techniques have been discussed in detail in Chapter 8.

Figure 9.1 shows the actual implementation of virtual memory. This diagram illustrates that (i) address translation of logical address to physical address should take place, (ii) This should be followed by a check, if the page is present in the main memory, (iii) the mapper enters this page in the available frame where this page is accommodated in the main memory, (iv) if the mapper detects that requested page is not present in main memory, (v) A page fault occurs and the page must be read into a frame in main memory, from secondary storage, (hard disk). This is known as demand paging and is one way of implementing virtual memory. The logical address here is also called virtual address, sometimes. Another way of implementing virtual memory is demand segmentation. The following sections discuss these methods in detail.

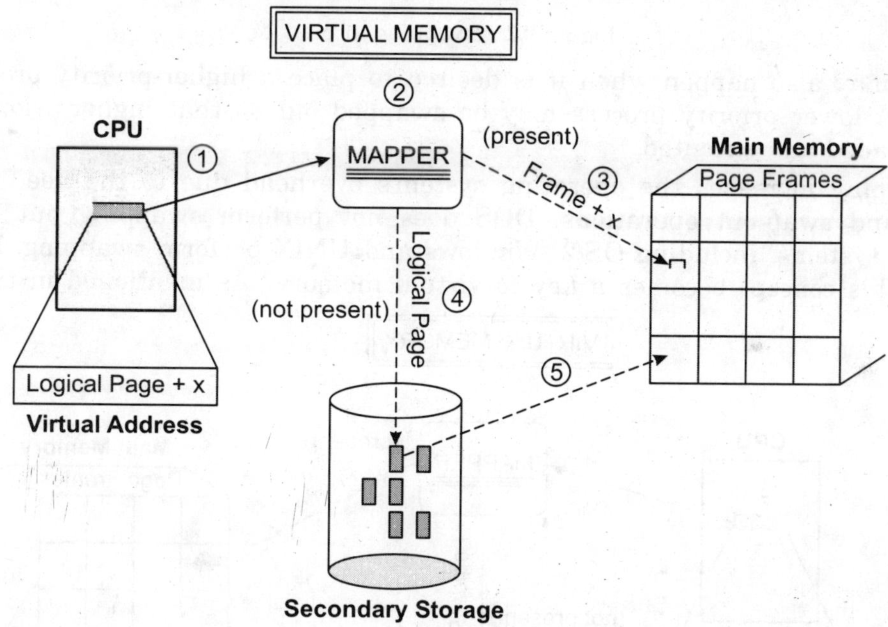

Figure 9.1 : Virtual Memory implementation

9.2. SWAPPING

Swapping is the technique of temporarily removing inactive programs from the main memory of a computer system. An inactive program is one that is neither executing nor performing an I/O operation. Figure 9.2 illustrates swapping as used in a practical situation. There is usually a set of active programs in memroy. Out of these only one executes on the CPU while others perform I/O. Whenever, an active program becomes inactive, the operating system begins to swap it (when system is falling short of main memory space). This involves writing the program's instructions and data areas onto the secondary storage, typically a disk. Once a program is completely swapped out, the memory area allocated to it become free. For example, this may happen in case of round robin scheduling. A process is swapped out when its time quantum finishes and later, it is brought into the memory for continued execution.

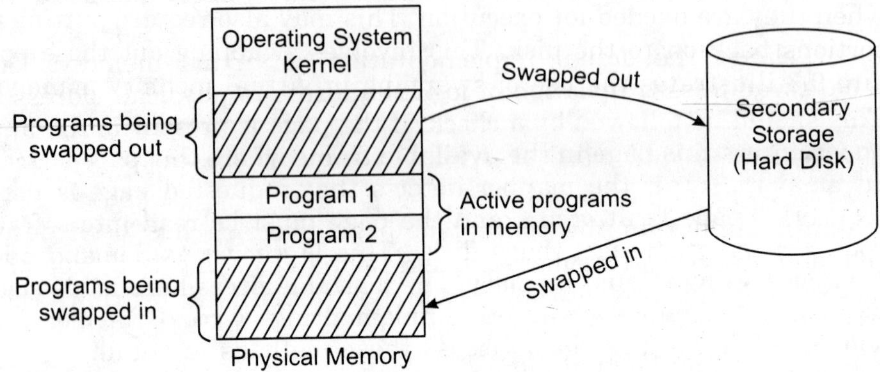

Figure 9.2 : Swapping in practice

This may also happen when it is desired to place a higher-priority process in the memory. A lower priority process may be swapped out so that higher-priority process may be loaded and executed.

Swapping increases the operating system's overhead due to the need to perform swap-in and swap-out operations. DOS does not perform swapping but most other operating systems, including OS/2, Windows and UNIX perform swapping. Now, let us see how this concept becomes a key to virtual memory? As mentioned in the previous

VIRTUAL MEMORY

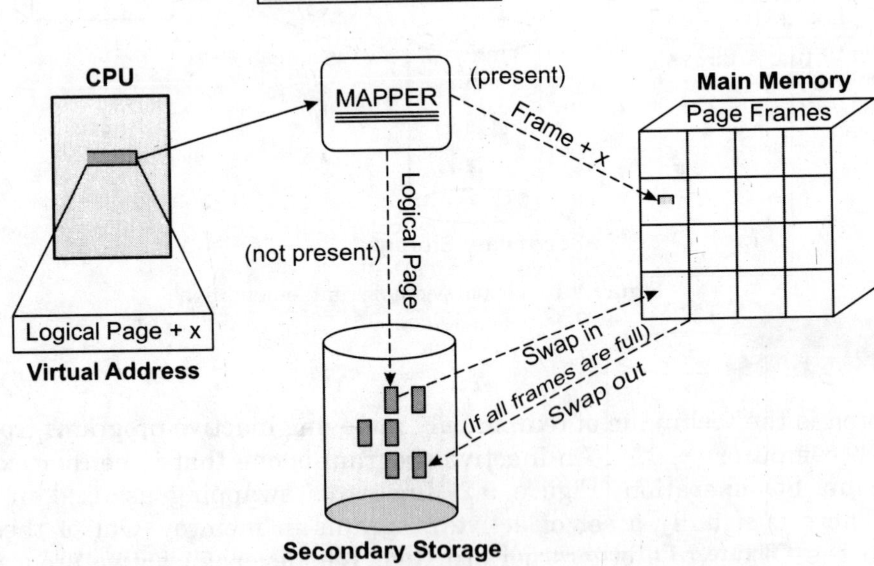

Figure 9.3 : The role of swapping in virutal memory management

section, the idea of virtual memory concept is to accommodate as many application processes (in main memory) as possible so as to increase CPU utilization and throughput. This is possible, by keeping only those portions of these programs in memory, which are currently needed for their execution. The remaining portions can be picked up as and when needed (from the secondary storage like disk). This means that portions of these programs have to be swapped in to the memory (by the operating system) when they are needed for execution. This may also require putting the currently unused portions back on to the disk. This involves swapping out these portions to the disk. Figure 9.3 illustrates the use of swapping in virtual memory management.

9.3. DEMAND PAGING AND ITS PERFORMANCE

It is almost similar to the concept of paging, which has been described in the previous chapter. In virtual memory system, demand paging is a type of swapping in which pages of programs are not copied from disk to main memory until they are needed for execution.

In demand paging, virtual address (logical address) is accessed by CPU, the corresponding page number is looked up in the page table and if it shows that currently this page is not in main memory, then this page must be brought into the main-memory. This requires some hardware support to distinguish between pages that are in memory and those that are on disk. A valid-invalid bit in the page table may be used to achieve this. If this bit for a page is invalid then either it is on disk or it is not within the logical

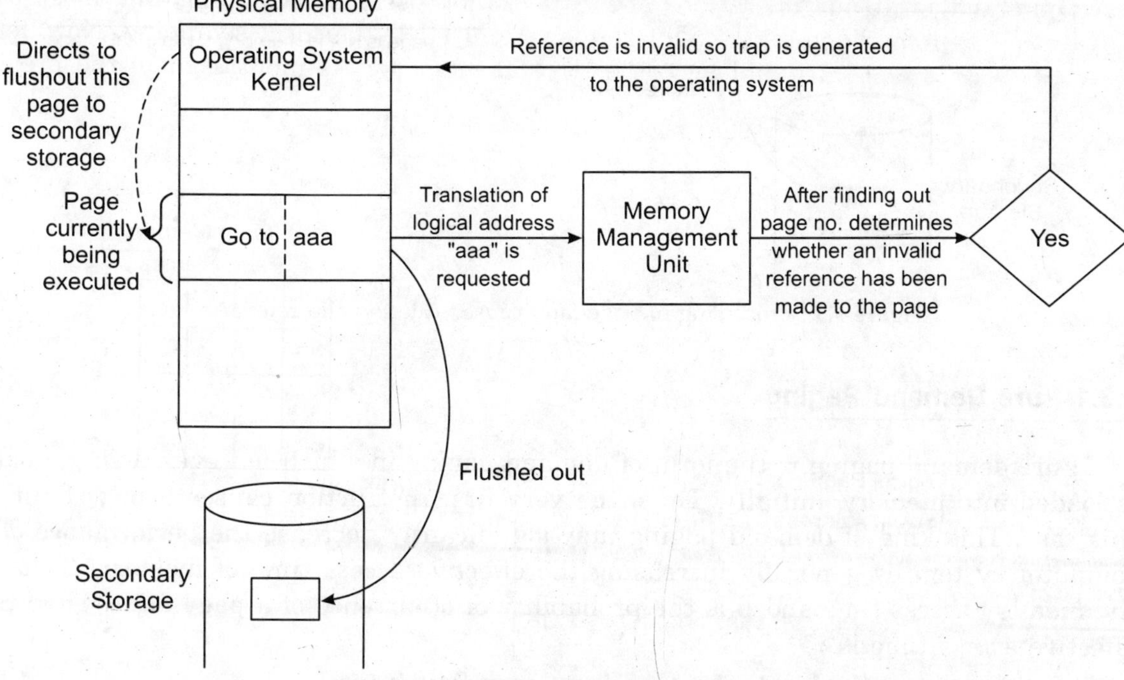

Figure 9.4 : Processing of page-fault caused due to invalid reference.

address space of the process i.e., it do not belong to the process in whose context it is being accessed. A page fault occurs when an invalid page is addressed. Page fault must be followed by swapping-in the page (demanded just now by the CPU) from disk to main-memory or a trap should be generated to the operating system if the page being demanded is not within the logical address space of the process. To determine whether the reference to the requested page is within the logical address space or not, an internal table may be consulted. Figure 9.4 and Figure 9.5 show the steps involved in servicing a page fault for invalid (where the page is outside the logical address space of the process) and valid (where the page is within the logical address space of the process) reference respectively.

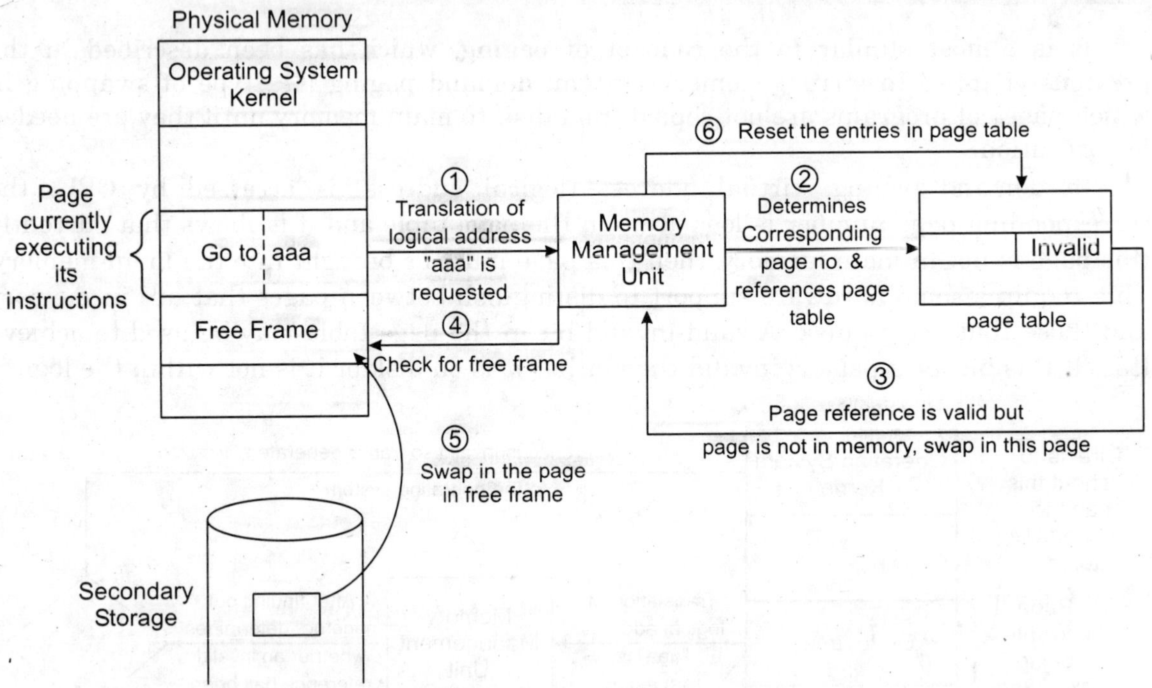

Figure 9.5 : Processing of page-fault caused due to valid reference.

9.3.1 Pure Demand Paging

Pure demand paging is the form of demand paging in which not even a single page is loaded into memory, initially. Thus, the very first instruction causes a page fault in this case. This kind of demand paging may significantly decrease the performance of a computer system by generally increasing the effective access time of memory. If ma is the memory access time and p is the probability of occurrence of a page fault. Then the effective access time is :

$$\text{effective access time} = (1 - p) \times ma + p \times \text{page fault time}$$

Example : Suppose the average page fault service time is 20 milli-seconds and memory access time is 200 nanoseconds. Suppose, we wish to have less than 10% degradation in the memory access when a page fault occurs, what must the page fault rate be less than?

This means that we want effective access time should be less than

$$\left(\frac{10}{100} \times 200 + 200\right) \times 10^{-9} \text{ seconds i.e., } 200 \times 10^{-9} \text{ seconds.}$$

Effective access time is obtained as :

$$(1 - p) \times 200 \times 10^{-9} + p \times 20 \times 10^{-3} = 2 \times 10^{-7} - 2 \times 10^{-7}\, p + 2 \times 10^{-2}\, p$$

Now, $2 \times 10^{-7} + 1.99 \times 10^{-2}\, p$ should be less than 220×10^{-9}

Thus, $2 \times 10^{-7} + 1.99 \times 10^{-2}\, p < 220 \times 10^{-9}$

$$\Rightarrow \quad 1.99 \times 10^{-2}\, p < 2.2 \times 10^{-7} - 2 \times 10^{-7}$$

$$\Rightarrow \quad 1.99 \times 10^{-2}\, p < .2 \times 10^{-7}$$

$$\Rightarrow \quad p < \frac{.2 \times 10^{-7}}{1.99 \times 10^{-2}}$$

$$\Rightarrow \quad p < \frac{.2 \times 10^{-5}}{1.99}$$

$$\Rightarrow \quad p < .10050 \times 10^{-5}$$

$$\Rightarrow \quad p < .00001 \text{ approximately}$$

This means that probability of occurring of a page fault should be less than .00001 so as to achieve a degradation of less than 10%. This implies that page fault rate should be kept as low as possible so that effective memory access time should not increase.

Page fault service time talked about in this example means the time it takes to serve the page fault. It usually includes the time taken to

1. Determine that the page being demanded is legal (reference is valid).
2. Read the page from disk.
3. Swap it in free space in memory if available. Otherwise make space available by swapping out some page of the same process or other process.
4. Restart the process, which has demanded this page.

9.4. PAGE REPLACEMENT

Once the main memory fills up, a page must be swapped out to make room for any pages to be swapped in. This is known as page replacement. The question arises which page should be swapped out of the memory? This is decided by various algorithms known as page replacement algorithms.

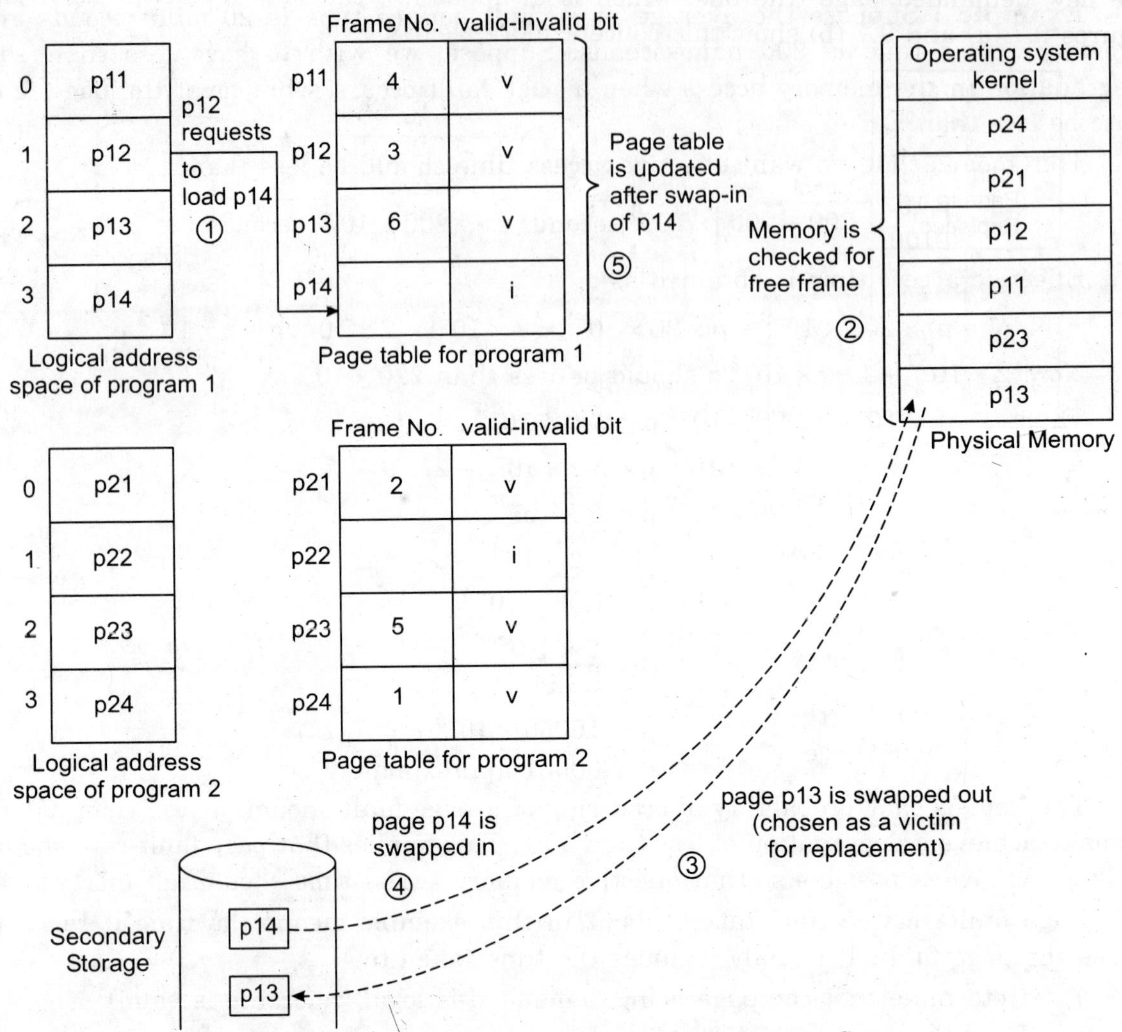

Figure 9.6 : Page replacement process

Figure 9.6 shows the need for page replacement and a generalized method to do it. The sequence of actions is labelled using numbers 1, 2, 3, etc.

Before taking up each of the page replacement algorithm in detail, we analyze the general working of page replacement. This involves the movement of two pages. One is copied from disk to main memory (to serve page fault) and other from main memory to disk (to create free space). This is a time consuming operation. To overcome this problem, a bit known as modify/dirty bit can be associated with a page. This bit is set whenever any word is written into this page and thus indicates that the page has been modified. Now, when a page is selected to be replaced, its modify bit is checked. If it is set, it implies that this page was modified (when it was in main memory) and therefore, must be written back to the disk, otherwise this page must not be written back to the disk, because no changes have been made to it after it was read from the disk into the memory.

The new demanded page (the one, which is swapped-in), can now replace it as it is. Figures 9.7 (a) and 9.7 (b) show this concept more clearly.

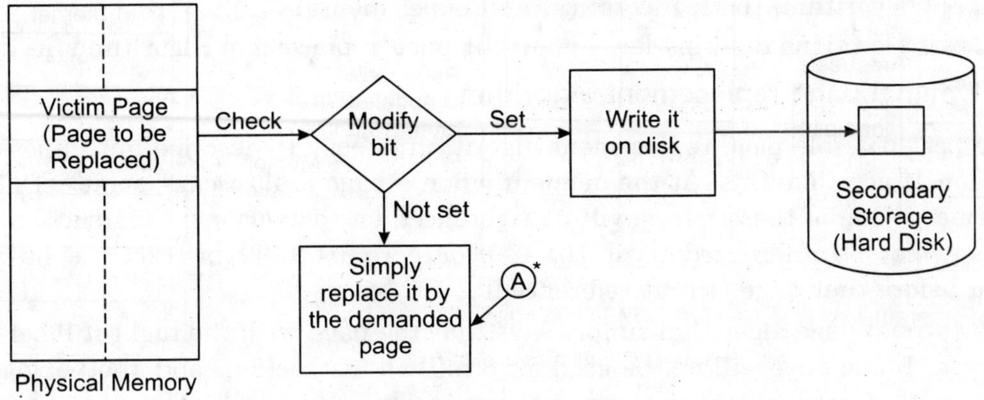

Figure 9.7(a) : Use of Modify bit in page replacement

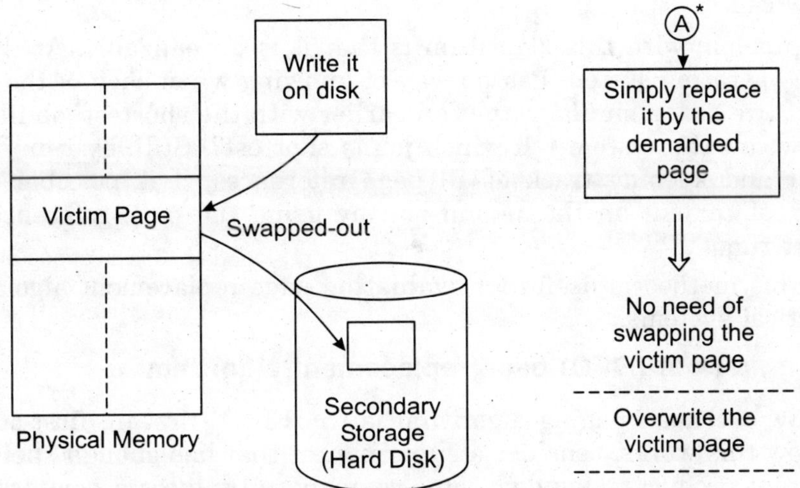

Figure 9.7 (b) : Reduced overhead by using modify bit

Let us now move on to discuss the page replacement algorithm.

9.4.1 Page Replacement Algorithms

When a page fault occurs, the operating system has to choose a page to remove from memory to make room for the page that has to be brought in. If the page to be removed has been modified while in memory, it must be rewritten to the disk to bring the disk copy upto date. If, however, the page has not been changed (i.e., it contains program text), the disk copy is already upto date, so no rewrite is needed. The page to be read in just overwrites the page being replaced.

While it would be possible to pick a random page to replace at each page fault, system performance is much better if a page that is not heavily used is chosen. If a heavily used page is removed, it will probably have to be brought back in the near future, resulting in extra overhead. Much work has been done on the subject of page replacement algorithms, both theoretical and experimental.

Following sections describe few important page replacement algorithms in detail.

9.4.1.1 Optimal page replacement algorithm

The best possible page replacement algorithm is easy to describe but impossible to implement. It goes like this. At the moment when a page fault occurs, some set of pages is in memory. One of these pages will be referenced on the very next instruction. Other pages may not be referenced until 10, 100, or perhaps 1000 instructions have been executed before that page is first referenced.

The optimal page algorithm simply says that the page with the highest label should be removed. If one page will not be used for 8 million instructions and another page will not be used for 6 million instructions, the former page should be removed, as it will not be used in the near future. Computers, like people, try to put off unpleasant events for as long as they can!

The only problem with this algorithm is that it is unrealizable. At the time of the page fault, the operating system has no way of knowing when each of the pages will be referenced next (we saw a similar situation earlier with the shortest job first scheduling algorithm—how can the system tell which job is shortest?) Still, by running a program on a simulator and keeping track of all page references, it is possible to implement optimal page replacement on the second run by using the page reference information during the first run.

Although this method is useful for evaluating page replacement algorithms, it is of no use in practical systems.

9.4.1.2 First-in, first-out (FIFO) page replacement algorithm

Another low-overhead paging algorithm is the FIFO (first-in, first-out) algorithm. To illustrate how this works, consider a supermarket that has enough shelves to display exactly k different products. One day, some company introduces a new product. It is an immediate success, so our supermarket has to get rid of one old product in order to stock the recently successful product.

One possibility is to find the product that the supermarket has been stocking the longest (*i.e.,* something it began selling 120 years ago) and get rid of it on the grounds that no one is interested any more. In effect, the supermarket maintains a linked list of all the products it currently sells in the order they were introduced. The new one goes on the back of the list; the one at the front of the list is dropped.

As a page replacement algorithm, the same idea is applicable. The operating system maintains a list of all pages currently in memory, with the page at the head of the list, being the oldest one and the page at the tail, being the most recent arrival. On a page fault, the page at the head is removed and the new page is added to the tail of the list. When applied to stores, FIFO might be useful. When applied to computers, problem arises because the page although being oldest, might be the heavily used page and may be needed immediately in the memory. This will thus lead to quick page faults. FIFO in its pure form is rarely used because this algorithm suffers from Belady's anomaly. This is named after Belady who in 1970 found a problem with FIFO algorithm. The problem is when more frames are allotted to a process (to accommodate more pages of the process), it generates more page faults whereas it should be the other way round. Figure 9.8 shows this anomaly in a very descriptive way.

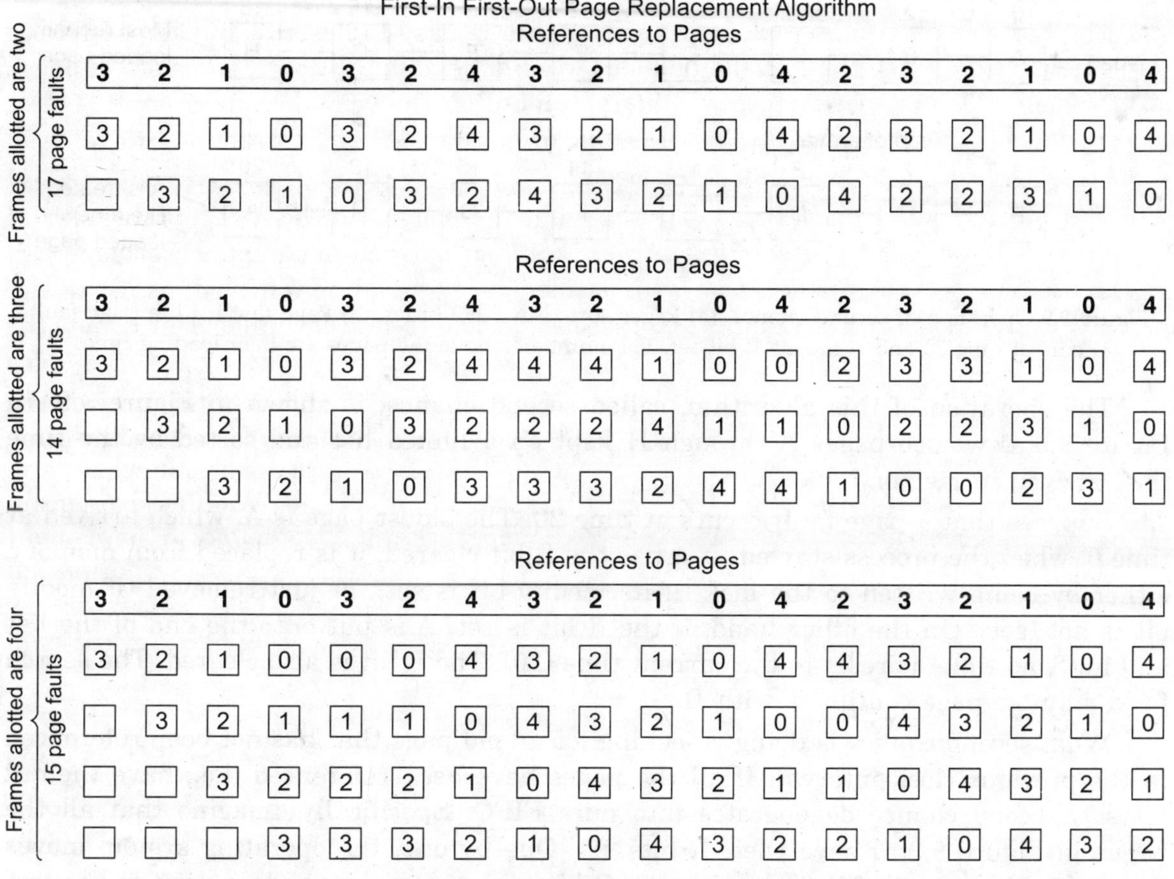

Figure 9.8 : Belady's Anomaly

The newest page is on the top and the oldest migrates to the bottom like a queue. All of the page faults are indicated here in this figure. Notice the expected improvements in the number of page faults when three frames are used. But, most unexpectedly, see that adding fourth frame results in an increase in the number of page faults whereas it should have been decreased. This is called Belady's anomaly and is the biggest disadvantage of FIFO algorithm.

9.4.1.3 Second chance page replacement algorithm

A simple modification to FIFO that avoids the problem of throwing out a heavily used page is to inspect the Referenced bit (R) of the oldest page. If it is 0, the page is both old and unused, so it is replaced immediately. If the R bit is 1, the bit is cleared, the page is put onto the end of the list of pages, and its load time is updated as though it had just arrived in memory. Then the search continues. This implies that this algorithm searches for an old page that has not been referenced. If a page is oldest but has been referenced, it will not be considered for replacement.

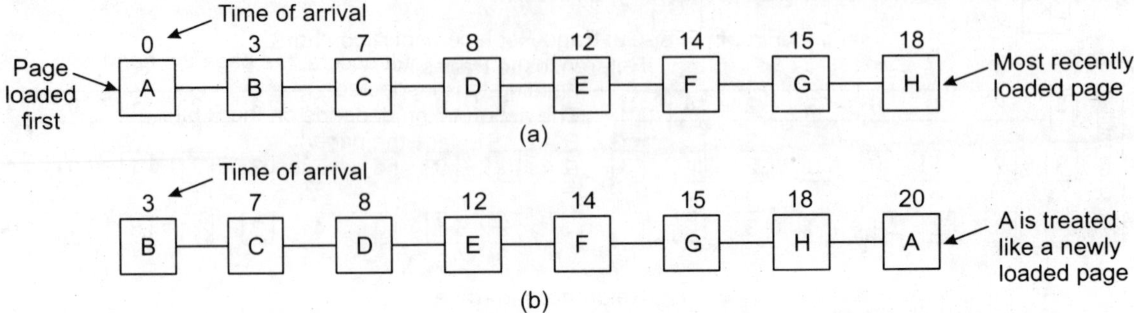

Figure 9.9 Operation of second chance. (a) Pages sorted in FIFO order. (b) Page first list if a page fault occurs at time 20 and A has its R bit set. The numbers above the pages are their loading times

The operation of this algorithm, called second chance, is shown in Figure 9.9. In Figure 9.9(a) we see pages A through H kept on a linked list and sorted by the time they arrived in memory.

Suppose that a page fault occurs at time 20. The oldest page is A, which arrived at time 0, when the process started. If A has the R bit cleared, it is replaced from memory, either by being written to the disk (if its modify bit is set), or just removed (if modify bit is not (set). On the other hand, if the R bit is set, A is put onto the end of the list and its “load time” is reset to the current time (20). The R bit is also cleared. The search for a suitable page continues with B.

What second chance is doing is looking for an old page that has not been referenced in the previous clock interval. If all the pages have been referenced (i.e., have their R bit set) second chance degenerates into pure FIFO. Specifically, imagine that all the pages in Figure 9.9(a) have their R bits set. One by one, the operating system moves the pages to the end of list, clearing the R bit each time it appends a page to the end of the list. Eventually, it comes back to page A, which now has its R bit cleared. At this point A is replaced. Thus, the algorithm always terminates.

9.4.1.4 Clock page replacement algorithm

Although second chance is a reasonable algorithm, it is unnecessarily inefficient because it is constantly moving pages around on its list. A better approach is to keep all the pages on a circular list in the form of a clock, as shown in Figure 9.10. A hand points to the oldest page.

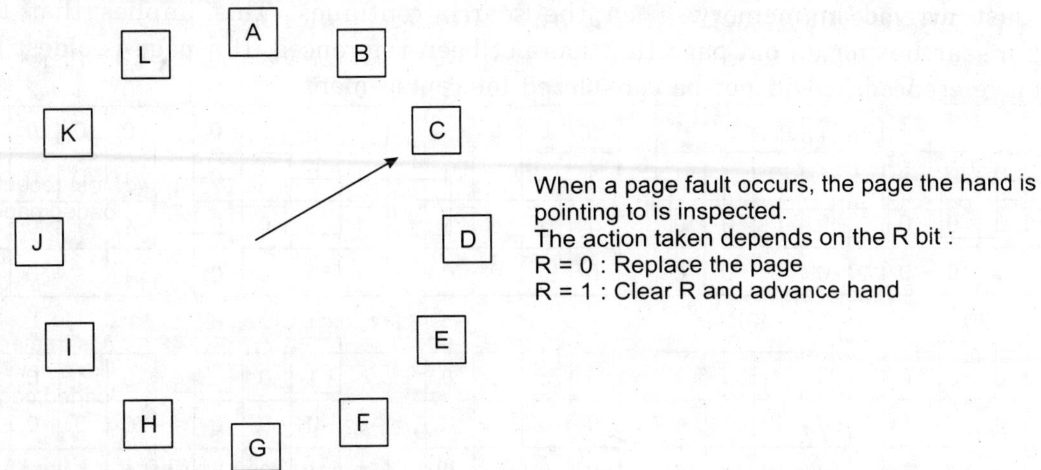

Figure 9.10 : The clock page replacement algroithm

When a page fault occurs, the page being pointed to by the hand of clock is inspected. It its R bit is 0, the page is replaced, the new page is inserted into the clock in its place, and the hand is advanced one position. If R bit is 1, it is cleared and the hand is advanced to the next page. This process is repeated until a page is found with R bit = 0. Not surprisingly, this algorithm is called clock. It differs from second chance only in the implementation.

9.4.1.5 Least Recently Used (LRU) Page Replacement Algorithm

A good approximation to the optimal algorithm is based on the observation that pages that have been heavily used in the last few instructions will probably be heavily used again in the next few. Conversely, pages that have not been used for ages will probably remain unused for a long time. This idea suggests a realizable algorithm : when a page fault occurs, throw out the page that has been unused for the longest time. This strategy is called LRU (Least Recently Used) algorithm.

Although LRU is theoretically realizable, it is not cheap. To fully implement LRU, it is necessary to maintain a linked list of all pages in memory, with the most recently used page at the front and the least recently used page at the rear. The difficulty is that the list must be updated on every memory reference. Finding a page in the list, deleting it, and then moving it to the front is a very time consuming operation, even in hardware (assuming that such hardware could be built).

Now let us look at hardware LRU algorithm. For a machine with n pages, the LRU hardware can maintain a matrix of $n \times n$ bits, initially all zero. Whenever page k is referenced, the hardware first sets all the bits of row k to 1, then sets all the bits of column k to 0. At any instant, the row whose binary value is lowest is the least recently used, the row whose value is next lowest is next least recently used, and so forth. The workings of this algorithm are given in Figure 9.11 for four frames and page references in the order

0 1 2 3 2 1 0 3 2 3

After page 0 is referenced, we have the situation of figure 9.11(a). After page 1 is referenced, we have the situation of Figure 9.11(b), and so forth.

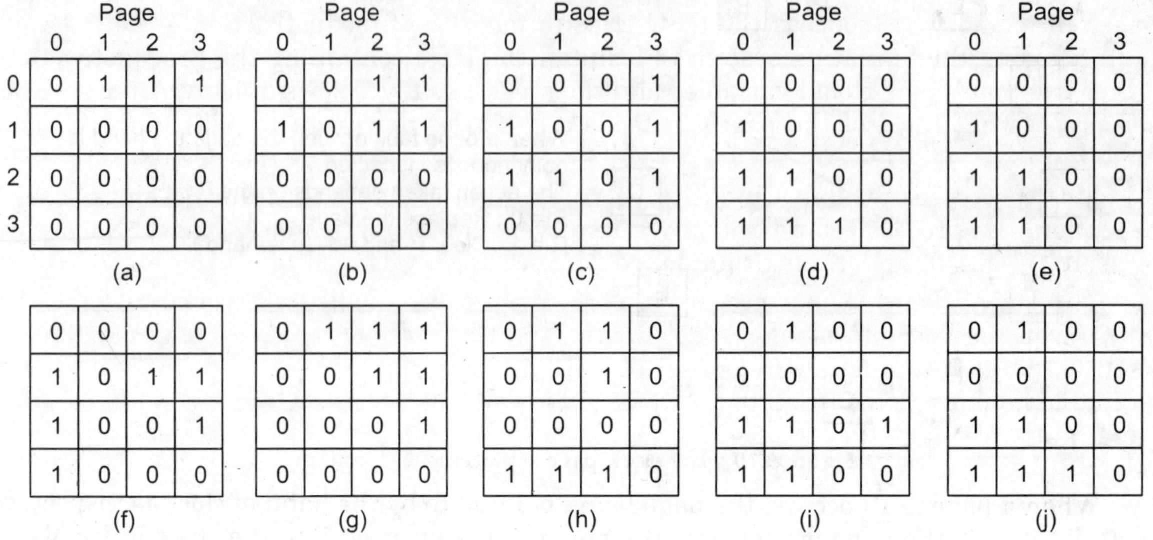

Figure 9.11 : LRU using a matrix when pages are referenced in the order 0, 1, 2, 3, 2, 1, 0, 3, 2, 3

At any instance, for example after (d), if a page is to be replaced then LRU page will be found by checking the row with least binary value. At instance (d), page number 0 is least recently used and it can be replaced.

9.4.1.6 Simulating LRU in Software

Although both of the previous LRU algorithms are realizable in principle, but only few machines have this hardware, so they are of little use to the operating system designer who is making a system for a machine that does not have this hardware. Instead, a solution that can be implemented in software is needed. One possibility is called the NFU (Not Frequently Used) algorithm. It requires a software counter associated with each page, initially zero. In effect, the counters are an attempt to keep track of how often each page has been referenced. When a page fault occurs, the page with the lowest counter is chosen for replacement.

The main problem with NFU is that it never forgets anything. For example, in a multipass compiler, pages that were heavily used during pass 1 may still have a high count well into later passes. In fact, if pass 1 happens to have the longest execution time of all the passes, the pages containing the code for subsequent passes may always have lower counts than the pass 1 pages. Consequently, the operating system will remove useful pages (of pass 2 and so on) instead of pages (of pass 1) no longer in use.

Another possibility of simulating LRU in software is to use stack of page numbers. Whenever a page is referenced, its number is removed from the stack and put on the top. In this way, the top of the stack is always the most recently used page number and the bottom is the LRU page number. This method may be time consuming when LRU page number is to be removed from the stack. However, this algorithm does not suffer from Belady's anomaly explained in Section 9.4.1.2.

9.4.1.7 Working Set Page Replacement Algorithm

In the purest form of demand paging, processes are started up with none of their pages in memory. As soon as the CPU tries to fetch the first instruction, it gets a page fault, causing the operating system to bring in the page containing the first instruction. Other page faults for global variables and the stack usually follows quickly. After a while, the process has most of the pages it needs and settles down to run with relatively few page faults.

Most processes exhibit a **locality of reference,** meaning that during any phase of execution, the process references only a relatively small fraction of its pages. Each pass of a multi-pass compiler, for example, references only a fraction of all the pages.

The set of pages that a process is currently using is called its working set. If the entire working set is in memory, the process will run without causing many page faults until it moves into another execution phase (*e.g.,* the next pass of the compiler). If the available memory is too small to hold the entire working set, the process will cause many page faults and run slowly since executing an instruction takes a few nanoseconds and reading in a page from the disk typically takes 10 milliseconds. At a rate of one or two instructions per 10 milliseconds, it will take ages to finish. A process causing page faults after every few instructions is said to be **thrashing.** Thus, thrashing refers to high paging activity of a process. This implies that a process is effectively spending more time in paging than executing therefore, frequent occurrence of thrashing can slow down the system and thus, it is not desirable.

In a multiprogramming system, processes are frequently moved to disk (*i.e.,* all their pages are removed from memory) to let other processes have a turn at the CPU. The question arises is what to do when a process is brought back in again. Technically, nothing need be done. The process will just cause page faults until its working set has been loaded. The problem is that having 20, 100, or even 1000 page faults every time a process is loaded, is slow, and it also wastes considerable CPU time, since it takes the operating system a few milliseconds of CPU time to process a page fault (page fault service time).

Therefore, many paging systems try to keep track of each process' working set and make sure that it is in memory before letting the process run. This approach is called the **working set model.** It is designed to greatly reduce the page fault rate. Loading the pages before letting processes run is also called pre-paging. Note that the working set changes over time.

It has been long known that most programs do not reference their address space uniformly, but that the references tend to cluster on a small number of pages. A memory reference may fetch an instruction, it may fetch data, or it may store data. At any instant of time, t, there exists a set consisting of all the pages used by the k most recent memory references. This set w(k, t), is the working set. Because thc k = 1 most recent references must have used all the pages used by the k > 1 most recent references and possibly others, w(k, t), is a monotonically non-decreasing function of k. The limit of w(k, t) as k becomes large is finite because a program cannot reference more pages than its address space contains, and few programs will use every single page.

Figure 9.12 depicts the size of working set as a function of k. The fact that most programs randomly access a small number of pages, but that this set changes slowly in time explains the initial rapid rise of the curve and then the slow rise for large k. For example, a program that is executing a loop occupying two pages using data on four pages, may reference all six pages every 1000 instructions, but the most recent reference to some other page may be a million instructions earlier, during the initialization phase.

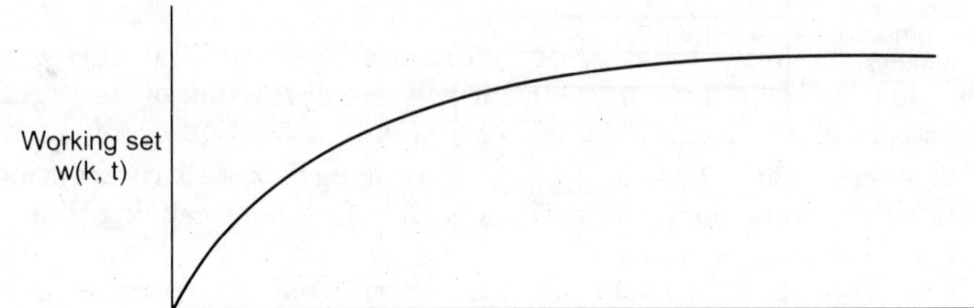

Figure 9.12 : The working set is the set of pages used by the k most recent memory references. The function w(k, t) is the size of the working set at time t.

Thus, there exists a wide range of k values for which the working set is unchanged. Because the working set varies slowly with time, it is possible to make a reasonable guess as to which pages will be needed when the program is restarted on the basis of its working set when it was last stopped. Pre-paging consists of loading these pages before the process is allowed to run again.

To implement the working set model, it is necessary for the operating system to keep track of which pages are in the working set. Having this information also immediately leads to a possible page replacement algorithm: When a page fault occurs, find a page not in the working set and replace it. To implement such an algorithm, we need a precise way of determining which pages are in the working set and which are not at any given moment of time.

As mentioned above, the working set is the set of pages used in the k most recent **memory** references (some authors use the k most recent **page** references, but the choice is arbitrary). To implement any working set algorithm, some value of k must be chosen in advance. Once some values has been selected, after every memory reference, the set of pages used by the previous k memory references is uniquely determined.

Now let us look at a page replacement algorithm based on the working set. The basic idea is to find a page that is not in the working set and replace it. In Figure 9.13 a portion of a page table for some machine can be seen. Because only pages that are in memory are considered as candidates for replacement, pages that are absent from memory are ignored by this algorithm. Each entry contains (at least) two items of information : the approximate time the page was last used and the R (Referenced) bit. The empty white rectangle symbolizes the other fields not needed for this algorithm, such as the frame number, the protection bits, and the M (Modified) bit.

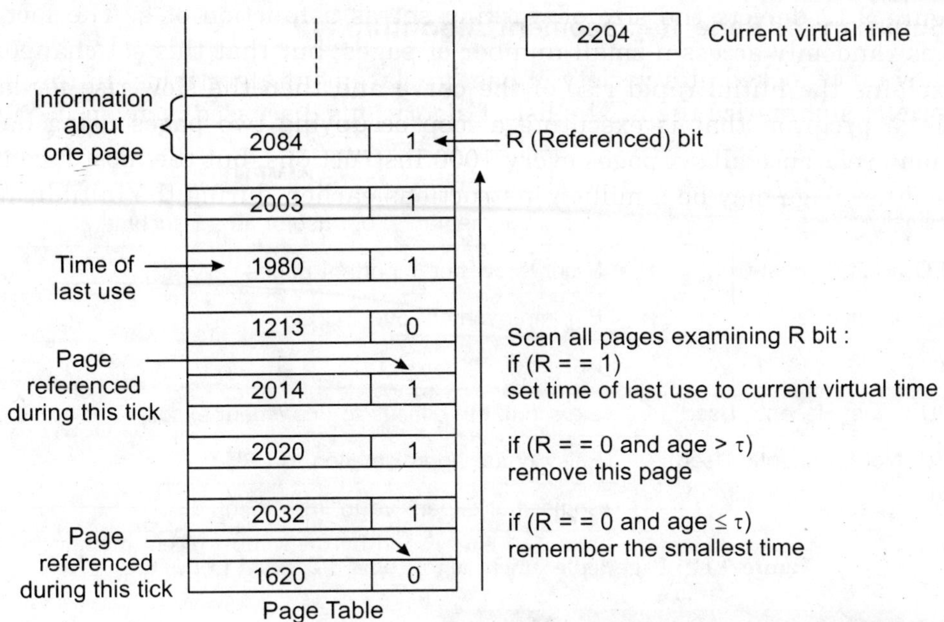

Figure 9.13 : The working set algorithm

The algorithm works as follows. The hardware is assumed to set the R and M bits, whenever a page is referenced or modified (as we have discussed before). Simialrly, a periodic clock interrupt is assumed to cause a software to run that clears the Referenced bit on every clock tick. On every page fault, the page table is scanned to look for a suitable page to be replaced.

As each entry is processed, the R bit is examined. If it is 1, the current virtual time is written into the *'Time of last use'* field in the page table, indicating that the page was in use at the time when the fault occurred. Since the page has been referenced during the current clock tick, it is clearly in the working set and is not a candidate for removal. (t is assumed to span multiple clock ticks).

If R is 0, the page has not been referenced during the current clock tick and may be a candidate for removal. To see whether or not it should be removed, its age, that is, the current virtual time minus its *'Time of last use'* is computed and compared to t. If the age is greater than t, the page is no longer in the working set. It is replaced and the new page is loaded here. The scan continues updating the remaining entries, however.

However, if R is 0 but the age is less than or equal to t, the page is still in the working set. The page is temporarily spared, but the page with the greatest age (smallest value of *'Time of last use'*) is noted. If the entire table is scanned without finding a victim, that means that all pages are in the working set. In that case, if one or more pages with R = 0 is found and the one with the greatest age is replaced. In the worst case, all pages have been referenced during the current clock tick (and thus all have R = 1), so one is chosen at random for removal, preferably the one whose modify bit is not set.

Besides the algorithms that have been discussed here, least frequency used (LFU) and most frequently used (MFU) are other algorithms that can be used for page replacement.

9.4.1.8 Summary of Page Replacement Algorithms

We have now looked at a variety of page replacement algorithms. In this subsection we will briefly summarize them. The list of algorithms discussed is given in Figure 9.14.

ALGORITHM	COMMENT
Optimal	Non implementable, but useful as a benchmark
FIFO (First-in, First-Out)	Might throw out important pages
Second chance	Big improvement over FIFO
Clock	Realistic
LRU (Least Recenty Used)	Excellent, but difficult to implement exactly
NFU (Not Frequently Used)	Fairly crude approximation to LRU
Working set	Somewhat expensive to implement

Figure 9.14 : Page replacement algorithms discussed in the text

9.5. PAGE REPLACEMENT POLICIES

So far, we have considered only 'local page replacement policy' in our page-replacement algorithms. What is this local page replacement policy? It means that when a process requests for a new page to be brought in and there are no free frames in the memory, we choose a frame allocated to only that process (and not of any other process), for replacement. Figure 9.6 shows this very clearly. Here program1 wants a page p14 to be loaded into the memory. This is done by choosing page p13 (by using some page replacement algorithm) of same program1.

Whereas in 'global replacement' policy, any frame from any other process can be replaced. For example, in our Figure 9.6, page p24 of program2 can be chosen to be replaced by p14, if global page replacement policy is used. Thus, here, the operating system has to decide the set of worst pages, *i.e.,* least referenced pages from all processes and then choose a page amongst them. In this case, process priorities and types also play a major role. Therefore, without going into any detail, we can say that the page replacement algorithms which use global page replacement policy, will be very difficult to implement and their discussion is outside the scope of this text.

9.6. DEMAND SEGMENTATION

Demand paging is generally considered to be the most efficient virtual memory system but a significant amount of hardware is needed to implement it. The lack of this hardware may sometimes be a hindrance in the implementation of demand paging.

Demand segmentation is another method of implementing virtual memory. Demand segmentation allocates segments rather than pages to processes. It keeps track of those segments in segment descriptors/segment table that are similar to a page table and store information about the segment size, location and protection. As virtual memory provided with paging enables the execution of the process without it being totally in memory, similarly, with segmentation all the segments do not have to be in memory to execute.

The segment descriptor contains a valid bit in the same way as in paging to show if the segment is in memory.

If the segment is in main memory, the access continues unhindered. If the segment is not in memory, a trap to the operating system occurs (segment fault), just as a page fault occurs in demand-paging implementations, and the required segment is swapped in from secondary memory.

In order to make the selection of a segment to be replaced by another segment, a bit in the segment descriptor called accessed bit is used. An accessed bit services the same purpose as a reference bit in demand paging. It is set whenever any byte in the segment is either read or written.

When an invalid-segment trap occurs, the memory management routines first determine whether there is sufficient free memory space to accommodate the segment. If there is not enough room in memory, the least recenty used segment is chosen for replacement and is written to disk. If the newly freed space is large enough to accommodate the requested segment, then the requested segment is read into the vacated segment, the segment descriptor is updated, and the segment is placed at the head of the queue. If the newly free space is not that large, then the requested segment cannot be read and probably one more segment has to be replaced.

Demand segmentation has the disadvantage of high overheads and is not an optimal means for making best use of the resources of a computer system. It suffers from external fragmentation. The problem of external fragmentation can be reduced by taking the size of segment (to be brought into the memory) into consideration when the segment replacement decision takes place.

EXERCISES

9.1 Explain the term `virtual memory'.

9.2 How is swapping used in the implementation of virtual memory?

9.3 How can a "dirty bit/modify bit" improve the performance of a virtual memory system?

9.4 How can the performance of demand paging mechanism degrade?

9.5 What is a page fault? How is it serviced?

9.6 Explain demand paging with the help of an example.

9.7 Is page fault a form of interrupt?

9.8 What is Belady's anomaly? Does LRU algorithm for page replacement, suffer from this anomaly? Justify your answer with the help of an example.

9.9 Consider that the pages are referenced in the following sequence :

1, 2, 3, 4, 2, 1, 5, 6, 2, 1, 2, 3, 7, 6, 3, 2, 1, 2, 3, 6.

How many page faults would occur for the following replacement algorithms, assuming one, two, three, and four frames?

1. LRU
2. FIFO
3. Optimal

9.10 If demand segmentation is used for virtual memory implementation, do you think that it will be necessary to consider "the size of the segment (in demand)" in the segment replacement algorithm.

9.11 What is thrashing? What is the cause of thrashing? How can the system eliminate the problem of thrashing?

9.12 Compare the different page replacement algorithms with respect to :

— Time complexity

— Cost of implementation.

9.13 Explain the steps that need to be taken when a page fault occurs in a paged virtual memory system (assume there is a free frame available).

9.14 Explain the steps that need to be taken when a page fault occurs in a paged virtual memory system (assume there is no free frame available).

CHAPTER

10

File System Interface and Implementation

OVERVIEW

The first part of this chapter introduces file : an abstract data type defined and implemented by the operating system. File concepts containing naming of files, file operations, file attributes have been discussed. File access methods – 'sequential' and 'random' have been described and their comparison has been done in brief. Directory structures, directory operations and access paths have been explained in detail. Hierarchical directory structures have been discussed. A brief notion of file protection has been introduced. The second part of this chapter deals with file system implementation issues. It involves the discussion of various methods of allocating space to the files on the disk and management of free space on the disk.

10.1. INTRODUCTION

It becomes essential to store information for **long-term** so that it can be accessed at any time. As seen in earlier chapters, it is also essential to make **data sharable** among various processes. Also that this information can be **huge in size** and therefore, must be accommodated on the appropriate storage devices. Thus, these are three essential requirements for long-term information storage. It indicates that information should be stored on disks and other external media in units called files. Processes running in the system can read or write these storage media via files. Information stored in files must be persistent *i.e.* it should not be affected by process creation and termination.

Files are managed by the operating system. How are they structurted, named, accessed, protected and implemented are few major considerations in operating system design. The part of operating system, which deals with files, is known as the file system.

10.2. FILE CONCEPTS

Physically, a file is the smallest allotment of secondary storage device *e.g.* disks. Logically a file is sequence of logical records *i.e.* a sequence of bits and bytes. A file has various attributes like name, type, location, size, protection, time and data of creation, user information etc. Let us look at various attributes from the user's point of view.

10.2.1 File Naming

The exact rules for file naming vary somewhat from system to system, but all operating systems allow strings of one to eight letters as legal file names. Thus 'ekta', 'walia', 'lecturer' are possible file names. Frequently digits and few special characters are also permitted therefore, file names like 'OSI', 'Sys_Prog' are also permitted. Similarly, some file systems distinguish between upper case and lower case letters, whereas others do not.

Almost every operating system supports two parts of a file name, where the two parts are separated by a period, as in 'ekta.c'. The part following the period is called the file extension, and usually indicates something about the file. The size of this extension can be upto 3 characters in MS-DOS whereas, UNIX permits that a file may have two or more extensions like 'ekta.c.z'., where '*.z*' indicates that a file has been compressed or zipped. Figure 10.1 shows some typical file extensions.

EXTENSION	MEANING
file.bak	Backup file
file.bas	BASIC source program
file.bin	Executable binary program
file.c	C source program
file.dat	Data file
file.doc	Documentation file
file.ftn	FORTRAN source program
file.hlp	Text for HELP command
file.lib	Library of object files used by the linker
file.man	Online manual page
file.obj	Object file (compiler output, not yet linked)
file.pas	Pascal source program
file.txt	General text file

Figure 10.1 : Some typical file extensions

File extensions are important to know because they indicate a particular software needed to open a particular file e.g. a C compiler will compile only '.c' files and not any other file. Looking at the file "ekta.c", the user can identify that this is a program file in 'C' language and can be opened and complied using a 'C' compiler.

10.2.2 File Attributes

A file has a name and data. Other than this, the operating system can associate other information like data and time of file creation, file's current size etc. with a file. These are known as attributes of a file. Figure 10.2 shows a list of possible attributes. The list of these attributes varies from system to system.

File Preparation

Files exist to store information and allow it to be retrieved later. Different systems provide different operations to allow storage and retrieval. The following list shows the most common file operations available via system calls :

1. Create. A blank file is created. The purpose of this call is to create a new blank file with the specified attributes.

2. Delete. The purpose of this system call is to delete this file from the disk when it is not needed.

3. Open. Before using a file either for reading or writing, it must be opened. The purpose of this call is to allow the sytem to fetch the attributes and list of disk addresses into main memory for rapid access on subsequent calls. This is a very important concept, which relates to caching.

4. Close. When a file is no longer accessed, it must be closed using this system call.

5. Read. When a file is only to be read, this call is used. The location of the data to be read must be specified. The size of data to be read must also be specified.

6. Write. Data can be written to file with this system call. The data is written at the current position in the file and if the current position is at the end of the file, then the file size increases automatically.

7. Append. This call is a restricted form of WRITE. It can only add data to the end of the file.

8. Seek. This call is used to reposition the current pointer to a specific place in the file. After this call succeeds the pointer is placed at the desired location and data is read or written there, using another system call (like READ or WRITE).

9. Get Attributes. Processes often need to know the attributes of some files to do their work. For example, a process might want to display the id of the person who created the file. Therefore, it can use this system call to get the attributes of that file.

10. Set Attributes. Using this system call, attributes of a file can be set. For example, a user may want to set its read-only flag to 1, so that it can only be read by the users and thus, cannot be written.

11. Rename. A user may need to change the name of a file very often. Therefore, this functionality is provided by RENAME system call.

FIELD	MEANING
Protection	Who can access the file and in what way
Password	Password needed to access the file
Creator	Id of person who created the file
Owner	Current owner
Read only flag	0 for read/write, 1 for read only
Hidden flag	0 for normal, 1 for do not display in listings
System flag	0 for normal file, 1 for system file
Archive flag	0 implies file has been backed up, 1 for needs to be backed up
ASCII/binary flag	0 for ASCII file, 1 for binary file
Random access flag	0 for sequential access only, 1 for random access
Record length	Number of bytes in a record
Key position	Offset of the key within each record
Key length	Number of bytes in the key field
Creation time	Date and time file was created
Time of last access	Date and time file was last accessed
Time of last change	Date and time file was last changed
Current size	Number of bytes in the file
Maximum size	Maximum size file may grow to

Figure 10.2 : Some possible file attributes

Protection, password, creator and owner attributes are basically used to protect a file from unauthorized access. Some systems provide the privilege to lock a file with some particular password. Only those users who know this password can then access this file. The flags mentioned in Figure 10.2, are used to enable or disable some specific property of a file. A file can be made read-only, hidden, system-file, and so-on by setting its read only flag to 1, its hidden flag to 1, its system flag to 1 and so on. The archive flag is a bit that keeps track of whether the file has been backed up or not? Once the backup of a file has been taken, its backup bit is set to 0. Operating system sets this bit to 1 whenever a change takes place in the contents of this file, so that it should again be backed up by the user, using a back up program. Record length, key position and key length fields are only present in files whose records can be searched using a key.

The various time attributes keep track of when the file was created, most recently accessed and most recently modified. This information may be necessary to know that if the source file has been modified after the creation of the corresponding object file, then it needs to be compiled again. Maximum size attribute is used by some systems, which require the maximum size to be specified when the file is created.

10.3. FILE ACCESS METHODS

Files can be categorized broadly into two types depending upon their access methods. Sequential files are those, which are read sequentially (one record, then another and so on) in an order, starting at the beginning to the end of the file. Sequential files can be rewound so that they can be read as often as needed. However, records in such files cannot be read out of order e.g. reading of 34th record followed by 5th record and then 1st record is not possible with sequential files. Sequential files are convenient when the storage media is serial-access *e.g.* magnetic tape rather than direct-access *e.g.* magnetic disk.

Files whose records can be read in any order are called random access files. Random access files are basically a collection of records stored on a disk and these records are numbered 1, 2, 3 and so on and therefore, can be referred to by their numbers instead of their position. Such files should be necessarily be stored on direct access media like disk.

Random access files are essential for many applications, for example, data base systems. In a banking application, a customer may want to look up his current balance. This can be easily done by locating this customer's record using his account number as a key, rather than sequentially reading the records for thousands of other customers before this customer's record is located and read.

It is worth mentioning here that not all operating systems support both sequential and random access for files. Some systems allow only sequential file access, others allow only random access. Some systems require that a file should be defined as sequential or random when it is created, so that it can be accessed in the way it has been declared.

10.3.1 Sequential Access

In this access method, data records are retrieved in the same order in which they have been stored on the disk. The organization is such that the length of each record is fixed and can not be changed. The data contents can only be replaced by fresh contents. The read and write operations are performed sequentially on file contents. This access method is the simplest one as the disk head moves in one direction to access the mentioned data records. It need not jump randomly to forward and backward disk blocks suring every next retrieval. Magnetic tapes store information in sequential manner and like wise the retrieval is performed. Printing and scanning devices provide efficiency in their performance while accessing data records in an order. In case of select or update operations where random access to data records is required, the sequential access gives inefficient results.

10.3.2 Random Access

In case of random access the record is searched from the disk based on its direct address information. The technique used is Hashing. In hashing every record is associated with a key number to preprocess the address calculation. Hash function is used to obtain absolute address of a particular record. Any further search algorithm is not required to fetch the mentioned data record. The only restriction here is that hash table used to store entries must be of fixed size and comparable to the number of data records so that all data records get uniformly distributed among all the table entries. e.g. suppose there are 10 records and hash table size is also 10. Every record will be assigned an address value from 1-10 based on the hash function result. Similarly with the help of hash function the data values will be retrieved at any moment of time. The complexity involved in this method is the selection of hash function. A hash function should be such that makes uniform distribution of records among the provided memory space. Also hash function must not generate similar address values for more than one data records. The situation where more than one records are assigned same address is called collision state. If the record count is limited or small the hashing technique proves to be very beneficial for query processing, but as the number of records increases the complexity of hash function increases to provided maximum unique address distribution among available records. There are many schemes provided to handle collisions. The important technique used in this concern is chaining. In chaining, a linked list is attached to every hash table entry and similar address data records are made to get added up to that list. Another technique is Rehashing, where the hash address obtained is further processed with another hash function to generate final hash address. Figure 10.3 shows how hashing is implemented.

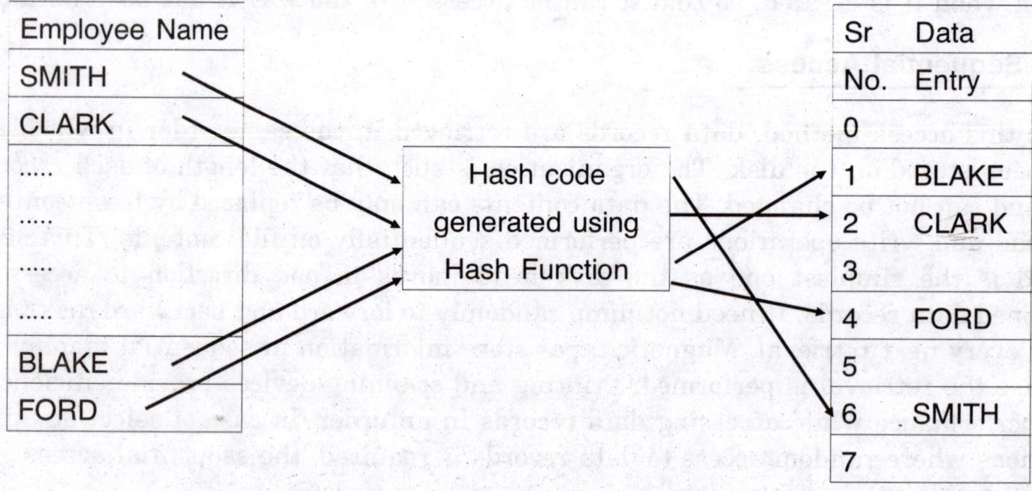

Figure 10.3 : Hashing implementation

10.3.3 Indexed Access

Indexed file approach is helpful with multiple attribute fields like in database files. In these files, every field is associated with an index key. While querying data the index key is kept in the memory and related records are fetched from the disk. These indexing keys help distinguishing one record from the other. Indexes are managed in various ways like single level index and multilevel index. These are also called dense and sparse index respectively. In single level, every record has an index value associated with it. These index values can get associated with primary or secondary index key. In case of multi level index, a group of entries have one index key associated and rest of the entries in that group are further being indexed based on another key criteria. Indexes require limited memory space for execution as only index key values are required at a moment in memory. In other cases whole data file need to be in main memory. This results in wastage of memory area allocated to a process. In query processing generally we deal with just one third of the whole contents and rest of the memory space occupied is always a waste. Indexed access method lies between sequential and random access and provide benefit in case of large size of record files. Figure 10.4 shows indexed access implementation.

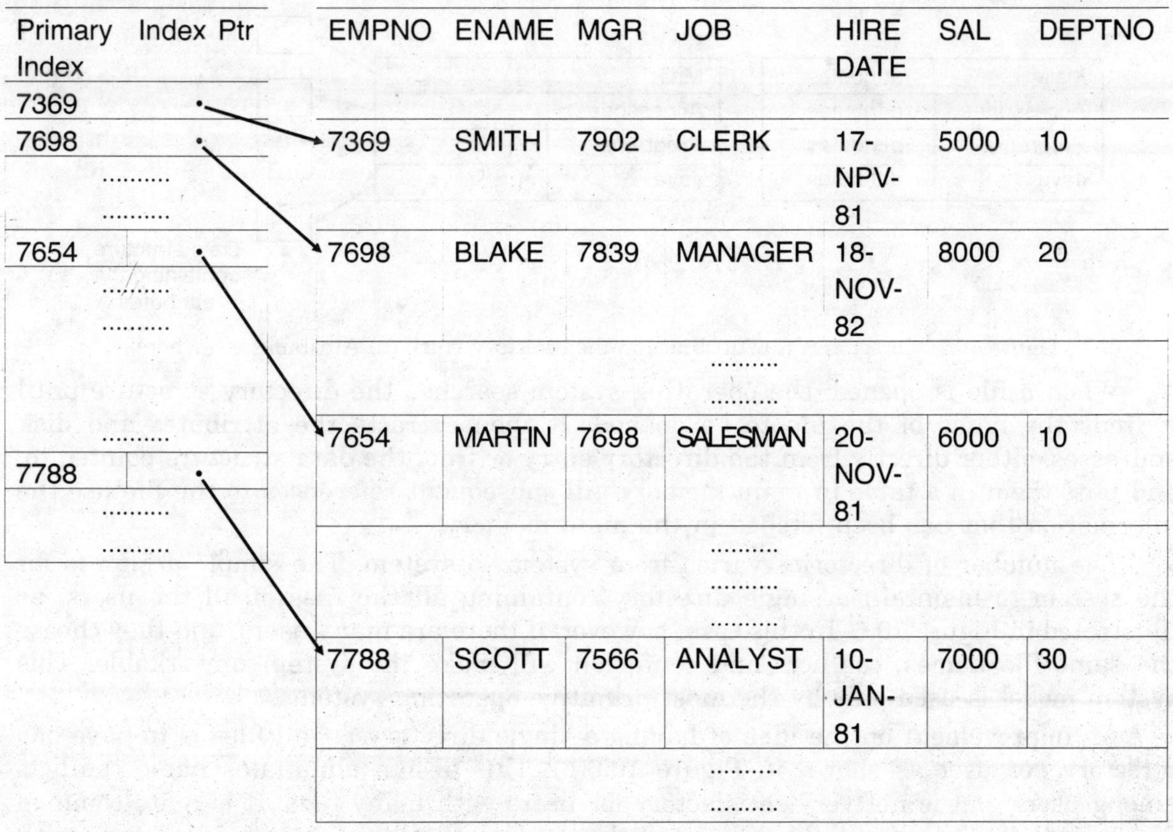

Figure 10.4 : Indexed Access Implementation

10.4. DIRECTORY STRUCTURE

To keep track of files, the file systems normally provide directories, which, in many systems, are themselves treated as files. A directory contains information about files. Thus, it is central to the functioning of the file system. A directory is used as a means to group the files owned by a user. This notion of grouping can be extended to permit grouping of files according to some user-defined criteria. This section focuses upon directories, their properties, organization and the operations that can be performed on them.

10.4.1 Hierarchical Directory Systems

A directory typically contains a number of entries, one per file. One possibility is that each entry contains the file name, the file attributes, and the disk address where the file is stored. Another possibility is that a directory entry holds the file name and a pointer to another data structure where the attributes and disk addresses are found. Both of these systems are commonly used. Figure 10.5 depicts the two ways to represent a directory.

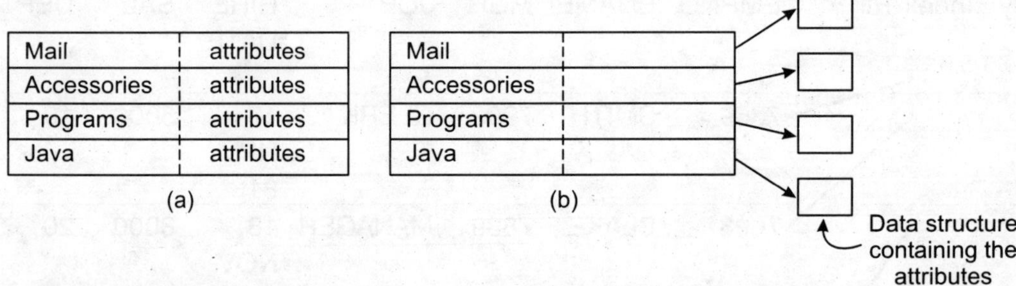

Figure 10.5 : Directories (a) Attributes in the directory entry (b) Attributes elsewhere

When a file is opened, the operating system searches the directory structure until it finds the name of the file to be opened. It then extracts the attributes and disk addresses, either directly from the directory entry or from the data structure pointed to, and puts them in a table in main memory. All subsequent references to the file use the information that has been fetched in the main memory.

The number of directories varies from system to system. The simple design is for the system to maintain a single directory containing all the files of all the users, as illustrated in Figure 10.6. In this case, however, if there are many users, and they choose the same file names, conflicts and confusion will make the system unworkable. This system model is used only by the most primitive operating systems.

An improvement on the idea of having a single directory for all files is to have one directory per user as shown in Figure 10.6(b). This design eliminates name conflicts among users, but is not very satisfactory for users with many files. It is quite common for users to want to group their files together in logical ways. For example, I may wish to have a collection of the files related to operating system concepts (to be consulted by

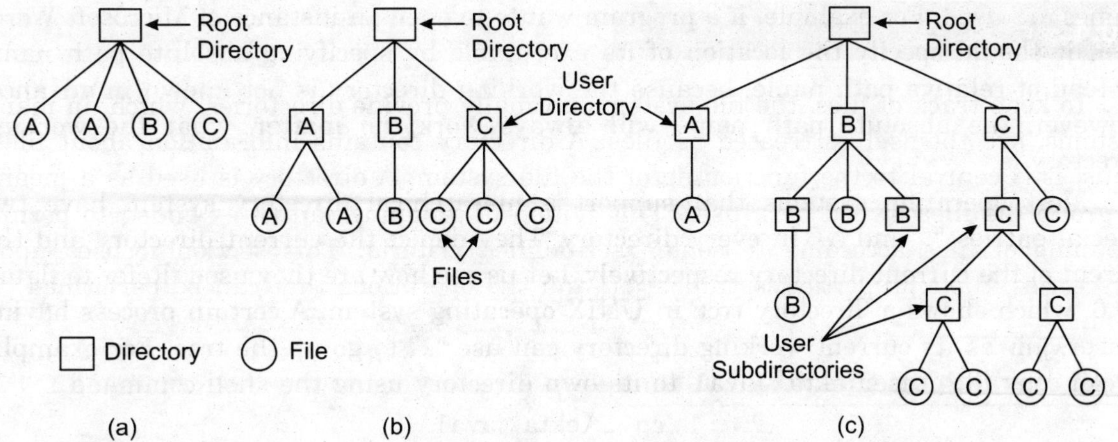

Figure 10.6 : Three file system designs (a) Single directory shared by all users; (b) One directory per user; (c) Arbitrary tree per user. The letters indicate name of files or directories

me while writing this book). Similarly, I may wish to have a collection of files containing assignments submitted by my students learning Java or a collection of files containing the source code of my project work etc.

A general hierarchy (*i.e.*, a tree of directories) is thus needed. With this approach, each user can have as many directories as are needed so that files can be grouped together in natural ways. This approach is shown in Figure 10.6 (c). Here the directories A, B and C contained in the root directory each belong to a different user and two (B and C) of them have subdirectories for two different projects.

10.4.2 Access paths

When the file system is organized as a directory tree, some way is needed to specify file names uniquely. Two methods are possible for specifying access paths :

(1) Absolute path name. It is a listing of the directories and files from the root directory to the intended file. For example, the path 'c:/windows/programs/spss.exe' means that the root directory contains a subdirectory 'windows', which further contains a subdirectory 'programs', that contains an executable "spss.exe".

Absolute path names are always unique as they start the specifications from the root directory. Mostly '/' is used as a separator in the path name string. Some operating systems use '\' or '>' as path name separators.

(2) Relative path name. This uses the concept of current directory (also known as working directory). A user can specify a particular directory as his current working directory and all the path names instead of being specified from the root directory are specified relative to the working directory. For example, if the current working directory is '\user\curr', then the file whose absolute path is '\user\curr\ekta' can be referred simply as 'ekta'. Thus, relative path name specifies the access path relative to the current working directory. What happens when a program needs to access a specific file without regard to what the working directory is ? This can lead to errors if relative path names are used. For example, if a program wants to open an instance of Microsoft Word, then it should specify the location of its executable by specifying absolute path name instead of relative path name, because the working directory is not known in advance. However, the absolute path name will always work, no matter, what the working directory is.

Most operating systems that support a hierarchical directory system have two special entries "." and ".." in every directory. They depict the current directory and the parent of the current directory respectively. Let us see how are they used. Refer to figure 10.6, which shows a directory tree in UNIX operating system. A certain process having '\user\jim' as its current working directory can use ".." to go up the tree. For example, it can copy file '\user\ekta\Java1' to its own directory using the shell command :

cp .. \ekta\java1

The first path instructs the system to go upwards (to the 'user' directory), and then to go down to the directory 'ekta' to find the file java1 there.

The second argument of this command specifies the current directory. Thus, this cp command copies the file 'java1' to the current working directory. This command is equivalent to

cp \user\ekta\java1 •

The use of dot here saves the user from the trouble of typing 'java1' again as the second argument.

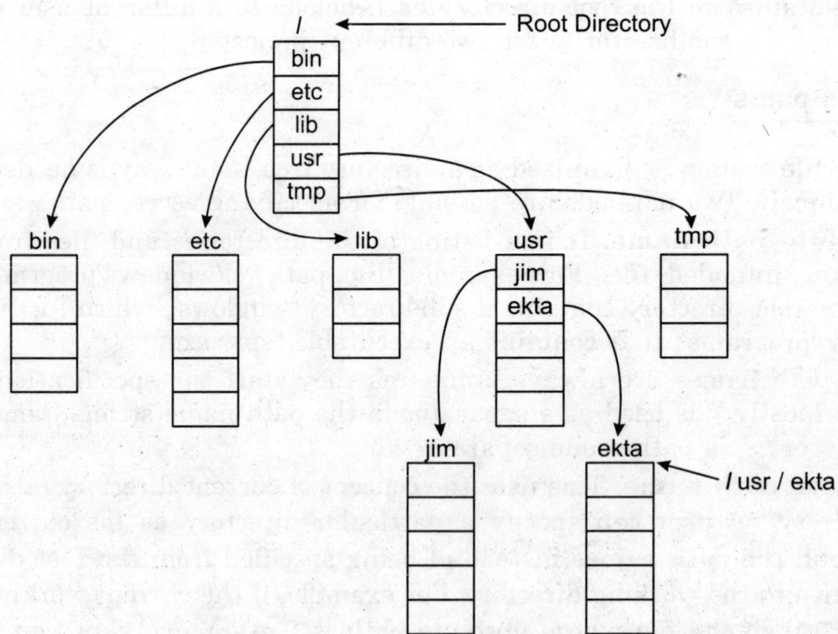

Figure 10.7 : A UNIX directory tree

Links

The access path information described so far has been based on the parent child relationship in the file system directory hierarchy. This can make access paths long and combersome to write. A link is a directed connection in the file system hierarchy between two existing files. A link is thus an ordered triple :

(<from_filename>, <to_filename>, <linkname>)

where <from_filename> is a directory, <to_filename> is a directory or a file and <linkname> is a symbolic name for the link. Once a link is established, the <to_filename> can be accessed as it were a child of <from_filename> i.e. as if it were a file named <linkname> in the directory <from_filename>. Figure 10.8 shows the implementation of a link. It considers A to be a user directory and establishes a link named *mylink* between the directory A and the file 'ekta' whose access path is /A/Projn/bookonos/ekta. Note that the existence of links makes the directory structure a *generalized graph* rather than a *tree*. A file may have multiple access paths in the file system. In fact, access paths may even contain loops.

The Figure 10.8 shows that the link permits \A\projn\bookonos\ekta to be accessed by the name \A\mylink.

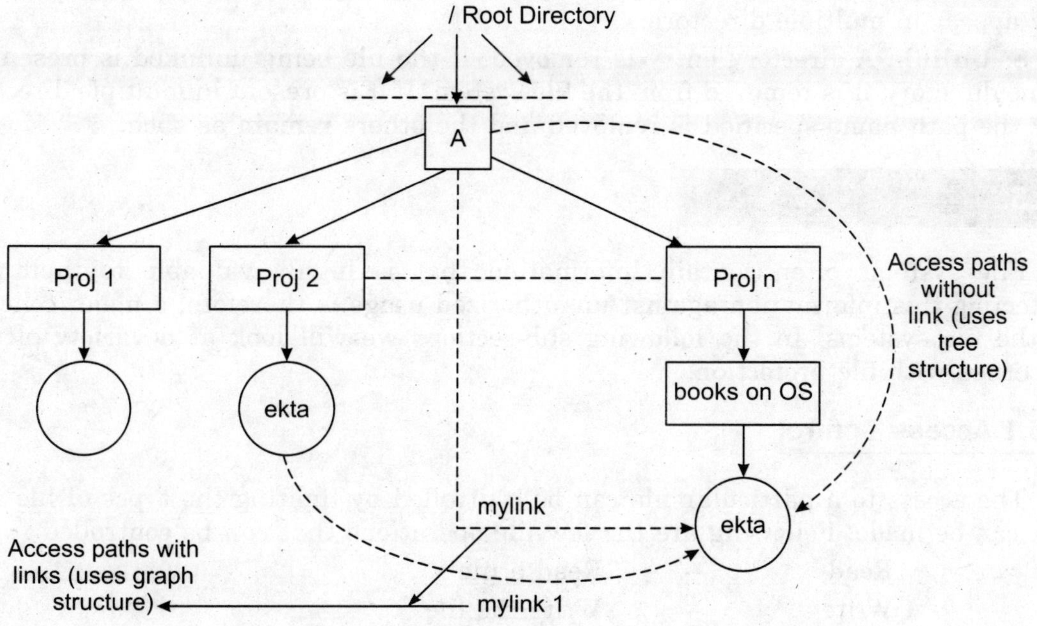

Figure 10.8 : Generalized graph structure using links

10.4.3 Directory Operations

Many system calls are allowed for managing directories. They vary from system to system. This part of text discusses some common system calls used to manipulate directories.

1. Create. A directory is created. It is empty except for dot (.) and dotdot (..), which are put there automatically by the system.

2. Delete. A directory is deleted. Only an empty directory can be deleted. A directory containing only dot and dotdot is considered empty, as these usually cannot be deleted. In order to delete a directory having subdirectories, first the subdirectories should be deleted.

3. Opendir. Directories can be opened for reading it. For example, to list all the files in a directory, a listing program opens the directory to read out the names of all the files it contains. Before a directory can be read, it must be opened.

4. Closedir. When a directory has been read, it should be closed to free up internal table space in main memory.

5. Readdir. This call returns the next entry in an open directory. Formerly, it was possible to read directories using the usual READ system call, but that approach has the disadvantage of forcing the programmer to know and deal with the internal structure of directories. In contrast, READDIR always returns one entry in a standard format, no matter which of the possible directory structures is being used.

6. Rename. Directories can be renamed just like files.

7. Link. This system call specifies an existing file and a path name, and creates a link from the existing file to the name specified by the path. In this way, the same file may appear in multiple directories.

8. Unlink. A directory entry is removed. If the file being unlinked is present only in one directory, it is removed from the file system. If it is present in multiple directories, only the path name specified is removed and the others remain as such.

10.5. FILE PROTECTION

File systems often contain information that is highly valuable to their users. Protecting this information against unauthorized usage is therefore, a major concern of all the file systems. In the following sub-sections we will look at a variety of issues concerned with file protection.

10.5.1 Access Control

The access to a particular file can be controlled by limiting the types of file access that can be made. Following are the few file operations that can be controlled :

Read	–	Read a file
Write	–	Write the file
Append	–	Append a file
Delete	–	Delete a file
List	–	List the name and attributes of a file
Rename	–	Rename a file
Edit	–	Chaning the contents of a file
Copy	–	Make a copy of a file.

One way to control these operations in through access control lists (ACLs) and groups. An access list may be associated with each file and directory. This list may contain the user name and the types of access allowed for each user. The operating system checks this access control list (accociated with a file) whenever a user requests an access to a particular file. If that user is listed for the requested access, the access is allowed. Otherwise, user is denied access to the file.

The main problem with access controls list (ACLs) is their length. If we want to allow every-one to read a file, we must list all users with read access. To overcome this problem many systems classify the users of a file into three types :

1. **Owner.** The user who created the file.
2. **Group.** A set of users who are sharing the file and need similar access.
3. **Universe.** All remaining users in the system constitute universe.

Thus, if a person has created a file, he/she is owner of the file. If the owner has given execute-only permission (on his file) to some set of users, then this set of users constitute a group and all users in this group have execute-only permission for the file. All the other possible users will fall into the universe category and probably may be given read-only access to the file. UNIX operating system uses this method to provide protection to the files. Access control lists should be created and maintained by some administrator, file owner or any other manager of the organization. These protection mechanisms have been taken up in detail in chapter 13 of this book.

10.5.2 Other protection mechanisms

Files can be protected by a password. The owner of a file can control its access by assigning a password. Thus, only those users who know the password, can access a particular file.

Disadvantages of this scheme are :

1. If a separate password is associated with each file, the user will have to remember so many passwords and the scheme will become impractical.
2. If only one password is used for protecting all files, then cracking of one password by an unauthorized user will enable him to access all the files.

This problem can be dealt by associating a password with a subdirectory rather than with an individual file.

10.6. FILE SYSTEM IMPLEMENTATION

So far, we have discussed the users' view of a file system. Let us now look at implementer's view. Users are concerned with how files are named, what operations are allowed on them, what the directory tree looks like, and similar interface issues. Implementers are interested in how files and directories are stored, how disk space is managed, and how to make everything work efficiently and reliably. Let us examine the file implementation issues here.

The key issue in implementing file storage is keeping track of which disk blocks go with which file. Various methods are used in different systems. In this section, we will examine a few of them.

10.6.1 Contiguous Allocation

The simplest allocation scheme is to store each file as contiguous block of data on the disk. Thus, on a disk having blocks of size 1k, a 25k file would be allocated 25 consecutive blocks. This scheme has two significant advantages :

(1) It is simple to implement because keeping a track of where a file's blocks are, is reduced to remembering one number only. This number is the disk address of the first block occupied by the file.

(2) Performance is good because entire file can be read from the disk in a single operation (just because it is stored contiguously).

Disadvantages of this scheme are :

(1) It is not feasible unless the maximum file size is known at the time of file creation. If it is not known, the operating system does not know how much disk space should be reserved.

(2) Fragmentation of the disk may occur as a result of this scheme. Therefore, space is wasted that might otherwise have been used. Compaction cannot be applied as a solution to this problem, because compaction of the disk is expensive.

10.6.2 Linked List Allocation

The second method for storing files is to keep each one as a linked list of disk blocks, as shown in Figure 10.9. The first word of each block is used as a pointer to the next one. The rest of the block is used for storing data.

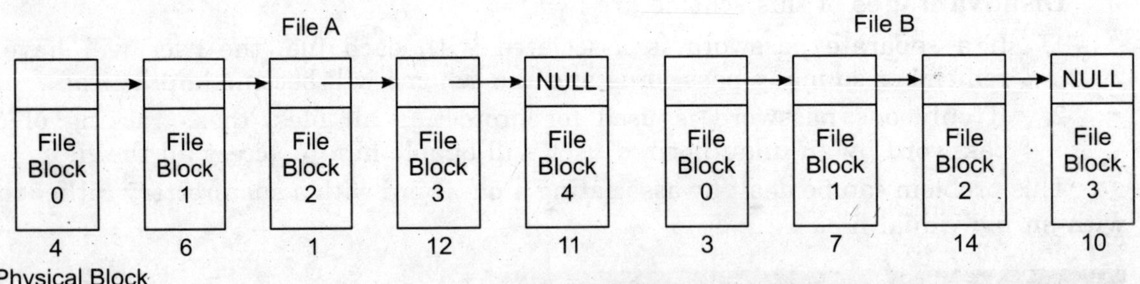

Figure 10.9 : Storing a file as a linked list of disk blocks

Advantages of this scheme are :

(1) Unlike contiguous allocation, every disk block can be utilized by this method. Thus there is least possibility of disk fragmentation.

(2) The directory entry can merely store the disk address of the first block and this can be used to find the rest of the blocks occupied by the file.

This scheme however, suffers from the following **disadvantages :**

(1) Although reading a file sequentially is easy, but random access becomes extremely slow.

(2) Pointer takes up space in each disk block and therefore, the amount of data storage in a block is no longer a power of two, which otherwise would have been a power of two. This is essential because most programs read and write data in blocks whose size is a power of two.

10.6.3 Linked List Allocation Using an Index

This scheme is an attempt to remove the disadvantages of the linked list allocation. Here, instead of having a pointer, an index is maintained. For the Figure 10.9, where the linked allocation of two files namely A and B has been shown, table or index like the one shown in Figure 10.10 can be used. Using the table of Figure 10.10, for file A we can start with the block 4 and follow the linked list all the way to the end. The same way for file B, we can start from block 3 and follow the linked list.

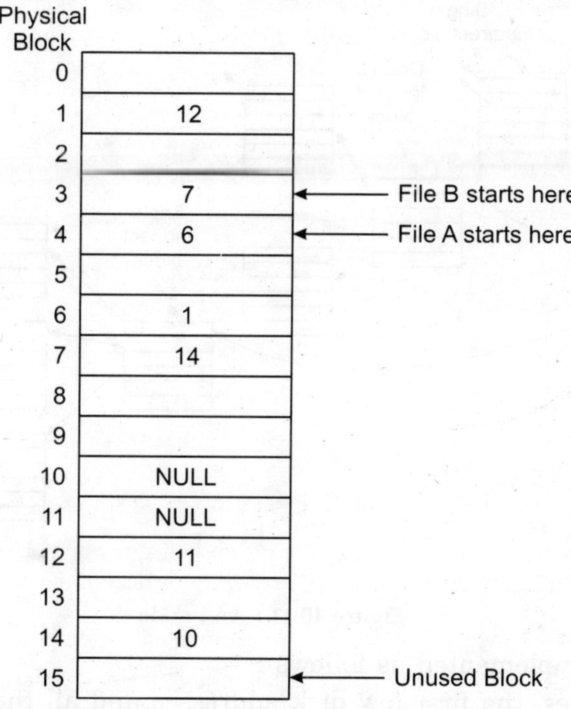

Figure 10.10 : Linked list allocation using a table in main memory

Advantages of this scheme are :

1. The entire block is available for data. No space is consumed by pointers etc.
2. Random access is easier. This is so because, no doubt, the chain has to be followed to locate a particular part of a file, but because the index is in memory, the seek operations do not involve disk references as in the previous case.

3. Here also, the directory entry can merely store the disk address of the first block and this can be used to find the rest of the blocks occupied by the file. This method is used by MS-DOS for disk allocation.

Disadvantages of this scheme are :

1. The entire index or table will have to be kept in main memory for all the time to make it work. This may prove to be hazardous if the disk is large and thus the table or index is also large.
2. Looking up for an entry in such a large index will also become very time consuming.

10.6.4 I-nodes

This method for keeping track of which block belongs to which file, is used by UNIX operating system. In this scheme, each file is associated with a little table called an i-node (index node), which lists the attributes and disk addresses of the file's blocks. I-nodes are shown in Figure 10.11.

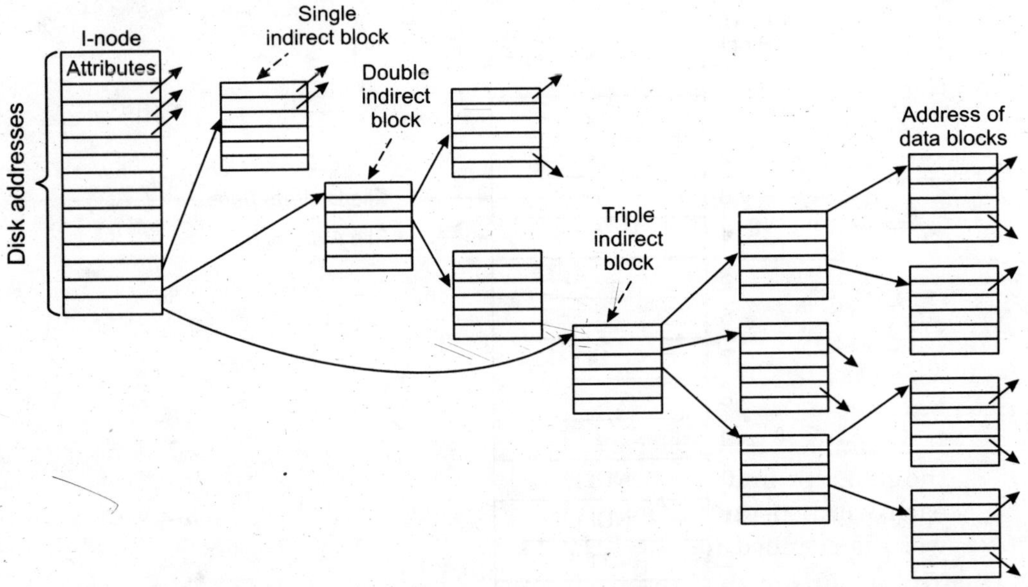

Figure 10.11 : An i-node

This scheme is implemented as follows :

1. For small files, the first few disk addresses and all the necessary information are stored in the i-node itself. Whenever a file is opened, all this information is fetched from disk to main memory.
2. For somewhat larger file, one of the addresses in the i-node is the address of a disk block called single indirect block. This block contains additional disk addresses.

3. For even more large file, the i-node may contain another address which is the address of a disk block called a double indirect block. This block contains the addresses of the blocks containing the lists of single indirect blocks. Each of these single indirect blocks point to a few hundred data blocks. Similarly, a triple indirect block can also be used.

10.7. FREE SPACE MANAGEMENT

It becomes necessary to reuse the disk space created after deleting the files so that new files can use it. The operating system maintains a free-space list to keep track of free disk space. Whenever, a new file is created, the free-space list is searched for the required amount of space. This free space is allocated to the newly created file and its entry is then removed from the free-space list. When a file is deleted, the disk space freed up by it is then added to the free-space list.

Let us now understand the various possible methods of implementing free-space list:

10.7.1 Bit map

The free space list is implemented as a bit map. Every bit represents a block on the disk. The bit for a block is 1 if it is free and it is 0 if the block is allocated. This bit map is stored on specific place on the disk. The free-space bit map is as shown in Figure 10.12.

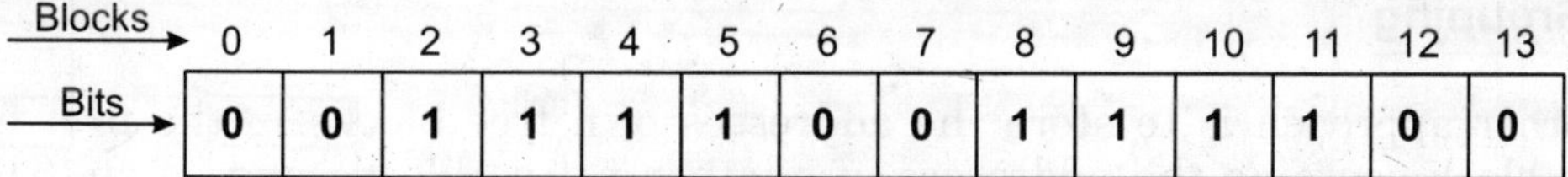

Figure 10.12 : Bit Map

The Figure 10.12 indicates that the blocks 2, 3, 4, 5, 8, 9, 10, 11 are free and rest of the blocks are allocated.

Advantages of this approach are :

1. It is simple and efficient to find the first block or n consecutive free blocks on the disk. To find the first free block, the operating system checks sequentially each word in the bit map to see whether that value is not 0. The first non-0 word is scanned for the first 1 bit, which is the location of the first free block.

Disadvantages of this approach are :

1. This may require special hardware support (bit operation) to find the first '1' in a word if it is not zero.
2. Bit maps are inefficient unless they are kept in main memory and are written to disk occasionally for recovery needs. If the disk size is large, the corresponding bit map is large and thus keeping it in the main memory is not possible. Consider that the disk size is 1 GB $\Rightarrow 2^{30}$ bytes and the block size is 2^{12} bytes then the number of blocks will be $2^{30}/2^{12} = 2^{18}$ and corresponding to each block, a bit will be there in the bit map. This implies that size of bit map will be 2^{18} bits = 256 KB.

10.7.2 Linked list

This approach maintains a linked list of all the free disk blocks. The first free block in the list can be pointed out by a head pointer, which is kept in a special location on the disk. Figure 10.13 shows the linked list of free blocks represented by bit map shown in Figure 10.12.

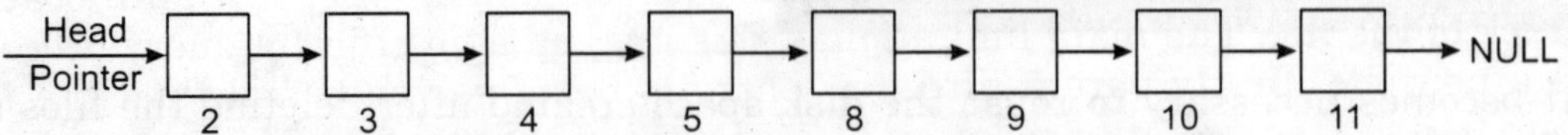

Figure 10.13 : Linked free space list on disk

Advantages of this approach are :

1. Whenever a file is to be allocated a free block, the operating system can simply allocate the first block in the free space-list and move the head pointer to the next free block in the list.

Disadvantages of this approach are :

1. Traversing the free space list will be very time consuming; each block will have to be read from the disk, which is read very slowly as compared to the main memory.
2. Pointers used in the linked list will consume disk space.

10.7.3 Grouping

Another approach is to store the addresses of n free blocks in the first free block. The last block contains the addresses of another n free blocks and so on. This means that first n–2 blocks of these blocks are actually free (as the first and last blocks of the group will contain addresses). The advantage of this approach over linked list approach is that by accessing only one block, the addresses of a large number of free blocks can be known at once.

10.7.4 Counting

Another approach takes into consideration that generally, several contiguous blocks may be allocated or freed simultaneously, particularly when contiguous allocation algorithm has been used for allocating disk space. Thus, instead of keeping a list of addresses of n free blocks, it is more convenient to keep the address of the first free blocks and the number n of free contiguous blocks that follow the first block. Therefore, each entry in the free space list then consists of a disk address and a count. This may make the overall list shorter in size.

10.8. DIRECTORY IMPLEMENTATION

Directory Structures are implemented in hard disk in various ways. These different techniques are designed to makes retrieval of files and data contents easy.

10.8.1 Linked List

The easiest way to manage directories is with linked list data structure. Every directory entry contains pointer to the list of file names. Every file is pointed to the starting address of its data contents. Directories manage the information regarding individual file associated with it. It maintains file id, name, type, size and location to keep track of the file. The main limitation of this method is in efficient query processing. To add a new file, firstly parent directory entry is being searched and then the link is added up to it. Like wise after deleting file contents, file entry from the parent directory entry has to be deleted. To improve processing time required for search and insert, caching technique is used. It keeps track of the recently used directories to make the process faster in case same directory is being fetched again and again. After deletion of a file entry, linked list node is managed in free node list. With the help of sorting technique we can make the search process quite efficient. By using binary search the time required will reduce to $\log_2 n$ for n number of entries. This technique is also not without its limitations as insertion and deletion requires proper positioning of file entries.

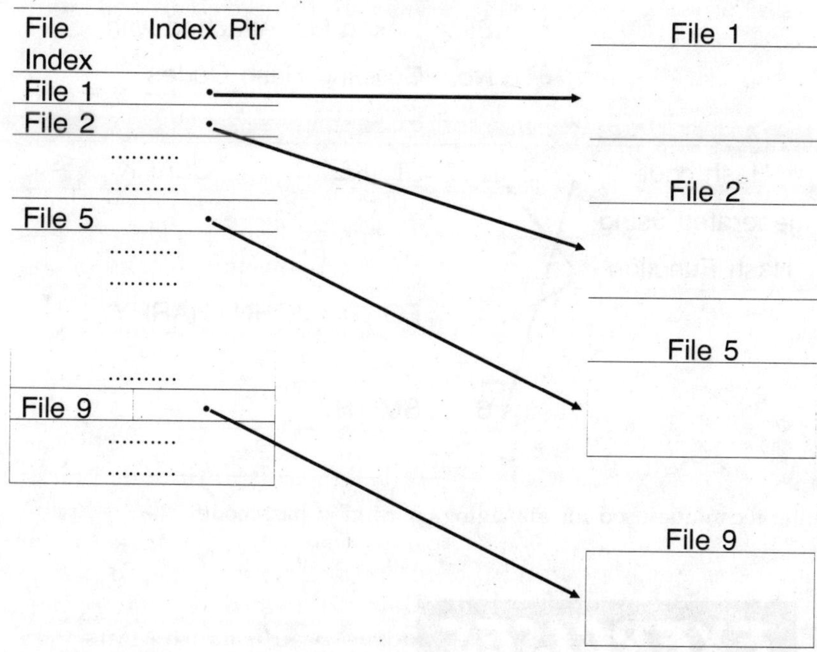

Figure 10.14 : Linked list directory implementation

10.8.2 Hashing

Due to limitations of the former technique, hash data structure is used along with the linked list. Hash table contains address entries for every file name calculated with the help of Hash Function. These entries are pointed in the linked list pointer field. In this way every file entry need just to check the corresponding hash table entry to get the respective address. The search is not required any more. The hash function is the main computation part in generating address entry. The selection of hash function should be such that it makes uniform distribution of file entries in the hash table.

The drawbacks of this technique are :

i. Hash table must be of the size comparable to the number of file entries available. Generally hash table is a fixed data structure.

ii. Hash function becomes complex with the increase in number of entries in the table.

iii. Some times hash function generates same address value for more than one file entries. This situation is called the collision state. This must not arise but if it happens, collision needs to be resolved. There are various algorithms provided to manage collision. The important one are : Chaining and Rehashing. In Chaining, a linked list is assigned to every hash table entry. The entries with similar address values are stored in these individual lists. Using rehashing, the coinciding entry is further being processed using another hash function. The next generated address becomes the final destination address for that file entry.

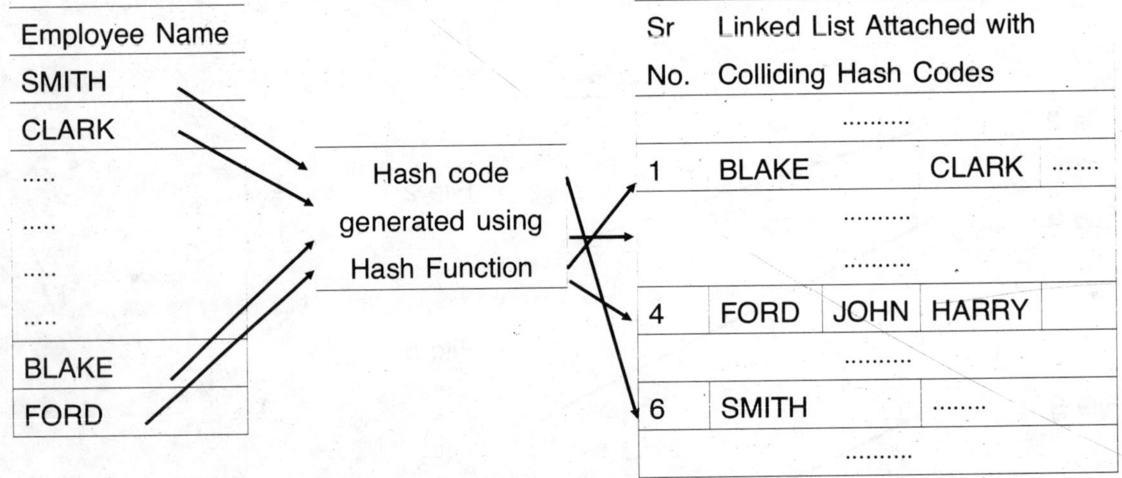

Figure 10.15 : Chaining technique used for managing collision in hash codes

EXERCISES

10.1 What is the difference between absolute and relative path name of a file ?

10.2 Compare sequential and random file access methods with respect to their usefulness in today's applications.

10.3 What is the necessity of different directories for different users ?

10.4 Explain various file allocation methods and compare them with respect to space and time consumed by each of them.

10.5 What is i-node ? How is it is better than simple indexed allocation method ?

10.6 We have learnt in this chapter that fragmentation on a disk could be eliminated by compaction. But disks do not have relocation or base registers (such as those that are used for memory compaction), so how can the files be relocated? Give three reasons why relocation of files on disks is often avoided.

10.7 We have learnt in this chapter that bit maps are inefficient unless the entire map is kept in main memory (and is written to disk occasionally for recovery needs). Do you think there is a possibility of inconsistency between the bit map loaded into the main memory and that on the disk? If yes, how will it be ensured that such inconsistency should not occur.

(**Hint:** situation like bit for block i is 1 in memory and is 0 on the disk should be avoided. Solution is to set bit for block i to 1 on disk. Allocate this block i and set bit for block i to 1 in memory).

10.8 Explain the purpose of links with the help of an example.

10.9 If you have to maintain a railway reservation application, what file organization will you choose for it and why ?

10.10 Consider a file system where a file can be deleted and its disk space reclaimed while links to that file still exist. What problems may occur if a new file is created in the same storage area or with the same absolute path name ? How can these problems be avoided?

10.11 What criteria should be used to decide which strategy (contiguous, linked, indexed allocation) is best utilized for a particular file?

CHAPTER

11

Device Management and Storage Structures

OVERVIEW

The first part of this chapter discusses the various device management functions of an operating system. It gives a brief introduction to the concept of dedicated, shared and virtual devices. It also discusses in brief, the various components of an I/O subsystem i.e. I/O channel, I/O control unit, I/O traffic controller, I/O device handler and I/O scheduler.

The second part of this chapter discusses the secondary storage device-magnetic disk and tertiary storage devices - floppy disk, CD-ROM etc. The magnetic disk structure and scheduling algorithms have been explained in depth. Disk management issues like and block recovery, low-level formatting etc. have been described next. Swap space management on the disk has also been explained with respect to the operating system's responsibilities. A brief introduction to various tertiary storage devices is being followed up by the discussion of operating system's capabilities to use these tertiary storage devices.

11.1. DEVICE MANAGEMENT FUNCTIONS

As the two main jobs of a computer are I/O and processing, therefore, it becomes essential to know the role of an operating system in managing and controlling the I/O operations and I/O devices.

The device management functions that must be performed by an operating system are :

1. Track the status of each device (such as tape drives, disk drives, printers, plotters and terminals).
2. Use algorithms to decide which process will get a device and for how long.
3. Allocate the devices.

4. Deallocate the devices at two levels :
   - At command level, when I/O command has been executed and the device has been temporarily released.
   - At process level, when process has terminated and the device has been permanently released.

11.2. ALLOCATING DEVICES

The devices can be managed and allocated by an operating system in three possible ways.

- Dedicated
- Shared
- Virtual

11.2.1 Dedicated devices

An operating system can use a device in a dedicated manner by assigning it to only one process at a time, such device will remain assigned to only one process at a time and will serve that process till it terminates. There are certain devices that can be managed and used in this manner only. Examples of such devices are tape drives, plotters etc. These devices demand this kind of allocation scheme, as it is difficult for them to be shared.

The **disadvantages** of this scheme are:

1. It can be a very inefficient scheme especially when device is not used 100 percent of time. System may not always get full utilization of that device.
2. Another obvious disadvantage of this scheme is that the device cannot be shared among different user processes.

11.2.2 Shared devices

In this scheme, the operating system can assign a device in such a way that it can be shared among several processes. Examples of the devices that can be shared include printers, hard disks etc. Several processes can share them at same time by interleaved execution of their requests.

However, the device manager must carefully control this interleaving of process requests. In case, two requests from two different processes arrive at the same time, then such conflicts must be resolved with the help of predetermined policies which can decide that which request should be handled first.

This may be done partially by software (the I/O scheduler and traffic controller) or entirely by hardware (as in some computer with very sophisticated channels and control units). Policy for establishing which process' request is to be satisfied first might be based on a priority list or on the system output (for example, by choosing whichever request is nearest to the current position of the head of the disk).

The advantage of this scheme is that the device utilization reaches almost 100 percent if it is shared among several processes and thus kept busy almost at every instance.

11.2.3 Virtual Devices

Some devices that would normally have to be dedicated (e.g. card readers, printers) may be converted into shared devices through techniques such as SPOOLing (Simultaneous Peripheral Operations On Line). For example, a SPOOLing program can read and copy all card input onto a disk at high speed. Later, when a process tries to read a card, the SPOOLing program intercepts the request and converts it to a read from the disk. Since several users may easily share a disk, we can easily convert a dedicated device to a shared device, changing one card reader into many "virtual" card readers. This technique is equally applicable to a large number of peripheral devices, such as teletypes, printers, and most dedicated slow input/output devices.

Another example is; Printers are converted to sharable devices through a SPOOLing program that re-routes all printing requests to the disk. The disk sends the output to the printer (for printing) only when all of the other requests that have been lined up before this request have been finished.

But to the user who has just now given a request for printing, it appears that this system has its own dedicated printer attached to it because the moment he gives printing command, and the SPOOLing occurs he can resume his work. Thus, this technique can convert one printer into several "virtual" printers, thus improving both its performance and use.

We further discuss the need for having virtual devices, the old solutions to meet the requirements and the new concept of virtual system.

Need for virtual devices

Devices such as card readers, punches, and printers present two serious problems that hamper effective device utilization.

1. Each of these devices performs best when there is a steady, continuous stream of requests at a specified rate that matches its physical characteristics (*e.g.*, 2000 cards per minute read rate, 2000 lines per minute print rate, etc.). If a program attempts to generate requests faster than the device's performance rate, the program must wait for a significant amount of time. On the other hand, if a program generates requests at a much lower rate, the device is idle much of the time and is substantially underutilized.
2. These devices must be dedicated to a single program at a time. Thus, since most programs perform some input and output, we would require as many card readers and printers as we have programs being multiprogrammed. This would normally be uneconomical because most programs use only a fraction of the device's capacity. Many other devices, such as plotters, graphic displays, and typewriter terminals, have similar problems.

11.2.3.1 Historical Solutions

These problems would disappear, or at least decrease, if it were possible to use Direct Access Storage Devices for all input and output. A single DASD can be efficiently shared and simultaneously used for reading and/or writing data by many programs.

Furthermore, DASDs provide very high performance rates, especially if the data are blocked, thereby decreasing the amount of wait time for programs that require substantial amounts of input/output.

Although theoretically appealing, the use of DASDs for all input and output is impractical. How do we get out input data into the DASD? What do we do with the output data recorded on the output DASD ? These problems are practically hard to solve.

1. Offline Peripheral Operations

A solution to this problem can be found in the three-step process illustrated in figure 11.1. At step 1 we use a separate computer whose only function is to read cards at maximum speed and record the corresponding information on a DASD. Computer 1 may use two or more card readers, depending upon the amount of input that must be transcribed.

At step 2 the DASD containing the input recorded by computer 1 is moved over to the main processing computer (Computer 2). This step corresponds to the one mentioned in Section 11.2.3.2. Multiple programs can be in execution, each reading its respective

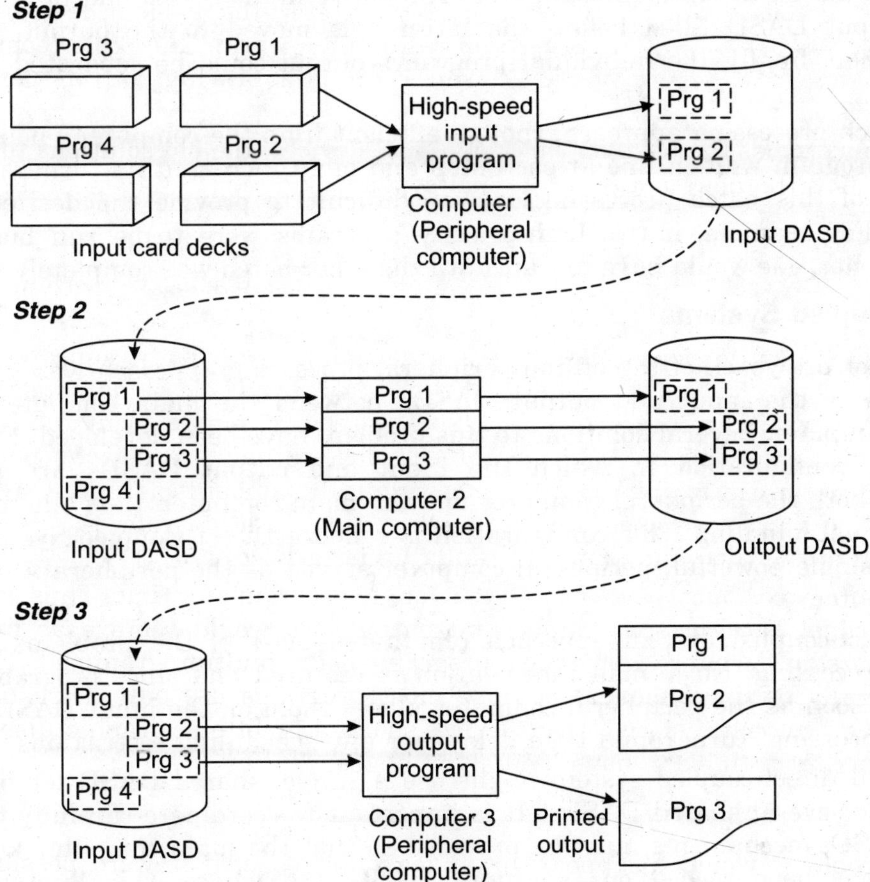

Figure 11.1. : Offline Peripheral Operations

input from the input DASD and writing its output onto an output DASD. Note in this example, that it is possible to multiprogram three programs even though only two physical card readers are assumed to exist (on computer 1 at step 1).

Finally, at step 3, the output DASD is moved to a third computer that reads the recorded output at high speed and prints the information on the printers.

The method described above was used quite extensively during the 1960s. The work performed by computers 1 and 3 was termed offline peripheral processing and the computers were called peripheral computers because they performed no computation but merely transferred information from one peripheral device to another. Since this operation was performed independent of the main computer, this was "offline" operation.

The offline peripheral processing technique solved the problems presented earlier, but it also introduced several new problems in regard to (1) human intervention, (2) turnaround, and (3) scheduling. Since human operators were required to move the input DASDs from the input peripheral computer to the main computer and to perform a simpler task for output processing, there were many opportunities for human error and inefficiency. Many programs (i.e., a batch of programs) were recorded on the input DASD before it was moved to the main computer. The entire input DASD had to be processed and the output DASD filled before the latter was moved to the output peripheral computer. Then, finally, the individual program's output could be separated and given to its owner.

This batch processing approach, though efficient from the computer's point of view, made each program wait in line at each step and often increased its turnaround time. As a result of this batch processing, it was difficult to provide the desired priority scheduling. For example, if two high-priority programs were to be run but were in separate batches, one would have to wait until the other batch was completely processed.

2. Direct-Coupled Systems

The major drawback of the offline peripheral processing approach was the need to physically move the input and output DASDs between the main computer and the peripheral computer. Several solutions to this problem have been developed. Figure 11.2 illustrates a configuration in which the input and output DASDs are physically connected to both the peripheral computer and the main computer, thus eliminating the need for manual handling. This configuration is called a Direct Coupled System (DCS). Normally, a single powerful, peripheral computer served as the peripheral computer to a main computer.

The direct-coupled system approach eliminates most of the problems of offline peripheral processing. No human intervention is required and since programs can be processed as soon as the peripheral computer places them on the input DASD, there is no "batch processing" turnaround time delay, nor any scheduling restrictions.

An actual direct-coupled system might use a single, shared DASD for both input and output or several shared DASDs. It is important to coordinate carefully the use of a shared DASD; mechanisms must be provided so that the main computer knows that a program has been placed on the input DASD and where it is located; similar requirements exist for output. This coordination may increase the complexity of the system. Furthermore, since both the peripheral computer and main computer may wish to use the same DASD at the same time, there are frequent access conflicts that can reduce performance.

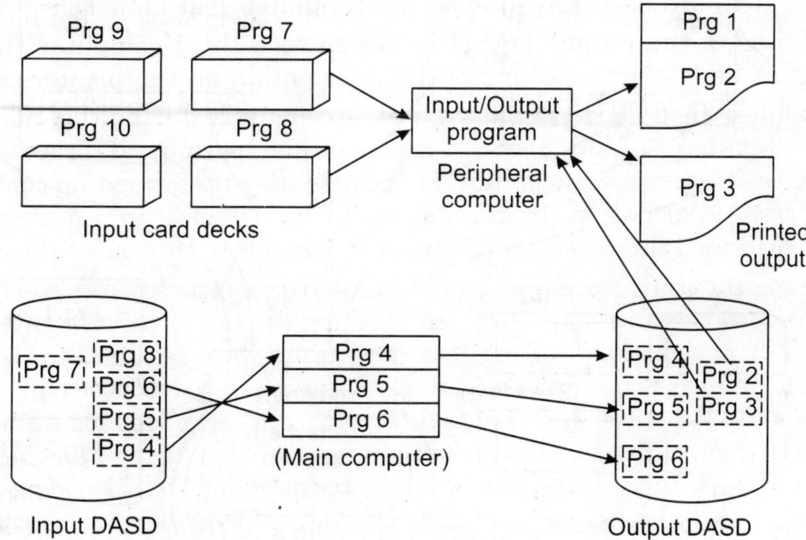

Figure 11.2 : "Direct-coupled system" configuration

3. Attached Support Processor

It is possible to directly connect the peripheral and main computers together via a high-speed connection, as illustrated in Figure 11.3(a). In this configuration the peripheral computer is called an Attached Support Processor (ASP). The support processor assumes all responsibility for controlling the input/output peripherals as well as the input and output DASD. It also performs all buffering and blocking, thereby simplifying the work required by the main computer. In this mode the attached processor has the appearance of multiple, very high-speed card readers and printers as shown in Figure 11.3(b). The attached processor produces the effect of virtual devices (*i.e.* many more and much faster devices than really exist).

The major disadvantages of this approach are that two or more processors are required, and since certain processors are assigned specific tasks (as a peripheral or main processor), it is possible that at times one processor may be idle or under-utilized while another is unable to handle its load. Thus, this configuration does not necessarily utilize all resources efficiently.

11.2.3.2 Virtual System

In all the solutions presented above it was assumed that one or more special computers were dedicated to the handling of input / output processing functions. It is possible to achieve the same by not having a separate computer system to handle the input/output. In a SPOOLing system, the main computer performs Simultaneous Peripheral Operations On Line (SPOOL), as illustrated in Figure 11.4.

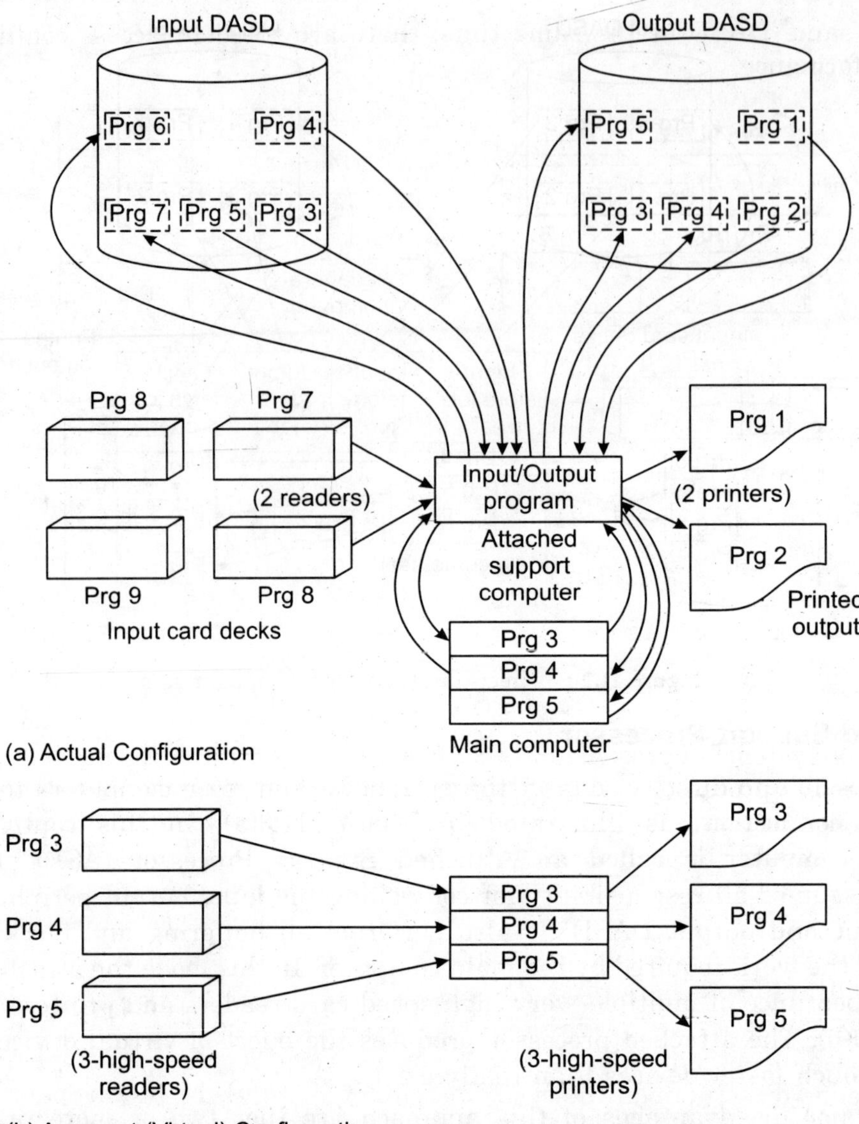

Figure 11.3 : "Attached Support Processor" Configuration

In such a system, certain programs are assigned the functions normally performed by the Attached Support Processor. These programs handle the input/output and reside permanently on the main computer. They share the use of the main computer with normal programs via multiprogramming. Since these programs are actually system programs rather than user programs, they are often given special names, such as "daemons". In modern operating systems, such special system programs perform many special functions.

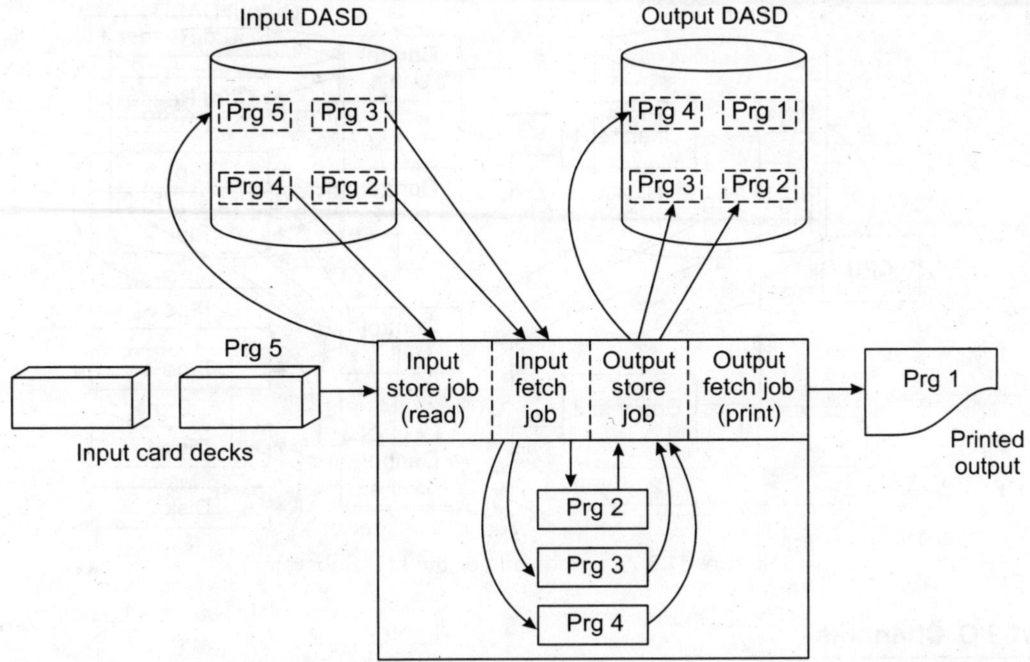

Figure 11.4 : SPOOLing system

SPOOL-systems represent a mechanism that interfaces extensively with memory management, processor management, device management, and information management. Because the programs that performs the SPOOL functions are special permanent system programs, memory management may handle these programs in different ways. As a matter of fact, in some systems these programs are incorporated into the operating system's memory area. Since there must be communication and coordination between these programs, various facilities of process management must be used. Finally, efficient buffering, blocking, and I/O control must be performed to attain good performance.

The ease of implementing a SPOOL mechanism, together with the approach to be used, depends directly upon the specific facilities provided by the memory management, processor management, information management, and device management components of the operating system.

11.3. I/O SUB-SYSTEM

Because I/O devices vary so widely in their functions and speed, a variety of methods are needed to control them. These methods form the I/O subsystem of the kernel, which separates the rest of the kernel from the complexity of managing I/O devices.

Look at the Figure 11.5, which shows the components of an I/O subsystem.

The two basic components of this subsystem are :

- I/O channels
- Control units

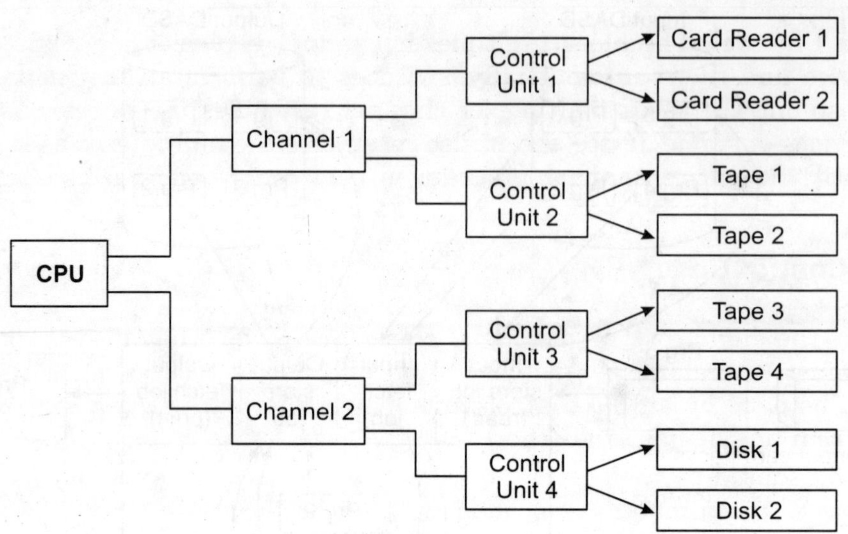

Figure 11.5 : Components of the I/O Subsystem

11.3.1 I/O Channels

They are used to provide a path or a channel for the data to flow between I/O devices and the main memory. I/O channels use channel programs that specify action to be performed by devices and control the transmission of data between main memory and control units. They are required to resolve the disparity in speed of the I/O devices and the CPU. They are in fact, specialized processing units intended to operate the I/O devices. Since these units may be simple, specialized and not too fast they are generally much less expensive than a conventional CPU. If all the input and output are performed via the channel, the CPU is free to perform its high-speed computations without wasting time on slow operations such as reading cards. It is also possible for the CPU to operate several channels simultaneously, therefore, many card readers, tape drives and printers can function at the same time. However, to obtain these benefits, the operating system may have to supervise these operations.

Types of I/O Channels

Basically I/O channels come in two types : Selectors and Multiplexors. In both cases, multiple devices can be connected to each channel.

Selector Channel. It can service only one of the devices at a time - i.e. one device is selected for service at one time. These channels are normally used for high-speed I/O devices such as magnetic disks and drums. Thus each I/O request is usually completed quickly and then another device is selected for I/O.

Multiplexor Channel. It is capable of servicing many devices, simultaneously. It is able to accomplish this only for slow I/O devices such as card readers, cardpunches and printers.

A third type of I/O channel which is a compromise solution that allows multiple channel programs for high-speed devices to be active on the same I/O channel, is Block

Multiplexor Channel. The block multiplexor channel performs one channel instruction for one device and then, automatically, switches to perform an instruction for another device and so on. The block multiplexor channel resembles the selector as at any given time, it services only one device and it also resembles the multiplexor as it does not have to wait until the entire channel program is completed before it can service another device.

11.3.2 I/O Control Units

Due to the high cost of channels, there are fewer channels than devices. The channels, must, therefore, be switched from one device to another. This switching of devices can be done by an I/O control unit, which interprets signal, sent by channel for switching from one device to another.

It can be shared by many similar type of I/O devices (such as tapes, disks etc.) and can interpret the commands associated with these devices. As shown in Figure 11.5, there is a control unit that manages card readers, a control unit for tapes and a control unit for disks.

11.3.3 Device Management Techniques

The device management routines must keep track of the status of (1) channels, (2) control units, and (3) devices. Since the channels and control units are usually scarce, they frequently create a serious bottleneck. Several hardware techniques can be used to reduce this problem: independent device operation, device buffering, multiple paths, and block multiplexing.

11.3.3.1 Independent Device Operation

In many cases there is sufficient capability in the device to complete an I/O operation without any further assistance from the channel or control unit. A disk seek operation, which might require 50 ms, only needs the channel long enough to transmit the seek address from memory to the disk which takes 10 or 20 ms. The seek can be completed by the device alone. Similarly, there are operations that may require both the device and the control unit but not the channel for completion.

When an I/O operation is initiated, the entire path must be available. In order to indicate when parts of the path become available, there may be separate I/O completion interrupts : channel end, control unit end, and device end. The status bits in the Channel Status Word designate completion interrupt. If more than one part of the path becomes available at the same time, there will be only one interrupt but the status bits will indicate all available parts (*e.g.*, both the channel end and control unit end bits will be on in the channel status word).

If a channel end occurs, the channel is no longer busy, although the device may still be busy. An I/O operation can then be initiated on some other device using that channel.

11.3.3.2 Buffering

By providing a data buffer in the device or control unit, devices that would ordinarily require the channel for a long period can be made to perform independent of the channel.

For example, a card reader may physically require about 80 ms to read a card and transfer the data to memory through the channel. However, a buffered card reader always reads one card before it is needed and saves the 60 bytes in a buffer in the card reader or control unit. When the channel requests that a card be read, the contents of the 60-byte buffer are transferred to memory at high speed (*e.g.*, 80 ms) and the channel is released. The device then proceeds to read the next card and buffer it independently. Card readers, cardpunches, and printers are frequently buffered.

11.3.3.3 Multiple Paths

The channel and control unit bottlenecks can be reduced by buying more channels and control units. Another alternative, however, is to use the channels and control units in a more flexible manner. This allows multiple paths to each device. Figure 11.6 illustrates such an I/O configuration. In this example there are four different paths to device E :

1. Channel A - Control Unit C - Device E
2. Channel A - Control Unit D - Device E
3. Channel B - Control Unit C - Device E
4. Channel B - Control Unit D - Device E

If channel A and control unit C were both busy due to I/O for device F, a path could be found through channel B and control unit D to service device E. An actual I/O configuration may have eight control units per channel and eight devices per control unit. A completely flexible configuration would make all control units accessible to all channels and all devices accessible to all control units, thus providing possibly 256 alternative paths between memory and each device.

In addition to providing flexibility, a multiple path I/O configuration is desirable for reliability. For example, if channel A becomes erroneous and must be repaired, all the control units and devices can still be accessed through channel B. It is the responsibility of the device management routines to maintain status information on all paths in the I/O configuration and find an available route to access the desired device.

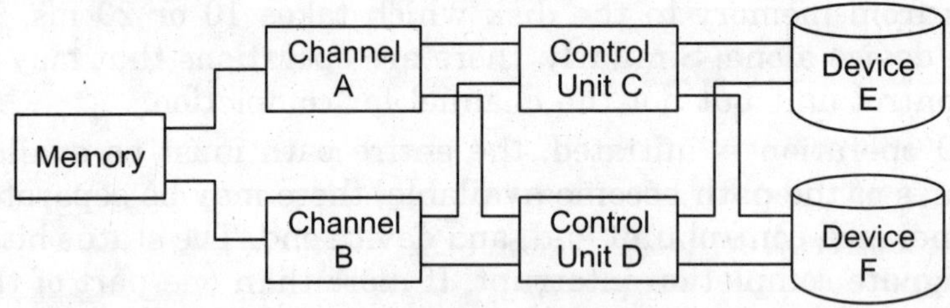

Figure 11.6 : I/O Configuration with Multiple Paths

11.4. DEVICE ALLOCATION CONSIDERATION

As discussed earlier, there are three major techniques of device allocation : dedicated, shared, or virutal. Virtual technique transforms a dedicated device into a shared device; thus, it is merely a special case of dedicated and shared allocation.

Need of Dedicated Devices

Certain devices require either manual actions or time-consuming I/O operations to be performed prior to use by a program, such as positioning a magnetic tape to the desired data record. To switch use of such a device among several programs would require an excessive amount of work. Thus, these devices are dedicated to one program at a time and are not reassigned until that program releases the device - usually at the termination of the program. The assignment of a device to a program is usually performed in conjunction the CPU scheduling algorithms.

Need of Shared Devices

Due to the relative ease and speed with which a direct access device such as a magnetic drum or disk can be repositioned, it is possible to share it among several programs running concurrently. A shared device is logically treated as if it were a group of dedicated devices. Each program using a shared device logically has a separate area to itself; the direct access property of the device makes it economical to switch back and forth among these areas. The device management routines may decide which shared device will be assigned to a program and what area of the device will be assigned.

For both dedicated and shared devices, static and dynamic allocation decisions must be made. The static decisions largely involve determining which dedicated and shared devices are to be assigned to the program. In general, device management tries to spread the allocation among devices so as to minimize channel and control unit bottlenecks. Often the user can provide information on the program control cards indicating which of the devices can be used concurrently (these should be on separate channels) and which can be used at different times (these can be safely assigned to the same channel).

Since channels and control units are so scarce, they are rarely permanently assigned to a program. Instead, an assignment is made when a program makes an I/O request to device management. This assigned channel and control unit are deallocated and become available for reassignment as soon as the I/O request is completed.

11.5. SOFTWARE COMPONENTS OF I/O SUB-SYSTEM

The functions of device management can be conveniently divided into three parts : Each function is handled by specific software component of I/O subsystem.

1. **I/O traffic controller** keeps track of the status of all devices, control units and channels.
2. **I/O scheduler** implements the policy algorithms used to allocate channel, control unit, and device to the I/O requests of the programs.
3. **I/O device handler** performs the actual dynamic allocation, once the I/O scheduler has made the decision by constructing the channel program, issuing the start I/O instruction, and processing the device interrupts. There is usually a separate device handler for each type of device.

11.5.1 I/O Traffic Controller

Whereas the I/O scheduler is mainly concerned with policies (*e.g.*, who gets the device and when), the I/O traffic controller is primarily concerned with mechanics (*e.g.*, Is it possible to assign the device?) The traffic controller maintains all the status information of a device.

The I/O traffic controller becomes complicated due to the interdependencies introduced by the scarcity of channels and control units, and the multiple paths illustrated earlier in Figure 11.6. The traffic controller has three basic tasks :

Unit Control Block (UCB)
Device unit identification
Status of device
List of control units connected to this device
List of processes waiting for this device

Channel Control Block (CCB)
Channel identification
Status of channel
List of control units connected to this channel
List of processes waiting for this channel

Control Unit Control Block (CUCB)
Channel unit identification
Status of control unit
List of devices connected to this control unit
List of channels connected to this control unit
List of processes waiting for this control unit

Figure 11.7. : Control Blocks

1. It must determine if there is at least one path available.
2. If there is more than one path available it must determine which one to select.
3. If paths are all busy, it must determine when one will become available.

In order to do these tasks, the traffic controller maintains a database reflecting the status and connections (between channels, control units etc.). This can be accomplished by means of Unit Control Blocks (UCB), Control Unit Control Block (CUCB), and Channel Control Blocks (CCB) as depicted in Figure 11.7.

The first task can be accomplished by starting at the desired UCB and working back through the connected control units and channels trying to find a combination that is available. In a similar manner it is possible to determine all available paths. The second task may be important especially when the I/O configuration is not symmetric, as shown in Figure 11.8. Since choosing one path may block out other I/O requests. Thus, one path may conflict with fewer I/O requests than another path. In Figure 11.8 there may be up to five different paths to device H, yet only one possible path for either device G or I.

Under heavy I/O loads, it is quite likely that there will not be a path available at the time an I/O request is issued by a process. When an I/O completion interrupt occurs, one or more components (i.e., device, control unit or channel) become available again. If, however, hundreds of I/O requests were waiting, this could be a time-consuming approach. A more efficient approach would be to list all I/O requests that are "interested" in the component, in the control block, as suggested in Figure 11.7. Only those particular I/O requests would then have to be examined.

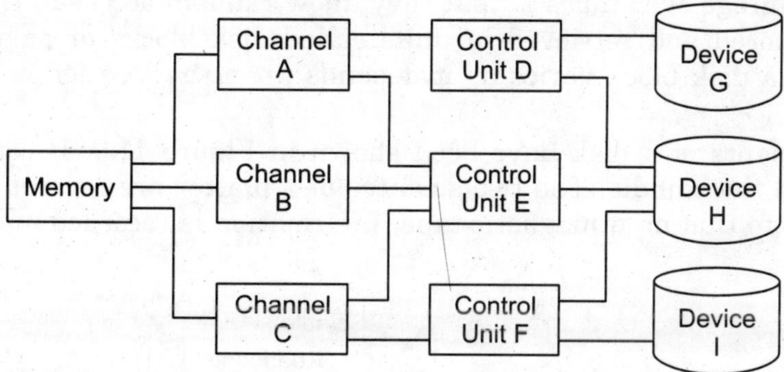

Figure 11.8 : Asymmetric I/O Configuration

11.5.2 I/O Scheduler

I/O Scheduler performs the same job as process scheduler. It allocates devices, control units and channels. If there are more I/O requests pending than available paths, it is necessary to choose which I/O requests to satisfy first.

I/O requests are not preempted i.e. once channel program has started it is allowed to continue towards completion, even though I/O requests with higher priorities may have entered the queue. This is feasible because most channel programs are relatively short (50 to 100 ms).

Many different policies may be incorporated into the I/O scheduler. For example, if a process has a high priority assigned by the process scheduler, it is reasonable also to assign a high priority to its I/O requests. This would help complete that program as fast as possible.

I/O scheduler must synchronize its work with traffic controller to make sure that a path is available to satisfy I/O requests.

11.5.3 I/O Device Handler

In addition to setting up the channel command words, handling error conditions and processing I/O interrupts, the I/O device handlers provide detailed scheduling algorithms that are dependent upon the type of the device. There is usually a different device handler algorithm for each type of I/O device. Scheduling algorithms for disks have been discussed later in this chapter. Every scheduling algorithm has the motive of minimizing three factors : arm movement, mean response time and variance in response time.

11.6. SECONDARY STORAGE (DISK) STRUCTURE

Before we discuss the disk structure, we should answer the obvious question of why not store everything in main memory ? The anwer is - firstly RAM costs too much, secondly, it is volatile but we want the instructions and data to remain in the system for a long time. Thus comparatively cheaper and non-volatile disks are very important for the storage of huge data almost forever. Disks are secondary storage devices of choice. Their main advantage over tapes is that they allow random access to the data stored on them. Data is stored and retrieved in units called disk blocks or pages. Unlike RAM, time to retrieve a disk block varies as it depends upon the location of the block on the disk.

The Components of a disk have been shown in Figure 11.9. It consists of platters that spin around the spindle. The two surfaces of a platter are covered with a magnetic material similar to that on a magnetic tape. Information is recorded magnetically on the platters.

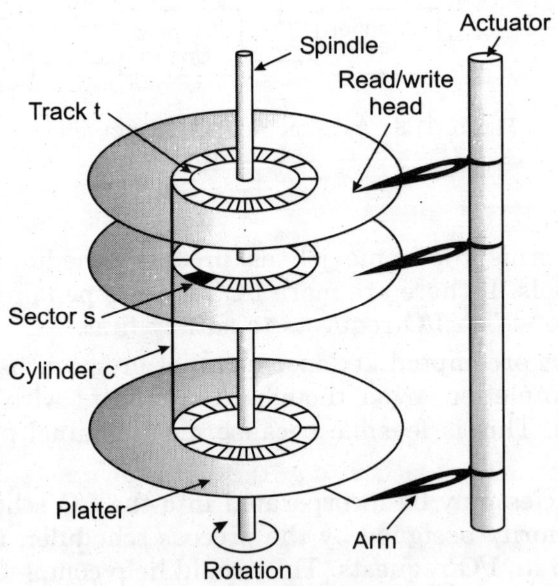

Figure 11.9 : Disk Structure

The surface of a platter is logically divided into circular tracks, which are sub-divided into sectors. The set of tracks that are at one arm position form a cylinder. There may be thousands of concentric cylinders in a disk drive, and each track may contain hundred of sectors. The storage capacity of common disks is measured in gigabytes (GBs).

The arm assembly is moved in or out to position a head on a desired track. Only one disk head reads/writes at any one time. An old style disk address actually consists of a cylinder number, a track number within that cylinder and a sector number within that track. Block size is a multiple of sector size (which is fixed). Modern disks are, however, organized into zones of cylinders. The number of sectors per track is constant within a zone. As we move from inner zones to outer zones, the number of sectors per track increases.

As the disk technology is improving, the number of sectors per track has increased and now, it is common to have more than 100 sectors per track in the outer zone of a disk.

Following times are associated with the access of a disk block

- **Seek time** – time taken to move arms to position disk head on the desired track.
- **Rotational delay** – time spent in waiting for desired block to rotate under the head.
- **Transfer time** – time spent in actually moving data to / from the disk surface.

Seek time varies from about 1 to 20 milli-seconds. Rotational delay varies from 0 to 10 milli-seconds. Transfer rate is about 1 milli-second per 4 KB block. Thus, seek time and rotational delay dominate transfer time and must be minimized probably by arranging the blocks in a file sequentially on the disk.

11.7. DISK SCHEDULING

In most systems, there are many processes that may be running simultaneously. Often, many processes request I/O operation from/to the hard disk. The algorithm used to select which I/O request is going to-be satisfied first is called "disk scheduling algorithm". In order to be able to understand and evaluate these algorithms, one should be familiar with the way hard disk works. As we know the disk structure, a brief idea of working of disk will be sufficient here. It goes like this - for each I/O request, first, a head must be selected. This is done electronically and the time it takes is not significant. Then the head is moved over the destination track. After that, the disk is rotated to position the desired sector under the head. Finally, the I/O operation is performed. Arm movements and disk rotations (as discussed earlier) are the points where the delay occurs.

There are two objectives for any disk-scheduling algorithm :

1. Minimizing the response time *i.e.* the average time that a request must wait before it is satisfied.
2. Maximize the throughout *i.e.* the average number of requests satisfied per unit of time.

There are many disk-scheduling algorithms. The following have been discussed here :

First-in-first-out (FIFO), Shortest Seek Time First (SSTF), SCAN, Circular Scan (C-SCAN), LOOK, Circular Look (C-LOOK).

11.7.1 First-in-first-out (FIFO)

This is the simplest algorithm. It processes the I/O requests in the same order as they arrive. This technique improves the response time as a request gets response in fair amount of time. However, the throughput is not efficient. It involves a lot of random head movements and disk rotations. Figure 11.10 shows an example of FIFO algorithm. This algorithm is used only in small systems where I/O efficiency is not very important.

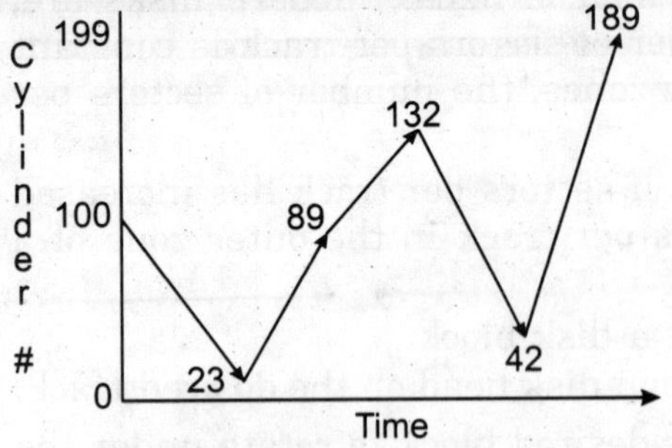

- The I/O request Queue : 23, 89, 132, 42, 187
- there are 200 cylinders numbered from 0-199
- the diskhead starts at number 100

- Total time is estimated by total arm motion :-

  $|100 - 23| + |23 - 89| + |89 - 132| + |132 - 42| + |42 - 189|$

Figure 11.10 : FIFO algorithm

11.7.2 Shortest Seek Time First (SSTF)

After each request is received, the disk controller selects the request that needs to access a track/sector, which is closest to the current location of the head. The throughput in this case is much better than in FIFO. However, some process may have to wait for a long time until its request(s) are satisfied, if new requests with shorter seek time keep arriving. Thus, it may cause starvation of some requests. Figure 11.11 shows an example of this scheduling algorithm.

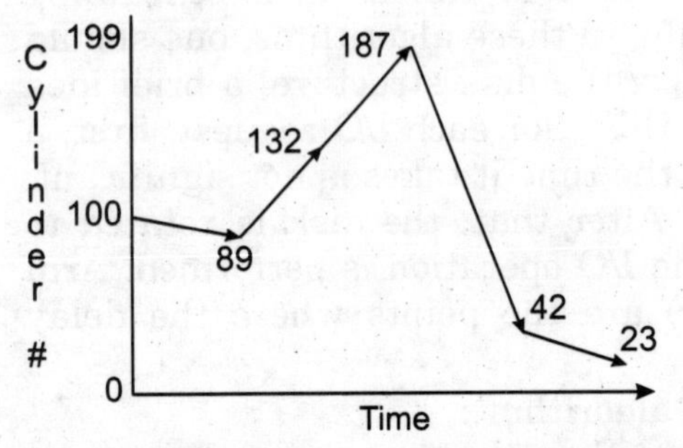

- The I/O request Queue : 23, 89, 132, 42, 187
- there are 200 cylinders numbered from 0-199
- the diskhead starts at number 100

- Total time is estimated by total arm motion :-

  $|100 - 89| + |89 - 132| + |132 - 187| + |187 - 42| + |42 - 23|$

Figure 11.11 : SSTF Algorithm

11.7.3 SCAN

In this algorithm, the head always constantly moves from the most inner cylinder to the outer cylinder, then it changes its direction back towards the center. As the head moves, if there is a request for the current disk position, it is satisfied. The throughput is better than FIFO. The SCAN algorithm is more fair than SSTF as far as starvation of requests is considered. An example of this algorithm is shown in Figure 11.12.

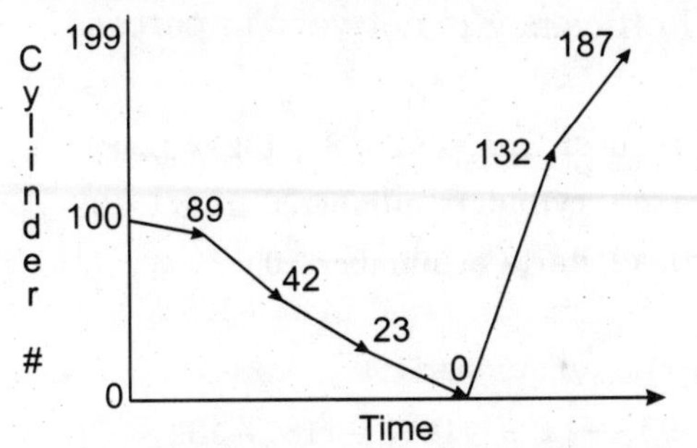

- The I/O request Queue : 23, 89, 132, 42, 187
- there are 200 cylinders numbered from 0-199
- the diskhead starts at number 100
- Assume that we are going inwards (i.e. towards 0)

- Total time is estimated by total arm motion :-
  $|100 - 89| + |89 - 42| + |42 - 23| + |23 - 0| + |0 - 132| + |132 - 187|$

Figure 11.12 : SCAN Algorithm

11.7.4 Circular Scan (C-SCAN)

This is an improvement over SCAN algorithm. In SCAN, the most outer and most inner cylinders have less opportunity to be accessed than the ones in the middle (as the middle is covered twice when the head moves from inner to outer and then outer to inner cylinders). C-SCAN eliminates this by satisfying requests only when the head moves in one direction and not satisfying any requests when it moves back. Figure 11.13 shows an example of this algorithm.

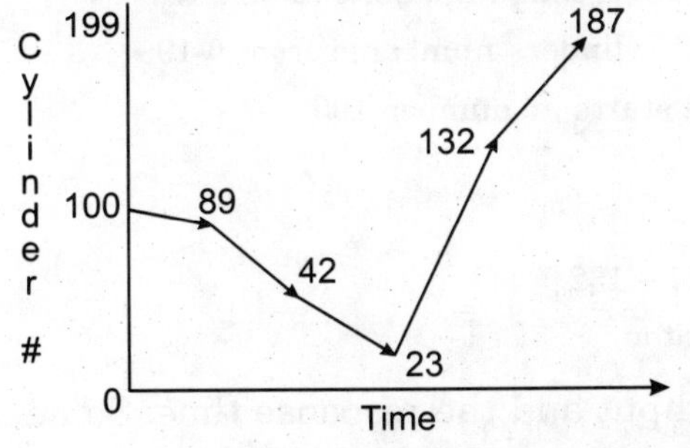

- The I/O request Queue : 23, 89, 132, 42, 187
- there are 200 cylinders numbered from 0-199
- the diskhead starts at number 100

- Total time is estimated by total arm motion :-
  $|100 - 89| + |89 - 42| + |42 - 23| + |23 - 132| + |132 - 187|$
- reduced variance compared to SCAN.

Figure 11.13 : C-SCAN Algorithm

11.7.5 LOOK

As in SCAN, requests are served when the head moves in both directions. The difference is that LOOK uses information about the requests to change the direction of the head. When it knows that there are no requests beyond the current point, it changes the direction of the head. This improves both the throughput and the response time. Figure 11.14 shows an example of this algorithm.

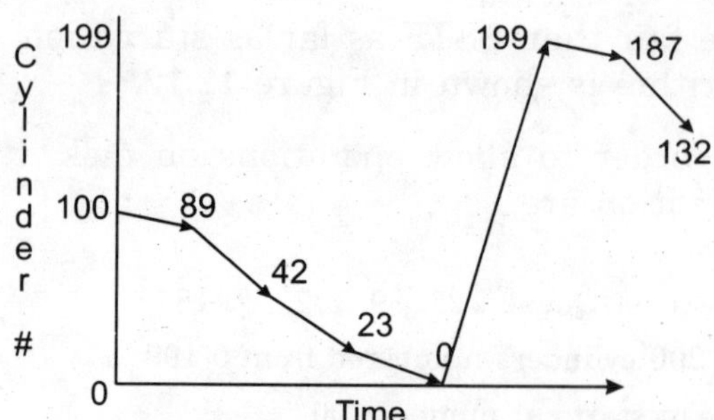

- The I/O request Queue : 23, 89, 132, 42, 187
- there are 200 cylinders numbered from 0-199
- the diskhead starts at number 100

- Total time is estimated by total arm motion :-

  |100 – 89| + |89 – 42| + |42 – 23| + |23 – 0| + |0 – 199| + |199 – 187| + |187 – 132|

Figure 11.14 : LOOK Algorithm

11.7.6 Circular Look (C-LOOK)

This is a variation of LOOK where requests are satisfied only when the head moves outwards, as in C-SCAN. Thus, no request is satisfied when the head moves inwards after determining that no requests are there beyond the current point. An example of therefore, this algorithm has been shown in Figure 11.15.

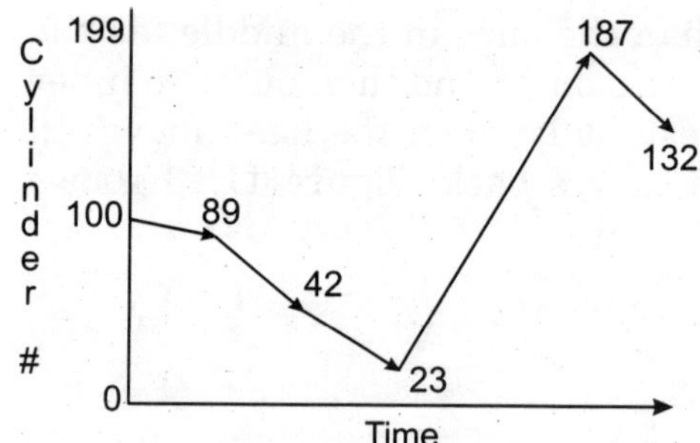

- The I/O request Queue : 23, 89, 132, 42, 187
- there are 200 cylinders numbered from 0-199
- the diskhead starts at number 100

- Total time is estimated by total arm motion :-

  |100 – 89| + |89 – 42| + |42 – 23| + |23 – 187| + |187 – 132|

Figure 11.15 : C-LOOK Algorithm

In general, there is a trade off between the throughput and the response time. Some algorithms focus more on the throughput. Others give more importance to the response time. The type of the system and the type of I/O requests, in terms of size and frequency, would determine the most suitable algorithm. A good algorithm would find the golden point somewhere in between the throughput and the response time. For a complicated system, a combination of more than one algorithm may be necessary to provide fair efficiency for all users.

11.8. DISK MANAGEMENT

Other than scheduling the I/O requests for the disk, the operating system should perform some other activities related to disk management. These involve initialization of the disk, booting from disk, and bad-block recovery etc.

11.8.1 Disk Initialization

Disk comes as a rough magnetic media. In order to allow operations on disk, it should be initialized. Three main steps of initialization are :

- Low-level formatting
- Partitioning
- Logical formatting

Low-level formatting

Its purpose is to divide disk into sectors. Each sector is capable of storing the same amount of byte, which is also known as block size. Here, we will use the term sector and block interchangeably. Sectors are separated from each other by special header and trailer chunks of bits that are put to each sector during the low-level formatting. Sectors are distinguished by disk-controller due to these bits. No doubt, that these bits introduce an overhead (wastage of storage space). This overhead is big when the sector size is small. Therefore, low-level formatting (usually done at factory) can be repeated manually to change the sector size (or block size).

Partitioning

The operating system may need to record its own data structures on the disk. This is done in two steps : - partitioning and logical formatting. Partitioning means that the disk is partitioned into one or more groups of cylinders. The partitions in a disk can be treated as separate and independent secondary storage device. For example, one partition can store all the files containing operating system's code and the other can hold user files.

Logical formatting

Its purpose is to make a file system on the disk. The operating system stores the file management structures and directory table on the disk. Logical formatting step may be bypassed if all the applications on the computer use raw I/O disk access rather than using file access. The raw I/O disk access is used by some databases that prefer raw I/O in order to control the exact disk location where each database record is stored.

11.8.2 Booting from disk

We know that in order to start computer running, the special (bootstrap) program is used. This program initializes all the hardware components and starts the operating system (finds the kernel on the disk, loads it into memory and jumps to the first instruction in it).

Originally, bootstrap program entirely resided in ROM and was not a disk concern. Adding the new device to the system or changing the characteristics of an old device then would demand change of the ROM chip. In the modern world, it would have to happen too frequently. Therefore, the solution for modern computer system is to store the small loader for bootstrap program in ROM. All the rest of this program is written to a dedicated area on the hard disk. This area of disk is known as boot sector.

This area can be few dedicated sectors or the whole dedicated partition. If a disk has a boot partition, it is called boot disk or system disk.

Then, to start the computer, the loader in ROM is started. This loader finds the boot sector on the disk, loads boot strap program from the boot sector into memory and then transfers the control to the boot step program (now loaded in memory), which in turn does the initialization job. This procedure is called booting from the disk.

Then, to start the computer, the loader in ROM is started. This loader finds the boot sector on the disk, loads boot strap program from the boot sector into memory and then transfers the control to the boot strap program (now loaded in memory), which in turn does the initialization job. This procedure is called booting from the disk.

11.8.3 Bad blocks recovery

More frequently, one or more sectors of a disk become defective. Most disks even come from the factory with bad blocks. Bad block's data are generally lost and need special application to recover them or restore them from backup copy. The bad blocks found are marked as bad through the file allocation methods. If the blocks are not marked as bad, the read/write errors may arise due to bad blocks reference. There are different ways to treat bad blocks on the disk.

- **Manually.** Bad blocks ons some disks with IDE (Integrated Drive Electronics) controllers can be handled manually. This approach uses some special system programs like format, chkdsk, etc., to search for bad blocks and lock them.
- **By Sectors Sparing.** This approach favours maintaining and updating the list of bad sectors and the list of spare sectors (which are not used for general allocation and are set aside by low-level formatting). The controller can be told to replace each bad sector logically with one of the spare sectors or in other words, each block from the list of bad blocks is mapped to the block from the list of spare blocks. Whenever, bad block is addressed, the corresponding spare block is referred, actually. Therefore, this method is known as sector sparing or sector formatting. SCSI controller uses this approach.
- **By Sectors Slipping.** Some controllers could be instructed to replace bad blocks by sector slipping. For example, if block 17 becomes defective and first available spare sector follows sector 61. Sector slipping would remap all the sectors from 18 to 61. Slipping the sectors by this way frees up the space of sector 18, so that sector 17 can be remapped to it. This has been shown in Figure 11.16.

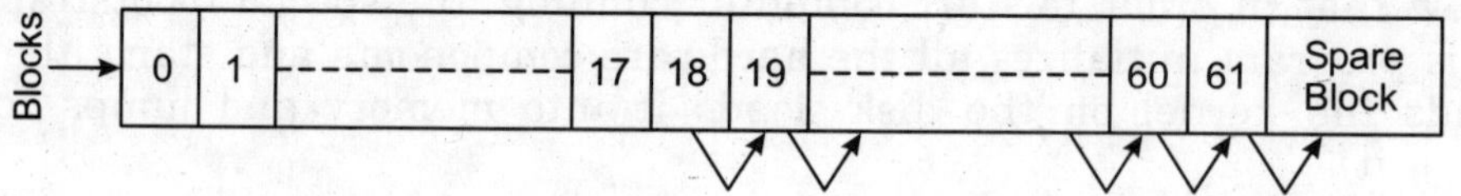

Figure 11.16. Sector slipping for recovery of bad block No. 17.

11.9. SWAP - SPACE MANAGEMENT

It is another important task of the operating system. We know that virtual memory when implemented using demand paging or demand segmentation uses swap space on the disk. Therefore, the optimized use of swap-space contributes a lot to the performance of virtual memory system. Swap space may be carved out of the normal file system or more commonly, it can be in a separate disk partition.

Swap Space Location

If the swap space is a large file within the file system, we can use all the file operations like create, rename, etc., to manipulate it. This is an easy implementation but suffers from external fragmentation as it may leave unused space holes on the disk that can not be further used by a single process or a page. If swap-space is created in a separated disk partition, a separate swap-space manager can be used to allocate or de-allocate the blocks. This manager can use algorithms to optimize speed. The only problem with this approach is that it creates a fixed amount of swap space during disk partition, which cannot be enhanced easily.

Swap-Space Size

The size of swap space depends upon the extent of its usage. Some systems may use swap space to hold the entire process image whereas others may simply use it to hold pages that have been pushed out of the main memory.

Swap Space Management in UNIX

Let us now see how swap-space is managed in UNIX.

In 4.3 BSD, swap space is allocated to a process when the process is started. Unix actually partitions its process into text segment, data segment and stack segment. Therefore, enough space is set aside to hold the program *i.e.* by setting aside the space for text pages or the text segment, and the data segment of the process. Pre-allocating all the needed space in this way therefore generally prevents a process from running out of swap space while it executes. When a process starts, its text is brought into memory from the file system. These pages are written out to swap when necessary, and are read back in from there. Pages from the data segment are read in from the file system, or are created (if they are uninitialized), and are written to swap space and paged back in as needed. One optimization (for instance, when two users run the same editor) is that processes with identical text pages share these pages, both in physical memory and in swap space.

Two swap maps per-process are used by the kernel to track swap-space use. One swap map is used for the text segment and another for the data segment of a process. The text segment is a fixed size, so its swap space is allocated in 512K chunks, except for the final chunk, which holds the remainder of the pages, in 1K increment as shown in Figure 11.17.

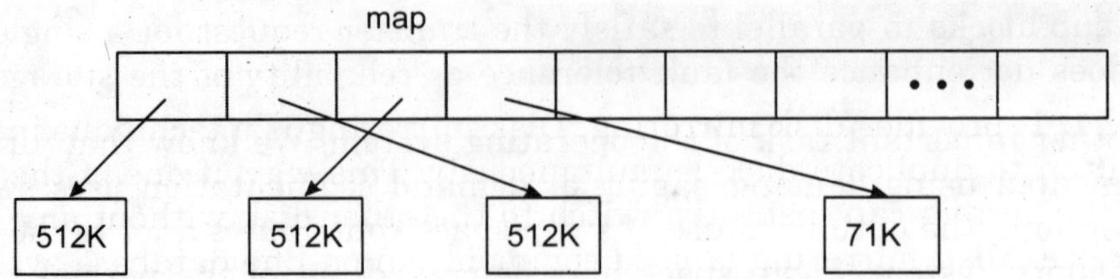

Figure 11.17 : 4.3 BSD text-sgement swap map

When a process tries to grow its data segment beyond the final allocated block in its swap area, the operating system allocated another block, twice as large as the previous one.

11.10. DISK RELIABILITY

When the operating system fails to read the stored data and instructions from a disk, the disk is said to have crashed. In case of a disk crash, the operating system begins to flash messages like :

Invalid media type error ....

Invalid partition table ....

General failure reading drive x ....

Data error reading drive x ....

Sector not found ....

The above messages indicate a serious disk problem. It may be logical or physical problem. The logical problems can be because either the boot sector/boot partition or the file system area has gone bad. Recovering from a disk crash may take hours. It may involve restoring of back up copies of the lost data on the new or the freshly formatted disk. Therefore, disk should be made more reliable. One of the important disk organization scheme meant to improve the disk reliability is RAID. It is a short form for "Redundant Array of Independent/Inexpensive Disks." It is a collection of multiple disks that work cooperatively. The basic purpose of this combination is to enhance fault tolerance and performance. The reliability of storage system is improved by storing redundant data. This enables the system to continue operation even if one of the disks crashes.

This organization is generally used on servers. There are a number of RAID levels. The most common are 0, 3 and 5 :

- **Level 0.** It provides disk striping but no redundancy. Disk striping is a technique for spreading data over multiple disks. It can speed up operations that retrieve data from disk storage. The computer system breaks a body of data into units and spread these units across the available disks. Systems that implement disk striping generally allow the user to select the unit size of stripe width. Data striping stores each unit of data in only one place and does not offer protection from disk failure. This improves performance as the time required to transfer a block to memory is reduced. This improves performance as the time required to transfer a block to memory is reduced. This is because all the disks can transfer their sub-blocks in parallel to satisfy the transfer request for a single block. But this does not enhance the fault tolerance or reliability of the storage system.

- **Level 1.** It provides disk mirroring. Disk mirroring is a technique in which data is written to duplicate disks simultaneously. This way, if one of the disk drives fails, the system can instantly switch to the other disk without any loss of data or service. Disk mirroring is used commonly in on-line database systems where it is critical that the data should be accessible at all times. For example, in railway reservation system, the existing database should be mirrored to recover from disk crash.
- **Level 3.** It is same as level 0, but also reserves one dedicated disk for error correction data. It provides good performance and some level of fault tolerance also.
- **Level 5.** It provides disk striping in which data as well as error correction information is divided at the byte level, across multiple disks. This results in excellent performance and good fault tolerance.

11.11. TERTIARY STORAGE DEVICES

Low cost and removability is the defining characteristics of tertiary storage. The removable and cheaper media like floppy disks, CD-ROMs etc. fall into the category of tertiary storage devices.

This section describes the types of storage devices used for tertiary storage.

1. **Floppy disk.** It is a thin flexible disk coated with magnetic material, enclosed in a protective plastic case. Most of the floppies can hold only about 1.44 MB of data. Thus, they have limited storage capacity.
2. **Removable Magnetic disk.** Removable magnetic disk can be as fast as hard disk and can hold about 1 GB of data. They are prone to damage from exposure.
3. **Magneto-optic disk.** This disk records data on a rigid platter coated with magnetic material. Laser light is used to read data from this disk. Its head moves much farther from the disk surface than a hard disk's head, and the magnetic material is covered with a protective layer of plastic or glass. Thus it is resistant to head crashes.
4. **Optical disks.** They do not use magnetism. They use special materials that are altered by laser light.
5. **WORM (Write - Once, Read-Many-times) disk.** These disks can be written only once. They are made of thin aluminium film sandwiched between two glass or plastic platters. When a bit is to be wirtten, the drive uses a laser light to burn a small hole through the aluminium. Because this hole cannot be reversed, any sector on the disk can be written for once only. These disks are very reliable and durable.
6. **Pre-recorded Read only disks** like CD-ROM and DVD (digital videodisk) use the same technology as that of WORM disks and are also durable.

7. **Magnetic tapes.** As compared to a disk, tape is less expensive and holds much more data. However, random access of a tape is much slower. It is thus an economical storage media where fast random access is not essential e.g. for taking back up copies of the disk data.

11.12. OPERATING SYSTEM CAPABILITIES

Whether the storage medium is a magneto-optic disk, a CD-ROM or a magnetic tape, the operating system needs to provide several capabilities to use removable media for data storage. These capabilities include :

11.12.1 Application Interface

Most operating systems handle removable disks almost like the fixed disks. A new cartridge is formatted and an empty file system is generated on the disk. This file system is used just like a file system on a hard disk.

Generally, tapes are treated as raw storage medium i.e. the application does not open a file on the tape and it opens the whole tape drive as a raw device. Usually, tape drive is reserved for the exclusive use of that application. As the file services offered by the operating system cannot be used (due to raw I/O), the application must decide how to use the array of blocks.

11.12.2 File Naming

The issue of naming files on removable media is especially difficult when we want to write data on a removable disk on one computer and then use it in another computer.

If both machines are of the same type and have the same kind of removable drive, the only difficulty is to know the contents and the layout on the disk. But if the machines or drives are different then additional problems can arise. Even if the drives are compatible, different computers may store bytes in different orders, and may use different encoding schemes for binary numbers and even for letters.

Today's operating systems generally leave the name-space problem unsolved for removable media, and depend on applications and users to figure out how to access and interpret the data. Fortunately, a few kinds of removable media are so well standardized that all computers use them the same way. One such example is the CD. Music CDs use a universal format that is understood by all CD drives.

EXERCISES

11.1 List the major device management functions that must be performed by an operating system.

11.2 Explain the functions of I/O traffic controller, I/O device handler and I/O scheduler.

11.3 What were the factors that led to the development of virtual devices ? How did the concept of virutal devices evolve ?

11.4 List two problems that force some operating system to use the technique of device dedication.

11.5 List three problems introduced by allowing users to share a device. What makes a disk more sharable than a tape ?

11.6 What advantages are there in using a Direct Access Storage Device (e.g., Disk) as opposed to a tape for input SPOOLing ? Do these advantages also apply to output SPOOLing ?

11.7 Out of all the disk-scheduling algorithms that have been discussed here, only FCFS is truly fair (i.e. never leads to starvation). Prove that all other algorithms are unfair (i.e. may lead to starvation).

11.8 Suppose that a disk drive has 5000 cylinders, numbered 0 to 4999. The drive is currently serving a request at cylinder 143, and the previous request was at cylinder 125. The queue of pending requests, in FIFO order is :

86, 1470, 913, 1774, 948, 1509, 1022, 1750, 130.

Starting from the current head position, what is the total distance that the disk arm moves to satisfy all the pending requests for each of the following disk scheduling algorithms ?

(a) FCFS

(b) SSTF

(c) SCAN

(d) LOOK

(e) C-SCAN

11.9 Explain why SSTF scheduling tends to favour middle cylinder over the innermost and outemost cylinders.

11.10 What is a bad block ? Compare the sector sparing technique with sector slipping technique of dealing with bad blocks.

11.11 What factors should be considered while deciding the swap-space size ?

11.12 Explain the term `RAID' and the usefulness of this technique to improve the storage system's reliability.

11.13 What all capabilities should be possessed by the operating system to use the tertiary storage devices ?

CHAPTER

12

Protection and Security

OVERVIEW

The first part of this chapter discusses protection issues related to various resources associated with a computer system. The concepts of domains and access rights have been explained. The access matrix has been explained as a general model of protection. A mention of its implementation using access list and capability list has been made. A comparison of these two implementations has also been made. The second part of this chapter discusses the security issues related to the external environment within which a system operates. It also explains various user authentication mechanisms such as passwords, biometrics techniques etc. An attempt has been made to introduce encryption as a security measure and also to chalk out the safeguards against computer viruses and worms. Methods to do threat monitoring have also been discussed.

12.1. WHY PROTECTION ?

We have already discussed in previous chapters about a few of the problems that can be overcome by enforcing protection mechanisms. The various processes (user and system processes) must be protected from one other's activities. Protection mechanisms deal with controlling the access of programs, processes or users to the resources of a computer system. Security, which is discussed later, is however, an issue that requires a control over the external environment within which the system operates. Internal protection is of no use if the computer system is accessed by an unauthorized individual who can remove some important files or insert a virus into the system and make it non-functional.

12.2. GOALS OF PROTECTION

The protection mechanism to be enforced into a system should have the following goals :

- In multi-programming systems, the operating system should enable the users to safely share a common logical address space such as files etc., It should also enable the users to share a common physical address space *i.e.* memory. In such systems, therefore, the goal should be to prevent accidental and intentional destructive behaviour.
- Ensure fair and reliable resource usage *i.e.* each program component active in a system should use the system resources only in accordance with certain policies (stated for the use of these resources). Since the policies for a resource usage may vary, depending upon an application, therefore, protection mechanisms should be provided as tools for the enforcement of these varying policies.

12.3. METHODS FOR ENFORCEMENT OF PROTECTION MECHANISMS

As we know that a computer system is a collection of processes and objects (resources). Objects means hardware objects like CPU, memory, disk, printer, etc., and software objects like files, programs, semaphores, etc. Each object has a specific kind of operation applicable to it. For example, memory can be read or written, CPU can be only executed on, disk can be read and written, data files can be created, deleted, opened, read, written and closed. Thus, if these operations are known, a control mechanism can be implemented for each resource. A process should be allowed to access only those resources it has been authorized to access. A process should follow "Need-to-know" principle so that it should be able to access the resources, which it currently needs. This can be one way of implementing protection because only those resources, which are currently required, will need to be protected and others will be totally safe.

12.3.1 Access rights

At any instance, protection should be provided to those resources, which may be currently used by a process. Thus, a domain known as protection domain can be defined for a process. Such a domain will contain the set of objects and the types of operations that can be invoked on each object. This means that domain is a set of <object, right> pair. 'Rights' refer to the operations that can be invoked by a process on the corresponding object. These rights are also known as access rights of a particular process on the corresponding object *e.g.* - if a process is executing in domain D = < data file F, {read, write} >; it can perform only read and write operations on the data file named 'F'.

The association of a process with a domain may be static or dynamic. The association can be static only when the set of resources available to a process is fixed throughout its lifetime. In case of static association, protection can be implemented by strictly adhering to the "need-to-know" principle. This implies that the domain should keep changing at different instances of a process' execution, as and when there is a change in the use of resources by this process. For example, consider a process P that needs read access (on a disk) in one phase and write access in another phase. Then in the first phase the domain should include only read access right on disk *i.e.* < disk, read > and in the later phase, the domain should be modified to contain < disk, write >.

In case of dynamic association, a process can switch from one domain to another. Thus, here instead of changing the contents of a domain (to which a process may be statically associated as in case of static association), a new domain may be created with the changed content and the process may be switched to this new domain.

Examples of implementation of protection mechanisms using domain are :

1. Dual mode (Monitor - User mode) model of operating system execution is an example of protection mechanism because it ensures that if a process is in monitor mode, it can execute privileged instructions only and if it executes in user mode, it can invoke only non-privileged instructions. Memory protection can be implemented in multiprogramming environment where more than one user program may be executing in the user mode and may sometimes, interfere with each other.
2. In UNIX, a domain is actually associated with a user. In this case, the sets of objects that can be accessed depend upon the identity of the user. Domain switching occurs when the user is changed - generally, this happens when one user logs out and another logs in or in a multiuser system when more than one user may be trying to access the same object. This can help in safe sharing of objects among diferent users. Therefore, the domain will contain < user - id, domain-bit >. This domain bit is also known as setuid bit. When a user (with user-id = A) starts executing a file (owned by user B), whose domain bit is off, the user-id of the process is set to A. This temporary user-id change ends when the process accessing the file exits or when the user logs off, whichever is earlier. When the domain bit is on, the user-id is not changed to A and remains B *i.e.* owner of the file. This implies that file is used by B and thus, should not be used by A.

12.3.2 Access Matrix

The access matrix model is the policy for user authentication and has several implementations such as access control lists (ACLs) and capability lists. It is used to describe which users have access to what objects (resources). Thus, basically it checks the access rights of users on system resources. The access matrix model consists of four major parts :

- A list of objects
- A list of subjects
- A function T that returns an object's type
- The matrix itself, with the objects (resources) making the columns and the subjects making the rows.

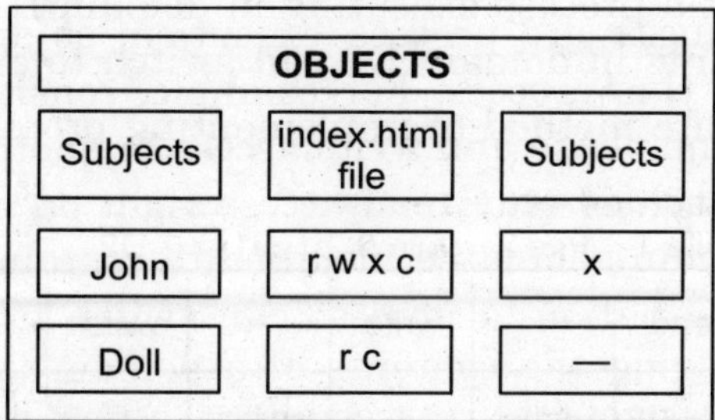

Figure 12.1 : Example Access Matrix

In the cells where a subject and object meet, lie the rights the subject has on that object. Some example access rights (as discussed in previous sub-section) are read, write, execute, list and delete. Figure 12.1 shows an example access matrix.

An access matrix has several standard operations associated with it :

- Entry of a right into a specified cell
- Removal of a right from a specified cell
- Creation of a subject
- Creation of an object
- Removal of a subject
- Removal of an object

The access matrix shown in Figure 12.1 considers users as subjects and states that John can read, write, execute and copy the index.html file and that Doll can only read and copy this file. The subjects can also be processes and procedures. This implies that access matrix model can be used to define the access rights for processes also. It means that subjects are in fact the domains, which can be realized either as a user, or a process or a procedure. The generalized access matrix model is shown in Figure 12.2.

Domain \ Object	File 1	File 2	Printer
D1	Read write	Execute	Output
D2	—	Execute	—
D3	—	Read write	Output

Figure 12.2 : Generalized access matrix

Advantages of access matrix as a mechanism for implementing protection are :

It provides an appropriate mechanism for defining and implementing strict control for both the static and dynamic association between processes and domains. When a process is switched from one domain to another, an operation called switch is used. Thus, domain switching by processes can be controlled by including domains among the objects of the access matrix. Figure 12.3 shows an access matrix with domains as objects.

This figure shows that a process executing in domain D1 can switch to domain D2. Similarly, a process executing in domain D2 can switch to domain D1 or domain D3.

It is thus an appropriate method of implementing protection mechanism.

Domain \ Object	File 1	File 2	File 3	D1	D2	D3	D4
D1	read	—	write	—	switch	—	—
D2	—	write	—	switch	—	switch	—
D3	read write	—	—	—	—	—	switch
D4	—	execute	—	switch	—	—	—

Figure 12.3 : Generalized Access Matrix with Domains as Objects

Disadvantages of this method are :

1. Although a useful model, access matrices are inefficient for storage of access rights in a computer system because they tend to be large and sparse.
2. Mechanisms must be enforced to protect the access matrices themselves from change.

12.3.2.1 Implementation of access matrices

The two most commonly used implementations are access control lists (ACLs) and Capability lists.

1. Access Control Lists (ACLs)

Access Control Lists (ACLs) are created by placing on each object a list of users and their rights to access that object. An example is already shown in Figure 12.1, where the two objects index.html file and Java VM have a list of users (John and Doll) associated with them whose access rights have been written in the corresponding cells.

2. Capability Lists

Capability Lists are implemented by stroing on each subject a list of rights the subject has for every object. This effectively gives each user, a sort of key ring. To remove access to a particular object, every user (subject) that has access to it must be "touched".

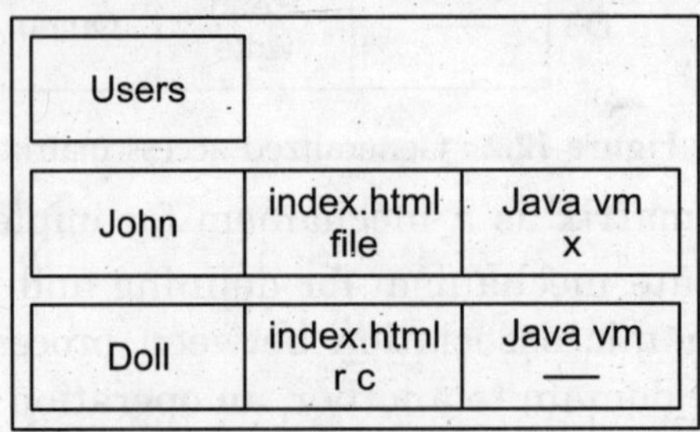

Figure 12.4 : Implementation of the access matrix using capability lists

A touch is an examination of a user's right to that object. Figure 12.4 shows an example of implementation of the access matrix using capability lists.

12.3.2.2 Comparison of access lists and capabilities

S.No.	Access Lists	Capabilities List
1.	Each object (resource) has a list of pairs of the form <subject, access rights>	Each subject (user, process or procedure) has a list of pairs of the form <object, access rights>
2.	It would be tedious to have separate listing for each subject (user), therefore, they are grouped into classes. For example, in UNIX, there are three classes : self, group, anybody else.	Here capabilities are the names of the objects. The objects not referred to in a capability list cannot be even named.
3.	The default is : Everyone should be able to access a file.	The default is : No one should be able to access a file unless they have been given a capability.
4.	Access lists are simple and are used in almost all file systems.	Capabilities are used in systems that need to be very secure as it prohibits sharing of information unless access is given to a subject.

12.4. SECURITY AND ITS GOALS

As discussed earlier, mechanisms are also needed to protect the external environment of a system.

Security violations (misuse) of the system can be either accidental or intentional. It is easier to protect against the accidental misuse than to protect against the intentional misuse. The intentional misuse can be of the following kinds :

- Theft of information
- Unauthorized modification of data
- Unauthorized destruction of data

System can be protected from such threats at two levels :

1. **Physical.** The site containing the computer systems must be physically secured so that the intruders can be prohibited to enter the site.

2. **Human**. Even the permitted users should be carefully screened so that the chance of authorizing a user who may give access to an intruder is reduced. It is obvious that if such a security system fails, the protection provided by the operating system will become almost useless.

Army databases, payroll databases and other such databases containing important financial data of an organization should be protected from intentional misuse. They are such sensitive data that remedy for the accidental loss should always be ready.

Even though such systems shall be kept under high security, there can be a chance of intruders coming in and trying to access the system. For this, the system hardware should also provide mechanisms to allow for the implementation of security features. Earlier operating systems like MS-DOS and Macintosh operating system did not provide much of the security as they were designed for the hardware which did not provide memory or I/O protection. Recent operating systems such as Windows NT, Windows 2000 have been designed to provide the needed security features. Since this book deals with operating system concepts, we will discuss only the security measures that must be provided by the operating system. Further discussion of security at the human and physical levels is out of the scope of this text.

12.5. AUTHENTICATION

Authentication of the user of a system is one of the major security issues associated with an operating system. This authentication is different from what we discussed in Section 12.3.2 as it deals with authenticating a user who tries to log into the computer system rather than authenticating the user who tries to access a system resource. Generally, authentication of a user is based on :

1. User identifier and password (Passwords)
2. Badge card possessed by a user (Artifacts)
3. Finger prints, retina pattern or signature (Biometrics techniques)

Let us discuss these techniques in detail.

12.5.1 Passwords

The password is the most common authentication mechanism based on sharing of a secret. In a password-based system each user has a password, which may initially be assigned by the system administrator. Many systems allow users to subsequently change their passwords. The system stores all user passwords and uses them to authenticate the users. When logging in, the system requests and the user supplies a presumably secret, user-specific password.

Passwords are popular because they require no special hardware and are relatively easy to implement. On the negative side, passwords offer limited protection, as they may be relatively easy to obtain or guess. Unencrypted passwords files stored in a system are obviously an easy prey. User-chosen passwords are frequently dictionary words or proper names. This makes them easy to remember and easy to guess. For example, user ids, names or surnames, and their backward spellings typically account for a significant percentage of passwords.

System-chosen passwords, on the other hand, are usually random combinations of letters and numbers that are hard to guess but are also hard to remember. As a result, the users tend to write them down and store them in a handy place near the terminal. This can be easily located by someone and thus may no longer be a secret.

Various techniques have been proposed to strengthen the level of protection availed by the password mechanism. Unfortunately, most of these have drawbacks that reduce either their effectiveness or user acceptance. For example, password schemes may be multilevel, and users may be required to supply additional passwords at the system's request at random intervals during computer use. This tends to annoy the actual authorized users. Another technique is to have the system issue a dynamic challenge to the user after log-in. This challenge can be in the form of a random number generated by the computer, to which the user is supposed to apply a secret transformation, such as squaring and incrementing the value. Failure to do so may be used to detect unauthorized users.

Another technique, which attempts to discourage unauthorized users who attempt to log in by trying a series of different passwords, is to limit the number of consecutive attempts to log in the system. The number of consecutive log-in attempts may be controlled by disabling the user's account after a certain number of unsuccessful attempts. The user may subsequently reinstate the account by establishing his or her identity with the manager or a system administrator. The danger of this approach is the potential denial of service. This happens when a mischievous user disables the accounts of others by intentionally attempting to log in using other persons' ids, which are usually public. Such a user could easily knock out the whole system by disabling the accounts of all the administrators. To counteract this problem partly, some systems prohibit disabling when the number of active administrative accounts drops to one.

12.5.2 Artifact-based Authentication

The artifacts commonly used for user authentication include machine-readable badges (usually with magnetic stripes) and electronic smart cards. Badge or card readers may be installed in or near the terminals, and users are required to supply the artifact for authentication. In many systems, artifact identification is coupled with the use of a password. That is, the user must insert the card and then supply his or her password. This form of authentication is common with automated teller banking machines. The artifact-based systems work especially well in environments where the artifact is also used for other purposes.

For example, in some compaines badges are required for employees to gain access to the organization's gate. The use of such a badge as an artifact for computer access and authentication can reduce the likelihood of the loss of an artifact. Smart cards can augment this scheme by keeping even the user's password within the card itself, which allows authentication without storage of passwords in the computer system. This makes it more difficult for mischievous users to uncover user passwords but the loss of such cards can be hazardous.

12.5.3 Biometrics Techniques

The third major group of authentication mechanisms is based on the unique characteristics of each user. Some user characteristics can be established by means of biometrics techniques. These fall into two basic categories :

1. Physiological characteristics, such as fingerprints, capillary patterns in the retina, hand geometry, and facial characteristics.
2. Behavioural characteristics, such as signature dynamics, voice pattern, and timing of keystrokes.

In general, behavioural characteristics can vary with a user's state and thus may be susceptible to higher false acceptance or rejection rates. For example, signature dynamics and keystroke patterns may vary with a user's stress level and fatigue.

The biometrics detection devices are usually self-contained and independent of the computer system, which increases their resistance to common computer penetration methods and improves the potential for tamper proofing.

The primary advantages of biometrics authentication are the largely increased accuracy of user authentication and reduction of errors in security-conscious environments. For example, some retinal-scan devices claim an error rate as low as 1 in 3 million (1 in trillion when both eyes are scanned).

The drawbacks of biometrics authentication include increased cost, potential invasion of privacy, and reluctance of some users.

12.6. ENCRYPTION

As computer networks gain popularity, more sensitive information is being transmitted over channels where eavesdropping and message interception is possible. Thus, the operating system should have some provision to fight such situations *i.e.* to protect the data that are transferred over the network.

Encryption is one such mechanism, which allows such data to be scrambled so that even if some one intercepts it on the network, it is not readable to him/her. Thus, the basic purpose of encryption is to make the data transfer secure over the network.

Encryption works as :

1. It transforms information from ("Clear" or "plain text") to coded information ("Cipher text"), which cannot be read by outside parties.
2. This transformation process is controlled by an algorithm and a key.
3. This process should be reversible so that the intended recipient can read the information transmitted to him in the form of cipher text. But for this a decryption mechanism which decrypts (decodes) the cipher text to plain text is must. Figure 12.5 shows a general encryption and decryption mechanism.

The main challenge in using this approach is the development of encryption schemes that are impossible to break.

There are two kinds of encryption :

1. 'Symmetrical Encryption' or secret key which uses a single key to encrypt and decrypt the transmitted data.

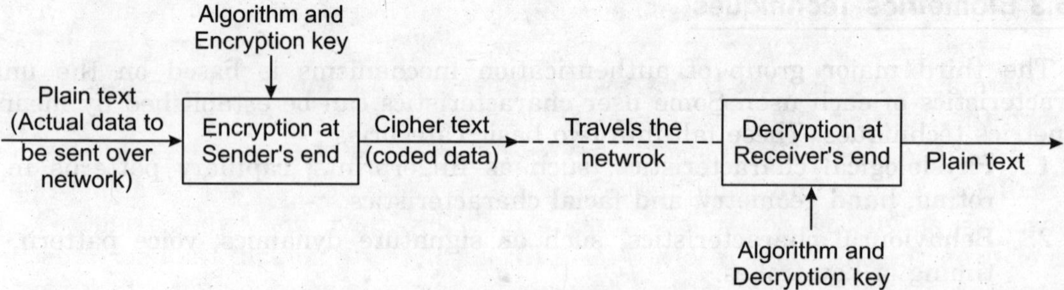

Figure 12.5 : General Encryption and Decryption Mechanism

2. 'Asymmetrical Encryption' which uses 'Private Key', in which one key is used to encrypt and another to decrypt the transmitted data.

Encryption Schemes

- One scheme (that uses single secret key) called Data Encryption Standard (DES), was once adopted as standard for encryption. This scheme, however, suffers from key-distribution problem. Before communication can take place, the secret keys must be sent securely to both the sender and the receiver. This task itself is prone to the threat of eves dropping by the unauthorized users who may be trying hard to know the secret keys.
- A solution to the problem encountered in DES is to use a scheme known as public-key-encryption scheme. In this scheme, each user has both a public and a private key, and two users can communicate knowing only each other's public key. The algorithms based on this concept are believed to be almost unbreakable and therefore, this scheme is the most preferred and reliable scheme for secure network communication.

12.7. VIRUSES, WORMS AND TROJANS

Let us first try to find out what is a Virus, a Worm and a Trojan ?

A computer virus is a small program written to alter the way a computer operates and it executes without the permission or knowledge of the user. A program is a virus if it meets the two criteria :

(i) It must execute itself.

(ii) It must replicate itself, for example, it may replace other executable files with a copy of the virus infected file. File infector viruses, boot sector viruses, master boot record viruses, multi-partite viruses and macro viruses are few kind of known viruses and this classification depends upon their target area or mode of operation.

Worms are basically the programs that replicate themselves from system to system without the use of a host file. They contain malicious code that can cause major damage to the files, software and data on a computer. The most insidious characteristics of a worm is its ability to distribute functional copies of itself to other computer systems. While viruses rely on attaching to another program to be executed, worms are free agents that can roam independently through networks and thus propagate and wreak havoc.

There are several ways that worms can get into a computer. The most common is through the Internet and E-mail. PrettyPark.worm is a prevalent example.

Trojan horses are impostors - files that claim to be something desirable, but in fact, arc malicious. A very important distinction from true viruses is that they do not replicate themselves, as viruses do. Trojans contain malicious code, that, when triggered, cause loss, or even theft of data. In order for a Trojan horse to spread, the user must invite these programs onto his computer - for example, by opening an e-mail attachment. The PWSteal.Trojan is a Trojan.

12.7.1 Dealing with Viruses

The existence of a computer virus typically encompasses four stages :

1. Dormancy
2. Propagation
3. Triggering
4. Damage

Upon infecting a new machine or a new program, the computer virus may remain dormant for a while so that its presence is not suspected. Computer viruses are commonly spread through acquisition of programs directly or indirectly obtained from computer network and bulletin boards in the form of shareware or public domain programs. Unlike worms, viruses need not propagate themselves via networks but may be spread by program sharing between users. A machine becomes infected by executing a contaminated program. However, networks can accelerate spreading of viruses, especially when shared programs residing in the server become contaminated.

The duration of the dormant period may vary depending on the type of mechanism being used. The virus may wait a certain number of executions of the host program or the elapsing of a certain period of time before progressing to the next stage - propagation. In the propagation stage, the virus attempts to infect other programs on the host machine. The target can also be the operating system and the boot block. For example, a floppy disk may be contaminated just by having its directory listed on the infected machine.

In order for the virus to spread, the infected carrier program must be executed. The virus spreads by searching the system, typically the disk, for uninfected programs and attaching itself to them. Although propagation of viruses is possible in any programmable computer, it is easier in personal computers with unprotected operating systems. Depending on the particular mechanism in use, the code of virus modifies an executable file in such a manner that it receives control upon program activation. When the infected program is executed, the virus code receives control, and performs the work appropriate for the stage that it is in. Control is then usually returned to the host program for normal operations. In this way, the virus can hide its existence all the way through the triggering stage.

After completing the self-propagation stage, the trigger is activated to facilitate transition to the damage stage. The trigger may be defined as a count of replications, or it can be timer-based so as to cause the damage at some specific time or date, such as September the 15th. The damage itself can range from printing a message announcing the presence of the virus to malignant damage such as erasure of files or damaging of the boot block.

Major safeguards against viruses are :

There is no known general vaccine for computer viruses. As usual, prevention is the best protection. Common preventive measures include careful screening of all newly acquired software, frequent backups and a combination of utilities such as integrity checkers, monitoring programs and virus removers.

1. **Integrity checkers** are programs that attempt to detect modifications of other programs by calculating their checksums. They should be run quite frequently, such as upon each boot. Since virus infection modifies the size of the affected program, the integrity checker can detect and report such changes.
2. **Monitoring programs** are permanent resident (daemon) programs that continuously check certain memory and I/O operations for suspicious behaviour that may be attributable to viruses. Monitoring programs are effectively an extension of operating system that try to plug the security holes known or likely to be exploited by viruses.
3. **Virus removers** are programs that scan system storage for signatures and patterns that belong to viruses known to the program author. They can detect and remove known viruses even in the dormant stage (the very first stage when a virus infects a machine or a new program). However, virus removers cannot cope with unknown viruses. Virus-remover programs need to be updated frequently in order to keep up with new types of viruses.
4. **Purchasing unopened software** from vendors, avoiding free or pirated copies from public sources, avoiding floppy-disk exchange are the safest ways of preventing virus infection.

12.7.2 Dealing with Worms

Computer-worm programs usually do not cause any direct damage to the other programs and files in a computer system that they invade. However, they tend to consume large amounts of resources for their own dissemination, thus denying service to users. A computer worm typically operates by sending copies of itself to other machines in a network. The usual line of attack is the users' mailing lists, which contain the names and addresses of other reachable machines. After gaining access to a mailing list, the worm sends copies of itself (an executable program) to some or all listed machines. Depending on its sophistication, upon arrival at a new destination, the worm may or may not check whether the new destination is already infected. If it is not infected or if no check is made, the worm will attempt to gain access to the local mailing lists for further spreading. As a result, computers on the network and the network itself become flooded with copies of executing and travelling worms. This infection usually spreads quickly and drowns the entire system by consuming processing time and network bandwidth so that only little or none of the any other works and communication can proceed.

Two major safeguards against computer worms are :

1. **Making penetration of each machine difficult.** Penetration attempts may be averted by strengthening system security, especially in the areas of mailing utilities, passwords, and access control to the mailing lists.
2. **Hindering worm spreading.** Spreading of executable programs may be curtailed by means of checkpoints in the communication system. For example, the network interface can prohibit transfers of executable programs and command files, or require explicit operator or user intervention as a condition for each particular acceptance.

12.8. THREAT MONITORING

The security of a system can be improved by some management techniques. One such technique is Threat-monitoring. Threat monitoring implies that the system can check for suspicious patterns of activity in an attempt to detect a security violation.

The techniques that can be used for threat monitoring are :

1. A time sharing system can keep the count of the number of incorrect passwords given, when a user is trying to log in. More than a few incorrect attempts may signal an attempt to guess a password.
2. Audit log is another common technique used for threat monitoring. An audit log records the time of use, the details of users, and types of all the accesses to an object. After the security has been violated, the audit log can be used to determine how and when the problem occurred and perhaps what amount of damage was done. This information can be useful for recovery from security violation as well as in the development of tighter security measures to prevent future problems.
3. The system can be scanned periodically for security holes. Scanning can be done when the system has less traffic. Such a scan can check a variety of aspects of the system. It can check for unexpectedly long running processes, existence of Trojans or some unauthorized programs in system directories, improper protection on system data files, such as the password file, device drivers, or even the operating system kernel itself.

   The problems encountered in the security scan can either be fixed automatically or reported to the system manager.
4. As the use of Internet is becoming very popular and as it is becoming an indispensable resource for many computers and individuals, protection from viruses and worms (that might invade the computer system through the Internet) is a very essential aspect of security. One solution to this problem is the use of a firewall. A firewall is basically a program (*i.e.* a software) or a hardware device that filters the information coming through the Internet connection into the company's private network or the individual user's system. Figure 12.6 shows how can a firewall be used. There are many ways that miscreant people may use to access or abuse unprotected computers. These include using remote login to control a remote computer and run some hazardous program on it. Other threats involve sending of spams (junk mails), hijacking of SMTP (Simple Mail Transfer Protocol) session and gaining access to a list of e-mail addresses, which can be used to send spams to thousands of users. All above stated threats and many more related to the unsecured use of Internet can be stopped by firewall. The entire network traffic can be restricted to travel through the firewall so that only certain types of information such as e-mail can get through. Spams cannot be filtered until the firewall stops an e-mail to get through which is not possible in today's world where almost everyone is using e-mail. It also stops (anyone outside), from remotely logging into a computer in a private network of an organization.

Figure 12.6 : Network security through firewall

12.9. ENCRYPTION

Encryption is used to provide secured data transmission over network. This technique encodes the original message in away that only destined users with its decoding key can fetch the original text. In a network, where more than one computer is attached and users are allowed to share information, security has become an utmost priority. Not only the authorized users but unauthorized users can also access data through malicious codes. Transmission of important text in its original form can be a dangerous task Encryption techniques were mainly used by the defense department for sending their confidential messages in such a way that only those users who have the key to decrypt the message got to know the same.

There are two main techniques for encryption.

Symmetric Encryption

Asymmetric Encryption

Symmetric Encryption. This encryption technique works with single key for encryption and decryption of the data. The algorithm works in a way that original text is converted into encrypted form using encryption algorithm with the help of a secret key. The other side of communication i.e. receiver end must use the decryption algorithm and the same secret key for retrieving the original message.

The steps for Symmetric Encryption are :

1. The original message is converted into encoded form (i.e. cipher text) by using encryption algorithm. e.g. Let the original message be "computer is a digital device" the encryption algorithm used will be "to replace every letter by the alphabet K step right of it in the word sequence".
2. Here 'K' is the public key used to manage the encoding of the text.
3. At the receiver end, decryption algorithm will be "to replace every letter of message by the alphabet K step left of it in the word sequence".
4. The secret key will be same on both sides.
5. Receiver can get secret key in the form of protected file attached along with the message.

The main advantage of this method is that only single key need to be managed among both communicating parties. In this way, the size of key remains small and it occupies less memory space. This helps in increasing the processor speed for computation. But this method is not without some weak points. The main drawback is that this technique is manageable only for small networks. If message has to be broadcasted among many users then it becomes difficult to keep the secret key a secret.

The main example algorithms of symmetric Encryption are :

Data encryption Standard (DES)

Advanced Encryption Standard (AES)

Asymmetric Encryption. In this scheme both communicating parties use a pair of encryption keys. Every time while sending data to another person, the sender can use either private or public key depending upon the requirement of sending data to one person or group of persons. Rather than applying digit mainpulation like in symmertric encryption, it performs numerical functions on the available data element. The technique used in asymmetric encryption is as follows :

1. Here, if sender wants to initiate connection with only one person in the network, he can use receiver's public key for sending message. On the other end, receiver can decode that message with his private key.
2. Like wise, if sender wants to communicate with more than one persons at a time, he can encrypt his message using his private key. Only those members having corresponding public key will be able to decrypt the message.

In this way everyone manages his own private key and public key of other members in the network to communicate with each other in a more secured way.

Asymmetric encryption provides more security in the way that different keys have been managed at both the sides.

At any moment if one feels like having some problem with his key, he can change the key and send the notice to concerned members.

The main drawback of this technique is :

1. The key size is kept large for security reasons, which makes processing speed slow.
2. It has been used by defense department for sending secured military messages, but destructive forces can also use the same technique to secure their messages. In the same way cryptanalysis becomes difficult on the defense side also.

   Cryptanalysis is the technique of breaking the code. If defense services use encryption for secure transmission of data then they also use cryptanalysis to crack the destructive message of terrorist parties, so it is good as well as bad on both the ends.

   Important example algorithms of asymmetric encryption are : Rivest-Shamir-Adleman (RSA) algorithm, Hashing, Digital Signatures.

Figure 12.7 shows difference between symmetric and asymmetric encryption techniques.

Sender ⇒ Encryption with secret key ⇒ Recipient ⇒ Decryption with password

(a)

Sender ⇒ Encryption with recipient's public key ⇒ Recipient ⇒ Decryption with recipient's private key

(b)

Figure 12.7 : (a) Symmetric and (b) Asymmetric encryption

EXERCISES

12.1 Compare capability lists and access lists.

12.2 Differentiate between static and dynamic association of a process with a domain.

12.3 What is the `need-to-know' principle ? Why is it important for a protection system to adhere to this principle ?

12.4 A password may become known to unwanted users in a variety of ways. Is there a simple method to detect that such an event has occurred ? Explain your answer.

12.5 The list of all passwords is kept within the operating system. If a user manages to read this list, password protection is no longer provided. Suggest a scheme to avoid this problem.

12.6 Make a list of six security concerns for a computer system in a bank. For each item on your list, state whether this concern relates to physical security, human security or operating system security.

12.7 Suggest some practical methods to deal with computer viruses and worms.

12.8 What are two advantages of encrypting the data stored in the computer system ?

12.9 Suppose that you share a file on a network with a fellow student so that he can copy this file from your system. What rights should he be given on this file ? What will be the contents of the cell of access matrix corresponding to this grant ?

12.10 What can be the purpose of installing a firewall in a college or an educational institute ?

12.11 Differentiate between symmetric and asymmetric encryption techniques.

OOOOO

CHAPTER

13

Operating System for Distributed Systems

OVERVIEW

This chapter introduces the concept of Distributed Systems, their advantages over independent PCs and centralized systems. A brief mention of their possible disadvantages has also been made. Sections 13.3 and 13.4 explain the concepts of Network operating systems and distributed operating systems. Section 13.5 explains the issues related with the design of a distributed operating system. The last Section 13.6 is a big one as it deals with all the synchronization issues related with distributed systems. Its various sub-sections explain the mechanisms for dealing with mutual exclusion requirements, concurrency control and deadlock handling in distributed systems. Various Election algorithms associated with the election of a coordinator site in a dfistributed system have also been explained. This chapter will be comparatively easy to understand as it just extends the previously known mechanisms (e.g., deadlock handling, concurrency control, etc.) to the concept of distributed environment.

13.1. INTRODUCTION

Starting in mid 1980s, two advances in technology changed the situation, when the computer used to be very huge in size and also very expensive. The first was the development of powerful microprocessors. Initially, these were 8-bit machines, but soon 16, 32 and even 64-bit CPUs became common. Many of these had the computing power of a decent-sized mainframe (i.e., large) computer, but for a fraction of the price.

The second development was the invention of high-speed local area networks or LANs. These systems allowed dozens, or even hundreds of machines to be connected in such a way that small amounts of information could be transferred between machines in a millisecond or so. Larger amounts of data can be moved between machines at the rate of 10 million bits/sec and more.

The net result of these two technologies is that it is now not only feasible, but also easy, to put together computing systems composed of large numbers of CPUs connected by a high-speed network. They are usually called distributed systems, in contrast to the previous centralized systems consisting of a single CPU, its memory, peripherals, and some terminals.

As distributed systems are quite different from the centralized ones, a totally different lot of software is needed for them. The very first software in this list is the most essential and most preliminary one *i.e.*, the operating system. A lot is being done and lot has to be done in the development of operating systems that serve to the needs of a distributed system.

13.2. GOALS

Just because it is possible to build distributed does not necessarily mean that it is a good idea. In this section we will discuss the motivation and goals of a typical distributed system, and look at their advantages and disadvantages compared to traditional centralized systems.

13.2.1 Centralized Versus Distributed Processing

Distributed processing implies that a number of computer systems are connected together to form a network. There are different ways of connecting computers, forming different topologies. Instead of a centralized computer system with centralized applications, data or control, you have a number of computers with distributed applications, data or control or combinations of these. Before, we move ahead the following terms should be clear to you.

- Distributed applications
- Distributed data
- Distributed control

13.2.1.1 Distributed Applications

The term 'Distributed Applications' really means that different applications or programs reside on different computers as shown in Figure 13.1. For instance, one computer can capture, store and process data required for a payroll application. Another may store and process the data for purchasing application, and so on. This scheme gives rise to the possibility of capturing the data where it originates. However, we still need computers to be connected, because there could be some data which is shared, for example, the purchasing application requires the inventory data which may be located on a different computer. Applications could be distributed in two ways :

- Horizontal distribution
- Vertical or hierarchical distribution

In **horizontal distribution,** all the computer systems are at the same level, i.e., they are equally capable of handling any functionality. Examples of this are office automation and airline reservation. Dozens or even hundreds of computers in the network are able to book or cancel any reservation, or enquire for any information.

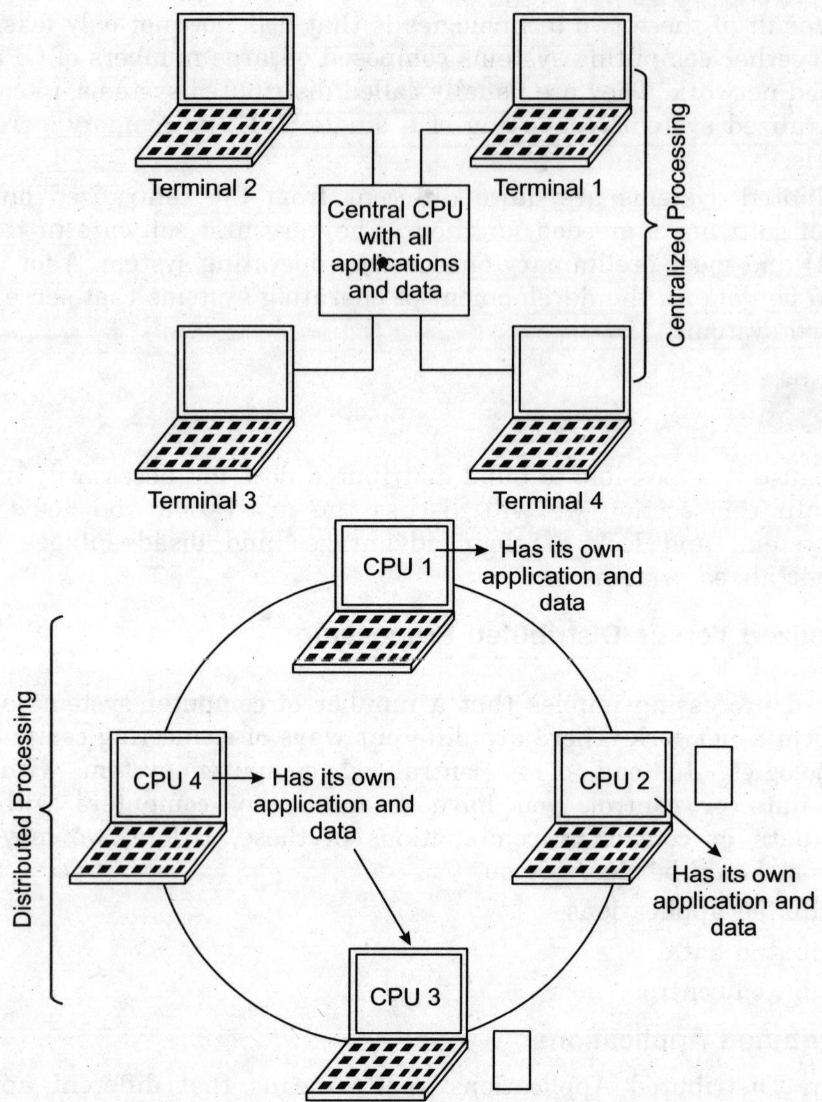

Figure 13.1 : Centralized versus Distributed Processing

In **vertical or hierarchical distribution,** there are various levels of functionality. These levels normally reflect the levels of an organization. For instance, a division of a company may have a number of zones and each zone in turn may have a number of branches. In such a case, a number of computers at the branch level will carry out the functions at various branches and send summaries to their higher level (zones). The computers at branch level can be networked together, if data sharing is required. This is shown in Figure 13.2. The computers at the zonal level also can be networked together, and they can share each other's information as depicted again by Figure 13.2.

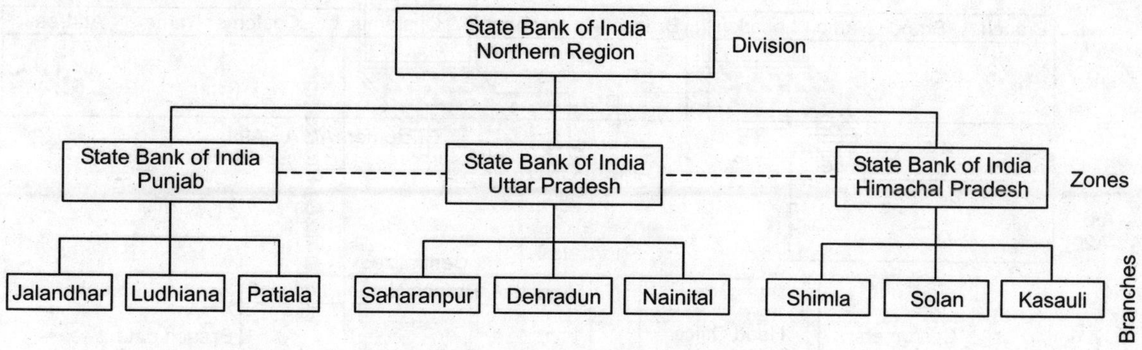

Figure 13.2 : Hierarchical distribution

The applications residing at the zonal level carry out all the zonal processing including processing of summaries received from branches and in turn producing summaries for the higher level. Therefore, one could map the distributed applications to truly hierarchical style of MIS of any organization.

13.2.1.2 Distribution of Data

In a distributed processing environment, the data required by various applications can be maintained as :

- Centralized data
- Replicated data
- Partitioned data

Figure 13.3 illustrates these concepts. The figure shows two branches of a bank networked together with their head office. It also shows three databases normally required for managing banking. One is *branch* database—containing information about different branches of the bank. Another is the *accounts* database which contains accounts and their balances for customers of each branch. Thus each branch should have this for its own accounts. The third database—*customers* should be available at all branches so that Branch1 can access the accounts of Branch2, if required and similarly, if required, Branch2 can access the accounts of Branch1.

In **centralized data,** the data resides at only one (preferably the central) node, but it can be shared amongst all the other nodes, *e.g.,* Branch database in Figure 13.3. In such a situation, this central node must run an operating system, which implements the functions of information management. It must keep track of various users, their files and directories. It must also handle sharing, protection and disk space allocation issues.

This node must also run a piece of front end software—normally a part of the operating system which receives requests for various pieces of data and then services them one by one. This software piece, and therefore, the entire node, is sometimes called a server. This scheme allows each node to have its local, private data but all the sharable data has to reside on a central server. In contrast to this scheme, we could distribute or spread our data on various nodes according to our needs. In fact, out of the total database, we could have only a part as centralized, and the rest distributed.

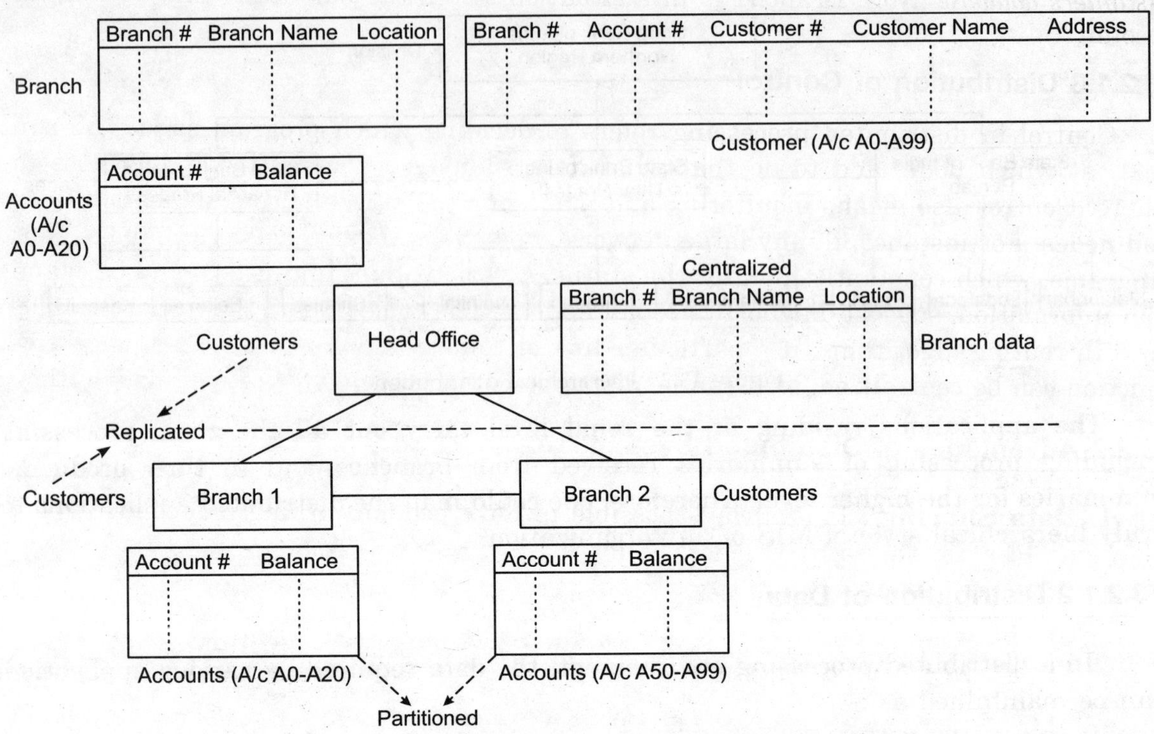

Figure 13.3 : Centralized, Replicated and partitioned Databases

If database is required very often at every node, and if transmitting it from a central node to the others is very expensive and time consuming, then that specific database could be **replicated or duplicated** at every node. But then, when any part of the data in the database changes the updates have to be made at all the desired locations immediately. Customers database shown in Figure 13.3 is replicated at two locations. It is present both at branch1 and branch2. In an airlines reservation system which connects the required computers at different locations worldwide, one can imagine that the flight timings and fares would need a lot of replication, because this information will be required very often at every node. Keeping it only at the central node would increase the network traffic tremendously and this would be very expensive. This replication also makes sense because it is a relatively stable data; changing only at a definite, pre-planned frequency when the time tables and fares change.

The third approach to the distribution of data is **partitioned data.** In this case, the database is sliced to multiple portions and different portions reside on different nodes according to the need. For example, the accounts database in Figure 13.3 is partitioned. A branch may not be physically storing the balances of all the accounts existing in the bank. The balances of only those accounts that belong to that branch can be maintained there. In case a customer of branch1 goes to branch2 for accessing his account and knows the branch# where his account is, his account number can be known by consulting the replicated *customers* database available with branch2.

If the customer does not know the Branch#, his account number can be known by first consulting the centralized *branch* database available at head office and then the *customers database.* Now, Branch1 is in a situation to tell the balance of this customer's account.

13.2.1.3 Distribution of Control

Control in distributed processing refers to deciding which program should be run next, at which node, and to do that what data should be transmitted from where to where. Control also means monitoring and managing the status of communication lines and nodes. For instance, in any large network, we always require network management programs, which constantly monitor the status of various lines and nodes, and based on that information, suggest diagnostics/repair actions. They also update the resource tables used in routing algorithms, if a particular link or a node fails for instance. This control function can be centralized, or it can be distributed with varying degrees of distribution.

13.2.2 Advantages of Distributed System over Independent PCs

1. Data Sharing : It is always possible to have people working independently on their own PCs, for the same business. But we know that users may need to share data. For example, airline reservation clerks need access to the master database of flights and existing reservations. Giving each clerk his own private copy of the entire database would not work, since nobody would be able to know which seats the other clerks have already sold. Shared data is absolutely essential to this kind of application and so, the machines must be interconnected.

2. Device Sharing : Data are not the only things to be shared. Expensive peripherals such as colour laser printers, photo-type setters and massive archival storage devices are also among the few things that should be sharable.

3. Communication : Another reason to connect a group of isolated computers into a distributed system is to achieve enhanced person-to-person communication. For many people, electronic mail has numerous attraction over paper mail, telephone and FAX as it makes various kinds of documents accessible by the people without changing their formats. This requires a good communication setup.

4. Flexibility : Finally, a distributed system is potentially more flexible than giving each user an isolated personal computer. If we have a mixture of personal and shared computers, perhaps of different sizes, and jobs run on the most appropriate ones rather than always on the owners' machine, then the workload can be spread over the computers more effectively and letting people run their jobs elsewhere may compensate for the loss of a few machines. This way the system will be more flexible.

13.2.3 Advantages of Distributed Systems over Centralized Ones

1. Speed : When used to implement parallel processing where only goal is to achieve maximum speed on a single problem, distributed systems can achieve very high speed as compared to the centralized ones.

2. Inherent Distribution : Another reason for building a distributed system is that some applications are inherently distributed. Banking, Airline reservation etc. are example of the applications that are inherently distributed. When all the branches or a bank are connected, we have a commercial distributed system.

3. Reliability : Another potential advantage of a distributed system over a centralized one is higher reliability. By distributing the workload over many machines, a single chip failure will bring down at most one machine, leaving the rest intact. Ideally, if 5 percent of the machines are down at any moment, the system should be able to continue to work with a 5 percent loss in performance. For critical applications, such as control of nuclear reactors or aircraft, using a distributed system to achieve high reliability may be a dominant consideration.

4. Incremental Growth : Finally, incremental growth is also potentially a big plus. Often a company will buy a mainframe with the intention of doing all its work on it. If the company prospers and the workload grows, at a certain point the mainframe will no longer be adequate. The only solution is to either replace the mainframe with a larger one (if its exists), or add a second mainframe. Both of these can cause management difficulties with the company's operations. In contrast, with a distributed system, it may be possible to simply add more processors to the system, thus allowing it to expand gradually as the need arises.

13.2.4 Disadvantages of Distributed Systems

Although, distributed systems have many advantages over centralized ones, yet there are some disadvantages that should be focused upon so that they can be removed totally in the next research phase of their development.

1. Very little software exists at present for the distributed systems : There are not much of experienced people involved in designing, implementing and using distributed software. What kinds of operating systems, programming languages, and applications are appropriate for these systems? How much should the users know about the distribution of data, control and applications? The experts differ on these issues. As more research is done, these problems may diminish, but for the moment it should not be underestimated.

2. Requirement for a strong communication network : Another problem is due to the communication network. It can lose messages and can become overloaded. When the network saturates, it must either be replaced or a second one must be added. In both the cases, some portion of one or more building may have to be rewired at great expense, or network interface boards may have to be replaced (e.g., by fiber optics). Once this system comes to depend on the network, its loss or saturation can negate most of the advantages, the distributed system was built to achieve.

3. Security issues : The easy sharing of data, which is an advantage, may turn out to be a disadvantage. If people can conveniently access data all over the system, they may equally be able to conveniently access data that they have no business looking at. In other words, security is often a problem. Here sometimes arises the need of an isolated personal computer with no network connections.

Despite these potential problems many people feel that the advantages outweigh the disadvantages, therefore it is expected that distributed systems will become increasingly important in the coming years.

13.3. NETWORK OPERATING SYSTEM

A network operating system provides an environment where users, who are aware of the multiplicity of machines, can access remote resources by either logging into the appropriate remote machine, or transferring data from the remote machine to their own machine.

13.3.1 Remote Login

An important function of a network operating system is to allow users to log in remotely on another computer. The Internet provides the *telnet* facility for this purpose. To illustrate this facility, let us suppose that a user at Punjabi University in Patiala wishes to access "cs.ttti_ed.wdu", a computer that is located at the TTTI (Technical Teachers' Training Institute) in Chandigarh. To do so, the user must have a valid account on that machine. To log in remotely, the user issues the following command :

telnet cs.ttti_ew.edu

This command results in a connection being formed between the local machine at Punjabi University and the "cs.ttti_ew.edu" computer at TTTI. After this connection has been established, the networking software creates a transparent, bi-directional link such that all characters entered by the user at Punjabi university are sent to a process on "cs.ttti_ew.edu" and all the output from that process is sent back to the user. The process on the remote machine asks the user for a login name and a password. Once the correct information has been received, this process can permit the user to compute on the remote machine just as any local user can.

13.3.2 Remote File Transfer

Another major function of a network operating system is to provide a mechanism for file transfer from one machine to another. In such an environment, each computer maintains its own local file system. If a user at one site 'TTTI' having computer ("cs.ttti_ew.edu") wants to access a file located on another computer at Punjabi University (cs.punb_ew.edu), then the file must be copied explicitly from the computer at "cs.punj_ew.edu" to the computer at TTTI.

The Internet provides a mechanism for such a transfer with the File Transfer Protocol (FTP) program. Suppose that a user on "cs.ttti_ew.edu" wants to copy a file *ekta.c* that resides on "cs.punj_ew.edu" into a local file *myekta.c*. The user must first invoke the FTP program, by executing

ftp cs.punj_ew.edu

The program then asks the user for the login name and a password. Once the correct information has been received, the user must connect to the sub-directory where the file *ekta.c* resides, and then copy the file by executing

get *ekta.c myekta.c*

In this scheme, the file location is not transparent to the user; the user must know exactly where each file is. Moreover, there is no real file sharing, because a user can only copy a file from one site to another. Thus, several copies of same file may exist, resulting in a waste of space. In addition, if these copies are modified, the various copies will be inconsistent.

Notice that in our example, the user at TTTI must have login permission on "cs.punj_ew.edu". FTP also provides a way to allow a user who does not have an account on the punjabi university computer (cs.punj_ew.edu) to copy files remotely. This remote copying is accomplished through the "anonymous ftp" method, which work as follows. The file to be copied (that is, *ekta.c*) must be placed in a special sub-directory (say FTP) with the protection set to allow the public to read the file. A user who wishes to copy the file uses the ftp command as before. When the user is asked for the login name, the user supplies the name "anonymous", and an arbitrary password.

Once anonymous login is accomplished, care must be taken by the system to ensure that this partially authorized user does not access inappropriate files. Generally, the user is allowed to access only those files that are in the directory tree of user "anonymous". Any files placed here are accessible to any anonymous user, subject to the usual file-protection scheme used on that machine. Anonymous users, however, cannot access files outside of this directory tree.

FTP requires the user to know a command set entirely different from the normal operating system commands. Telnet requires a smaller shift, in which the user must know appropriate commands of the remote system. For instance, a user on UNIX machine who telnets to a VMS machine must switch to VMS commands for the duration of the telnet session. It would be more convenient if users do not have to remember different set of commands. Distributed operating systems are designed to solve this problem.

13.4. DISTRIBUTED OPERATING SYSTEMS

In a distributed operating system, the users access remote resources in the same manner as they do local resources. The presence of the remote files is transparent to the user. Data and process migration from one site to another is under the control of the distributed operating system.

13.4.1 Data Migration

Suppose that a user on site 1 wants to access data (such as a file) from site 2. There are two basic methods for the system to transfer the data. One approach is to transfer the entire file to site 1. From that point on, all access to the file is local. When the user no longer needs access to the file, a copy of the file (if it has been modified) is sent back to site 2. Even if only a small change has been made to a large file, all the data must be transferred. This mechanism can be thought of as an automated FTP system. Unluckily, this is an inefficient approach.

The other approach is to transfer to site 1 only those portions of the file those are actually necessary for the immediate task. If another portion is required later, another transfer will take place. When the user no longer wants to access the file, any part of it that has been modified must be sent back to site 2.

Clearly, if only a small part of a large file is being accessed, the latter approach is preferable. If significantly large portions of the file are being accessed, it is more efficient to copy the entire file.

It is not sufficient merely to transfer data from one site to another. The system must also perform various data translations if the two sites involved are not directly compatible (for example, if the systems represent integers differently, then compatibility of such systems must be ensured).

13.4.2 Computation Migration

In some circumstances, it may be more efficient to transfer the computation, rather than the data, across the system. For example, if a job needs to access various large files that reside at different sites, in order to obtain a summary of those files. Then it would be more efficient to operate the files at the sites where they reside and return the desired results to the site that initiated the computation. Generally, if the time to transfer the data is longer than the time to execute the remote command, the remote command should be used.

Such a computation can be carried out in a number of different ways.

Suppose that a process P at site 2 wants to access a file at site 1. Access to the file is carried out at site 1 and could be initiated by a Remote Procedure Call (RPC). An RPC uses a datagram protocol (such as UDP) to execute a routine on a remote system. Process P invokes a predefined procedure at site 1. The procedure executes appropriately and then returns the result to process P on site 2.

Alternatively, process P on site 2 can send a message to site 1. The operating system at site 1 would then create a new process P_1 whose function is to carry out the designated task. When process P_1 completes its execution, it sends the needed result back to P via the message system. Note that, in this scheme, process P may execute concurrently with process P_1, and, in fact, may have several processes running concurrently on several sites.

Both methods could be used to access several files residing at various sites. One remote procedure call might result in the invocation of another remote procedure call, or even in the transfer of messages to another site.

13.4.3 Process Migration

A logical extension to computation migration is process migration. When a process is submitted for execution, it is not always executed at the site in which it is initiated. It may be advantageous to execute the entire process, or parts of it, at different sites. This scheme may be used for several reasons :

Load balancing : The processes (or sub-processes) may be distributed across the network to evenly distribute the workload.

Computation speedup : If a single process can be divided into a number of sub-processes that may run concurrently on different sites, then the total process turnaround time can be reduced.

Hardware preference : The process may have characteristics that makes it more suitable for execution on some specialized processor (such as matrix inversion on an array processor, rather than on a microprocessor).

Software preference : The process may require software that are available at only one particular site, and therefore, the process should be moved there.

Data access : Just as in computation migration, if the data used in computation are numerous, it may be more efficient to have a process run remotely, rather than to transfer all the data locally.

There are basically two techniques that can be used to move processes in a computer network. In the first, the system can attempt to hide the fact that (the process has migrated) from the client. This scheme has the advantage that the user does not need to code his program explicitly to accomplish the migration.

The other approach is to allow (or require) the user to specify explicitly how the process should migrate. This method is usually employed in a situation when the process must be moved to satisfy a hardware or software preference. Some examples of existing distributed operating system are Amoeba, Chorus, QNX, Tao etc.

13.5. DESIGN ISSUES

Let us now, look at some of the design issues that must be dealt with while building a distributed operating system.

13.5.1 Transparency

What does transparency really mean? Let us look at a few examples to make the idea clearer. To start with, imagine a distributed system consisting of workstations each running some standard operating system. Normally system services (*e.g.*, reading files) are obtained by issuing a system call that traps to the kernel. In such a system, remote files should be accessed the same way.

A system in which remote files are accessed by explicitly setting up a network connection to a remote server and then sending messages to it is not transparent because remote services are then being accessed differently than local ones. The programmer can tell that multiple machines are involved, and this is not allowed.

Thus the issue of transparency deals with giving the users an impression that they are using single processor sharing system instead of a distributed system. This goal implies that the distributed nature of the system should be transparent.

This transparency can be achieved at two different levels.

One way is that the distribution should be kept completely hidden from the users. The user should not know that his command actually gets divided into sub-commands, which are executed on different machines. In terms of commands issued from the terminal and results displayed on the terminal, the distributed system can be made to look just like a single processor system.

At a lower level, it is also possible, but harder, to make the system look transparent to programs. In other words, the system call interface can be designed so that the existence of multiple processors is not visible.

The concept of transparency can be applied to severals aspects of a distributed system, as shown in Figure 13.4. This includes location, migration, replication, concurrency, and parallelism transparency.

Location Transparency

Location transparency refers to the fact that in a true distributed system, users cannot tell where hardware and software resources such as CPUs, printers, files, and databases are located. The name of the resource must not secretly encode the location of the resource, so names like *"tti_ew.ekta.c"* or *"/ttti_ew/ekta.c"* are not acceptable.

Kind	Meaning
Location transparency	the users cannot tell where resources are located
Migration transparency	Resources can move without changing their names
Replication transparency	The users cannot tell how many copies exist
Concurrency transparency	Multiple users can share resources automatically
Parallelism transparency	Activities can happen in parallel without users knowing about it

Figure 13.4 : Different kinds of transparency in a distributed system

Migration Transparency

Migration transparency means that resources must be free to move from one location to another without having their names changed.

Suppose that a system administrator realizes that a portion of data (data 1) residing at site A should actually be located at site B, and thus migrates "data 1" to site B. Later this "data 1" is accessed by some user at site C assuming that it is still at site A.

Now, this user finds that "data 1" no longer exists at site A and this implies that the system is not migration transparent. If the system would have been migration transparent, it should have not reflected the absence of "data 1" on site A and the link to "data 1" on site B should have been automatically restored and "data 1" should have been accessed from site B without user's knowledge.

Replication transparency

If a distributed system has replication transparency, then the operating system is free to make additional copies of files and other resources on its own without the users noticing. To see how replication transparency might be achievable, consider a collection of n servers logically connected to form a ring. Each server maintains the entire directory tree structure, but holds only a subset of the files themselves. To read a file, a client sends a message containing the full path name to any of the servers. The server checks to see if it has the file. If so, it returns the data requested. If not, it forwards the request to the next server in the ring, which then repeats the algorithm. In this system, the servers can decide by themselves to replicate any file on any or all servers, without the users having to know about this at all. Such a scheme is replication transparent because it allows the system to transparently make copies of heavily used files without the users even being aware of this happening.

Concurrency transparency

Distributed systems usually have multiple, independent users. What should the system do when two or more users try to access the same resource at the same time? For example, what happens if two users try to update the same file at the same time? If the system incorporates concurrency transparency, the users will not notice the existence of other users. One mechanism for achieving this form of transparency would be for the system to automatically lock a resource once someone had started to use it, unlocking it only when the access was finished. In this manner, all resources would only be accessed sequentially, never concurrently.

Parallelism transparancy

The hardest issue is parallelism transparency. In principle, a distributed system is supposed to appear to the users as a traditional uniprocessor timesharing system. What happens if a programmer knows that his distributed system has 1000 CPUs and he wants to use a substantial fraction of them for executing some parts of a sophisticated program in parallel? The answer is that together the compiler, runtine system, and operating system should be able to figure out how to take advantage of this potential parallelism without the programmer even knowing it. Unfortunately, the current state is not allwoing this to happen. Programmers who actually want to use multiple CPUs for a single problem are required to program this explicitly. Parallelism transparency can be regarded as a challenge for distributed system designers.

13.5.2 Flexibility

The second design issue is flexibility. It is important that the system should be flexible because we are just beginning to learn about how to build distributed systems. It is likely that this process will incur many false starts and considerable backtracking. Design decisions that now seem reasonable may later prove to be wrong. The best way to avoid problems is thus to keep one's option open.

There are two thoughts concerning the structure of distributed systems. One thought, each machine should run a traditional kernel that provides most services itself. The other maintains that the kernel should provide as little as possible, with the bulk of the operating system service available from user-level servers. These two models known as the monolithic kernel and microkernel, respectively, are illustrated in figure 13.5. This is something you should have already read in chapter 3 of this book.

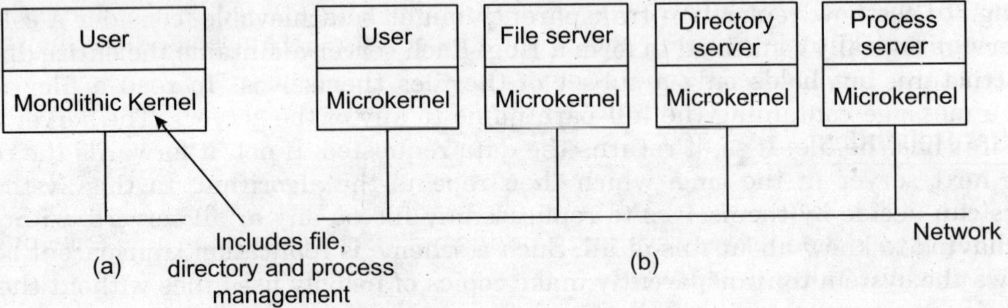

Figure 13.5 : (a) Monolithic Kernel (b) Microkernel

The monolithic kernel is basically today's centralized operating system augmented with networking facilities and the integration of remote services. Most system calls are made by trapping to the kernel, having the work performed there, and having the kernel return the desired result to the user process. Many distributed systems that are extensions of UNIX use this approach because UNIX itself has a large, monolithic kernel.

Most distributed systems that have been designed from scratch use the microkernel approach. The microkernel is more flexible because it does almost nothing. It basically provides just for minimal services :

1. An inter-process communication mechanism
2. Some memory management
3. A limited amount of low-level process management and scheduling
4. Low-level input/output.

In particular, unlike the monolithic kernel, it does not provide the file system, directory system, full process management, or much of system call handling. The goal is to keep the kernel small.

All the other operating system services are generally implemented as user-level services. To look up names, read a file, or obtain some other service, the user sends a message to the appropriate server, which then does the work and returns the result. The advantage of this method is that it is highly modular : there is a well-defined interface to each service (the set of messages the server understand), and every service is equally accessible to every client, independent of location. In addition, it is easy to implement, install, and debug new service since adding or changing a service does not require stopping the system and booting a new kernel, as is the case with a monolithic kernel. It is precisely this ability to add, delete, and modify services that gives the microkernel its flexibility.

As a simple example of this power, it is possible to have a distributed system with multiple file servers, one supporting MS-DOS file service and another supporting UNIX file service. Individual programs can use either or both, if they choose. In contrast, with a monolithic kernel, the file system is built into the kernel, and users have no choice but to use it.

The only potential advantage of the monolithic kernel is performance. Trapping to the kernel and doing everything there will be faster than sending messages to remote servers. However, a detailed comparison of two distributed operating systems, one with a monolithic kernel (Sprite), and with a microkernel (Amoeba), has shown that in practice this advantage is nonexistent.

13.5.3 Reliability

One of the original goals of building distributed systems was to make them more reliable than single process system. The idea is that if some machine goes down, some other machine takes over the job.

It is important to distinguish various aspects of reliability.

1. Availability

Availability is the time for which a system is usable. Availability can be enhanced by a design that does not require the simultaneous functioning of a substantial number of critical components. Another tool for improving availability is redundancy : key pieces of hardware and software should be replicated, so that if one them fails the others will be able to take up.

A high reliable system must be highly available, but that is not enough. Data entrusted to the system must not be lost or garbled in any way, and if files are stored redundantly on multiple servers, all the copies must be kept consistent. In general, the more copies that are kept, the better the availability, but the greater the chance that they will be inconsistent, especially if updates are frequent. The designers of all distributed systems must keep this problem in mind at all times.

2. Security

Another aspect of overall reliability is security. Files and other resources must be protected from uanuthorized usage. Although the same issue occurs in single-processor systems, in distributed systems it is more severe. In a single-processor system, the user logs in and its authenticated. From then on, the system knows who the user is and can check whether each attempted access is legal. In a distributed system, when a message comes in to a server asking for something, the server has no simple way of determining who it is form. No name or identification field in the message can be trusted, since the sender may try to deceive the receiving server.

3. Fault Tolerance

Still another issue relating to reliability is fault tolerance. Suppose a server crashes and then quickly reboots. What happens ? Does the server crash bring down users with it ? If the server has tables containing important information about ongoing activites, recovery will be difficult.

In general, distributed system can be designed to hide failures them from the users.

13.5.4 Performance

Performance is an issue associated with the design of every kind of system. When running a particular application on a distributed system, it should not be appreciable worse than running that same application on a single processor.

Various performance metrics can be used. Response time, throughput (number of jobs completed per hour), system utilization, and amount of network capacity consumed are few such metrics.

The performance problem is compounded by the fact that communication, which is essential in a distributed system is typically quite slow. Sending a message and getting a reply over a LAN takes about 1 msec. Most of the time spent is due to protocol handling on both ends, rather than the time the bits spend on the wire. Thus to optimize performance, one often has to minimize the number of messages. The difficulty with this strategy is that the best way to gain performance is to have many activities running in parallel on different processors, but doing so requires sending many messages.

One possible way out is to pay considerable attention to the size of all computations. Starting up a small computation remotely, such as adding two integers, is a good idea, because the communication overhead is much more than the extra CPU cycles gained. On the other hand, starting up a long CPU-bound job remotely is a good idea.

13.5.5 Scalability

Consider the interactive access to all kinds of databases and services ranging from electronic banking to reserving places in planes, trains, hotels, theatres and restaurants. These distributed systems have millions of users. It is to be ensured that the methods we are currently developing should scale to such large systems.

Although little is known about such huge distributed systems, one guiding principle is clear : avoid centralized components, tables, and algorithms. Having a single mail server for 50 million users would not be a good idea. Even though it has enough CPU and storage capacity, the network capacity into and out of it would surely be a problem. Furthermore, the system would not tolerate faults well. A single power outage could bring the entire system down. Lastly, most mail is local. Having a message sent by a user in Chandigarh to another user who is two sectors away, pass through a machine in Paris is obviously inefficient.

Centralized tables are almost as bad as centralized components. How should one keep track of the telephone numbers and addresses of 50 million people ? Suppose each data record could be fit into 50 characters. A single 2.5 GB disk would provide enough storage. But here again, having a single database would undoubtedly saturate all the communication lines into and out of it. It would also be vulnerable to failures (a speck of dust could cause a head crash and bring down the entire service).

Thus centralization should be avoided to make distributed systems scalable.

13.6. SYNCHRONIZATION ISSUES IN DISTRIBUTED SYSTEMS

We know that process in distributed system should connunicate with each other using some fixed set of rules (protocols). The methods for this communication include layered protocols, request/reply message passing including RPC (Remote Procedure Call) and group communication (i.e. multicasting, broadcasting etc.).

Another important thing that should be focused upon is how these processes should cooperate and synchronize with one another. This implies that methods to implement solutions for the critical section problem and resource allocation in a distributed system must be known.

This section deals with inter-process cooperation and synchronization in distributed systems. It is clear that the methods to implement inter-process cooperation and synchronization in distributed systems will be more complex and difficult to implement as compared to those in single CPU systems.

13.6.1 Event Ordering

In a centralized system, it is always possible to determine the order in which two events have occurred, since there is a single common memory and clock. In many applications, it is of high importance to be able to determine order of events. For example, in a resource-allocation scheme, we specify that a resource can be used only after the resource has been granted. In a distributed system, however, there is no common memory and no common clock. Therefore, it is sometimes impossible to say which of two events in distributed systems happened first. Since the ability to define a total ordering is crucial in many applications, a distributed algorithm for extending the happened-before relation to a consistent total ordering of all the events in the system has been described here :

13.6.1.1 The Happened-Before Relation

Since we are considering only sequential processes, all events executed in single process are totally ordered. It is also known that a message can be received only after it has been sent. Therefore, we can define the happened-before relation (denoted by →) on a set of events as follows (assuming that sending and receiving a message constitutes an event) :

1. If A and B are events in the same process, and A was executed before B, then A → B *i.e.* A happened before B.
2. If A is the event sending a message by process and B is the event of receiving that message by another process, then A → B *i.e.* A happened before B.
3. If A → B and B → C then A → C *i.e.* A happened before C.

Since an event cannot happen before itself, the → relation is an irreflexive partial ordering.

If two events, A and B, are not related by the → relation (that is, A did not happen before B, and B did not happen before A), then we say that these two events were executed concurrently. Such events cannot affect each other. If, however, A → B, then it is possible for event A to affect event B in some way or the other.

A diagram, such as that in Figure 13.6 can best illustrate the definitions of concurrency and of happened-before relation. The horizontal direction represents space (that is, different processes) and the vertical direction represents time. The labelled vertical lines denote processes (or processors). The labeled dots denote events. A wavy line denotes a message sent from one process to another. From this diagram, it is clear that events A and B are concurrent if and only if no path exists either from A to B or from B to A.

For example, consider Figure 13.6. Some of the events related by the happened-before relation are :

$a_1 \rightarrow b_2$,

$c_0 \rightarrow b_4$,

$b_3 \rightarrow c_1$,

$a_1 \rightarrow b_4$, (since $a_1 \rightarrow b_2$, and $b_2 \rightarrow b_4$).

Some of the concurrent events in the system are :

b_0 and a_2,
c_0 and b_3,
c_0 and a_3,
b_3 and a_3.

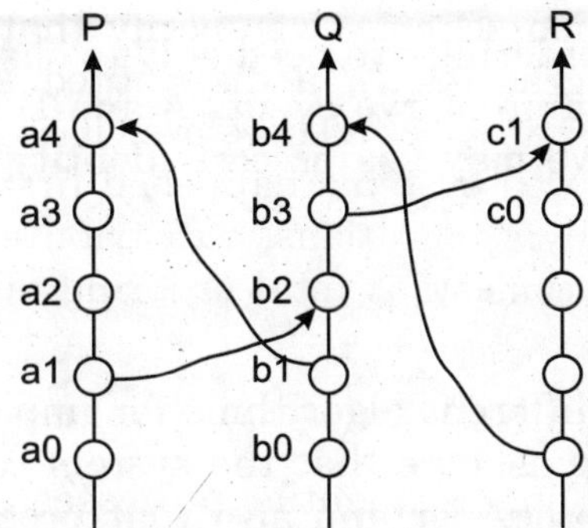

Figure 13.6 : Relative time for three concurrent processes

We cannot know which of the two concurrent events, such as b_0 and a_2, happened first.

13.6.1.2 Implementation

To determine that an event A happened before an event B, we need either a common clock or a set of perfectly synchronized clocks. Since, in a distributed system neither of these is available, we must define the happened-before relation without the use of physical clocks.

We associate with each system event a timestamp. We can then define the global-ordering requirement : For every pair of events A and B, if A → B, then the timestamp of A is less than the timestamp of B. We will see here that the converse does not need to be true.

Let us see how to enforce the global ordering requirement in a distributed environment ? We define within each process P a logical clock, LC. The logical clock can be implemented as a simple counter that is incremented between any two successive events executed within a process. Since the logical clock has an increasing value, it assigns a unique number to every event, and if an event A occurs before events B in process P, then LC(A) < LC(B). The timestamp for an event is the value of the logical clock for that event. Clearly, this scheme ensures that, for any two events in the same process, the global ordering requirement is met.

Unfortunately, this scheme does not ensure that the global ordering requirement is met across processes. To illustrate the problem, we consider two processes P_1 and P_2 that communicate with each other. Suppose that P_1 sends a message to P_2 (event A) with $LC_1(A) = 100$, and P_2 receives the message (event B) with $LC_2(B) = 95$ (because the processor for P_2 is solwer than the processor for P_1 and so its logical clock ticks slower). This situation violates our requirement, since A → B, but the timestamp of A is greater than the timestamp of B.

To resolve this difficulty, we require a process to advance its logical clock when it receives a message whose timestamp is greater than the current value of its logical clock. This implies that if a process P_i receives a message (even B) with timestamp t and $LC_i(B) \leq t$, then it should advance its clock such that $LC_i(B) = t + 1$. Thus, in our example, when P_2 receives the message from P_1, it will advance its logical clock such that $LC_2(B) = 101$.

Finally, to realize a total ordering, we need only to observe that, with our timestamp ordering scheme, if the timestamp of two events A and B are the same, then the events are concurrent. In this case, we may use process identity numbers to break ties and to create a total ordering.

13.6.2 Mutual Exclusion

There exist a number of different algorithms for implementing mutual exclusion in a distributed environment. We assume that the system consists of n processes, each of which resides at a different processor and also that processes are numbered uniquely from 1 to n, and that there is a one-to-one mapping between processes and processors (that is, each process has its own processor). Now let us concentrate on mutual exclusion algorithms mentioned here.

13.6.2.1 Centralized Approach

In a centralized approach to providing mutual exclusion, one of the processes in the system is chosen to coordinate the entry to the critical section. Each process that wants to invoke mutual exclusion sends request message to the coordinator. When the process receives a reply message from the cooordinator, it can proceed to enter its critical section. After exiting its critical section, the process sends a release message to the coordinator and proceeds with rest of its execution.

On receiving a request message, the coordinator checks to see whether some other process is in its critical section. If no process is in its critical section, the coordinator immediately sends back a reply message. Otherwise, the request is queued. When the coordinator receives a release message, it removes one of the request messages from the queue (in accordance with some schedulig algorithm) and sends a reply message to the requesting process.

It should be clear that this method ensures mutual exclusion. This scheme requires three messages per critical-section entry : a request, a reply, and a release.

If the coordinator process fails, then a new process must take its place. In the sub-section 13.7, various algorithms for electing a unique new coordinator have been described. Once a new coordinator has been elected, it must poll all the processes in the system, to reconstruct its request queue. Once the queue has been constructed, the computation may resume.

13.6.2.2 Fully Distributed Approach

If we want to distribute this decision-making job (that decides which process should execute its critical section next) across the entire system, then the solution is far more complicated. We present an algorithm that is based on the event-ordering scheme described in Section 13.6.1.1.

When a process A wants to enter its critical section, it generates a new timestamp, TS, and sends the message request (A, TS) to all other processes including itself. On receiving a request message a process may reply immediately (that is, send a reply message back to A), or it may defer sending a reply back (because it is already in its critical section, for example). A process that has received a reply message from all other processes in the system can enter its critical section. After exiting its critical section, the process sends reply messages to all its deferred requests.

The decision whether process A replies immediately to a request (B, TS) message or defers its reply is based on three factors :

1. If process A is in its critical section, then it defers its reply to B.
2. If process A does not want to enter its critical section, then it sends a reply immediately to B.
3. If process A wants to enter its critical section but has not yet entered it, then it compares its own request timestamp with the timestamp TS of the incoming request made by process B. If its own request timestamp is greater than TS, then it sends a reply immediately to B. Otherwise, the reply is deferred.

This algorithm has the advantage that the mutual exclusion is obtained in a simple manner. It is also free from deadlock and starvation.

13.6.2.3 Token-Passing Approach

Another method of providing mutual exclusion is to circulate a token among the processes in the system. A token is a special type of message that is passed around the system. Possession of the token entitles the holder to enter the critical section. Since there is only a single token in the system, only one process can be in its critical section at a time.

The ring talked about here should be logical and not physical i.e. we assume that the processes in the system are logically organized in a ring structure; the physical communication network does not need to be a ring. To implement mutual exclusion, the token is passed around the ring. When a process receives the token, it may enter its critical section, keeping the token. After this process exits its critical section, the token is passed around again. If the process receiving the token does not want to enter its critical section, keeping the token. After this process exits its critical section, the token is passed around again. If the process receiving the token does not want to enter its critical section, it passes the token to its neighbour.

Since there is only a single token, only one process at a time can be in its critical section. In addition, if the ring is unidirectional, freedom from starvation is ensured.

Two types of failures must be considered. First, if the token is lost, an election must be called to generate a new token. Second, if a process fails, a new logical ring must be established. There are several different algorithms for election and for reconstructing a logical ring. In sub-section 13.7 an election algorithm has been explained.

13.6.3 Deadlock Handling

The deadlock-prevention, deadlock-avoidance, and deadlock-detection algorithms presented in Chapter 7 can be enhanced so that they can also be used in a distributed system. In the following sub-sections we describe these distributed algorithms.

13.6.3.1 Deadlock Prevention

The deadlock prevention and deadlock-avoidance algorithms presented in Chapter 7 can also be used in a distributed system, provided that appropriate modifications are made.

1. We can use the resource-ordering deadlock-prevention technique by simply defining a global ordering among the system resources. That is, all resources in the entire system are assigned unique numbers, and a process may request a resource (at any processor) with unique number i only if it is holding a resource with a unique number greater than i.
2. We can use the banker's algorithm in a distributed system by designating one of the processes in the system as the process that maintains the information necessary to carry out the banker's algorithm. Every resource request must be channeled through the banker's algorithm.

   These two schemes can be used in dealing with the deadlock problem in a distributed environment. The first scheme is simple to implement and requires little overhead. The second scheme can also be implemented easily, but it may require too many overheads. Since the number of messages to and from the process executing banker's algorithm may be large, therefore, the banker's scheme does not seem to be of practical use in a distributed system.
3. Another scheme based on time stamp-ordering approach is being mentioned as under :

   To control the preemption, we assign a unique priority number to each process. These numbers are used to decide whether a process A should wait for process B. For example, we can let A wait for B if A has a priority higher than that of B; otherwise A is rolled back. This scheme prevents deadlock because, for every edge A → B in the wait-for graph, A has a higher priority than B. Thus, A can wait for B but B cannot wait for A and therefore, a cycle cannot exist.

   One difficulty with this scheme is the possibility of starvation. Some processes with extremely low priority may always be rolled back. This difficulty can be avoided through the use of timestamps. Each process in the system is assigned a unique timestamp when it is created. Two deadlock-prevention schemes using timestamps have been explained below :

- **The wait and die scheme :** This approach is based on a non-preemptive technique. When process A requests a resource currently held by B, A is allowed to wait only if it has a smaller timestamp than that of B. Otherwise A is rolled back (dies). For example, suppose that processes P_1, P_2 and P_3 have timestamps 2, 5 and 10 respectively. If P_1 requests a resource held by P_2, P_1 will wait. If P_3 requests a resource held by P_2, P_3 will be rolled back. In this scheme, an older process must wait for a younger one to release its resource. Thus, the older the process gets the more it tends to wait.

- **The wound and wait scheme :** This approach is based on a preemptive technique and is a counterpart to the wait and die system. When process A requests a resource currently held by B, A is allowed to wait only if it has a larger timestamp than does B (that is, A is younger than B). Otherwise, B is rolled back. Looking at our previous example, with processes P_1, P_2 and P_3 if P_1 requests a resource held by P_2, then the resource will be preempted from P_2 and P_2 will be rolled back. If P_3 requests a resource held by P_2, then P_2 will wait. In this scheme, an older process never waits for a younger process.

The major problem with these two schemes is that unnecessary rollbacks may occur.

13.6.3.2 Deadlock Detection

The deadlock-prevention algorithm may preempt resources even if no deadlock has occurred. To prevent unnecessary preemption, we can use a deadlock-detection algorithm. We construct a wait-for graph describing the Resource-allocation State. Since we are assuming only a single resource of each type, a cycle in the wait-for graph represents a deadlock (as we have already studied in Chapter 7 of this text).

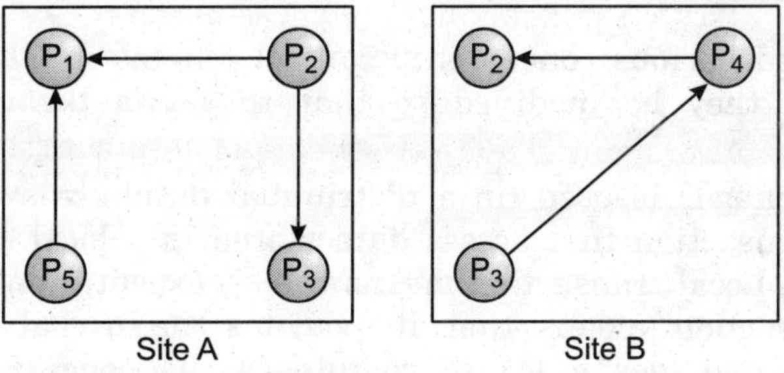

Figure 13.7 : Two local wait-for graphs

The main problem in a distributed system is deciding how to maintain the wait-for graph. There are many different schemes to deal with this problem. These schemes require that each site keep a local wait-for graph. The nodes of the graph correspond to all the processes (local as well as non-local) that are currently either holding or requesting any of the resources local to the site. For example, in Figure 13.7 we have a system consisting of two sites, each maintaining its local wait-for graphs. Note that processes P_2 and P_3 appear in both graphs, indicating that these processes have requested resources at both sites.

These local wait-for graphs are constructed in the usual manner for local processes and resources. When a process P_i in site A needs a resource held by process P_j in site B, a request message is sent by P_i to site B. The edge $P_i \rightarrow P_j$ is then inserted in the local wait-for graph of site B.

Clearly, if any local wait-for graph has a cycle, deadlock has occurred. On the other hand, the fact that there are no cycles in any of the local wait-for graphs does not mean that there are no deadlocks. To illustrate this problem, we consider the system depicted in Figure 13.7. Each wait-for graph is acyclic; nevertheless, a deadlock exists in the system. To prove that a deadlock has not occurred, we must show that the union of all local graphs is acyclic. The wait for graph (shown in Figure 13.8) that we obtain by taking the union of the two wait-for graphs of Figure 13.7 contains a cycle, implying that the system is in a deadlock state.

There are a number of different methods for organizing the wait-for graph in a distributed system. The description of schemes for organizing the wait-for graph in a distributed system is out of the scope of this text.

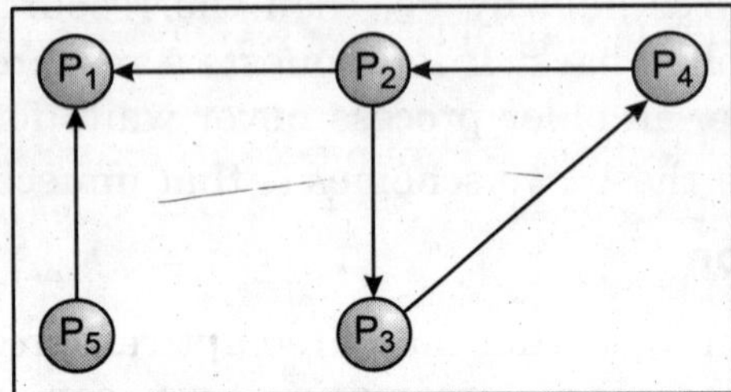

Figure 13.8 : Global wait-for graph for Figure 13.7

13.6.4 Concurrency Control

We have discussed various concurrency control schems in Chapter 6 of this book. Let us see how can they be modified so that they can be used in a distributed environment.

A transaction manager is used (in a distributed database system) to manage the execution of those transaction that access data stored in a local site. Such transaction can be local or global. Local transaction means that it executes only at a particular site whereas global transaction means that it executes at several sites. At every site, transaction manager manages a log to coordinate the concurrent execution of the transactions executing at that site. Two basic schemes : locking protocols and timestamping have been discussed with respect to concurrency control in distributed systems.

13.6.4.1 Locking

It is the most widely used concurrency control technique. When an object is to be read or written, it must be first locked by a process. Locking can be done using a centralized lock manager, or with a local lock manager on each machine for managing local files. In both cases the lock manager maintains a list of locked files, and rejects all attempts for locking the files that are already locked by another process. Locks are normally acquired and released by the transaction manager and do not require any action by the programmer.

Locks should be distinguished as read locks and write locks. If a read lock is set on a file, other read locks are permitted. Read locks are set to make sure that the file does not change, but there is no reason to stop other transactions from reading the file. In contrast, when a file is locked for writing, no other locks of any kind are permitted. Thus read locks are shared, but write locks must be exclusive.

For simplicity, we have assumed that the unit of locking is the entire file. In practice, it might be a smaller item, such as an individual record or page, or a larger item, such as entire database. The issue of size of the item to be locked is called the granularity of locking. The finer the granularity, the more precise the lock can be, and the more parallelism can be achieved. For example, a process that wants to use the end of a file can acquire a lock on only this portion of the file and therefore, should not be held up by some other process using the beginning of the file. On the other hand, find-grained locking requires more locks and is therefore, more expensive, and can lead to deadlocks also.

Now let us see how this locking technique can be applied in various distributed systems with different characteristics.

13.6.4.1.1 Non-Replicated Scheme

If no data are replicated in the system, then the locking scheme can be applied as follows :

Every site has its own local lock manager which manages the locking and unlocking of the data items stored at that site. Whenever, a transaction wishes to lock a data item at site S, it sends a message to lock manager at site S, requesting a lock (either shared or exclusive). If that data item is already locked in exclusive mode, then the request is delayed until that lock is released.

Once it has been determined that the lock request can be granted, the lock manager sends a message back to the initiator indicating that lock request has been granted.

This scheme is simple, as it requires two message transfers for handling lock requests and one message transfer for handling unlock requests.

13.6.4.1.2 Single Coordinator Scheme

In this scheme, the lock manager is centralized and resides at a single site S. All the lock and unlock requests are made at this site S. Whenever, a transaction needs to lock a data item, it sends a lock request to S. The lock manager determines whether lock can be granted. If so, then it sends a message that lock has been granted, to the site from where the lock request was initiated. Otherwise, the request is delayed until it can be granted. The requesting transaction can read the data from any one of the sites at which the replica of the data item resides. In case the contents have to be written, all the sites where a replica of the data item resides must be involved in the writing.

This scheme has following **advantages :**

1. It is simple, as it requires only two messages for handling lock requests and one message for handling unlock requests.
2. As all the lock and unlock requests are made at one site, the deadlock can be handled much easily as compared to complex deadlock handling in case of single non-replicated scheme.

This scheme has the following **disadvantages :**

1. Site S will always be heavily overloaded.
2. If site S fails, the concurrency control is lost.

13.6.4.2 Timestamps

A completely different approach to concurrency control is to assign each transaction a timestamp at the moment when it starts executing itself.

Our first task, then, in generalizing the centralized scheme to a distributed scheme is to develop a scheme for generating unique timestamps. Once this scheme has been developed, the previous protocols mentioned in Chapter 6 can be applied directly to non-replicated environment.

13.6.4.2.1 Generation of Unique Timestamps

There are two primary methods for generating unique timestamps; centralized and distributed. In the centralized scheme, a single site is chosen for distributing the timestamps. The site can use a logical counter or its own local clock for this purpose.

In the distributed scheme, each site generates a unique local timestamp using either a logical counter or the local clock. The global unique timestamp is obtained by concatenation of the unique local time stamp with the site identifier, which must be unique. The order of concatenation is important.

We may still have a problem if one site generates local timestamps at a faster rate than do other sites. In such a case, the fast site's logical counter will be larger than that of other sites. Therefore, all timestamps generated by the fast site will be larger than those generated by other sites. Therefore, a mechanism is needed to ensure that local timestamps are generated fairly across the system. To accomplish the fair generation of timestamps, we define within each site S, a logical clock, which gnerates the unique local timestamp. The logical clock can be implemented as a counter that is incremented after a new local timestamp are generated fairly across the system. To accomplish the fair generation of timestamps, we define within each site S, a logical clock, which generates the unique local timestamp. The logical clock can be implemented as a counter that is incremented after a new local timestamp is generated. To ensure that the various logical clocks are sycnhronized, we require that site S advance its logical clock whenever a transaction T with timestamp <t, r> visits that site and t is greater than the current value of LC. In this case, site S advances its logical clock to the value t + 1.

If the system clock is used to generate timestamps, then timestamps are assigned fairly provided that no site has a system clock that runs fast or slow. Since clocks may not be perfectly accurate, a technique similar to that used for logical clocks must be used to ensure that no clock gets far ahead or far behind another clock.

13.6.4.2.2 Timestamping technique in Distributed Systems

Every file in the system has a read timestamp and a write timestamp associated with it, telling which committed transaction last read and wrote it, respectively. If transactions are short and widely spaced in time, then it will normally occur that when a process tries to access a file, the file's read and write timestamps will be lower than the current transaction's timestamp. This ordering means that the transactions are being processed in the proper order.

When the ordering is incorrect i.e. a transaction that started later than the current one has managed to get in there, access the file, and commit. Then this situation means that the current transaction is too late, so it is aborted.

It is easiest to explain the timestamp method by means of an example. Imagine that there are three transaction, A, B and C. Transaction A ran a long time ago using every file needed by B and C, so all their files have read and write timestamps set to A's timestamp. B and C start concurrenlty, with B having a lower timestamp than C (but higher than A of course).

Let us first consider B writing a file. Let its timestamp be, T, and take the read and write timestamps of the file to be written as T_R and T_W, respectively. Unless C has committed, both T_R and T_W will be A's timestamp, and thus less than T. In Figures 13.9(a) and 13.9(b) we see that T is larger than both T_R and T_W (C has not already committed), so the write is accepted and done tentatively. It will become permanent when B commits. B's timestamp is now recorded in the file as tentative write.

In Figures 13.9(c) and 13.9(d) B does not get chance. C has either read (c) or written (d) the file and committed. B's transaction is aborted. However, it can apply for a new timestamp and start all over again.

Now look at reads. In Figure 13.9(e), there is no conflict, so the read can happen immediately. In Figure 13.9(f), some other transaction has got the chance and is trying to write the file. This transaction's timestamp is lower than B's so B simply waits until this transaction commits, at which time it can read the new file and continue.

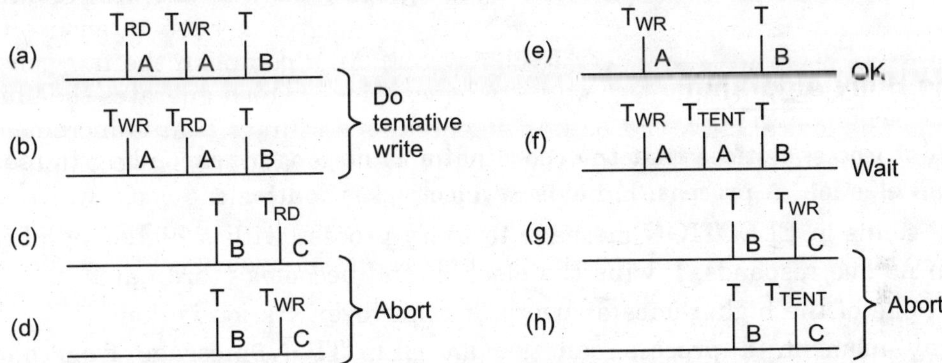

Figure 13.9 : Concurrency control using timestamps

In Figure 13.9(g), C has changed the file and already committed. Again B must abort. In Figure 13.9(h), C is in the process of changing the file, although it has not committed yet. Still, B is too late and must abort.

Timestamping has different properties than locking. When a transaction encounters a larger (later) timestamp, it aborts, whereas under the same circumstances with locking it would either wait or be able to proceed immediately. On the other hand, it is deadlock free, which is a big advantage.

Transactions offer many advantages and thus are good technique for building reliable distributed systems.

13.7. ELECTION ALGORITHMS

Many distributed algorithms require one process to act as coordinator, initiator, sequencer, or otherwise perform some special role. We have already seen several examples, such as in the centralized mutual exclusion algorithm and sometimes, in token-ring mutual exclusion algorithm also. In general, it does not matter which process takes on this special responsibility, but one of them has to do it. In this sub-section we will look at algorithms for electing a coordinator.

If all processes are exactly the same, with no distinguishing characteristics, there is no way to select one of them to be special. Consquently, we will assume that each process has a unique number, for example, its network address (for simplicity, we will assume one process per machine). In general, election algorithms attempt to locate the process with the highest process number and designate it as coordinator. The algorithms differ in the way they do this.

Furthermore, we also assume that every process knows the process number of every other process. What the processes do not know is which ones are currently up and which ones are currently down. The goal of an election algorithm is to ensure that when an election starts, it concludes with all processes agreeing on who the new coordinator is to be.

13.7.1 The Bully Algorithm

When a process notices that the coordinator is no longer responding to requests, it initiates an election. A process, P, holds an election as follows :

1. P sends in ELECTION message to every process with a higher number.
2. If no one responds, P wins the election and becomes coordinator.
3. If one of the higher-ones answers, it takes over. P's job is done.

At any moment, a process can get an ELECTION message from one of its lower-numbered colleagues. When such a message arrives, the receiver sends an OK message back to the sender to indicate that it is alive and will take over. The receiver then holds an election, unless it is already holding one. Eventually, all processes give up but one and that one is the new coordinator. It announces its victory by sending to all processes, a message telling them that from now onwards it is the new coordinator.

If a process that was previously down comes back up, it holds an election. If it happens to be the highest numbered process currently running, it will win the election and take over the coordinator's job. Thus the biggest guy in town always wins, hence the name is "bully algorithm".

In figure 13.10 we see an example of how the bully algorithm works. The group consists of eight processes, numbered from P_0 to P_7. Previously P_7 was the coordinator, but it has just crashed. Process P_4 is the first one to notice this, so it sends *ELECTION* messages to all the processes higher than it, namely P_5, P_6 and P_7 as shown in Figure 13.10(a). Processes P_5, P_6 both respond with OK, as shown in Figure 13.10(b). Upon getting the first of these responses P_4 knows that its job is over. It knows that one of these big bosses will take over and become coordinator. It just sits back and waits to see who the winner will be.

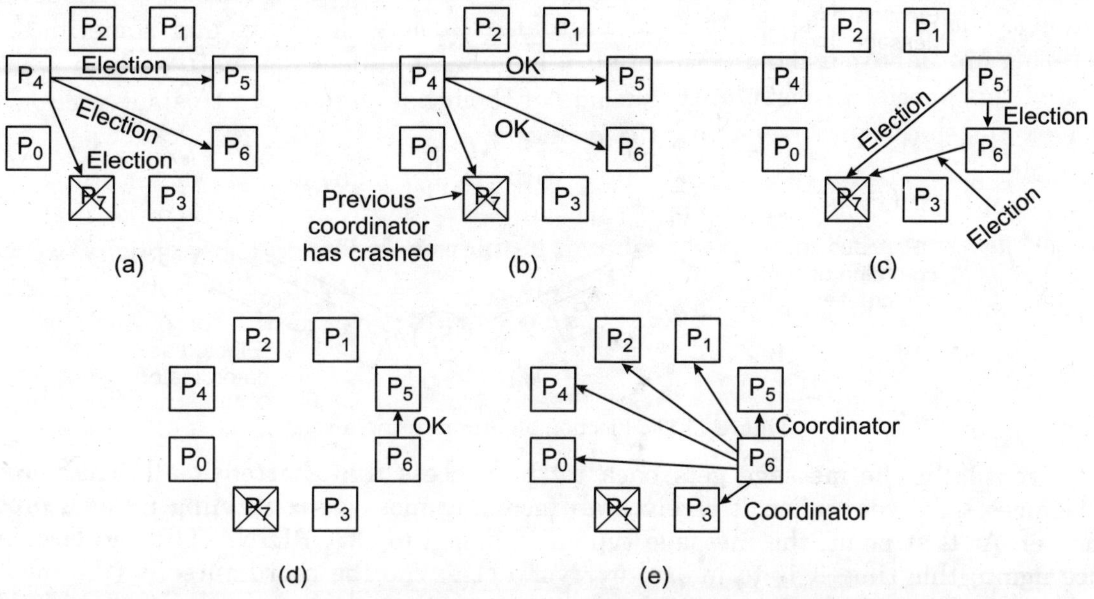

Figure 13.10 : The bully algorithm

In Figure 13.10(c), both P_5 and P_6 hold elections, each one sending messages to only those processes higher than it is. In Figure 13.10(d) process P_6 tells P_5 that it will take over. At this point P_6 knows that P_7 is dead and that it (P_6) is the winner. If some state information is to be collected (from disk or elsewhere) to know that where the old coordinator left off, P_6 must now do it. When it is ready to take over, P_6 announces this by sending a COORDINATOR message to all the running processes. When P_4 gets this message, it can continue with the operation it was trying to do when it discovered that P_7 was dead, now using P_6 as the coordinator.

If process P_7 is ever restarted, it will just send all the others a COORDINATOR message and bully them into submission.

13.7.2 A Ring Algorithm

Another election algorithm is based on the use of a ring, only unlike the previous ring, this one does not use a token. We assume the processes are physically or logically ordered, so that each process knows who its successor is. When any process notices that the coordinator is not functioning, it builds an ELECTION message containing its own process number and sends the message to its successor. If the successor is down, the sender skips over the successor and goes to the next process along the ring, or the one after that, until a running process is located. At each step, the sender adds its own process number to the list in the message.

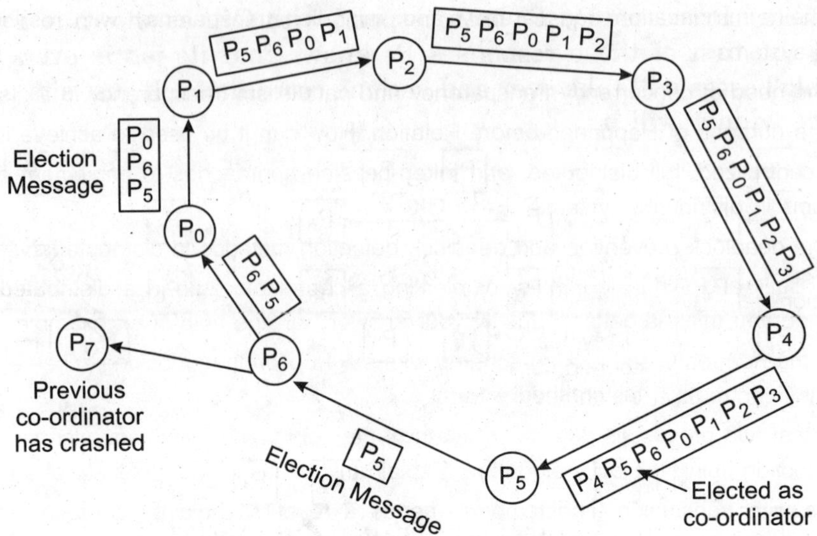

Figure 13.11 : Election algorithm using a ring

Eventually, the message gets back to the process that started it all. That process recognizes this event when it receives an incoming message containing its own process number. At that point, the message type is changed to COORDINATOR and circulated once again, this time it is to inform everyone else who the coordinator is (the member with the highest number) and which processes are the members of the new ring. When this message has circulated once, it is removed and everyone goes back to work.

In Figure 13.11, the working of election algorithm using a ring has been shown. Here, process P_5 detects that the previous coordinator P_7 has crashed and sends the ELECTION message around the ring. Finally, when the same message returns to P_5, it finds that P_6 has been elected as the new COORDINATOR and this information can be circulated by it around the ring.

EXERCISES

13.1 Explain with the help of an example, the working of a distributed application.

13.2 Distinguish between horizontal and vertical distribution of applications in a distributed system.

13.3 In what three ways the data required by various applications can be maintained in a distributed system. Differentiate between them with the help of an example.

13.4 List all the advantages and disadvantages of a distributed system.

13.5 What are the functions of a distributed operating system? In what ways it can deal with a situation where a user on site1 wants to access data that resides on site2 ? How is its way of dealing different from the way, a network operating system would handle the same situation ?

13.6 What are the key design isues that must be dealt with, in building a distributed operating system ?

13.7 Explain the terms `location transparency' and `migration transparency' with respect to distributed operating systems.

13.8 Explain the need of concurrency transparency and parallelism transparency in a distributed system.

13.9 Explain the purpose of Happened-before-Relation. How can it be used to achieve its purposes?

13.10 Contrast centralized, full distributed, and token-passing approaches to implement mutual exclusion mechanisms in distributed systems.

13.11 Explain the deadlock prevention and deadlock detection methods in distributed systems.

13.12 Compare Bully and Ring algorithms for electing a coordinator site in a distributed system. Which algorithm do you think is better ? Justify your answer with the help of an example.

13.13 Compare the non-replicated locking scheme with single coordinator locking scheme of implementing concurrency control in a distributed system.

13.14 Suppose that two processes detect the death of the coordinator simultaneously and both decide to hold an election using the bully algorithm. Explain this situation with the help of an example.

13.15 A process with transaction timestamp 50 needs a resource held by a process with transaction timestamp 100. What happens if the following methods are used to prevent deadlocks :

1. Wait and die Deadlock Prevention Scheme
2. Wound and die Deadlock Prevention Scheme.

13.16 How can a wait-for-graph be used for detecting deadlocks in a distributed environment ?

Case Studies - UNIX and Windows NT

OVERVIEW

The goal of this chapter is to discuss UNIX and Windows NT with respect to their architecture, file system, memory management, process management etc. The first part of this chapter takes up the case study of UNIX operating system. The concepts of shell and command language in UNIX have been discussed in detail. Its file management, process management, I/O management methods have also been explained. The second part of this chapter explains the NT architecture in detail. NT's various layers and their functions have been described in detail. File system, CPU scheduling and process management in Windows NT has been discussed in depth. The last section describes virtual memory management in Windows NT.

14.1. UNIX, ITS HISTORY AND CAUSES OF ITS POPULARITY

Most discussions of UNIX begin with the history of UNIX without explaining why the history of UNIX is important to understand UNIX. All of UNIX's strengths and weaknesses can be directly related to the history of its development and hence a discussion of history is very useful. The first part of this section will describe the history of UNIX and its second part will describe some strengths and weaknesses of UNIX and attempt to explain why UNIX is becoming popular.

UNIX was originally developed at Bell Laboratories as a private research project by a small group of people in 1969. This group had experience with a number of different operating system research efforts in the 1970's. The goals of the group were to design an operating system to satisfy the following objectives :

- Simple and elegant
- Written in a high level language rather than assembly language
- Allow re-use of code

Typical vendor operating systems of that time were extremely large and all written in assembly language. UNIX had a relatively small amount of code written in assembly language (this is called the kernel) and the remaining code for the operating system was written in a high level language called C.

The group worked primarily in the high level language in developing the operating system. As this development continued, small changes were necessary in the kernel and the language to allow the operating system to be completed. Through this evolution the kernel and associated software were extended until a complete operating system was written on top of the kernel in the C language.

UNIX Application Programming Interface

Many proprietary operating systems have a simplified view of application behaviour. A typical application reads some data from disk, tape or a terminal and does some processing. Output is produced onto disk, tape, terminal, or printer. Such operating systems generally provide easy to use, well-implemented facilities to support these types of applications.

As applications become more sophisticated they need new features such as network access, multi-tasking, and inter-process communications. In traditional operating systems, these features are often hard to use, not well-documented, and only callable from assembly language. When a program makes use of these features, the program may be much more complex and much more difficult to maintain.

In UNIX because the C language is used to implement an operating system, implementation of these sophisticated features is quite easily done from the C language without writing any assembly language. In addition, the documentation for these sophisticated features is in the same format and location as the documentation for the normal application calls.

When UNIX was distributed, users could write applications in C and easily make use of all of the operating system facilities. This allowed application developers to quickly develop much more sophisticated applications using these facilities.

The pattern of development in UNIX when adding new features such as networking is to provide an application program interface from the C language to access the new features.

In general UNIX system developers and application developers write programs in the same language using the same application-programming interface. Whereas, in a typical proprietary operating system, the operating system programmers do programming in assembly language and have access to a many capabilities which are not available to the application developer.

UNIX Networking

In 1984, the University of California at Berkeley released version 4.2BSD, which included a complete implementation of the TCP/IP networking protocols. Systems based on this and later BSD releases provided a multi-vendor networking capability based on Ethernet networking.

The networking support included remote login, file transfer, electronic mail, and other important features.

As UNIX was ported onto more and more different types of computer hardware, the UNIX networking allowed many different types of systems to share and mutually use data. Networks consisting of many different systems could be used as a large distributed system.

When SUN Microsystems added NFS (Network File System), this ability to share and mutually use data was significatly enhanced.

UNIX Popularity

The application portability and system programming issues have caused many hardware and software vendors to choose UNIX.

The effect of many vendors choosing UNIX is that there are a wide variety of UNIX systems available to users at attractive prices. There are three primary causes for UNIX's popularity (and none is user interface) :

- Only a very small amount of code in UNIX is written in assembly language. This makes it relatively easy for a computer vendor to get UNIX running on their system. UNIX is nearly the unanimous choice of operating system for computer companies started since 1985. The user benefit, which results from this, is that UNIX runs on their systems in additon to their proprietary operating systems.
- The application program interface allows many different types of applications to be easily implemented under UNIX without writing assembly language. These applications are relatively portable across multiple vendor harware platforms. Third party software vendors can save costs by supporting a single UNIX version of their software rather than four completely different vendor specific versions requiring four times the maintenance.
- Vendor-independent networking allows users to easily network multiple systems from many different vendors.

These features of UNIX have contributed to its rise in popularity in mid 1980's.

User Interface

So far, there has been no mention of the user interface for UNIX. UNIX is a good operating system for experienced programmers. The operating system was designed and implemented by experienced programmers so everything which the experienced programmer needs, is present but not much else. A perfect example of this is the on-line documentation called "man-pages" or manual pages. The material is completely reference oriented with very little tutorial information. Experienced programmers find the man pages very useful but the beginning user often finds them overwhelming.

In the last few years, there has been extensive work to improve the user interface to UNIX. The most dramatic effort has been the addition of windowing interfaces on top of UNIX such as X-windows, Suntools, NextStep, Motif, OpenLook, etc. These windowing interfaces do not change UNIX itself but are built on the top of UNIX to provide a more intutive interface to UNIX. Each of the different user interfaces has some advantages and some disadvantages. Currently intensive development effort is being done on all of these Graphical User Interfaces (GUIs).

Vendors providing UNIX have also done a work to improve the user interface of their particular versions of UNIX for users without windowing interfaces. Even with all of these efforts, UNIX is weak in the end-user interface area.

User Portability

Even with a relatively poor user interface, non-programmer users have adopted UNIX. The primary reason for this is because UNIX can run on so many different computer systems ranging from small desktops to the largest computers in the world. Once a user has learned UNIX, the skills can be used on many different systems. This ability for a user to work on many different makes of computer systems without re-training is called "user portability".

Open Systems

There is a recent effort to define what is an "open system" in the international standards area. An open system is a system, which allows application protability, system inter-operatability, and user portability between many different computer vendor harware platforms. UNIX is a good example of an "open system".

Thus, from a simple beginning as a personal research project to an important role in the operating system on a wide range of computer systems from desktop micros to the largest mainframes, UNIX has and will have a lot of impact. The strength of UNIX is its portability across multiple vendor hardware platforms, vendor independent networking, and the strength of its application-programming interface.

These benefits are so strong that the relative weak end-user interface has not significantly affected the adoption of UNIX.

The end users are not the direct beneficiaries of the portability and the application-programming interface. However, end-users have already seen the dramatic drop in the cost of computing when multiple vendors can provide the same operating system and software solutions.

End users are currently making the choice for inexpensive and flexible computing rather than for best user-interface in choosing UNIX.

14.1.1 Architecutre of UNIX

The UNIX operating system can be divided into pieces. These pieces can be thought of as building blocks of the operating system, and fit into a sort of hierarchy. The lowest level of the operating system controls the computer's hardware, while higher levels of the operating system provide higher level services by manipulating the lower levels of the system.

As shown in Figure 14.1, at the most basic level of the operating system is a compact collection of software, which directly controls the computer's hardware. This compact, central part of the operating system is termed the kernel. In most situations, you will never notice the UNIX kernel, but virtually everything you do on cne of the UNIX workstations eventually requires services provided by the kernel. It is the UNIX kernel, which controls your keyboard and mouse, your screen, and the various disk drivers and other peripheral devices attached to your computer.

Running "on top of" the kernel are a number of higher-level system programs which provide higher-level services, such as network access, user account maintenance, and printing services.

At the highest level of the operating system software hierarchy is the UNIX shell (sh). The UNIX shell acts as a command interpreter. It is the piece of software which provides you with a system prompt, and which interprets the commands you type and sends them to the proper lower levels of the operating system for processing. For example, when you sit down at one of the UNIX workstations and log in to the system running a copy of the UNIX shell and type a command, it is the UNIX shell which reads the command, interprets it, and executes whatever application software or system software is necessary to execute the command you typed. Because the shell sits at the top of the operating system software hierarchy, many people prefer to view it as application software, rather than system software, but here we will treat it as operating system software.

One of the more attractive features of the UNIX operating system is its ability to run a variety of different shells (C shell, Bourne shell, TC shell, Korn shell, etc.) each providing slightly different command syntax. Each UNIX account is configured when it is created with a default shell, which is the shell started automatically for you when you log in. You can run other shells, but most of the time, you will work in your default shell.

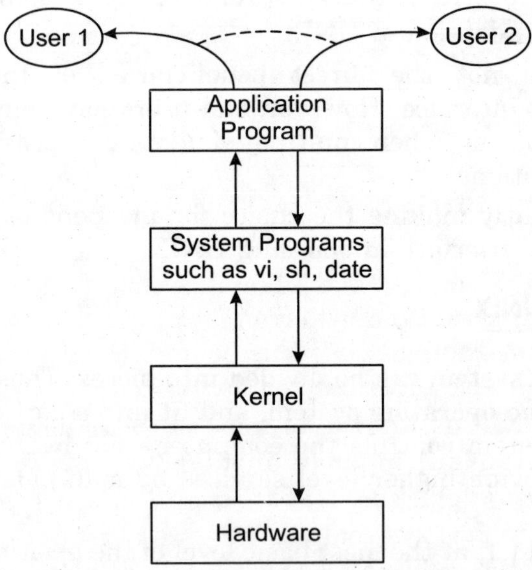

Figure 14.1 : The Unix Environment

14.1.2 Command Language of UNIX

As mentioned in the previous section, UNIX users invoke commands by interacting with a command-language interpreter called the shell. In addition to interpreting user requests and invoking the corresponding system services, the shell is also a programming language suitable for construction of elaborate command files called shell scripts. When a user logs in, the system invokes a copy of the shell to handle interactions with the related user. Although the shell is the standard system interface, it is possible to invoke any other user-specified process to serve in place of the shell as a system interface for each particular user. This allows dedicated interfaces developed for users of specialized applications, such as clerks using text-processing facilities, to coexist with the shell and thus provide quite different views and working environments for different users of the same system.

Let us examine shell's role as a command-language interpreter. The shell supports I/O redirection, pipes, filters and concurrent execution of user programs. These features have been explored briefly as :

All programs that run under the shell start out with three predefined files : standard input, which is normally the terminal keyboard, standard output, and error output. Both standard and error output are normally assigned to the terminal display. Symbols > and < are used to indicate temporary redirection of standard input and output. For example, the command

ls

lists contents of a directory on the standard output, that is, on the display of the terminal from which it is invoked. By using the redirection operator, this output can be diverted to a file named file1 as follows :

ls > file1

Similary, input to a program or a command may be taken from the standard input, the keyboard, or from any other file. For example, the command

ed < file2

instructs the program ED (editor) to take its input from the file named file2. The purpose of the standard error output is to allow error messages, if any, to be displayed on the user's terminal even when standard output is being redirected to another file or device. Standard error output can also be redirected as desired.

Another utility of UNIX is known as 'pipe'. *Pipes* allow standard output of one program to be used as standard input of another program. Several programs can be connected via pipes to form a pipeline. It is through this facility that UNIX tools, called filters, may be combined to perform complex compund functions. The shell is instructed to form pipes by means of the vertical bar character, |. For example, the UNIX command *who*, which lists logged-on users, can be combined with the filter *sort* to provide a sorted listing of users as follows.

who | sort

In this simple example of a pipe, the output of *who* is piped to *sort*, which sorts the list of users and outputs it to the standard output - the terminal display in this case. *sort* is one of the many UNIX filter programs that take standard input, perform some processing (sorting) on it, and output the result to the standard output. Depending on the particular command line, standard input may come from a device, a file, or a pipe.

The following command uses *pr* as the print formatter.

who | sort | pr-2

Thus, the output of *sort* is formatted. The same example could be expressed without pipes by several command lines involving the creation and removal of temporary files. However, pipes provide a much more economical and convenient way to combine several programs.

I/O redirection and pipes allow UNIX utilities built as filters to be combined in order to accomplish more complex tasks. As mentioned earlier UNIX designers advocate the view that tools should be simple to build, to learn, and to use. This flexibility should be provided by allowing basic commands to be combined in an arbitrary way. For example, the *who* command can be combined with the *wc* filter, which counts characters, lines, and words in a file, to obtain the number of logged-on users :

who | wc

To find out whether the user named 'ekta' is currently on the system without going over the possibly long listing of users generated by *who*, the following command can be used :

who | grep ekta

grep is another UNIX filter, and it outputs only those lines from its input that contain the specified pattern *ekta* in our example.

Even these simple examples illustrate the flexibility and power of the UNIX command system.

Another capability of the shell is concurrent activation of programs. Users indicate their intention to invoke several programs concurrently by putting the ampersand, &, character at the end of a command line. Thus, the command sequence :

cc myprog &

causes the shell to return to the user with a prompt immediately upon launching compilation (as directed by the command *cc*) of the program named 'myprog', without waiting for the compilation to finish. This mode of operation allows users to do some other unrelated work while potentially lengthy operations are being performed on their behalf. Figure 14.2 shows some other commands used in UNIX.

Commands	Purpose
bc	programmable calculator
cat	Concatenate file and write them to standard output
cc	Compile a C program
chmod	Change protection mode for files
cmp	Compare two files to see if they are identical
comm	Returns lines common to two sorted files
cp	Make a copy of a file
cut	Make each column in a document into a separate file
date	Returns the date and time
diff	Returns all the differences between two files
echo	Returns the arguments (used mostly in shell scripts)
ed	Original line-oriented text editor
find	Find all the files meeting a given condtion
grep	Search a file for lines containing a given pattern
head	Returns the first few lines of one or more file
kill	Send a signal to process
ln	Create a link to a file
lp	Print a file on the line printer
ls	List files in a directory
make	Recompile those parts of a large program that have changed
mkdir	make a directory
mv	move or rename a file
paste	Combine multiple files as columns in a single file
pr	Format a file for printing
pwd	Displays present working directory
rm	Remove a file
rmdir	Remove a directory
sh	Invoke the shell
sleep	Suspend execution for a given number of seconds
stty	Set terminal options such as the characters for line editing
sort	Sort a file consisting of ASCII lines
tail	Displays the last few lines of a file
tr	Translate character codes
uniq	Returns unique lines in a file
wc	Count characters, words, and lines in a file

Figure 14.2 : Some of the common UNIX utility programs

14.1.3 The UNIX File system

In the UNIX operating system, as in many other operating systems, data is stored in files. In UNIX, a file is a collection of data stored together on a mass storage device (such as a disk drive) and given a name. Files in UNIX can contain any sort of data, and can be of virutally any size. You might, for instance, have a file, which contains a digitized picture of your car, another, which contains your grocery list, and another, which contains the text of a paper you are writing for a class. Other files contain the executable code for various commands you will use.

Files, in turn, are stored in a hierarchical system of directories. You can think of directories as being the electronic equivalent of drawers in filing cabinets, except that unlike file drawers, directories can contain not only files, but also other directories. When a directory is contained within another directory it is termed as subdirectory. The directory it is contained in is called its parent directory. A UNIX file system is the collection of all directories, subdirectories, and files.

Full Pathnames

In any UNIX system there is a single, top-level directory. Because the structure of the UNIX file system is sometimes referred to as a tree, owing to its hierarchical nature, this top-level directory is called the root directory. In all cases, the root directory's name is the same : a single slash, /.

To name a file or a directory stored somewhere under the root directory on a UNIX system, you simply string together the list of directories and subdirectories which contain it, separated by slashes. For example, the file called vmunix in the root directory is named as :

/vmunix

The subdirectory called *font* stored in the directory called *lib*, which is under the directory named *usr* under the root directory, is named as :

/usr/lib/font

Because the filenames denote the route or path through the maze of directories and subdirectories, which make up a UNIX file system, they are sometimes referred to as full pathnames. But as explained later, these unwieldy full pathnames are not the only way to name files in the UNIX file system.

Relative Pathnames and the Current Working Directory

As you might guess, if a UNIX file system contains a few thousand directories in tens of levels of its hierarchy, the names of files could become unmanageably long. To simplify the naming of files in the UNIX file system, the UNIX shell gives you a current working directory. That is, the shell remembers the full pathname of one directory in the file system for you at all times. If you specify a filename, say, as the argument of a command, and you do not begin the filename with a slash, the UNIX shell automatically prefixes your current working directory's name to the name you specify. If you do begin a filename with a slash, the UNIX shell assumes that you intend to specify a full pathname for the file, and does nothing to what you type. Filenames, which do not begin with slashes, are sometimes termed as relative pathnames, since they are relative to the shell's current working directory. As you will see in later sections, there are commands available for checking and for setting your current working directory.

As an added convenience, all directories in a UNIX file system contain two specially named directories : one called · (pronounced dot) and another called ·· (pronounced dot-dot). The name · can be used as shorthand for your current working directory. The name ·· can be used as shorthand for the parent directory of your current working directory. For example, if your current working directory had the full pathname :

/usr/local/lib/emacs

and you specified the relative pathname :

foo

in a shell command, you shall be referring to the file whose full pathname is :

/usr/local/lib/emacs/foo

If you instead used the relative pathname :

··/foo

You shall be referring to the file whose full pathname is :

/usr/local/lib/foo

The relative pathname operators · and ·· can be used to refer to files and directories far away from your current working directory. For example, if your current working directory were :

/afs/acpub/users/h/i/hiro/private/messages

and you wanted to refer to the file whose full pathname is

/afs/acpub/users/h/i/hiro/public/sports/cricket

You could use the full pathname, or you could use the somewhat shorter as shown below :

··/··/public/sports/cricket

·· is used twice to go back to the directory : **/afs/acpub/users/h/i/hiro** which is further appended by **public/sports/cricket** to obtain the intended path name.

Standard Directores

Although files of any type can conveniently be stored anywhere within the UNIX file system, there are a few standard directories where certain types of files can usually be found. A description of few standard directories goes like :

/dev	where special device files are kept. There is one special file for each device.
/bin	where executable system utilies like sh, cp, rm are kept. Only the utilities available as binary files are kept.
/etc	where system configuration files and databases are kept.
/lib	where operating system and programming libraries are kept.
/tmp	contains temporary data files. Sometimes, files in /tmp directory of a workstation are subject to automatic removal after two days.
/usr/local	The top-level directory for storing application software and data written or modified by local system staff.
/usr/local/bin	where locally written or locally modified application software is stored. Many useful applications reside here.

/usr/local/lib	where configuration files for locally adapted software and parts of some locally adapted applications reside.
/usr/man	the manual pages (help pages) are kept here.

14.1.4 Process Management in UNIX

Processes are active entities in the UNIX system. Each process runs a single program and has a single thread of control. In other words, it has one program counter, which keeps track of the next instruction to be executed.

UNIX is a multiprogramming system, so multiple independent processes may be running at the same time. Each user may have several active processes at once, so on a large system, there may be hundreds or even thousands of processes running. In fact, on most single-user workstations, even when the user is absent, dozens of background processes, called daemons, are running. These are started automatically when the system is booted.

A typical daemon is the cron daemon. It wakes up once a minute to check if there is any work for it to do. If so, it does the work. Then it goes back to sleep until it is time for the next check.

This daemon is needed because it is possible in UNIX to schedule the activites minutes, hours, days, or even months in the future. For example, suppose a user has some appointment at 3 o'clock next Tuesday. He can make an entry in the cron daemon's database telling the daemon to beep at say, 2 : 30 on Tuesday. When the appointed day and time arrives, the cron daemon sees that it has work to do, and starts up the beeping program as a new process.

The cron daemon is also used to start up periodic activities, such as making daily disk backups at 4.00 a.m. Other daemons handle incoming and outgoing electronic mail, manage the line printer queue, check if there are enough free pages in memory, and so forth. daemons are straightforward to implement in UNIX because each one is a separate process, independent of all other processes.

Process Creation

Processes are created in UNIX in a simple manner. The fork() system call creates an exact copy of the original process. The calling processs is called the parent process. The new process is called the child process. The parent and child each have their own, private memory images. If the parent subsequently changes any of its variables, the changes are not visible to the child, and vice versa.

Open files are shared between parent and child. That is, if a certain file was open in the parent before the fork(), it will continue to be open in both the parent and the child afterwards. Changes made to the file by either one will be visible to the other. This behaviour is reasonable, because these changes are also visible to any unrelated process that opens the file as well.

The fact that the memory images, variables, registers, and everything else are identical in the parent and child leads to a small difficulty : How do the processes know which one should run the parent code and which one should run the child code ? The solution is that the fork() system call returns a zero to the child and a nonzero value, known as the pid (process identifier of the child) to the parent. Both processes normally check the return value, and act accordingly, as shown in Figure 14.3.

```
pid = fork () ;     /*if the fork succeeds, pid > 0 in the parent */
if (pid < 0)   {
        /* Fork failed, usually because memory or some table is full. */
} else if (pid > 0) {
        /* parent code */
} else {
        /* Child code */
}
```

Figure 14.3 : Process creation in UNIX

Processes are named by their pids. As we have seen, when a process is created, the parent is given the child's pid. If the child wants to know its own pid, there is a system call, getpid(), that provides it. Pids are used in a variety of ways. For example, when a child terminates, the parent is given the pid of the child that just finished. This can be important because a parent may have many children. Since children may also have children, an original process can build up an entire tree of children, grandchildren, and further descendants.

This ability to form a tree of process is the key to how timesharing works in UNIX. When the system is booted, the kernel starts a process called **init.** This process then reads a file /etc/ttys that tells how many terminals the system has, and provide certain information describing each one. **Init** then forks off a child process for each terminal and goes to sleep until some child terminates. Each child runs the login program, which prints

login :

on the terminal's screen and tries to read the user's name from the keyboard. When someone sits down at the terminal and provides a login name, login then asks for a password, encrypts it, and verifies it against the encrypted password stored in the password file : /etc/passwd. If it is correct, login overlays itself with the user's shell, which then waits for the first command. If it is incorrect, login just asks for another user name.

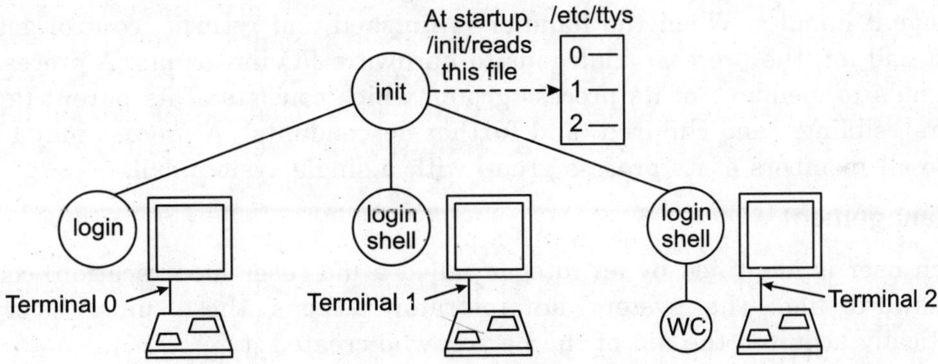

Figure 14.4 : Init with three children and one grandchild

This mechanism is illustrated in Figure 14.4 for a system with three terminals. The login process running on behalf of terminal 0 is still waiting for input. The one running on behalf of terminal 1 had a successful login, and is now running the shell, which is awaiting a command. A successful login has also occurred on terminal 2, only here the user has started the 'wc' program, which is running as a child of the shell. The shell is blocked, waiting for the child to terminate, at which time the shell will type another prompt and read from the keyboard. If the user at terminal 2 had typed 'cc' instead of 'wc', the main program of the C compiler would have been started, which in turn would have forked off more processes to run the various compiler passes.

Inter-process Communication

Processes in UNIX can communicate with each other using a form of *message passing*. It is possible to create a kind of channel between two processes into which one process can write a stream of bytes for the other to read. These channels are called pipes (explained in Section 14.1.2). Synchronization is possible because when a process tries to read from an empty pipe it is blocked until data are available.

Pipes

Shell pipelines are implemented with pipes. When the shell sees a command such as :

sort < f | head

it creates two processes, *sort* and *head*, and sets up a pipe between them in such a way that *sort's* standard output is connected to *head's* standard input. In this way, all the data that *sort* writes go directly to the *head*, instead of going to a file. If the pipe fills up, the system stops running *sort* until *head* has removed some data from the pipe.

Software Interrupts

Processes can also communicate through software interrupts. A process can send what is called a signal to another process. Processes can tell the system what they want to happen when a signal arrives. The choices are to ignore it, to catch it, or to let the signal kill the process (default). If a process elects to catch signals sent to it, it must specify a signal handling procedure. When a signal arrives, control will abruptly switch to the signal handler. When the handler is finished and returns, control goes back to where it had left the process, analogous to hardware I/O interrupts. A process can only send signals to members of its process group, which consists of its parent (and further ancestors), siblings, and children (and further descendants). A process may also send a signal to all members of its process group with a single system call.

User Management

Each user is identified by an integer called a uid (user identification) contained in the password file. The system adminstrator assigns these uids. Every process automatically acquired the uid of the person who created it.

The user with uid 0 is special and is called the superuser (or root). The superuser has the power to read and write all files in the system, no matter who owns them and no matter how they are protected. Processes with uid 0 also have the ability to make a small number of protected system calls denied to ordinary users. Normally only the system administrator knows the superuser's password.

The power of the superuser is exploited to prohibit the users from doing certain dangerous things. For example, many UNIX systems have programs that allow users to ask how much disk space is left. This information is stored on each disk in block 0, but normally the disks are protected in such a way as to prohibit ordinary users from just reading the raw bytes. The superuser can find out this information easily enough, but telling everyone the superuser's password would defeat the entire protection system.

Instead, UNIX has a bit associated with each executable program called the setuid bit. This bit is actually a part of the protection mode word (the protection part only uses 9 bits, so there are a few left over for other purposes). When a program with the setuid bit 'on' is executed, the effective uid for that process becomes the uid of the executable file's owner instead of the uid of the user who invoked it. By making the program (that reports on disk space) be owned by the superuser but with the setuid bit on, any user can execute it, and get superuser privileges for that process. Thus it is possible for the superuser to make available to ordinary users a collection of programs that make use of superuser power, but in a limited and a controlled way.

14.1.5 Memory Management in UNIX

When the UNIX kernel is first loaded into memory (at boot time), it sets aside a certain amount of RAM for itself as well as for all system and user processes. Main categories into which RAM is divided are :

- **Text :** To hold the text segments of the running processes.
- **Data :** To hold the data segments of the running processes.
- **Stack :** To hold the stack segments of the running processes.
- **Standard Memory :** This is an area of memory, which is available to all the running programs if they need it.
- **Buffer Cache :** All the read and writes to the file system are cached here first. You may have experienced situations where a program that is writing to a file does not seem to work (nothing is written to the file). You wait a while, then a sync occurs, and the buffer cache is dumped to disk and you see that the file size increases.

As mentioned above, every UNIX process has an address space consisting of at least three segments : text, data and stack.

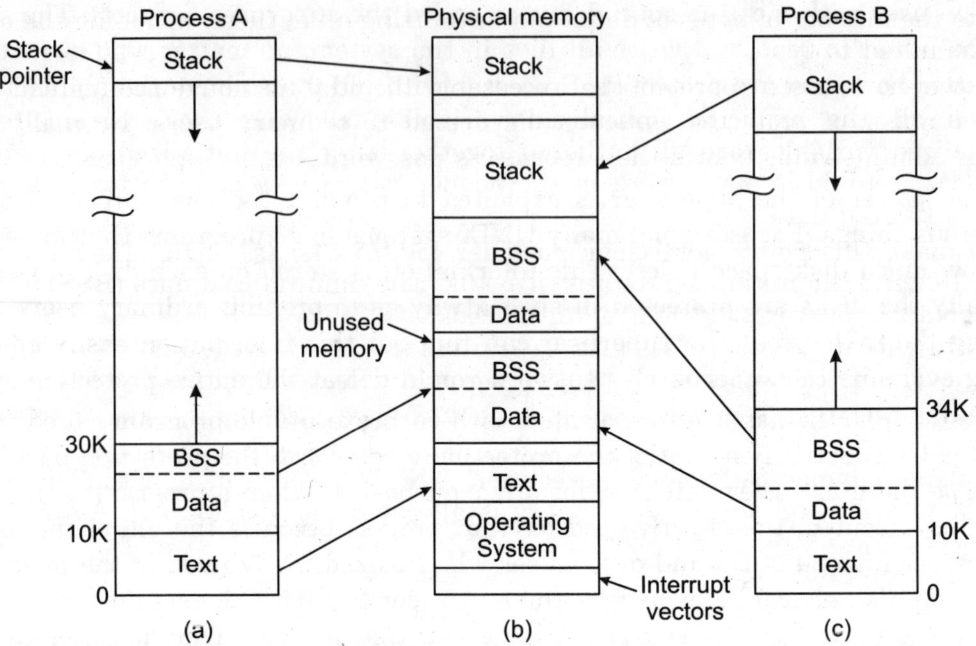

Figure 14.5 : (a) Process A's virtual address space. (b) Physical memory, (c) Process B's virutal address space

An example process' address space is depicted in Figure 14.5(a).

Text Segment

The text segment contains the machine instructions that form the program's executable code. The compiler or the assembler produces it by translating the C, Pascal, or other program into machine code. The text segment is normally read-only. The text segment neither grows nor shrinks or changes in any other way.

Data Segment

The data segment contains storage for the program's variables, strings, arrays, and other data. It has two parts, the initialized data and the uninitialized data. For historical reasons, the letter is known as the BSS. The initialized part of the data segment contains variables and compiler constants that need an initial value when the program is started.

For example, in C it is possible to declare a character string and initialize it at the same time. When the program starts up, it expects that the string has its initial value. To implement this, the compiler assigns the string a location in the address space, and ensures that when the program is started up, this location contains the proper string. From the operating system's point of view, initialized data are not at all that different from program text - both contain bit patterns produced by the compiler that must be loaded into memory when the program starts.

The existence of uninitialized data is actually just an optimization. When a global variable is not explicitly initialized, the semantics of the C language says that its initial value is 0. In practice, most global variables are not initialized, and are thus 0. This could be implemented by simply having a section of the executable binary file exactly equal to the number of bytes of data, and initializing all of them, including the ones that have defaulted to 0.

However, to save space in the executable file, this is not done. Instead, the file contains all the explicitly initialized variables following the program text. The uninitialized variables are all gathered together after the initialized ones, so all the compiler has to do is put a word in the header telling how many bytes to allocate for the uninitialized data.

To make this point more clear, consider Figure 14.5 (a) again. Here the program text is 10k and the initialized data is also 10k. The uninitialized data (BSS) is 10k. The executable file is only 20k (text + initialized data), plus a short header that tells the system to allocate another 10k after the initialized data and zero it before starting the program. This trick avoids strong 10k of zeros in the executable file.

Unlike the text segment, which cannot change, the data segment can change. Programs modify their variables all the time. Furthermore, many programs need to allocate space dynamically, during execution. UNIX handles this by permitting the data segment to grow and shrink as memory is allocated and deallocated. A system call is available to allow a program to set the size of its data segment. The C library procedure *malloc*, commonly used to allocate memory, makes heavy use of this system call.

Stack Segment

The third segment is the stack segment. On most machines, it starts at the top of the virtual address space and grows down towards 0. If the stack grows below the bottom of the stack segment, a hardware fault normally occurs, and the operating system lowers the bottom of the stack segment by a few thousand bytes (*e.g.*, on page). Programs do not explicitly manage the size of the stack segment.

When a program starts up, its stack is not empty. Instead, it contains all the environment (shell) variables as well as the command typed on the shell to invoke it. In this way a program can discover its arguments. For example, when the command

cp source dest

is typed, the cp program is started up with the string "cp source dest" on the stack, so it can find out the names of the source and destination files (*i.e.* **cp** program can now discover its two arguments i.e. **source** and **dest**).

Sharing of Programs

When two users are running the same program, such as the editor, it would be possible, but inefficient to keep two copies of the editor's program text in memory at once. Instead, most UNIX systems support shared text segments. In Figure 14.5(a) and Figure 14.5(c) we see two processes that have the same text segment. In Figure 14.5(b) we see a possible layout of physical memory, in which both processes share the same piece of text. The mapping is done by the virtual memory hardware.

Data and stack segments are never shared. If either one needs to grow and there is no room adjacent to it to grow into, it is moved elsewhere in memory.

Memory Protection for Kernel

How the kernel protects itself from user processes ? When the kernel loads, it uses RAM to keep itself memory resident. Consequently, it has to ensure that user programs do not overwrite/corrupt the kernel data structures (or overwrite/corrupt other users' data structures). It does so by designating part of RAM as kernel or system pages (which hold kernel text and data segments) and user pages (which hold user stacks, data, and text segments). Strong memory protection is implemented in the kernel memory management code to keep away the users from corrupting the system area. For example, only the kernel is allowed to switch from the user to the system area. During the normal execution of a UNIX process, both system and user areas are used.

A common system call when memory protection is violated is sigsegv() (you see a "Segmentation violation" message on the screen when this happens. The culprit process is killed using the kill() system call and its memory contents are dumped to a disk file called "core").

Let us now see how memory is managed for running a process in UNIX :

Paging and swapping are used to do memory management.

Paging when a process starts in UNIX, not all its memory pages are read in from the disk at once. Instead the kernel loads into RAM only a few pages at a time. After the CPU digests these, the next page is requested. If it is not found in RAM, a page fault occurs, signaling the kernel to load the next few pages from disk into RAM. This is called demand paging and is a perfectly normal system activity in UNIX.

In a variant of Unix(UNIX SVR4), a daemon which performs the paging out operation, is called pageout. It is long running daemon and is created at boot time. The pageout process cannot be killed. There are three kernel variables, which control the paging operation :

- **minfree** - the absolute minimum of free RAM needed. If free memory falls below this limit, the memory management system does its best to get back above it. It does so by page stealing from other running processes, if practical.
- **desfree** - the amount of RAM the kernel wants to have free at all times. If free memory is less than desfree, the pageout() system call is called every clock cycle.
- **lotsfree** - the amount of memory necessary before the kernel stops calling *pageout*. Between *desfree* and *lotsfree*, pageout is called 4 times a second.

Swapping

Let us say you start ten heavy weight processes (for example, a couple of netscapes, a sendmail, and a couple of pines) on an old 486 computer running Linux with 16MB of RAM. Basically, you 'do not have' enough physical RAM to accommodate the text, data and stack segments of all these processes at once. Since the Kernel cannot find enough RAM to fit things in, it makes use of the available virtual memory by a process known as swapping. It selects the least busy process and moves it in its entirety (meaning the program's text, stack, and data segments that are in RAM) to disk. As more RAM becomes available, it swaps the process back in from disk into RAM. While this use of the virutal memory system makes it possible for you to continue to use the machine, it comes at a very heavy price. Remember that disks are relatively slower (by the factor of a million) than CPUs and you can feel this disparity rather severely when the machine is swapping.

In UNIX SVR4, the process handling swapping is called sched (in other UNIX variants, it is sometimes called swapper). It always runs as process 0. When the free memory falls so far below minfree that pageout is not able to recover memory by page stealing, sched invokes the systemcall sched(). System call swapout() is then called to free all the memory pages associated with the process chosen for being swapped out. On a later invocation of sched(), the process may be swapped back in from disk if there is enough memory.

14.1.6 Input/Output in UNIX

Like all computers, those running UNIX have I/O devices such as terminals, disk, printers, and networks connected to them. Some way is needed to allow programs to access these devices. The UNIX treats devices as special files, Each I/O device is assigned a path name, usually in /dev. For example, the printer might be /dev/lp, terminal1 might be /dev/tty1, and the network might be /dev/net.

These special files can be accessed the same way as any other files.No special commands or system calls are needed. The usual read() and write () system calls will do just fine. For example, the command

cp file /dev/lp

copies the file to printer, causing it to be printed. Programs can open, read, and write special files the same way as they do regular files, In fact, the copy program 'cp' in the above example is not even aware that it is printing. In this way, no special mechanism is needed for doing I/O.

An additional advantage is that the usual file protection rules apply automatically to I/O devices. If the protection bits for /dev are set up to prohibit everyone except the superuser from directly accessing the files in it, then users are prohibited from doing direct I/O themselves. Restricted access to selected I/O devices can be given by installing setuid programs that have permission to read and write the files in /dev.

For example, a common way to manage access to the printer is to make /dev/lp readable for no one and writable for only the superuser. A program called lpr is offered to allow users to print files. What lpr does is copy the files specified in its arguments to a SPOOling directory, where a daemon with access to /dev/lp takes them out and prints them in order. It should be clear that the superuser need not necessarily own dev/lp. By having the I/O devices integrated into the file system like this, great flexibility in access can be achieved.

As devices are of two types, special files are also divided into two categories, block and character. A **block special file** is one consisting of a sequence of numbered blocks. The key property of the block special file is that each block can be individually addressed and accessed. In other words, a program can open a block special file and read, say, block 124 without first having to read blocks 0 to 123. Block special files are used for disks.

Character Special files are normally used for devices that input or output a character stream. Terminals, printers, networks, mice, plotters, and most other I/O devices that accept or produce data for people use character special files. It is not possible (or even meaningful) to seek to block 124 on a mouse.

Although character special files cannot be randomly accessed, they often need to be controlled in ways that block special files do not. Consider, for example, a terminal. In addition to accepting read and write requests, a terminal has a number of special characteristics that must be managed. For example, when the user makes a typing error and wants to erase the last character typed, he presses some key. Some people prefer to use backspace, and others prefer DEL. Likewise, to interrupt the running program, some special key must be hit. Here too, different people have different preferences.

Rather than making a choice and forcing everyone to use it, UNIX allows all these special functions and many others to be customized by the user. A special system call is generally provided for setting these options. This system call also handles tab expansion, enabling and disabling of character echoing, conversion between carriage return and line feed, and similar items. Such system call is not permitted on regular files or block special files.

An example of I/O is networking, as pioneered by Berkeley and UNIX. The central concept in the Berkeley design is the socket. Sockets are analogous to mailboxes and telephones as they allow users to interface to the network, just as mail boxes allow people to interface to the postal system and telephones allow them to interface to the telephone system. The position of the sockets is shown in Figure 14.6.

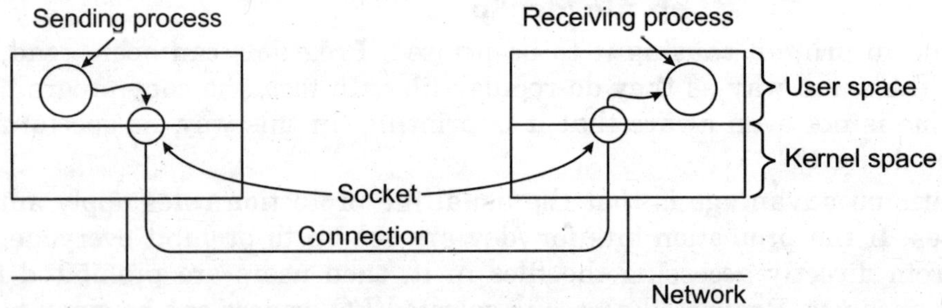

Figure 14.6 : The use of sockets for networking

Sockets can be created and destroyed dynamically. Creating a socket returns a file descriptor, which is needed for establishing a connection, reading data, writing data, and releasing the connection. Each socket supports a particular type of networking, which is specified when the socket is created. The most common types are :

1. Reliable connection-oriented byte stream. This socket type effectively allows two processes on different machines to establish the equivalent of a pipe between them. Bytes are pumped in at one end and they come out in the same order at the other end.

2. Reliable connection-oriented packet stream. This type is similar to the first one, except that it preserves packet boundaries. If the sender makes five separate calls to write(), each for 512 bytes, and the receiver asks for 2560 bytes, with a type1 socket, all 2560 bytes will be returned at once. With a type2 socket only 512 bytes will be returned. Four more calls are needed to get the rest.

3. Unreliable packet transmission. This type of socket is used to give the user access to the raw network. This type is especially useful for real-time applications, and for those situations in which the user wants to implement a specialized error-handling scheme.

When a socket is created, one of the parameters specifies the protocol to be used for it. For reliable byte and packet streams, the most popular protocol is TCP/IP. For unreliable packet-oriented transmission, UDP (User Datagram Protocol) is the usual choice. Both of these protocols originated with the U.S. Department of Defense's ARPANET, and are now widely used throughout the world.

Before a socket can be used for networking, it must have an address bound to it. This address can be in one several naming domains. The most common domain is the Internet naming domain, which uses 32-bit integers for naming endpoints.

Once sockets have been created on both the source and destination computers, a connection can be established between them (for connection-oriented communication). One party makes a listen() system call on a local socket, which creates a buffer and blocks until data arrive. The other one makes a connect() system call, giving as parameters the file descriptor for a local socket and the address of a remote socket. If the remote party accepts the call, the system then establishes a connection between the sockets.

Once a connection has been established, it functions analogously to a pipe. A process can read and write from it using the file descriptor for its local socket. When the connection is no longer needed, it can be closed in the usual way.

14.1.7 Key features of UNIX

The key features of UNIX are :

1. Time sharing operating system, which uses round robin CPU scheduling, for user processes.
2. Highly portable and is thus available for a variety of process or classes ranging from microprocessors to supercomputers.
3. Has hierarchical file system that spans volume boundaries.
4. Specialized versions of UNIX are available for program development and document preparation.
5. A variant of indexing (I-nodes, which have been discussed in chapter 10,) is used to keep track of and to access data blocks of files.
6. To reduce physical I/O and effective disk access time, UNIX provides extensive buffering of disk blocks.
7. Uses signals for process - synchronization while pipes provide for communication between related processes.
8. UNIX processes form a family tree and strong ties exist between children and their parent processes.

14.2. WINDOWS NT OPERATING SYSTEM

Let us look into how and why Windows NT developed. During NT's development period, from 1988 to 1993, the computing world was different from what it is today. DOS was the predominant PC operating system, and both Windows and OS/2 were gaining momentum. Servers and scientific and engineering workstations ran UNIX exclusively.

Because all these operating systems were popular, Microsoft built support in NT for DOS, Windows 3.x, OS/2, and POSIX (a variant of UNIX). This support created a compatibility mode in NT for DOS and Windows users, and also enabled OS/2 and POSIX users to migrate to NT.

Microsoft realized that although NT's DOS and Windows 3.x support made its PC customers happy, enterprise-level (which at that time meant 32-bit) customers were more interested in the POSIX and OS/2 32-bit APIs (Application Programming Interface). Microsoft saw that if it wanted to capture enterprise-level customers, it would have to develop its own 32-bit API (Application Programming Interface). Thus, Win32, Microsoft's answer to OS/2 and POSIX, became NT's primary API (Application Programming Interface).

Throughout NT's development period, most PCs used Intel's x86 processor. To keep its PC customer base, as well as to accommodate the desires of high-end users, Microsoft decided to make NT as portable as possible and the company designated NT to run out of the box on any of the RISC processor chips. Microsoft reasoned that NT's portability across different processors would ensure its viability regardless of which chip came out on top in the market.

Although Windows 3.1 had a good graphical user interface, it had no native networking support, and Windows 3.11's networking capabilities were cumbersome and relatively slow. Microsoft intended to avoid repeating these networking mistakes, and it outfited NT with support for most of the APIs and networking protocols that were in widespread use in the 1980s. Those APIs included NetBIOS, Remote Procedure Call (RPC), file server and redirector, mail slots, named pipes, and Berkely sockets. The protocols included TCP/IP, NetBEUI (Microsoft's Lanmanager protocol), IPX/SPX (Novell's NetWare Protocol), Apple Talk Data Link Control (DLC), and SNA. By including protocols in NT that its competitors owned (*i.e.* Apple Talk and IPX/SPX), Microsoft opened that door to the sites that were dominated by Macintosh or NetWare.

In addition to these high-level requirements, Microsoft included two important low-level operating system capabilities in NT. First, NT's developers designed its security subsystem as a centralized module that can be easily and thoroughly validated. This security configuration earned NT a high security rating.

Secondly, its developers gave NT a multitasking preemptive scheduling system whereas neither DOS nor Windows 3.x is capable of true multitasking with preemptive scheduling. Without add-on software, DOS can execute only one program, or task, at a time. Windows 3.x can execute several programs concurrently, but they must be well behaved; that is, each program must be aware that other programs may need to run, and it must therefore, yield the machine at regular intervals. This design means that a malicious program can halt the computer simply by entering an infinite loop in which it never yields. In NT, a centralized scheduling authority divides CPU time to programs that need it. Once a program's turn has ended, the scheduler has the power to preempt it and give another program a turn.

Microsoft wanted NT to incorporate one final major feature : it has to be truly 32-bit and provide protected address spaces. DOS and Windows 3.x are 16-bit operating systems. Programs running on them cannot easily access large amounts of memory. Using 32-bit addressing enables programs on NT to access 4GB(2^{32} bytes) of memory efficiently.

14.2.1 An Overview of NT Architecture

Figure 14.7 shows Windows NT architecture. As we know that most of the operating systems provide protection by allowing two modes - kernel mode (monitor mode) and user mode. Windows NT also supprots these two modes. User mode is the least-privileged mode NT supports; it has no direct access to hardware and only restricted access to memory. For example, when programs such as Word and Lotus Notes execute in user mode, they do not have direct acess to hardware devices, and they cannot touch parts of memory that are not specifically assigned to them. Kernel mode is privileged mode. Those parts of NT that execute in kernel mode, such as device drivers and subsystems such as the Virtual Memory Manager, have direct access to all the hardware and memory.

Modified Microkernel Architecture

NT takes a unique approach, known as modified microkernel that falls between pure microkernel and monolithic design. In NT's modified microkernel design, operating system environments execute in user mode as discrete processes, including DOS, Win16, Win32, OS/2, and POSIX (DOS and Win16 are not shown in Figure 14.7). The basic operating system subsystems, including the Process Manager and the Virtual Memory Manager, execute in kernel mode, and they are compiled into one file image. These kernel-mode subsystems are not separate processes, and they can communicate with each other by using function calls for maximum performance.

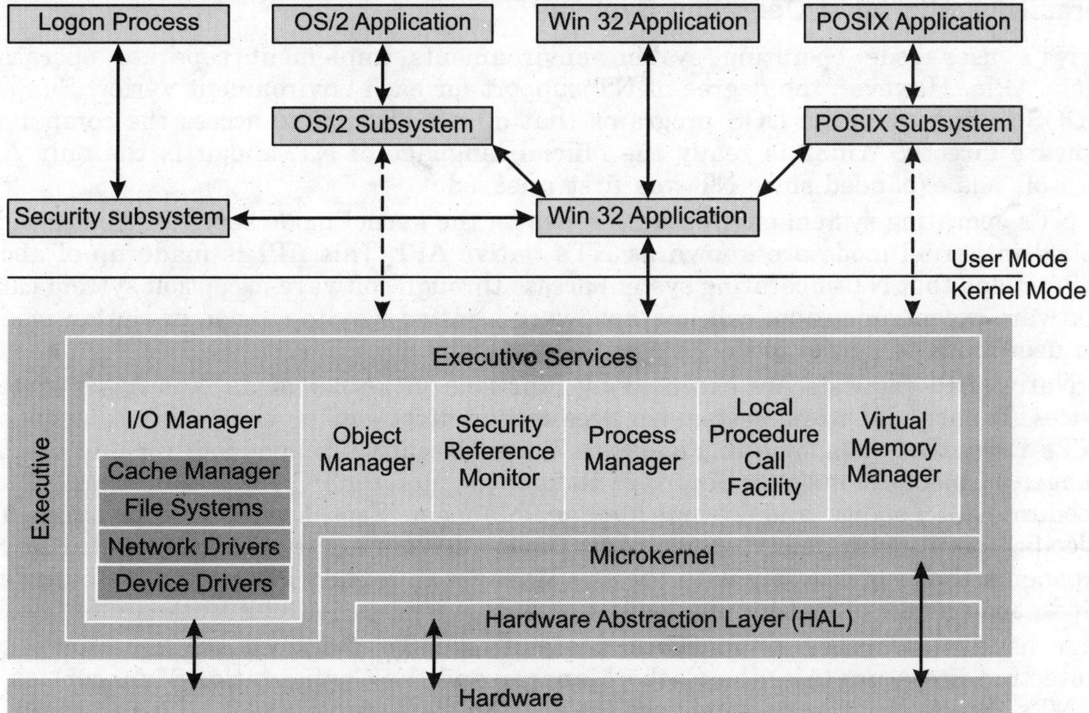

Figure 14.7 : Windoes NT Architecture

What makes NT unique is where it draws the line between the two. NT is sometimes referred to as a microkernel-based operating system. As we know that the idea behind the microkernel concept is that all operating system components except a small core (the microkernel) execute as user-mode processes, just as word processors and spreadsheets do. But the core components in the microkernel execute in priviledged mode, so they can access the hardware directly.

Microkernel architecture gives a system configurability and fault tolerance. Because an operating sytem subsystem like the Virtual Memory Manager fails, thanks to the fault-tolerance possible in a microkernel design, the operating system can restart it with minimal effect on the rest of the system. In monolithic operating system design (*e.g.* in DOS and Windows 3.1), the entire operating system must be rebuilt to change any subsystem. If the Virtual Memory Manager has a bug in a monolithic system, the bug is likely to bring down the whole machine.

As discussed in the first part of this chapter, a disadvantage of pure microkernel design is slow performance. Every interaction between operating system components in microkernel design requires an inter-proces message. For example, if the Process Manager requires the Virtual Memory Manager to create an address map for a new process, it must send a message to the Virtual Memory Manager. In addition to the overhead costs of creating and sending messages, the inter-process message requirement results in two context switches : the first from the Process Manager to the Virtual Memory Manager, and the second back to the Process Manager after the Virtual Memory Manager carries out the request.

Interactivity with other Operating Systems

NT's user-mode operating system environments implement separate operating system APIs. However, the degree of NT support for each environment varies. Support for DOS is limited to the DOS programs that do not attempt to access the computer's hardware directly. Win32 is really the official language of NT, and it is the only API Microsoft has expanded since NT was first released.

NT's operating system environment relies on the kernel mode services. The services invoked in kernel mode are known as NT's native API. This API is made up of about 250 functions that NT's operating system access through software-exception system calls. A software-exception system call is a hardware-assisted way to change execution modes from user mode to kernel mode.

Native API requests are executed by functions in kernel mode, known as system services. To carry out work, system services call on functions in one or more components of NT's Executive. As shown in Figure 14.7, the Executive components include the I/O Manager, Object Manager, Security Reference Monitor, Process Manager, Local Procedure Call Facility, and Virtual Memory Manager. Each Executive component has a specific operating system responsibility. Device drivers are dynamically added to NT components that work closely with the I/O Manager to connect NT to specific hardware devices, such as disks and inputs devices.

A handful of other components are not usually described in Microsoft's NT architecture literature (e.g., the Cache Manager and the Configuration Manager).

NT's Executive Components use basic hardware functionality implemented is microkernel. The microkernel, which is known in NT as the kernel, contains the scheduler. The Kernel also manages the Executive's use of NT's hardware and software interrupt handlers.

Device drivers and the Kernel use the HAL (Hardware Abstraction Layer) to interact with the computer's hardware. The HAL exports its own API, which translates abstract data into processor-specific commands.

NT is **portable** across processor types because processor-specific code is restricted to the kernel and the HAL (Hardware Abstraction Layer). This situation means that when NT is ported to a new processor, only the Kernel and the HAL must be converted. The rest of the NT's code is written in C and C++ and can simply be recompiled for the new processor.

14.2.2. NT's Executive, Kernel, and HAL (Hardware Abstraction Layer)

What we discussed just now are the basics of NT's architecture. Now let's delve into NT's operating system environments and system services more deeply.

OBJECT TYPE	REPRESENTS	OWNING SUBSYSTEM
Object type	Object type object	Object Manager
Directory	Object namespace	Object Manager
Symbolic Link	Object namespace	Object Manager
Event	Synchronization primitive	Executive
EvenPair	Synchronization primitive	Executive
Mutant	Synchronization primitive	Executive
Timer	Timer notifications	Executive
Semaphore	Synchronization primitive	Executive
Windows Station	Interactive logon	Win 32
Desktop	Windows desktop	Win 32
File	Tracks open files	I/O Manager
I/O Completion	Tracks I/O completion notifications	I/O Manager
Adapter	Direct memory access (DMA) resource	I/O Manager
Controller	DMA controller	I/O Manager
Device	Logical or Physical device	I/O Manager
Driver	Device driver	I/O Manager
Key	Doorway to the Registry	Configuration Manager
Port	Communications channel	Local Procedure Call (LPC) Facility
Section	Memory mapping	Memory Manager
Process	Active process	Process Manager
Thread	Active thread	Process Manager
Token	Process security profile	Process Manager
Profile	Performance monitoring	Kernel

Figure 14.8 : NT 4.0 Object Types and Kernel-Mode Subsystems that Manage them

As seen in Figure 14.7, the NT architecture is a layered system of modules. The three main layers are HAL, kernel and the Executive. This section deals with the detailed discussion of these layers.

14.2.2.1. The Executive

NT's Executive subsystems make up the meatiest layer in kernel mode, and they perform most of the functions traditionally associated with operating systems. Figure 14.7, shows their position in NT's architecture. These subsystems have separate responsibilities and names, so you might think that they are different processes. For example, when a program like Microsoft Word requests an operating system service such as memory allocation, the flow of control proceeds from Word into kernel mode through NT's native system service interface. A system service handler for memory allocation then directly invokes the Virtual Memory Manager's allocation function. The requested allocation executes in the context of the process (Word) that requested it-there is no context switch to a different system process.

If you have seen the system process in NT's Performance Monitor (Perfmon), you might think that the Executive subsystems are different processes. However, the purpose of the system process in Perfmon is to own Executive threads (commonly called worker threads) that carry out work, usually of a background nature, for Executive subsystems. For example, the Cache Manager creates system process threads for lazy-write operations : Every few seconds these threads will flush dirty (modified) disk data from memory back to the disk (Just like daemons do in UNIX).

Object Manager

The Object Manager is probably the least known of NT's Executive subsystems. It is also one of the most important Executive subsystems. An operating system's primary role is to manage a computer's physical and logical resources. Other Executive subsystems use the Object Manager to define and manage objects that represent these resources. For example, through the Object Manager, the Process Manager defines a process object to track active processes. Figure 14.8 lists the NT 4.0-defined objects and the kernel-mode subsystems that manage them.

The Object Manager performs object-management duties that include identification and reference counting. When an application opens a resource, the Object Manager either locates the associated object or creates a new object. Instead of returning an object pointer to the application that opened the resource, the Object Manager returns an opaque identifier called a handle. The handle's value is unique to the application that opened the resource, but it is not unique to the system across different applications. The application uses the handle to identify the resource in subsequent operations. When the application is finished with the object, the application closes the handle. The Object Manager uses reference counting to track how many system parts, including applications and Executive subsystems, are accessing an object that represents a resource. When the reference count goes to zero, the object representing the resource is no longer in use and the Object Manager deletes the object (but not necessarily the resource).

The Object Manager implements NT's namespace to provide object identification. All shareable resources in NT have names that are rooted in this name sapce. For example, when a program opens a file, the Object Manager parses the file's name to locate the file-system driver for the disk that stores the file. Similarly, when an application opens a Registry key, the Object Manager determines from the Registry key's name that the Configuration Manager must be called.

The Object Manager calls other Executive subsystems when necessary. Every object type has functions that execute when NT perform particular operations on objects of that type. Thus, when the Object Manager creates a file object to represent an open file, the Object Manager invokes the I/O Manager's function for opening files. Similarly, the Object Manager creates an associated process object for an open process and invokes the Process Manager's function for opening processes.

Security Reference Monitor

The Security Reference Monitor is closely associated with the Object Manager. The Object Manager calls the Security Reference Monitor for an access check before letting an application open an object. The Object Manager also calls the Security Reference Monitor before it lets applications perform other operations on objects, such as reading from the object or writing to it.

The Security Reference Monitor implements a security model based on identifiers and Access Control Lists (ACLs). Every process in NT has an associated access token object that contains the ID identifying the user that owns the process and the IDs of the group the user belongs to. When a security check takes place, the IDs in the access token of the process describe the user trying to complete an action on an object. Figure 14.9 gives an example of ACL that does not let the process owner, named Mark to read the object, although it lets the group to which the owner belongs (Administrators) read from and delete the object.

NT's security model has a powerful capability that lets a process impersonate any user other than the user associated with the process. Server applications such as NT's built-in file server (SRV) rely heavily on impersonation. When a client on a different machine opens a file on the server, the server impersonates the client by temporarily adopting an access token that identifies the server as the remote client. NT creates the token on the server, but the token contains the client's IDs. When the server opens the file, it invokes the Object Manager, which then calls the Security Reference Monitor to make the appropriate access check. The client can have more or less privilege than the server (the server might not be allowed to open the file), but impersonation lets the server temporarily identify as the client and thus hides the discrepancy.

ACLs specify the action that particular IDs can perform on an object. An ACL can contain any number of access control entires (ACEs), including no entries, which contain the information, about the actions that IDs can perform. Each ACE contains an ID, a flag specifying whether the ACE is of the deny type or allow type, and an operations mask (*i.e.,* read, write, delete). Every object can have an ACE connected to it, such as the example in Figure 14.9 shows. NT references the ACE when a user attempts to open the object.

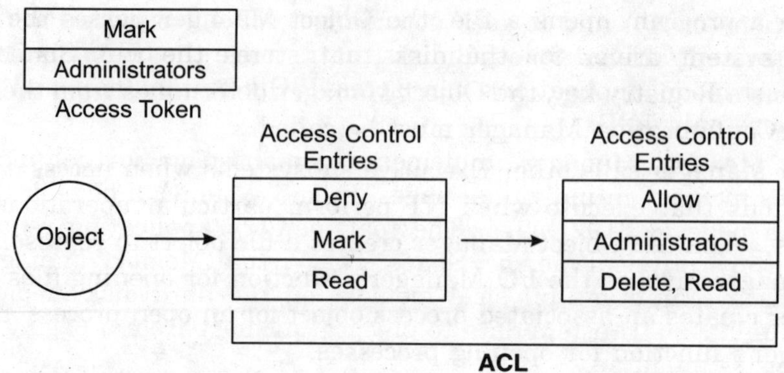

Figure 14.9 : Function of Security Reference Monitor

Given the access token object and the ACL in Figure 14.9, the Security Reference Monitor would deny the owner named Mark, read access to the object, even though it allows the members of the Administrator group to read the object. The Security Reference Monitor would deny Mark read access to the object because the 'deny' ACE is in front of the 'allow' ACE in the ACL.

When a process wants to open an object, it must indicate the access it desires (*e.g.*, read, write, and delete). The Object Manager calls the Security Reference Monitor for an access check, and the Security Reference Monitor takes the desired access and the IDs from the process' access token and goes through the object's ACL until it finds matching information. The Security Reference Monitor then looks at the ACL's ACE type : If the ACE is an allow type, the process can open the object. If the ACE is a deny type, the process cannot access the object. Two special case exist in ACL security. First users can fully access an object that does not have an ACL. Second users cannot access an object with an existing but empty ACL.

When an object opens successfully, NT associates the access types granted to the calling process (and that match the access types specified during the open function) with the handle that NT returns to the calling process. When the calling process later performs an operation on the object, all the Security Reference Monitor must do is verify that the granted access types permit the operation-there is no need for the Security Reference Monitor to rescan the ACL.

The Security Reference Monitor also implements System Access Control Lists (SACLs), which are similar to ACLs, ACLs tell the system to log specific actions when particular users perform those actions. System administrators typically use SACLs to monitor and record attempted security violations.

Virtual Memory Manager

The Virtual Memory Manager has two main duties : to create and manage address maps for processes and to control physical memory allocation. NT4.0 implements a 32-bit (4GB)-address space; however, applications can directly access only the first 2GB, as Figure 14.10 shows. This portion of the address space is the user-mode half of the address map, and it changes to reflect the currently executing program's address map (*e.g.*, Netscape, Notepad, Word). The 2GB to 4GB portion of the address space is for the kernel-mode portions of NT, and it does not change. NT 4.0 Service Pack 3 (SP3) and NT Server, Enterprise Edition 4.0, let administrators move the boundary in the address space so that user-mode applications can access 3GB of the map and kernel-mode components can use only 1GB.

The Virtual Memory Manager implements demand-page virtual memory, which means it manages memory in individual pages. In x86 systems, a page is 4096 bytes; in Alpha systems, a page is 8192 bytes. The toal memory application requirement can exceed the computer's physical memory space. The Virtual Memory Manager stores the data that exceeds a computer's physical memory on the hard disk in page files. The Virtual Memory Manager transfers data to physical memory from a paging file when an application requests the data.

NT uses memory sharing to enhance physical memory use and to communicate between processes. For example, multiple instances of a program share a memory-mapped file image, and this sharing increases memory efficiency.

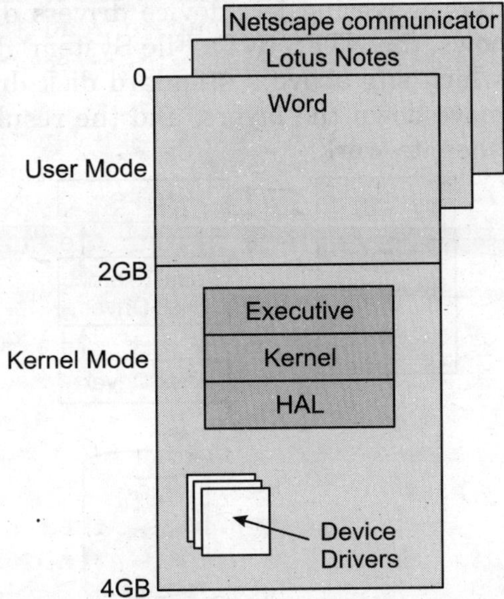

Figure 14.10 : Managing Virtual Memory in Windows NT

The Virtual Memory Manager divides physical memory among several executing programs. It uses a function called working-set tuning to allocate additional memory to programs that require it and ensure that other executing programs have enough memory to keep running.

I/O Manager

The I/O Manager is responsible for integrating add-on device drivers with NT. Microsoft did not build support for various hardware devices into NT. Device drivers, that are dynamically loaded kernel-mode components, provide hardware support. A device driver controls a specific type of hardware device by translating the commands that NT and applications direct to the device and manipulating the hardware to carry out the commands. Microsoft supplies several device drivers for common hardware. If you purchase a non-standard hardware item, the hardware vendor will provide a device driver for it.

The I/O Manager supports asynchronous I/O. For example, when a program such as Lotus Notes reads from a file, the read-file system service, NtReadFile, allocates an I/O request packet (IRP) that describes everything a device driver needs to know to complete the program's request. The I/O Manager takes the IRP and passes it to the device driver—in this example, a file system driver is responsible for reading the target file.

After the I/O Manager gives an application's request (and an IRP) to a device driver, the I/O Manager returns control to the application. The application can continue performing useful work while the device driver is transferring data and can check the device driver after the data transfer.

The I/O Manager supports 64-bit file offsets and layered device drivers. Using 64-bit offsets lets NT's file systems address extremely large files and lets disk device drivers address extremely large disks. Layering lets device drivers divide their labour. As the example in Figure 14.11 shows, the NTFS (NT's File System) driver is layered above the fault-tolerant disk driver which sits above a standard disk driver. As the I/O Manager processes requests, IRP's move down the layers, and the results pass back up from the bottom as each driver finishes its work.

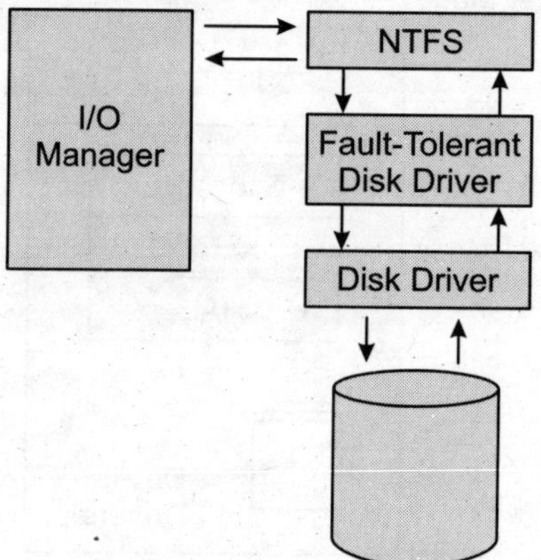

Figure 14.11 : Layered device drivers

Cache Manager

The Cache Manager works closely with the Virtual Memory Manager and file system drivers. The Cache Manager maintains NT's global (shared by all file systems) file system cache. The working set tuner assigns physical memory to the file system cache. The NT cache is file oriented rather than disk-block oriented as Windows 95's cache. When the working set tuner takes memory containing modified file data away from the Cache Manager, the I/O Manager invokes file systems that manage the moved files to write their data back to the disk.

Local Procedure Call Facility

NT's local Procedure Call (LPC) Facility optimizes communications for applications, including operating system environments. The LPC function is based on two types of port object : connection ports and communication ports. A server creates a connection port, which a client connects to. After the client establishes that connection, the server creates communications port which the server and client transmits data through.

Three kinds of LPC exist : data copying, shared memory, and shared memory with event pairs (Quick-LPC). NT uses data copying for small mesages (less than 256 bytes). One end of the communications link (client or server) copies a message to a port, and the other end of the link copies the message out of the port.

NT uses shared memory for messages larger than 256 bytes. In shared-memory LPC, the connected client and server share a region of memory. When one end of the communication link wants to send a message larger than 256 bytes to the other it sends through the communications port a short message whose only function is to point to the location of the primary message in the shared memory.

Win32 under NT 3.51 uses Quick-LPC. Win32 does not send messages through ports. Instead, one end of the communications link uses an event-pair synchronization object to signal the other end of the communications link that it has placed a message in shared memory. Using event-pair synchronization objects avoids the overhead of communicating through a port but as a trade-off has even higher resource overhead than other LPC methods.

Configuration Manager

Microsoft rarely discusses the Configuration Manager in its NT architecture documentation, but Configuration Manager is an important Executive subsystem. The Configuration Manager manages the Registry, and Win32 Registry API Functions rely on NT native APIs the Configuration Manager implements. The Configuration Manager also exports functions to the I/O Manager, and the I/O Manager uses these functions to assign physical resources to device drivers. The Configuration Manager stores this assignment information in the Registry to detect and help prevent resource conflicts.

Process Manager

The Process Manager works with the kernel to define process and thread objects. The Process Manager wraps the kernel's process object and adds to it a process identifier (PID), the access token, an address map, and a handle table. The Process Manager performs a smaller operation on the kernel's thread object, adding to it a thread identifier (TID) and statistics. These statistics include process and thread start and exit times and various virtual-memory counters.

The Process Manager exports an interface that lets other Executive subsytems and user-mode applications manipulate processes and threads. For example, applications can access Process Manager functions to create processes, delete them, and modify their characteristics (such as their priority). You can access many Process Manager functions in user mode through system services.

Plug-and-Play Manager and Power Manager

Two new Executive subsystems will debut in NT 5.0: the Plug-and-Play Manager and the Power Manager. The Plug-and-Play Manager notifies device drivers and the I/O Manager when hardware devices come on-line or are removed. The Power Manager maintains central control of the computer's power level, letting it shift into low power modes when possible. Both new subsystems work primarily with the I/O Manager and device drivers.

14.2.2.2 The Kernel

NT's Kernel operates more closely with hardware than the Executive does, and it contains CPU-specific code. NT's thread scheduler, called the dispatcher by NT's developers, resides in the Kernel. The dispatcher implements 32 priority levels, 0-31. The dispatcher reserves priority level 0 for a system thread that initializes memory pages to zeros as a background task. Priority levels 16 through 31 are fixed priority levels that only administrators can access.

The NT dispatcher is a preemptive scheduler. The CPU's time is divided into slices called quantum. When a thread runs to the end of its quantum and does not yield the CPU, the dispatcher will step in and preempt it or schedule another thread of equal priority that is waiting to run.

NT implements most synchronization primitives in the Kernel. NT has a rich set of synchronization types, including semaphores, events, and spin locks. The Kernel implements and manages its own object types, and Kernel objects represent NT's synchronization primitives. In most cases, NT wraps Kernel objects with Executive objects so that applications can access them from user mode through the native API. As described previously, the Process Manager wraps its process and thread objects around the Kernel's objects. NT stores all priority-related information and statistical information related to scheduling (e.g., context switches, and user time) in the Kernel's objects. The Kernel manages interrupts also.

14.2.2.3 The Hardware Abstraction Layer (HAL)

The HAL is NT's interface to the raw CPU. Microsoft wanted to make NT portable across different processors. To make this portability feasible, NT's developers isolated as much CPU-specific code as possible into a separate, dynamically replaceable module, the HAL. The HAL exports a common processor model that masks the difference in various processor chips from NT. Device drivers use this common processor rather than a particular CPU type. Even different motherboards in the same processor family can differ significantly, but hardware vendors can ensure that NT will work with their boards by writing a custom HAL to work with NT.

A common diference between motherboards in the same processor family is that some are for multiprocessor systems and other are for uniprocessor systems. A multiprocessor HAL is different from a uniprocessor HAL. Based on this, Microsoft provides three versions of each NT release: the uniprocessor version, the multiprocessor version, and the debug version (or the checked-built version). In addition to having different HALs, uniprocessor and multiprocessor versions of NT have different ntoskrnl.exe images. The uniprocessor version of kernel executable (ntoskrnl.exe) does not include code that is necessary for correct execution on multiprocessors. Microsoft provides the debug version of NT for device-driver developers. The debug version contains additional sanity checks and symbolic information not contained in the uniprocesor and multiprocessor machines.

14.2.3 NT File System

Historically, MS-DOS systems have used the file-allocation table (FAT) file system. The 16-bit FAT file system has several shortcomings, including internal fragmentation, a size limitation of 2 GB, and a lack of access protection for files. The 32-bit FAT file system has solved the size and fragmentation problems, but the performance and features are still weak by comparison with modern file systems. The NTFS (NT file system) is much better. It was designed with many features in mind, including data recovery, security, fault tolerance, UNICODE names, and file compression. For compatibility, NT provides support for the FAT and OS/2 HPFS file systems.

The fundamental entity in NTFS is a volume. A volume is created by the NT disk administrator utility, and is based on a logical disk partition. The volume may occupy a portion of a disk, may occupy an entire disk, or may span across several disks. In NTFS, all metadata such as information about the volume - are stored in a regular file.

NTFS does not deal with individual sectors of a disk, but instead uses clusters as the unit of disk allocation. A cluster is a number of disk's sectors that is a power of 2. The cluster size is configured when an NTFS file system is formatted. The default cluster size is the sector size for volumes up to 512 MB, 1 KB for volumes up to 1 GB, 2 KB for volumes up to 2 GB, and 4 KB for larger volumes. This cluster size is much smaller than that for the 16-bit FAT file system, and the small size reduces the amount of internal fragmentation. As an example, consider a 1.6 GB disk with 16,000 files. If you use a FAT-16 file system, 400 MB may be lost to internal fragmentation because the cluster size is 32 KB. Under NTFS, only 17 MB would be lost when storing the same files. NTFS uses logical cluster numbers (LCNs) as disk addresses. It assigns them by numbering clusters from the beginning of the disk to the end. Using this scheme, the system can calculate a physical disk offset (in bytes) by multiplying the LCN by the cluster size.

A file in NTFS is not a simple byte stream, as it is in MS-DOS or UNIX; rather, it is a structured object consisting of attributes. Each attribute of a file is an independent byte stream that can be created, deleted, read, and written. Some attributes are standard for all files, including the file name (or names, if the file has aliases), the creation time, and the security descriptor that specifies access control. Other attributes are specific to certain kind of files. For instance, Macintosh files have two data attributes : the resource fork and the data fork. A directory has attributes that implement an index for the file names in the directory.

Every file in NTFS is described by one or more records in an array stored in a special file called the master file table (MFT). The size of a record is determined when the file system is created; it ranges from 1 to 4 KB. Small attributes are stored in the MFT record itself, and are called resident attributes. Large attributes, such as the unnamed bulk data, called nonresident attributes, are stored in one or more contiguous extents on the disk, and a pointer to each extent is stored in the MFT record. For a tiny file, even the data attribute may fit inside the MFT record. If a file has many attributes, or if it is highly fragmented (remember linked list allocation of files discussed in Chapter 10), and therefore, many pointers are needed to point to all the fragments, one record in the MFT might not be large enough. In this case, the file is described by a record called the base file record, which contains pointers to overflow records that hold the addition pointers and attributes.

Each file in an NTFS volume has a unique ID called a file reference. The file reference is a 64-bit quantity that consists of a 16-bit file number and a 48-bit sequence number. The file number is the record number (i.e., the array slot) in the MFT that describes the file. The sequence number is incremented every time when an MFT entry is reused. This incrementation enables NTFS to perform internal consistency checks, such as catching a stale reference to a deleted file after the MFT entry has been reused for a new file.

As in MS-DOS and UNIX, the NFTS name space is organized as a hierarchy of directories. Each directory uses a tree like structure to store an index of the file names in that directory. The index root of a directory contains the top level of the tree. For a large directory, this top level contains pointers to disk portions that hold the remainder of the tree. Each entry in the directory contains the name and file reference of the file, and also a copy of the update timestamp and file size taken from the file's resident attributes in the MFT. Copies of this information are stored in the directory, so it is efficient to generate a directory listing–all the file names, sizes, and update times are available from the directory itself, so there is no need to gather these attributes from the MFT entries of each of the files.

In addition to MFT, there are some other special files that contain NTFS volume's metadata. These files are log file, volume file, attribute definition table, root directory, bitmap file, boot file and bad-cluster file.

14.2.4 Process Management and CPU Scheduling in NT

Windows NT is a preemptive multithreading operating system. That is, NT lets several programs run simultaneously and switches among them often enough to create the illusion that each program is the only program running on the machine. Well, that is the idea anyway. How to smoothly share one CPU (or mulptile CPUs) among many threads of control is a complicated problem. Solving this problem dynamically many times per second is the job of the NT scheduler. The NT scheduler must honour the relative priorities that the application programmers designate for each thread and attempt to provide responsiveness to user interactive threads.

Threads and Priorities

The basic scheduling unit in NT is a thread. A thread is a point of control within a process. Processes consist of a virtual address space that includes executable instructions, a set of resources such as file handles, and one or more threads that execute within its address space. Typical applications consist of only one process, so program and process are often used synonymously. Most programs today are single-threaded, which means they run as one process with one thread. However, multithreaded programs are becoming more common. An example of a multithreaded program is a program that lets a user sort a list, with an option to cancel. One thread in the program's process might perform the CPU-intensive sorting task while another thread in the process displays a how-to-cancel message to the user and waits for a response. The scheduler does not differentiate between threads of different processes. Instead, the scheduler examines the priorities of all the threads ready to run at a given instant to pick which thread to execute.

NT assigns each thread a priority number from 1 to 31, where higher number depicts higher priorities (NT uses priority 0 for the system idle thread, which executes when no other thread is able to). NT reserves priorities 16 through 31 (real-time priorities) for use by time-critical operations. Only a user with administrator privileges can direct the system to execute threads in this range. NT uses priorities 1 through 15 (dynamic priorities) for the program threads of typical applications (*e.g.*, Notepad, Word, Lotus Notes etc.).

Whose Turn is It ?

Threads must take turns running on the CPU so that one thread does not prevent other threads from performing work. One of the scheduler's jobs is to assign units of CPU time (quantums) to threads. A quantum is typically very short in duration, but threads receive quantum so frequently that the system appears to run smoothly even when many threads are performing work. One difference between NT server and NT Workstation is the length of a user thread's quantum. On most x86 system running NT Workstation, a quantum can be 20 ms, 40 ms, or 60 ms, depending on your system setting and whether the thread is a background or foreground application thread.

The scheduler must make a CPU scheduling decision every time one of three situations occurs :

- A thread's quantum on the CPU expires
- A thread waits for an event to occur
- A thread becomes ready to execute

When a thread's quantum expires, the scheduler executes the 'Find Ready Thread' algorithm to decide whether another thread needs to take over the CPU. If a higher priority thread is ready to execute, it replaces (or preempts) the thread that was running.

In many cases, threads perform processing and then wait for an event to occur. For example, a client/server application might have a server thread that performs processing when it receives client requests and then waits for more requests. A waiting (or blocked) thread gives up its quantum early, and the scheduler must execute the 'Find Ready Thread' algorithm to find a new thread to run.

When a new thread or a blocked thread becomes ready to execute (e.g., when the client/server application server thread receives another client request), the scheduler executes the 'Ready Thread' algorithm. This algorithm determines whether the ready thread will take over the CPU immediately or it should be placed in an eligible-to-execute list.

'Find Ready Thread' and 'Ready Thread' are the key algorithms the NT scheduler uses to determine how threads take turns on the CPU. The uniprocessor versions of 'Find Ready Thread' and 'Ready Thread' are straighforward algorithms. Let us examine how 'Find Ready Thread' and 'Ready Thread' work.

Find Ready Thread Algorithm

Find Ready Thread locates the highest-priority thread that is ready to execute. The scheduler keeps track of all ready-to-execute threads in Dispatcher Ready List. The Dispatcher Ready List contains 31 entries, each of which corresponds to a priority level and a queue of threads assigned to that priority level. The Find Ready Thread algorithm scans the Dispatcher Ready List and picks the front thread in the highest-priority nonempty queue. Figure 14.12 shows an example Dispatcher Ready List with three ready threads - two at priority 10 and one at priority 7. Find Ready Thread algorithm directs the scheduler to choose the first thread in priority 10's queue as the next thread to run.

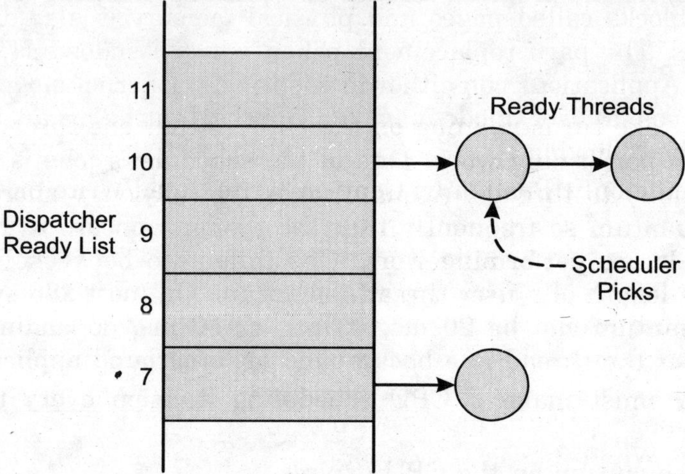

Figure 14.12 : Dispatcher Ready List Scheduling Algorithm

Ready Thread Algorithm

Ready Thread is the algorithm that places threads in the Dispatcher Ready List. When Ready Thread algorithm receives a ready-to-execute thread, it checks to see whether the thread has a higher priority than the executing thread. If the new thread has a higher priority, it preempts the current thread and the current thread goes to the Dispatcher Ready List. Otherwise Ready Thread algorithm places the ready-to-execute thread in the appropriate Dispatcher Ready List. At the front of the queue, Ready Thread algorithm places threads from which the scheduler pulls off the CPU before they complete at least one quantum; all other threads (including blocked threads) go to the end of the queue.

Preventing Starvation

Left alone, 'Find Ready Thread' algorithm and 'Ready Thread' algorithm might prevent low-priority threads from getting a chance to execute. For example, a priority 4 thread running on a system which is continuously running priority 8 threads would be starved for CPU time. However, NT provides a mechanism that gives low-priority threads a shot at the CPU. The NT Balance Set Manager is a system thread that wakes up every second or so to perform memory tuning. As a secondary responsibility, Balance Set Manager executes the 'Scan Ready Queues' algorithm, which implements NT's anti-CPU starvation policy.

'Scan Ready Queues' scans the Dispatcher Ready List, working down the list from priority 31. It looks for threads that have not executed in more than 3 seconds. When it finds one, 'Scan Ready Queues' gives the thread a special anti-starvation boost, doubles its quantum and calls 'Ready Thread' algorithm with the thread as a parameter.

14.2.5 Memory Management in Windows NT

Windows NT's memory architcture is a demand-paged virtual memory system that utilizes a linear address space and is addressed by 31-bit addresses. Up to 4GB of virtual memory is available with 2 GB available to user applications. Its virtual memory is divided into 4 KB blocks called pages and physical memory is also divided into 4 KB blocks called frames. The page replacement policy, which Windows NT utilizes, is first in, first out (FIFO). Applications run either in user mode or kernel mode and each virtual page is designated as a user mode page or a kernel mode page as well as being designated one of the following :

No-access, Execute-only, Read-only, Copy-on-Write, Read/Write or Guard-page.

Virtual Memory

Windows NT utilizes Virtual Memory Management technique, which allows it to use more memory than the computer, physically has available to be used. Each process is allocated a set of virtual memory addresses (called a virtual address space). Whenever a thread uses one of these virtual memory addresses the Virtual Memory Manger along with hardware (i.e. page table as discussed in chapter 9) translates them into physical memory addresses. When physical memory becomes over-committed then data is temporarily transferred to a file on disk. This paging file is called PAGEFILE.SYS in Windows NT. When the application requires access to the physical memory it is transferred back to physical memory.

Linear Address

Windows NT utilizes a linear address space, which is addressed by 32-bit addresses. Linear addressing starts at 0 and extends byte by byte to the uppermost boundary of the address space. The 32-bit address allows 4 gigabytes (2^{32}) of virtual memory to be accessed with 2GB for program storage and 2GB reserved for system storage. This approach of using a linear address space helps make NT portable, as this type of memory addressing is compatible with numerous processors such as MIPS R4000, DEC Alpha AXP and 32-bit Intel based machines. Another factor, which determines the portability of an operating system, is whether the operating system code interfaces with virtual memory hardware. If these interfaces exist then the operating sytem is not portable and must be modified to execute on different hardware. In Windows NT these interfaces are minimal and are well isolated.

Paging

Windows NT divides virtual memory into equal size blocks called pages. Similarly it divides physical memory into blocks called frames which are used to hold pages in memory.

A page size of 4 Kilobytes (2^{12}) has been used that was established by the Intel 386. Internal Fragmentation occurs when numerous pages have unused space, which creates unusable areas of memory. Due to the small page size (4K), which Windows NT uses, unused space is kept to a minimum.

Pages, which are in physical memory, are called valid pages and those on disk are called invalid pages. When an invalid page is accessed (called a page fault) the required page is located on disk and is loaded into a free frame in physical memory. Note that retrieved pages for a process do not have to be contiguous, they can be placed in any free frame. When the number of free frames begins to run low, selected pages are copied to disk. This process of moving pages is called paging and is transparent to programmers.

As mentioned earlier Windows NT memory architecture is a demand-paged, virtual memory system. Demand paging refers to the fetch policy which brings a page of virtual memory into main memory when a process references that page.

The virtual memory manager can transfer pages to multiple page files. If the page files are located on separate physical disk then multiple pages can be transferred to separate files simultaneously. This technique is used to increase swapping speed and improves system performance.

To translate virtual memory addresses to physical memory addresses a page table is used. Intel processors implement a page table format in hardware. The Virtual Memory Manager can also mimic this format used by Intel. The page table consists of a two level table look-up operation. The first level table (called a page directory), which contains 1024 entries, points to pages in the second table. The second level table points to the frames in physical memory.

To facilitate fast page table look-ups a cache (called a Translation Look aside Buffer (TLB) is used to store page table entries. This cache stores the most recently used entries. Hardware is used to read the entries simultaneously and compare them with the target address. If the entry does not exist in the cache then software is used to access to page table in memory.

Frame Database

The Virtual Memory Manager also needs to track the state of physical memory (i.e. whether a frame is free and who is using the frame). The Frame Database is an array, which contains entries for each frame. Page table entries point to entries in Frame Database and similarly entries in Frame Database point to entries in the Page table which are using the frame. Frame can be in one of the following states :

- **Valid.** Page is there in the frame.
- **Zeroed.** The page is not used and has been initialized with zeros.
- **Free.** Free but not initialized.
- **Standby.** This frame was in use and the page table entry is invalid and has been marked with a transition flag.
- **Modified.** Same as standby except changes have not yet been written to disk.
- **Bad.** Can not be used due to parity or other hardware error.

The database will also link together those pages, which are of the same state.

When the number of zeroed, free and standby entries falls below a given threshold, a thread called the *modified page writer* is initiated and writes the modified page frames to disk and changes their state to standby. If the number of modified entries falls below a given threshold, the Virtual Memory Manager begins automatic working set trimming (See Replacement Policy). The trimmed entries then have their status changed to modified or standby.

Replacement Policy

When the number of free frames beings to run low, selected pages are copied to disk. The set of rules that determine which pages are to be copied to disk is called a page replacement policy (as discussed in Chapter 9). The replacement policy, which Windows NT uses, is first-in, first-out (FIFO). This means that those pages, which have been in memory the longest, will be copied to disk (regardless of how often they are used). To enable the Virtual Memory Manager to determine the oldest page, it must keep track of the pages currently in memory for each process (called process's working set). When a process is created it is assigned a minimum working set size. This represents the minimum number of pages, which the process will have in physical memory while it is executing.

If there are sufficient free frames available then more frames can be assigned to a process. However, if there are insufficient free frames available and a page fault occurs, the Virtual Memory Manager will copy the oldest page to disk.

If a process incurs no page faults for a given period of time (*i.e.,* the code the process's threads are executing fit within the minimum working set size or none of the process's threads are executing) then the Virtual Memory Manager will reduce the process's working set until a page fault occurs.

When Physical memory becomes low the Virtual Memory Manager begins comparing each process' minimum working set size with its current working set size. If process's current working set size is greater than its minimum working set size, pages are removed from its working set (called automatic working set trimming).

Some processes, for performance reasons, may require a page to stay in physical memory. The process may lock the appropriate page, which will prevent it from being removed from memory while any thread in the process is executing. For example, if an index to a data structure was kept in memory, it would significantly reduce the number of page faults.

Shared Memory

Windows NT allows processes to share memory when either a process has requested it or it would be more efficient for the operating system to do so. The following example shows how sharing memory would be more efficient for an operating system :

1. Process 1 initiates a Compiler.
2. The Compiler is loaded into memory and process 1 is mapped to its physical location.
3. Process 2 initiates the same Compiler.
4. Process 2 is mapped to the physical location of the compiler, which already exists.

Note that this example prevents either process from manipulating the compiler image.

As each process has its own virtual address space, the Virtual Memory Manager can map the virtual addresses of each process to the same physical frames.

Another use may include sharing data between processes, which would require changes to the shared memory. This is particularly important on the computer system with multi-processors. For example, a process may have two threads executing on different processors trying to access the same data structure. This is addressed in the following discussion on Memory Protection.

Memory Protection

Memory is protected in Windows NT using the following techniques :

1. Hardware disallows a thread from accessing the virtual memory addresses of another process;
2. User mode can be used to restrict access to system data and code.
3. Each virtual page has a set of flags, which indicate the types of access, which is allowed in user and kernel mode;
4. When a process accesses an object the Windows NT Security Reference monitor checks whether the process has access to the object.

When a thread uses a virtual address, the Virtual Memory Manager and hardware translate the address into a physical address. This automatic translation prevents threads from one process accessing a frame of another process.

Each virtual page in process is designated as a user mode page or kernel mode page. Each page is then designated as one of the following :

- No-access
- Copy-on-Write
- Execute-only - (only if there is hardware support)
- Read-only
- Read/Write
- Guard-page

When a guard page is accessed the Virtual Memory Manager generates a guard page exception and sends a message to the process indicating that the guard page was touched.

When two processes read and write to the same page but do not want to share it, copy-on-write protection is placed on the page. Therefore, both processes can read the physical memory. If one thread attempts to write to the page the Virtual Memory Manager copies that page to another frame, makes the changes to the new frame and sets the protection level to read/write.

EXERCISES

14.1 Why there are so many different versions of UNIX currently available? In what ways this is an advantage to UNIX? In what ways it is a disadvantage?

14.2 What is the purpose of `pipes' in UNIX? Explain your answer with the help of an example.

14.3 What are the advantages of relative path names over absolute ones in UNIX.

14.4 Explain the process creation operation in UNIX. How do the processes distinguish between parent and child code?

14.5 Explain how UNIX manages a process address space.

14.6 In BSD UNIX, the data and stack segments are paged and swapped to a paging area on disk, but the text segment uses the executable binary file instead, why?

14.7 CPU Scheduling in NT uses two algorithms - Find Ready Thread and Ready Thread. Compare them with respect to

(a) Average waiting time for a process

(b) Starvation

14.8 What is the purpose of Security Reference Monitor Subsystem of NT? How does it actually implement the Access Control Lists to achieve security?

14.9 List and compare the key characteristics of Windows NT and UNIX operating system.

14.10 Prepare a list of the versions (of UNIX and Windows NT) that are available in market.

14.11 Does NT have any utility comparable to daemons in UNIX? If yes, what is that?

14.12 Explain the purpose of working set trimming in Windows NT.

14.13 Compare block and character device files in UNIX.

14.14 What is the purpose of Master File Table (MFT) in Windows NT ?

14.15 Explain the purpose of `minfree', `lotsfree' and `desfree' kernel variables in UNIX SVR4?

14.16 What is the use of the following system calls used in UNIX?

(a) fork()

(b) getpid()

(c) sigsegv()

(d) kill()

(e) pageout()

(f) sched()

(g) swapout()

(h) listen()

(i) connect()

14.17 What features of UNIX and Windows NT make them portable across different machine types?

14.18 Explain the purpose and function of Local Procedure Call (LPC) facility in Windows NT.

OOOOO

Solutions to Selected Exercises

CHAPTER 1

1.1 In parallel processing environment, there are several processors, all of which have their own memory, and they work simultaneously, whereas, in symmetric multi-processing, a single task is completed with several processors that share memory and work simultaneously.

1.3 The basic diference between network operating system and distributed operating system is that network operating system allows the user to access remote computer systems only if he/she knows the address of those computer systems, whereas distributed operating system is used by the user to share data and programs across many computers that are networked together. Here, the user need not know the address of these computers. The operating system automatically takes care of the location and name of the computer from which the data should be fetched.

1.8 Multiprogramming makes efficient use of the CPU by overlapping the demands of various users for the CPU and the input / output devices. It attempts to increase the CPU utilization by always having something for the CPU to execute. The throughput is increased as now more programs are executed in a given time interval as compared to the number of programs (i.e one program) being executed in a uniprogramming environment.

CHAPTER 2

2.2 An interrupt is a hardware-generated change of flow within a system. Interrupt is handled by an interrupt service routine that gains control when operating system directs it to do so. After servicing the interrupt, this routine returns control to the interrupt context and instruction.
A trap is a software generated interrupt. A trap can be used to call operating system routines that deal with exceptions like the memory violation, page fault, divide by zero etc.

2.3 DMA is useful for transferring large quantities of data between memory and input / output devices. It eliminates the need for the CPU to be involved in the transfer, allowing the transfer to complete more quickly and the CPU can perform other tasks concurrently, whereas, in interrupt based input / output, CPU is never that free to perform its other tasks concurrently as it can always be interrupted to serve an interrupt.

2.8 Following instructions should be privileged :

(a) Set the value of a timer

(b) Clear memory

(c) Turn of interrupts

(d) Switch from user to monitor mode

(f) Set the priority of an interrupt

(g) Set the base and limit registers

CHAPTER 3

3.4 Virtual machine is a software technique that subdivides a single computer system into multiple, virtual computer systems, each with its own processor, disk storage, and other input / output devices. Each of these small computers, simulated in software, acts as an independent and complete computer system. It basically divides all the resources - CPU, storage and input / output devices into may users at the same time.

For an operating system designer who uses virtual machine architecture, the system is easy to debug and security problems are easy to solve. Virtual machines also provide a good platform for operating system research since many different operating systems may run on one physical real system.

3.7 Command interpreter reads commands given by the user or from a file of commands and executes them, usually by converting them into one or more system calls. It is not a part of the kernel as it is subject to changes. Another reason is that it is usually written in a high level language like 'C' whereas the kernel is usually coded in assembly language.

3.8 As we know that a modular design is always advantageous, designing an operating system in a modular way has several advantages. The system is easier to debug and modify because changes affect only limited sections of the system rather than touching all the sections of the operating system. Information is kept only where it is needed and is accessible only within a defined and restricted area, so many bugs affecting that data must be limited to a specific module or layer.

CHAPTER 4

4.3 (i) **Short-term scheduler** selects from jobs in memory those jobs that are ready to execute and allocates the CPU to them.

(ii) **Medium term scheduler** used especially with time-sharing systems as an intermediate scheduling level. A swapping scheme is implemented to remove partially run programs from memory (to create more space for the programs that are currently running) and reinstate them later to continue where they left off.

(iii) **Long term scheduler** determines which jobs should be brought into memory (from secondary storage device) for processing.

4.6 (i) User-level threads are unknown by the kernel whereas kernel is aware of the kernel threads.

(ii) Kernel threads need not be associated with a process whereas every user thread belongs to a process.

4.8 Windows NT 4.0, Windows 2000, Windows 95, Windows 98, UNIX are few examples of multithreaded operating systems.

4.14 Multiple processors can be best utilized when multithreading is implemented because in multithreading, multiple threads should execute simultaneously and this simultaneous eexecution can be done efficiently in a multiprocessing environment with each thread being executed on a separate processor. This will increase the speed of a multithreaded program. For example a web server that services each request in a separate thread if uses multiple processors to execute these threads, can become very fast as compared to when it uses only a single processor.

CHAPTER 5

5.13 (1) Gantt chart for the different scheduling algorithms will be :

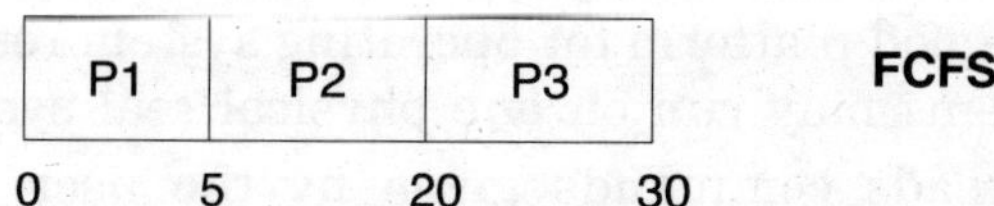

FCFS

$$\text{Average waiting time} = \frac{0+5+20}{3} = \frac{25}{3} \text{ units of time}$$

P1 | P2 | P3

0 5 15 30

SJF preemptive

$$\text{Average waiting time} = \frac{0+5+15}{3} = \frac{20}{3} \text{ units of time}$$

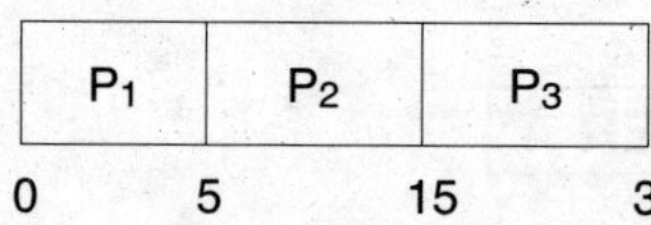

SJF non-preemptive

$$\text{Average waiting time} = \frac{0+5+15}{3} = \frac{20}{3} \text{ units of time}$$

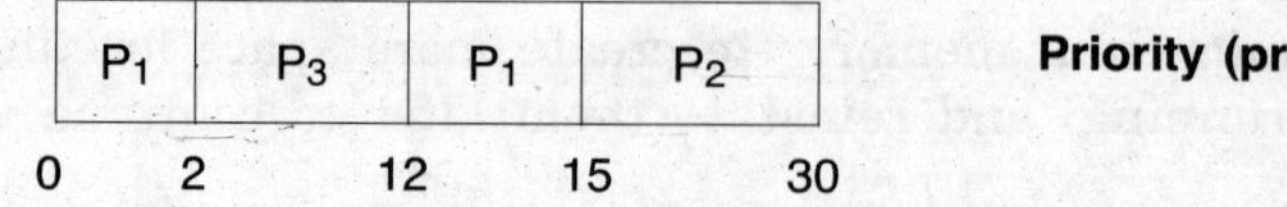

Priority (preemptive)

$$\text{Average waiting time} = \frac{0+2+10+15}{3} = \frac{27}{3} \text{ units of time}$$

P_1	P_3	P_2

0 5 15 30

Priority non-preemptive

$$\text{Average waiting time} = \frac{0+5+15}{3} = \frac{20}{3} \text{ units of time}$$

(2) **FCFS**

Turn around time = time of completion of job - time of submission of job

turn around time for $P_1 = 5 - 0 = 5$

turn around time for $P_2 = 20 - 1 = 19$

turn around time for $P_3 = 30 - 2 = 28$

$$\text{Average turn around time} = \frac{5+19+28}{3} = \frac{52}{3} \text{ units of time}$$

SJF (preemptive)

$$\text{Average turn around time} = \frac{5+13+28}{3} = \frac{47}{3} \text{ units of time}$$

SJF Priority (preemptive)

Turn around time for $P_1 = 15 - 0 = 15$

Turn around time for $P_2 = 30 - 1 = 29$

Turn around time for $P_3 = 12 - 2 = 10$

$$\text{Average turn around time} = \frac{15+29+10}{3} = \frac{54}{3} \text{ units of time}$$

SJF (Non-preemptive)

$$\text{Average turn around time} = \frac{5+29+13}{3} = \frac{47}{3} \text{ units of time}$$

(3) **RR Scheduling**

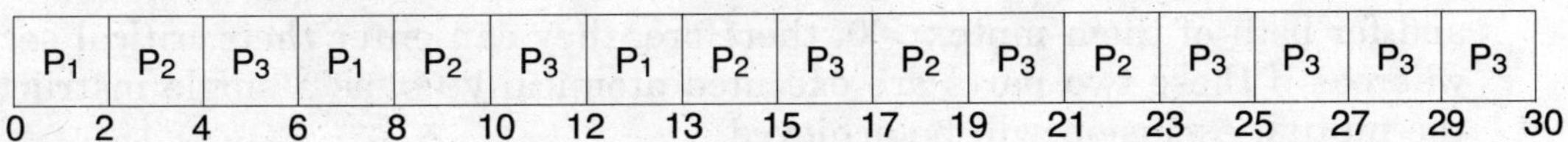

Waiting time for $P_1 = 0 + 4 + 4 = 8$

Waiting time for $P_2 = 2 + 4 + 3 + 2 + 2 = 13$

Waiting time for $P_3 = 4 + 4 + 3 + 2 + 2 = 15$

$$\text{Average waiting time} = \frac{8+13+15}{3} = \frac{36}{3} = 12 \text{ units of time}$$

$$\text{Average turn around time} = \frac{(13-0)+(23-1)+(30-2)}{3} = \frac{47}{3} \text{ units of time}$$

$$= \frac{13+22+28}{3} = \frac{63}{3} = 21 \text{ units of time}$$

CHAPTER 6

6.11 Monitors are nothing but operating system structuring mechanisms that address the issue of resource sharing in a systematic manner. The main idea behind monitors is to provide structural data abstraction, in addition to this concurrency control. Signal and wait operations on a condition variable differ from signal and wait operations on a semaphore as

- Signal (of condition variable) has no effect if no process is waiting on the condition.
- Signal (of semaphore) has some effect if a process is waiting or not.
- Wait (of a semaphore) checks the condition and blocks only if necessary.
- Wait (of condition variable) is explicit. It does not check the condition.

6.13 Consider the use of a semaphore named 'mutex' having initial value = 1 for achieving mutual exclusion by any process P.

```
Mutex → P ()
Critical section
Mutex → V()
Remainder section
```

Process structure

Now, if wait operation i.e., Mutex → P () is not atomic then execution of its two parts i.e. "while mutex ≤ 0 do nothing" and "mutex = mutex - 1" can be interleaved by two processes like :

while mutex ≤ 0 do nothing	while mutex ≤ 0 do nothing
mutex = mutex - 1	mutex = mutex - 1
critical section	critical section
Process P_1	Process P_2

and for both of them mutex > 0, therefore, they can enter their critical section whereas if these two parts are executed atomically i.e. as a single instruction, the mutual exclusion will be achieved.

CHAPTER 7

7.8 (1) Need matrix

	A	B	C
P_0	7	4	3
P_1	1	2	2
P_2	6	0	0
P_3	0	1	1
P_4	4	3	1

(2) A safe sequence

$$< P_1, P_3, P_0, P_2, P_4, >$$

exists after applying the Banker's algorithm.

(3) A safe sequence

$$< P_1, P_3, P_2, P_4, P_0 >$$

exists after applying the Banker's alogorithm (assuming that the request of process P_4 is granted). Therefore, the request can be granted immediately as it will not cause deadlock in the system.

CHAPTER 8

8.10 No, in a uniprogramming environment there is no need of any memory allocation scheme. In such an environment only the operating system and the single user program (which is to be executed) reside in the memory. No other user program can be brought into memory till this one finishes off its work. So, there is no question of memory allocation schemes as such.

8.12 Number of pages = $8 = 2^3$

Size of each page = $1024 = 2^{10}$

Number of frames = $32 = 2^5$

Size of each frame = $1024 = 2^{10}$

Logical address will have $3 + 10 = 13$ bits and physical address will have $5 + 10 = 15$ bits.

8.13 Logical address = 18 bits

Page size = 1 K = 1024 bits = 2^{10} bits

As mentioned in the text, if size of logical address space = 2^1 and size of each page is 2^P then the p lower-order bits designate page offset. Here, page size is 2^{10}, therefore : p = 10.

Thus 10 bits for for the page offset and remaining bits in the logical address i.e. $18 - 10 = 8$ bits designate page number.

Now, using a page table an entry can be found for each page number, which indicates the frame number where this page resides in the physical memory (if it is loaded into the memory) otherwise its entry is empty.

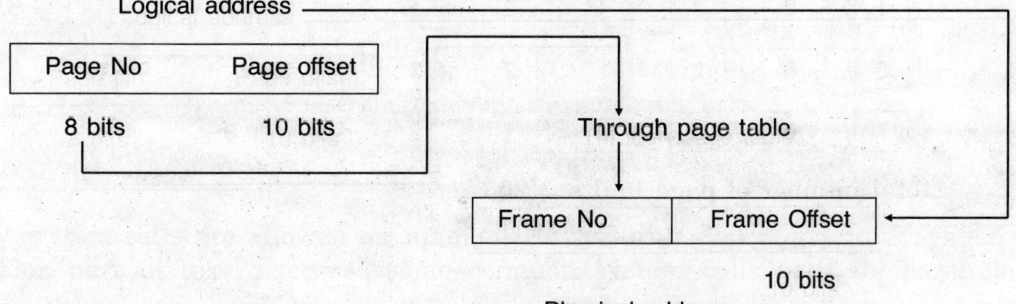

8.15 After consulting the segment table :

- Physical address of the logical address 0, 430 will be 219 + 430 = 649.
- Physical address of the logical address 0, 10 will be 2300 + 10 = 2310
- Reference to the physical address of the logical address 2, 500 will result in illegal reference and a trap to the operating system will be generated.
- Physical address of the logical address 3, 400 will be 1327 + 400 = 1727.
- Reference to the physical address of the logical address 4, 112 will result in illegal reference and a trap will be generated to the operating system.

CHAPTER 9

9.3 Dirty bit / modify bit is set if a page is modified after being brought into the memory. Now, if this page is to be replaced by some other page (due to the occurrence of some page fault) then it should be copied back to the disk only if it has been modified in the memory. If no change has been made in it then it should be simply flushed off from the memory (as disk contains its latest copy). This way a page is copied to the disk only if its contents were changed in the memory. Therefore, by reducing the number of disk write operations, dirty bit helps improving the performance of a virtual memory system.

9.9 We assume the situation when all frames are initially empty so our first unique pages will cause one fault each. The no. of page faults for each algorithm will be as shown below :

Number of page faults

Number of frames	With LRU	With FIFO	With Optimal
1	20	20	20
2	18	18	15
3	15	16	11
4	10	14	8

Let us see how do we get these answers for FIFO.

For 1 frame the page faults will be as indicated :

1	2	3	4	2	1		
5	6	2	1	2	3		
7	6	3	2	1	2	3	6

Total number of page faults = 20.

For 2 frames, the page faults using FIFO will be as indicated :

1	1	3	3	2	2
	2	2	4	4	1

5	5	2	2	3	3
1	6	6	1	1	7

6	6	2	2	3	3
7	3	3	1	1	6

Total number of page faults = 18.

For 3 frames, the page faults using FIFO will be as indicated :

7	6	3	2	1	2	3	6
7	6	3	2	1	2	3	6
7	6	3	2	1	2	3	6

7	6	3	2	1	2	3	6
7	6	3	2	1	2	3	6
7	6	3	2	1	2	3	6

Total number of page faults = 16.

Similarly for four frames the number of page faults (using FIFO) turn out to be 14.

9.10 Yes, it will be necessary to consider the size of the segment (in demand) for segment replacement. Because, segments are of varying size and whenever a new segment is to be brought into the memory, there should be a hole (contiguous space) in memory whose size is greater than or equal to the size of new segment to be brought into the memory. If such a hole is to be created by replacing a segment (either by flushing off if its dirty bit is not set or by copying it to the disk if its dirty bit is set, then this segment should be of the size greater than or equal to the size of the new segment to be brought into the memory. If we do not have such a big segment, then second choice should be to replace two (or three) segments whose size taken together should be greater than or equal to the size of the new segment to be brought in.

9.11 Thrashing is caused when not even the minimum number of pages required by a process (to start) is accommodated in the physical memory. This leads to repetitive page faults. The system can detect thrashing by evaluating the level of CPU utilization as compared to the level of multiprogramming. It can be reduced by reducing the degree of multiprogramming (i.e. by allocating more space for the process which is thrashing).

CHAPTER 10

10.6 Relocation of files on secondary storage involves considerable overhead - data blocks would have to be read into main memory and written back out to their new locations i.e. only possibility of relocation is by bringing the different data blocks into memory, relocate them and store them on the disk again. Further more, relocation registers apply only to sequential files, and many disk files are not sequential. Another, reason is that disk space can be best utilized by storing different data blocks at different places on the disk i.e. even sequential files can be allocated non-contiguous blocks if links between logically sequential blocks are maintained by the disk system. Therefore, there may not be any need for the relocation at all.

10.7 Yes, there is a posibility of inconsistency between the bit map loaded into the main memory and that on the disk. Actually, there is always a chance of inconsistency whenever copy of the same matter (here bit map) is kept at more than one place.

For avoiding such a situation, a situation like bit for block i is 1 in memory and is 0 in the disk should be avoided. If this ever occurs, solution is to set bit for block i to 1 on the disk, allocate this block i and set bit for block i to 1 in memory.

10.9 In railway reservation application, the records may have to be accessed directly (i.e. not sequentially), therefore, random access file organization should be chosen.

10.10 Let filel be the old file and file2 be the new file. A user wishing to access file1 through an existing link will actually access file2. Note that the access protection for file1 is used rather than the one associated with file2. This problem can be avoided by ensuring that all links to a deleted file are also deleted. This can be accomplished in several ways.

(a) Maintain a list of all links to a file and remove each of them when the file is deleted.

(b) Another possibility is to retain the links, removing them when an attempt is made to access a deleted file.

(c) Maintain a count of links to the file and delete the file only after all the links to that file has been deleted i.e this count of links becomes zero.

10.11 (1) Contiguous allocation strategy should be used if file is usually accessed sequentially and is relatively small.

(2) Linked allocation strategy should be used if file is large and usually accessed sequentially.

(3) Indexed allocation strategy should be used if file is large and usually accessed randomly.

CHAPTER 11

11.4 The two problems that force an operating system to adopt dedicated device allocation are :

(1) Some devices like magnetic tape require manual actions or other time consuming operations to be performed before their usage can actually begin. Therefore, it becomes difficult to share such devices.

(2) An input / output bound program may specify that the device it needs should not be shared by other programs. In such a case, an operating system cannot do anything other than to allocate the device in the dedicated manner.

11.5 Problems introduced by allowing users to share a device are :

(1) Device management becomes complex.

(2) Device scheduling becomes very complex.

(3) Device protection also becomes very difficult.

A disk is more sharable than a tape as it does not require any manual actions (like rewinding the tape etc.) to be performed. Its functions are totally automatic and therefore it can be easily shared by implementing the appropriate device (disk) scheduling algorithm.

11.8 (a) The schedule using FCFS algorithm is 143, 86, 1470, 913, 1774, 948, 1509, 1022, 1750, 130. The total distance that the disk arm moves is 7081.

(b) The schedule using SSTF algorithm is 143, 130, 86, 913, 948, 1022, 1470, 1509, 1750, 1774. The total distance that the arm moves is 1745.

(c) The schedule using SCAN algorithm is 143, 913, 948, 1022, 1470, 1509, 1750, 1774, 4999, 130, 86. The total distance that the arm moves is 9769.

(d) The schedule using LOOK algorithm is 143, 913, 948, 1022, 1470, 1509, 1750, 1774, 130, 86. The total distance that the arm moves is 3319.

(e) The schedule using C-SCAN algorithm is 143, 913, 948, 1022, 1470, 1509, 1750, 1774, 4999, 86, 130. The total distance that the arm moves is 9813.

11.9 The center of the disk is the location having the smallest average distance to all other tracks. Thus the disk head tends to move away from the edges of the disk. Here is another way to think of it. The current location of the head divides the cylinders into two groups. If the head is not in the center of the disk and a new request arrives, the new request is more likely to be in the group that includes the center of the disk; thus the head is more likely to move in that direction.

11.10 Certain blocks on the disk get corrupted such that their data is lost and may need to be recovered by some method or the other. Such blocks are called bad blocks.

Sectors sparing and sectors slipping are two methods of treating bad blocks. Sectors sparing uses spare (free) sectors to replace the bad blocks (sectors), whereas, sectors slipping require the shifting of all the good blocks (following a bad block) so that the bad block does not contain any useful data. Sector slipping may involve a lot of overhead of shifting the good blocks (sectors). This technique can require the reading and writing of an entire track's data to slip the sectors past the bad block.

With sectors sparing, when a bad block is accessed, a lot of time may be consumed in determining its mapping to a spare block and rotating the disk so that now the spare blocks (to which that bad block is mapped) can be read. This may cause an unlucky request to wait for an extra 8 ms of time.

CHAPTER 12

12.1 An access list is a list for each object consisting of the domains with a non-empty set of access rights for that object, whereas, a capability list is a list of objects and the operations allowed on those objects for each domain.

12.4 To know that whether such an event has occurred or not, the system can do the following :

Whenever a user logs in, the system can print the last time when the user logged in the system. With this the user can check whether the time of his last login is correct or not. If not, it implies that someone else used his user name and password to log in the system at that time.

12.5 The passwords stored in this list should be encrypted so that even though a user manages to read this list, he/she cannot know the actual password.

12.6 (1) A bank should be located in a protected location, well guarded : physical, human.

(2) Its network should be tamper proof : physical, human, operating system.

(3) If modem is used, its access should be eliminated or limited : physical, human.

(4) Unauthorized data transfers should be prevented : human, operating system.

(5) Backup media should be guarded : physical human.

(6) Trustworthy employees : human.

12.7 (1) Install the antivirus software on every computer system of an organization and schedule the scanning of the system after a fixed interval of time.

(2) Avoid the use of floppies, pen drives and other detachable storage devices as much as possible. If their use for data transfer is unavoidable, then first scan them for viruses and then access them.

(3) Update the antivirus software (installed on the system). These updates are now available on the websites of the antivirus software companies. They contain the antivirus utilities for detecting and removing newly emerging viruses.

12.8 Encrypted data are guarded by the operating system's protection facilities, as well as by a password that is needed to decrypt them.

12.9 "Read-only" right should be given to him. The access matrix cell will contain

	File 1
John	r

where 'John' is assumed to be the name of the fellow student and 'file1' to be the name of the file which is shared.

12.10 The purpose can be to stop the access of all the websites except the educational ones.

CHAPTER 13

13.2 In horizontal distribution of the application, all the computer systems are at the same level i.e. they are equally capable of handling any functionality. Examples of this are office automation and airline reservation. Dozens or even hundreds of computers in the network are able to book or cancel any reservation, or inquire on any information.

In vertical or hierarchical distribution of the application, there are various levels of functionality. These levels normally reflect the levels in an organization. For instance, a division of a company may have a number of zones and each zone in turn may have a number of branches. In such a case, a number of computers at the branch level will carry out the functions at various branches and send summaries to their higher level (zones). The computers at branch level can be networked together, if data sharing is required. The computers at the zonal level also can be networked together, and they can share each other's information.

13.3 In a distributed processing environment, the data required by various applications can be maintained as :

- Centralized data
- Replicated data
- Partitioned data

Figure 13.3 of chapter 13 illustrates these concepts. The figure shows two branches of a bank networked together with their head office. It also shows three databases normally required for managing banking. One is *branch* database - containing information about diferent branches of the bank. Another is the *accounts* database which contains accounts and their balances for customers of each branch. Thus each branch should have this database for its own accounts. The third database - *customers* should be available at all branches so that Branch 1 can access the accounts of Branch 2, if required and similarly, if required, Branch 2 can access the accounts of Branch 1.

Thus, *branch* database is centralized, *accounts* database is partitioned and *customers* database is replicated.

13.4 Advantage of Distributed Systems over Centralized Ones are :

1. Speed
2. Inherent Distribution
3. Reliability
4. Incremental Growth

Disadvantages of Distributed Systems are :

1. Very little software exists at present for the distributed systems
2. Requirement for a strong communication network (these days networks are not very reliable)
3. Security issues

13.5 In a distributed operating system, the users access remote resources in the same manner as they do local resources. The presence of the remote files is transparent to the user. Data and process migration from one site to another is under the control of the distributed operating system.

If a user on stie 1 wants to access data from site 2, the distributed operating system can facilitate this operation by data migration (i.e. copying the file on site 2 to site 1). To the user it appears as if the site 1 contains that file locally. The same situation if handled by the network operating system will have a difference that the data migration will not be transparent to the user. The user will be required to know the machine address of site2's computer system. In addition to this, the user should have a valid user name and password for activating FTP for transferring file from the site2's computer system.

13.6 Key design issues are :

1. **Transparency**

This consists of :

- Location transparency
- Migration transparency
- Replication transparency
- Concurency transparency
- Parallelism transparency

2. **Flexibility**

3. **Reliability**

This consists of :

- Availability
- Security
- Fault Tolerance

4. **Performance**

5. **Scalability**

13.10 The three Mutual Exclusion mechanism in distributed systems are :

1. Centralized Approach. In a centralized approach to providing mutual exclusion, one of the processes in the system is chosen to coordinate the entry to the critical section. Each process that wants to invoke mutual exclusion sends a request message to the coordinator. When the process receives a reply message from the coordinator, it can proceed to enter its critical section. After exiting its critical section, the process sends a release message to the coordinator and proceeds with rest of its execution.

The disadvantage is :

- This scheme requires three messages per critical-section entry : a request, a reply, and a release and is therefore more time consuming as compared to the other two.
- If the coordinator goes down, the mutual exclusion mechanism fails. This requires immediate execution of an election algorithm so that a new coordinator can be elected.

2. Fully Distributed Approach. Here this decision-making job (that decides which process should execute its critical section next) is distributed across the entire system. This method uses timestamps.

When a process A wants to enter its critical section, it generates a new timestamp, TS, and sends the message request (A, TS) to all other processes including itself. On receiving a request message a process may reply immediately (that is, send a reply message back to A), or it may defer sending a reply back (because it is already in its critical section, for example). A process that has received a reply message from all other processes in the system can enter its critical section. After exiting its critical section, the process ends reply messages to all its deferred requests.

The advantages are :

- This algorithm has the advantage that the mutual exclusion is obtained in a simple manner.
- It is also free from deadlock and starvation.

3. Token-Passing Approach. Another method of providing mutual exclusion is to circulate a token among the processes in the system. A token is a special type of message that is passed around the system. Possession of the token entitles the holder to enter the critical section. Since there is only a single token in the system, only one process can be in its critical section at a time.

To implement mutual exclusion, the token is passed around the ring. When a process receives the token, it may enter its critical section, keeping the token. After this proces exits its critical section, the token is passed around again. If the process receiving the token does not want to enter its critical section, it passes the token to its neighbour.

The advantages are :

- Since there is only a single token, only one process at a time can be in its critical section.
- As the ring is unidirectional, freedom from starvation is ensured.

The disdavantages are :

- If the token is lost, an election must be called to generate a new token.
- If a process fails, a new logical ring must be established.

13.14 If two processes detect the death of the coordinator simultaneously and both decide to hold an election using the bully algorithm, then both of them will send the election message to all processes higher than it. For example consider that there are 7 processes numbered from 1 to 7 and 7 was the previous coordinator that has been now found to be dead. If 4 and 5 detect that 7 has crashed, both will send ELECTION messages to 5, 6, 7 and 6, 7 respectively. Process 5 and 6 will respond back to 4 with OK and similarly 6 will respond back to 5 with OK. 4 will now know that its job is over and at the same time 5 will also know that its job is done. Both of them will sit to see that 6 sends an ELECTION message to 7 but 7 does not respond back (with OK) to 6 as it is dead. Then 6 declares itself as coordinator by sending COORDINATOR message to all. Thus, even though two processes detected the death of coordinator and initiated the election process, there is no conflict regarding the coordinator, which in every case is process 6 only.

13.15 1. In wait and die scheme, the process with timestamp 50 should wait for the process with timestamp 100.

2. In wound and wait scheme, the resource will be preempted from process with timestamp 100 and it will be rolled back.

CHAPTER 14

14.1 AT & T made the source code of UNIX available to universities and other sites, where experimentation and expansion took place. This allowed many people to have an influence on UNIX and to try out their own ideas. These ideas were circulated, and the best ones were included in the standard varieties of UNIX. The disadvantage of this is that there is no "standard" version of UNIX. Programs written for UNIX may only run on one, or some, versions of UNIX but rarely on all.

14.10 UNIX - BSD (1 BSD, 2 BSD, 3 BSD, 4 BSD, 386 BSD), Free BSD, Net BSD, Open BSD, Linux, BSDi, SysV, aos, Sunos, tandem, Unixware.
Windows NT–Windows NT server and Window NT workstation.

14.11 Yes, NT has some system process threads that carry out the same operations as daemons in UNIX e.g., there is a system process thread that copies dirty (modified) data from memory to the disk, after a fixed interval of time.

14.12 Working set trimming is used for memory management when the physical memory becomes low. The virtual memory manager begins comparing each process' minimum working set size with its current working set size. If process' current working set size is greater than its minimum working set size, pages are removed from its working set. This is known as automatic working set trimming.

14.16 (a) fork ( ) - creates a child process (an exact copy) of the original process.

(b) getpid ( ) - returns the process id of a process.

(c) sigsegv ( ) - indicates memory protection is violated.

(d) kill ( ) - kills (stops) a particular process.

(e) pageout ( ) - paging out operation is performed by it.

(f) sched ( ) - it is called when the memory becomes low and pageout operation is not able to recover memory by page stealing. It actually further calls swapout ( ).

(g) swapout ( ) - Frees all the memory pages associated with the process chosen for being swapped out.

(h) listen ( ) - creates a buffer and blocks until data arrives on the receiver's side.

(i) connect ( ) - Sender uses this call to connect to the receiver using sockets.

14.17 The use of 'C' language for writing UNIX and Windows NT makes them highly portable.

OOOOO

Frequently Asked Questions & Their Solutions

Q. Discuss the term 'Swapping'.

Ans : The technique of shifting a process from memory to disk and vice versa to manage multiprogramming in the computer is called swapping. During swapping, the process state of currently executing process is managed in the stack and after the completion of the new process or when the sufficient memory for its execution is available then it is again swapped in to the main memory. The state of reloading a process in memory is called swapping in and moving it out of the memory to make space for another process execution is called swapping out. This shift requires a lot to be done on operating system part. If the program has absolute addressing for its instructions then it needs to be shifted back to the same place in memory, but if the program keeps relative addressing then we can place the program at any point in main memory as instructions are fetched by the relocating loader on the basis of the base address mentioned at the starting point. Operating system manages all this placement and replacement. Similarly the memory space has to be protected against unauthorized access by other processes. The relocation and protection is also handled by the operating system.

Advantages :

1. Swapping is beneficial in providing multiprogramming.
2. By using swapping user gets a feel of huge amount of memory available to process for its execution. ❑

Q. What is busy waiting ?

Ans : The repeated execution of a piece of code while waiting for an event to occur is called busy waiting. During concurrent execution, many processes keep executing simultaneously. Every process is assigned a list of resources to work on at a particular moment. If some process requires a resource which is already engaged with another process then it starts sending access requests again and again. During this wait period, process stays idle and do not get involved in some constructive work. Busy waiting leads to waste of time and low resource utilization.

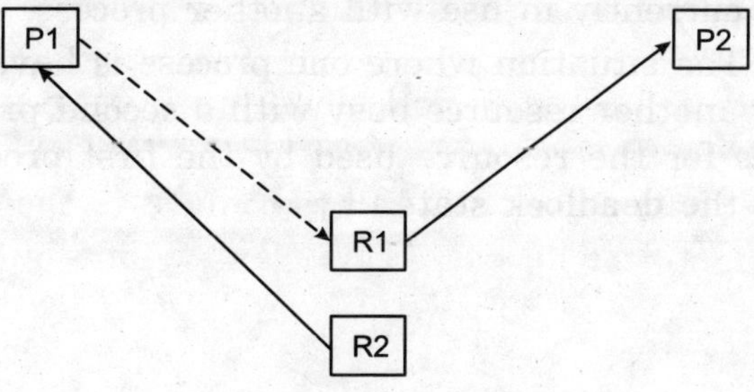

Fig. 1 : Busy waiting.

In the above shown figure, processes are having exclusive mode access on respective resources i.e. P1 is engaged with R2 and P2 is engaged with R1. If at any moment process P1 requires access to R1 then it has to wait till the process P2 relinquishes its access with that resource. Till that time it will not involve itself with any further processing and keeps on sending the access requests to resource R1. This leads to the waste of time and process cycles resulting in delayed execution. ❑

Q. What are the reasons for process suspension ?

Ans : Being in execution a process can be made to suspend its working due to many reasons :

1. If a high priority process requests for processor time then the currently executing process has to relinquish its CPU access.
2. At any time if operating system requires space for a new process then working of any one of the currently executing process is temporarily being suspended to make that process execute.
3. If a system loses its safe state and a process is found responsible for the fault then it is shifted to a suspended state till the recovery management.
4. During time slicing scheduling, a process periodically waits for its turn. During this wait some time a process got terminated.
5. When a process requests for a resource access or an event to happen which is not possible at a moment then process is shifted to suspend state till it gets the required access.
6. Sometimes a parent process requests suspension of a process due to requirement of its current involvement with some other process.

In all these above mentioned cases, the current state of the process is saved on the stack till its next execution. The process control block keeps track of the current parameters associated with the process. ❑

Q. When is the system in safe state ?

Ans : A system is in safe state if all the conditions to avoid deadlock are met in the execution sequence of set of processes present in the system. In case any of these conditions are violated, the system risks being in a deadlock state. The conditions are :

1. Mutual Exclusion : Every process is provided with an exclusive access to a particular instance of the resource. No any other process can gain its access till the time it's busy with a particular process.
2. Hold and Wait : While working with a resource a process cannot ask for a resource access currently in use with another process.
3. Circular Wait : The situation where one process is having access to a resource and waiting for another resource busy with a second process while that second process requests for the resource used by the first process leads to a circular wait and hence the deadlock state.

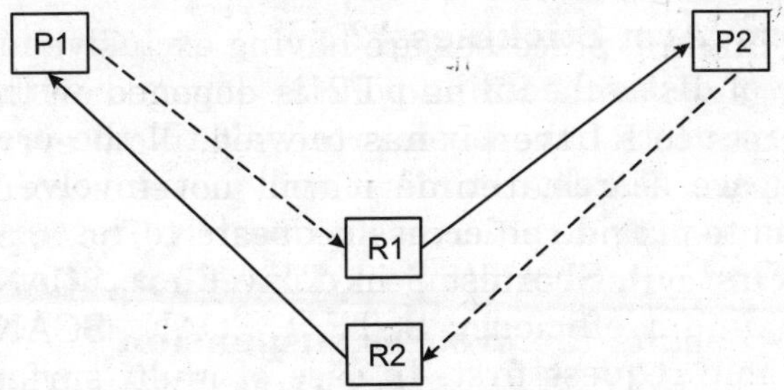

Fig. 2 : Deadlock state

4. No-Preemption : Any process working with a resource must not be forced to relinquish its access till the execution of that process. ❑

Q. Discuss FCFS scheduling.

Ans : FCFS stands for First Come First Serve. This scheduling is a non preemptive scheduling scheme where jobs are being processed on the basis of their entry time. No job with higher priority can preempt the execution of a process. In all other scheduling techniques like SJF, Round Robin, high priority either as a resource access or execution time can preempt the working of a currently executing process. In FCFS no any extra overhead is required on preprocessing with the incoming jobs. Every next job is placed on the ready queue to get executed in the same order.

But FCFS is also not without limitations :

1. During FCFS sometimes processor remains busy with a longer job and shorter jobs are made to wait for a long time even compared to their execution time. ❑

Q. What is the difference between Preemptive Scheduling and Time Slicing ?

Ans :

Preemptive Scheduling	Time Slicing
1. In this Scheduling technique a higher priority process can suspend the execution of current process and starts accessing processor time.	1. Here every process present in the system is allowed to takes processor access periodically for a definite time slice.
2. The state of the process is changed to suspend state.	2. The process after using its time slice is placed at the end of the ready queue to wait for its next turn.
3. The Scheduler decides the next execution of suspended process.	3. The next execution of a process is decided as per the task sequence.
4. Some times the lower priority processes go on waiting for their turn for an unlimited time and lead to a state called starvation.	4. No process can face starvation as processor time is provided to every process after a particular time limit.

❑

Q. Discuss the term 'Arm Stickiness' ?

Ans : The efficiency of disk scheduling policies depends on the maximum seek time measured after all the requests have been processed. Now every time a new request approaches for a disk space search, the disk arm moves according to the scheduling technique working behind to provide efficient disk search. The important disk scheduling techniques are First in First out, Shortest Seek Time First, SCAN, C-SCAN and LOOK. In order to achieve maximum efficiency SSTF, C-SCAN, SCAN all these techniques process the nearest possible request first. In case of multi surface disks, the disk arm goes on processing the request with in same track resulting in no movement of the arm. This situation leads to the arm stickiness. In case of lower density disks this kind of situation is rarely seen. To provide a solution to the problem the disk request queue can be divided into segments and every next request is stored on a new segment. Once the request in one segment gets completely processed the disk arm got moved to the next segment. Every segment is assigned a maximum limit of requests that it can have at a time. ❑

Q. What is Convoy Effect ?

Ans : In First Come First Serve scheduling technique, the jobs are processed based on their entry time in the system. The job arrived earlier in the system are served first. In that case if short jobs are lined up behind a longer job then they have to wait a long time as compared to even their execution time. The state where this kind of situation arises is called convoy effect. Take an example of the system with one longer process being processed by the processor and rest of the shorter jobs with I/O requests lined up behind it. Now here no resource dependency comes into play but still the jobs have to wait till the execution of the current process. This can even end up in starvation or termination of few shorter jobs while waiting. The major metrics taken care while scheduling techniques are CPU throughput, turn around time, response time and waiting time. Now if a CPU-bound process is making other jobs wait then system throughput will obviously get affected. Similarly individual performance issue will get lowered down. Only CPU has been kept busy and rest all other resources are sitting idle. ❑

Q. Explain the working of Dispatcher Subsystem ?

Ans : The subsystem which provides the process or control to the process selected by the scheduler is known as dispatcher. In multiprogramming system, more than one process resides in main memory at a particular time. The decision of assigning processor time to any one of the process present is taken by the short term scheduler. After the decision short term scheduler passes control to dispatcher for actual allocation of the processor control to that very process. The functions performed by the dispatcher includes context switch (The state of shifting processor control from one process control to another). During context switch the state of current process gets saved on to the stack and the process control block of new process becomes activated. The dispatcher switches the system mode to the user mode so that user can pass its commands to the processor. It lets the control jump to the proper location in the user program to start the particular program. In short dispatcher makes the allotment of selected process to CPU possible.

❑

Q. What are Internal Fragmentation and External Fragmentation ?

Ans : While keeping multiple process execution possible, it requires proper memory management issues to be taken care of. From memory management we mean placement of more than one process in main memory at any instance of time and making their simultaneous execution possible. To place different processes in main memory, the memory space is being partitioned into fixed or variable size blocks. In fixed size partitioning system every new process is placed in the available free block. Either these fixed partitions are made of same size or different size. e.g. if the block size is kept at 4k, then every process up to 4k size is made to reside in the blocks of 4k. If a process is of smaller size then the rest of the space is left empty. The empty space is wastage as this space can not be allocated to any other process. This insufficient memory use leading to the wastage is called internal fragmentation.

The other technique used to store processes in memory is variable size memory partitioning also called segmentation. In this case every new process is stored in the available free space. If the required space is not available in the memory then the selected process is moved out of the memory. Now every new process can be of same size or less size than the current process and leads to the wastage of memory space in between different processes present in the memory. Again this wasted memory didn't get used up anywhere in the execution of a different process. This wastage is called external fragmentation. The solution to manage external fragmentation is the compaction. In this technique the free space is collected together to give a contiguous memory block by shifting all the processes downwards. But this is not an easy task. All the respective address references need to be managed before doing compaction. ❑

Q. Describe the Buddy System of memory allocation.

Ans : In case of fixed and variable size partitions we face internal and external fragmentation respectively. Also the multiprogramming limit is fixed in the former case while latter requires complex algorithms to manage proper process allocation. A flexible solution to this problem is buddy systems. In buddy system whole memory space is taken as a single unit of memory. The moment a process comes for space requirement the present memory size is compared to the process size. Then if the size of the process is much smaller than the actual available size, the memory area is divided into equal partitions till we get a block size comparable to the request of the process. This increases utilization efficiency of the memory space as well as manages the dynamic multi-programming. Every new program is assigned a memory space according to its requirement leading to minimum wastage in between two processes. When a block gets freed up after the process execution the similar size blocks are combined to give new list of free blocks. ❑

Q. Discuss User Mode and Kernel Mode.

Ans : Operating system acts as an interface between user programs and hardware. Users issue commands in the programming language of their choice. The system programs working behind convert that program into hardware understandable code to let them execute for desired results. During this process operating system works as a resource and control manager. It assigns various resources to all the processes executing in the system. No any process is allowed to work in a way that leads to the misuse of system resources. To protect system from unauthorized access of user programs, the operating system provides two separate modes of execution in the system: User mode and Kernel Mode. The user programs present in the system always execute in the user mode. The command issued by each of the process works in the user mode. In case if user calls a system function or try to perform a faulty execution, the system mode is shifted to the kernel mode. The kernel mode is the secure mode where operating system handles function execution. Operating system is made responsible for assigning resources and shifting them from one process to another. During execution if any user program tries to interfere into the working of other processes like illegal access to memory space, processor control or tries to execute any system privilege the control gets shifted to the kernel mode. The indication of current execution mode is given by the mode bit present in the process control block. ❑

Q. What is Process Migration ?

Ans : When a process is made to suspend its execution from one system to restart it on another system this process is called process migration. After this the state of the process shifted to the destined system is also changed so that it can restart its execution as before. Earlier it was found quite difficult but now with the help of preemption the state of the process can be saved on to the stack and the current status of process control block can be made to shift to another system for further execution. These days in distributed network, systems are connected in such a way that they can share their resources among different processes present in the system. In order to share the load among various processors, to enhance the communication efficiency and to use the advanced resources present on the various systems, process migration has helped in an effective way. The only point in migration is that process has to be removed completely from the current system to move to the new processing unit. Any references to that process in current system have to be removed completely to avoid dangling pointers. The process migration comes into play when user feels like migrating process from one system to another or operating system wants to share network load among various processors to make network performance better. ❑

Q. Define the term 'Overlays'.

Ans : In case of fixed partition, programmer and system programs both are made responsible for utilization of the assigned memory space. If a process require more space than the available one we use overlays. According to this scheme, every process is divided into independent modules. During process execution only those modules are kept in the memory that are required for the current processing. Rest of them are made to stay in the disk space. When the instructions or data elements present on the disk space are required they are moved back in by replacing those modules which are not needed at present. Unlike dynamic loading overlays can be managed by programmer only. It does not require any help from operating system. The developer has to design an efficient program design to manage the overlays process. It must know each and every step of the instruction code so that to make efficient memory management. Till now overlays is used for only small programs. With the increase in the program length it becomes complex to manage the execution with swapping. Now a days some compilers provide programming support to the user. This has made work much easier for user and helped executing larger programs with this facility. e.g. A program has four modules: Module A has size 60K; Module B has size 70K; Module C has size 50K; Module D has size 80K. The total size allocated to the process is 130K The present state of memory is that Module A and B are in memory. Now if module C is required and working of module A is over then the memory space occupied by A can be made available for C by swapping A out to disk. In any way the total memory space will remain 130K. ❑

Q. What are Mission Critical Systems ?

Ans : The operating systems that help executing the real time processes efficiently are called mission critical systems. The real time processes work in their time constraints associated with them. The execution of such processes requires extra effort on the part of operating system. The real time processes need to be processed by the CPU the moment they enter the system so they are provided with the higher priority as compared to the other processes present in the system. The scheduling technique used by the operating system must manage the timely execution of these tasks so that to let them complete at their desired time limits. The preemption facility is provided with the general scheduling technique to manage mission critical tasks. Round robin technique and Shortest job first scheduling techniques are managed based on the preemption scheme.

The application areas where mission critical tasks are required are: flight control system, Medical Systems (Digital Imaging and operating Machines) Scientific and Industrial control system, Defense systems and various display systems.

The real time systems are of two types : hard real time and soft real time. Hard real time systems are those where time limits have to be met strictly. In case of any delay the results can harm the whole system. The soft real time systems are also with their time limits but here the time constraints can be delayed to some extent. ❑

Q. What is Relocation ?

Ans : To make the execution of more than one processes possible in main memory, it becomes necessary to keep the currently executing processes in memory and swap out the rest of the processes to disk so that to use them later at some time. Well every time a process is swapped in to main memory it can either get loaded into the same memory address as earlier or can be relocated to another memory address. The programs having absolute addressing of all the instructions can only be placed at their definite address locations. While the programs in which instructions keep their addressing relative to some starting point in the program can be placed at any free location in the memory. The concept of relative addressing with relocation has helped in achieving runtime loading of different modules in the program. Here loader just keeps track of the starting point and fetches rest of the instructions based on the relative addresses. Dynamic memory management can be handled in this way for multiple processes present in the system.

Relative Address + Base Address ⟶ Absolute Address

Fig. 3 : Relocating address.

The programmer need to know only the relative address also called logical address and rest of the processing is handled by the relocation loader. ❑

Q. Is Stack Allocation better than Heap Allocation ?

Ans : Stack allocation is a simple memory allocation scheme where related pages are kept in the contiguous memory locations. The size of the stack allocation is limited and has to be mentioned at compile time itself. The heap allocation scheme provides unpredictable storage allocation for the associated objects. It is a non linear data structure used for arbitrary list structures and complex data organizations. The size of heap storage is unlimited and the only limit is the memory size. If stack requires more pages for allocation then it has to manage from disk while heap manages more memory allocation from RAM itself. Due to contiguous allocation scheme, stack allocation is quite easy to handle. In case of heap the respective reference has to be searched out and fetched for making the concerned request execute. Similarly, the de-allocation scheme is simple in stack handling while heap requires proper garbage collection to avoid dangling pointers and memory leaks. The implementation of heap is expensive as compared to stack. The stack executions are much faster than the heap. In case of programming languages, stack variables keep their stay till the function execution while heap objects stay till the program execution. ❑

Q. Discuss the Term 'Reentrancy' ?

Ans : The property of a procedure through which more than one user is allowed to share the same procedure simultaneously is called reentrancy. The master copy of one procedure is kept into the disk space and more than one process is provided with the temporary access to that procedure in their individual memory space. The original code remains same but users can modify their local copy for that particular process. e.g. the clip art procedure provided by MS Office has one existence in the disk but can simultaneously be accessed by different users in MS Word, MS Excel and MS Power Point. They can manage different images in their application and work with them according to their requirement. The attributes associated with each temporary instance (activation) is called the respective activation record. It contains the properties of that procedure currently being used by the process. The data structure that works behind this scheme is the stack. In stack every process keeps its entry for a particular procedure. By this we mean that activation block entry is managed in the stack. ❑

Q. What is Physical and Logical Address Space ?

Ans : Physical address space is the actual memory address locations available in the memory for storing different user programs. The memory space provided to a user program is either fixed or variable size. Accordingly the modules keep on moving in and out of the memory as per their requirement during execution. Now every time a module is swapped into the memory it is being mapped onto a different address location in case of relative addressing. User is made unaware of this address mapping with the concept of logical address space. Logical address space is the memory addresses mentioned by the user program or generated by CPU. This logical address is managed by the concerned processor and is converted into physical address with the help of memory management unit. With this scheme, user programs get an illusion that the current program is in the main memory along with the sub modules and is present for entire processing time. The logical addresses and physical addresses are same during compile time and load time but become different in case of run time binding. If the user program provides absolute addresses then it has to be replaced in the memory every time at the same location. But in case of relative addressing all the instructions keep their addresses relative to the starting point of the program.

E.g.

1	I–1st
2	I–2nd
3	I–3rd
4	I–4th
5	I–5th

In the above figure the instructions (I1-I5) are stored on the address (1-5) respectively. Now with the base address as 1, we can fetch the respective 3rd or 4th instruction because of the relative addressing. ❑

Q. Define Turn around time, Response Time and Waiting Time.

Ans : The Turn around time is the total time for which a process keeps its stay in the system i.e. service time and waiting time. The turn around time is used to measure the system efficiency, the faster the execution of tasks the more will be its efficiency. The ratio of turn around time and service time gives the amount of delay caused to the process by various factors in the system. A process suffers delay due to concerned scheduling technique, preemption and suspension due to unavailable resources or interrupts in between the execution.

Response time is the factor of user and system interaction. The total time taken by the process from submission to the first response provided to the user by the system is called the response time. This is measured in interactive systems where user can interfere into the execution of a task. The user can input commands and can access the results in between the execution. In simulation, process results at every state are kept as a record for comparison with final execution. Similarly the intermediate results are compared in the next turn to find out the system efficiency with different input conditions.

Waiting time is the time taken by the process to wait for the processor time during its execution. Every job has to be processed by the CPU, whether it is a CPU- bound or I/O-bound job. If processor is busy with one job the other jobs are made to wait till the current execution is over. This wait can be due to scheduling technique or an interrupt. In case of time slicing scheduling, every process gets a periodic access to processor time for a given time quantum. Similarly in preemptive scheduling, a process is made to wait till the higher priority process executes. If a process requires an unavailable resource i.e. a resource which is currently engaged with another process then it has to wait for it in the device queue. Any other system interrupt can also lead to the waiting time in between process execution. ❑

Q. Explain Process and Thread.

Ans : Process is the unit of execution which occupies its individual memory space. These are also called heavy weight processes because shifting of processor control from one process to another requires context switching. During context switching the state of currently executing process is saved onto stack and the new process control block is made to activate. Process control block keeps track of the attributes associated with each process like process id, memory status, current state, data registers etc.

Thread is an entity associated with a process. Threads are called light weight processes because processor control transfer in this case requires less effort than in case of process shift. The context switch requires change in system mode from user to kernel while thread communication hardly require any interference from operating system. Threads share memory space, state information and other resources associated with the same process. Threads can get associated with only one process while one process can have multiple threads. While inter process communication among different processes require the system mode to be shifted to the secure mode which is quite expensive but it leads to secure communication i.e. one process can not interfere into the memory space of another process while threads work in an insecure mode where one thread can use the memory space of another thread contained in the same process. The creation of new process requires assignment of separate memory space, processor control and all resource allocations but thread creation is much simpler as it does not require any separate space or resource allocation. ❑

Q. What are System calls and Library Routines ?

Ans : System call acts as an intermediary function between user program and kernel. In order to provide protection to the system, user programs are kept away from performing system level instructions while execution. Whenever user wants to deal with system function, it makes a request to the kernel in the form of system call to execute that particular instruction. During system call the system mode gets shifted from user mode to kernel mode. Kernel mode is a secure mode where whole system functioning is handled by the operating system itself. e.g. if user wants to access a system resource it can request kernel to provide that access through system call. If that access is possible at that moment the kernel will suspend the current process and execute the system call request. It is taken as the high privilege instruction or we can say system calls perform high priority tasks.

Library routines are the functions available in the system that are made available for use to all user programs. These are also called shared libraries. This helps in developing different software applications where more than one user can access the same copy. Library routines are stored in system at one place. When a user program requires performing a task using any of the available library routines then they are provided with their own temporary code of that library routine. User can make required changes into the application facility and can use it in his program. Library routines act as system calls when the concerned functions are system level procedures. Otherwise we need to change the system mode to secure mode while using library routines. Library routines are present with the compiler code in programming language or in the form of intermediate language (e.g. byte code) understandable to all user programs. e.g. C provides standard library routines called GNU C library. Similarly OpenGL provides GLUT to provide complex graphic functionalities in a simple way to users. ❑

Q. What is Trap and Trapdoor ?

Ans : Trap is software initialized high priority interrupt. During trap the system mode gets shifted from user mode to kernel mode. Generally user programs access system resources by passing a request to the kernel in the form of system call. If possible kernel issues that system resource immediately by suspending the current process. It is an exception statement in the form of urgent request or faulty condition execution. In both of the cases, kernel will take charge of the system execution till the processing of that system call.

Trapdoor is a secret path to access the normal processing of software that is otherwise provided through an authorized access. Trapdoor is managed by the developer to enter into the system to debug or monitor the working of the system without following the actual-working path. This does not affect the actual processing of the software and in fact helps in providing maintenance and security in case of any damage. If used in a constructive way it can act as a very useful concept but on the other hand destructive minds can enter into the system through this secret path and can access the private information. The concept of trapdoor was shown in the movie "War Games", where unauthorized access to the system is gained. ❑

Q. What is Cycle Stealing ?

Ans : Direct Memory Access (DMA) processor is provided with the I/O resources to help them in gaining direct access to the memory without any interference from the processor side. Earlier the I/O resources need to have permission to access memory resources but with the help of DMA it can directly use such resources. The DMA controller is provided with the functionality that it can use data bus whenever it is free or it can force CPU to relinquish its access with data bus; the latter one is called cycle stealing. In this case DMA can temporarily suspend the current execution with CPU and can allow I/O controller to mange transfer of data to/from memory. No doubt it affects performance of CPU but overall system efficiency is increased. Many times I/O bound requests keep on waiting for processor time even if the work is related to only the memory unit. They are made to acquire prior permission from processor to perform any task but in cycle stealing scheme, DMA asserts the HOLD pin to request for the transfer. The CPU after suspension of the current process passes the HOLDA, the acknowledgement to let DMA start transferring the data by putting address on MEMR (Memory Read) or MEMW (Memory Write). After the completion of its data transfer it relinquishes access to the HOLD pin and let CPU continue with its task. This enables lot of work to be done that is otherwise kept on wait due to processor. ❑

Q. Discuss Placement and Replacement Algorithm ?

Ans : The **Placement Algorithms** are described while placing the incoming pages into one of the free frames. During variable size block allocation, compaction is not possible every time a frame is set free by an earlier executing process. So when a new process arrives, the concerned pages are placed in one of the available free blocks based on the placement algorithms. These algorithms take care of the size of the incoming page or the available free block or none of these. After comparing both of them the incoming page is allocated to the one of the free frame. The available placement algorithms are : first fit, best fit, next fit.

In first fit, the incoming page will be placed into the first choice available among the free blocks. The size comparison is not taken into care while applying this scheme. The main disadvantage of this scheme is that sometimes the size of available block is too large in comparison to the incoming page. It leads to the wastage of memory space.

The next algorithm is best fit. After getting the size of the incoming page, the best comparable free block size will be allocated to the incoming request. This scheme requires preprocessing for comparing the size of new page with the free blocks. The main advantage of this method is that wastage of memory is less. The last choice is next fit algorithm. In this scheme the last placement position is taken into care. To allocate new free block the system starts searching from the last pointer position and place the new page in to next available free block without concerning the size of the incoming page.

Replacement Algorithm : During dynamic loading scheme when the situation arises that no free block is available for the incoming page request then one of the present pages have to be replaced to provide the sufficient space. Now the decision regarding which occupied space to be set free for the incoming page is made. The replacement algorithms help solving this problem: Optimal, Least Recently Used (LRU), First-in-first-out (FIFO).

In case of optimal algorithm technique the page to be replaced is one which is going to get referenced at the farthest position in future. In this algorithm operating system has to keep track of the future forecasting to select next possible replacement. This is quite tough to implement. The least recently used algorithm replaces the page which has not been referenced in the recent past. This scheme takes care of the point that the farthest referenced page in the past might no longer be required in the future requests. But sometimes this leads to next page faults as the one being kept in the memory for so long may be required in the next step.

The first-in-first-out is the simple strategy that the page entered into the system at first position will be the one to move out. This case can also leads to increased page faults as the next or past reference scheme is not been taken into consideration. ❑

Q. Discuss Resident Set and Working Set of a process.

Ans : Due to limited size of main memory as compared to the disk space available, all the processes cannot reside in the memory at all the times. Also every process executing in the system is provided with a specific memory space to perform its execution. The processes are divided into pages in the virtual memory so that to place them into memory blocks available. Now as the required pages are kept in the memory at any instance and rest are swapped out on to the disk. The number of memory blocks assigned to a process to keep up with its execution is called the resident set. The resident set is either fixed or variable. In case of fixed size resident set, every time a process requires a new page to be swapped into the memory, one of the currently present pages in the resident set are replaced. By variable size we mean that resident set can change its size by adding free blocks of memory along with the currently used frames for making new allocation. Here comes the next term: working set. Working set is the size of the resident set for the particular process during the last execution time. It goes on changing with the allocation and de-allocation of the pages as per the requirement. In this case the free blocks are made available to other processes to let their new pages come into the memory along with the currently executing pages. If there are no free block available at that time the replacement is done from the current resident set to make space for the new page. ❑

Q. What are Local and Global replacements ?

Ans : While working with the resident set associated with each process, replacement algorithm is the major issue in concern. Whenever a new page is required in the process one of the existing pages has to be moved back. This replacement can be done in two ways :

- When a page is replaced by another page of the same process, then it is called local page replacement.
- When a page is replaced by another page of a different process, then it is called global page replacement.

Now application of these two replacement policies depend on the resident set properties. The fixed resident set allows only local replacement as the number of blocks associated with a process can not be increased or decreased while the process is in execution. In case of variable size, the resident set can make both local and global replacement. At any moment, a process can replace page from its current resident set or it can occupy the available frame with in the memory. With global replacement scheme, a list of unlocked blocks has to be managed to allocate one of them to the required process. ❑

Q. A block manager for a variable size region strategy has a free list of blocks of size 600, 1400, 1000, 2200, 1600 and 1050 bytes. What block size will be selected to honor the request for 1605 bytes using best fit policy ?

Ans : Best fit policy manages the allocation of free block size to the next requesting process which has the size comparable to the process requirement.

Ex. :

1050 bytes free
Process 6
1600 bytes free
Process 5
2200 bytes free
Process 4
1000 bytes free
Process 3
1400 bytes free
Process 2
600 bytes free
Process 1
Operating System

To honor the request of 1605 bytes the best fit block size should be 2200; because this block size is provided with space more than the required demand. All other block sizes are smaller in size and will not be able to accommodate the request. ❑

INDEX